About CROP

CROP, the Comparative Research Programme on Poverty, is a response from the academic community to the problem of poverty. The programme was initiated in 1992, and the CROP Secretariat was officially opened in June 1993 by the director-general of UNESCO, Dr Federico Mayor.

In recent years, poverty alleviation, poverty reduction or even the eradication and abolition of poverty has moved up the international agenda, and the CROP network is providing research-based information to policy-makers and others responsible for poverty reduction. Researchers from more than one hundred countries have joined the CROP network, with more than half coming from so-called developing countries and countries in transition.

The major aim of CROP is to produce sound and reliable knowledge that can serve as a basis for poverty reduction. This is done by bringing together researchers for workshops, co-ordinating research projects and publications, and offering educational courses for the international community of policy-makers.

CROP is multi-disciplinary and works as an independent non-profit organization.

For more information you may contact:

CROP Secretariat, Nygårdsgaten 5
N-5020 Bergen, Norway
tel: +47-5558-9739 fax: +47-5558-9745
e-mail: <crop@uib.no>
CROP on the Internet: <http://www.crop.org>

CROP is a programme under the International Social Science Council (which has also helped finance this publication).

CROP International Studies in Poverty Research published by Zed Books in association with CROP

ALREADY AVAILABLE

The International Glossary on Poverty, David Gordon and Paul Spicker (eds), CROP International Studies in Poverty Research, 1999, 162 pp.

Poverty Reduction: What Role for the State in Today's Globalized Economy?, Francis Wilson, Nazneen Kanji and Einar Braathen (eds), 2001, 372 pp.

The Poverty of Rights: Human Rights and the Eradication of Poverty, Willem van Genugten and Camilo Perez-Bustillo (eds), 2001, 209 pp.

Best Practices in Poverty Reduction: An Analytical Framework, Else Øyen et al (eds), 2002, 144 pp.

Law and Poverty: The Legal System and Poverty Reduction, Lucy Williams, Asbjørn Kjønstad and Peter Robson (eds), 2003, 303 pp.

Elite Perceptions of Poverty and Inequality, Elisa P. Reis and Mick Moore (eds), 2005, 288 pp.

Indigenous Peoples and Poverty: An International Perspective, Robyn Eversole, John-Andrew McNeish and Alberto D. Cimadamore (eds), 2005

IN PREPARATION

International Poverty Law: An Emerging Discourse, Lucy Williams (ed), 2006

Poverty and Social Deprivation in the Mediterranean: Trends, Policies and Welfare Prospects in the New Millennium, Maria Petmesidou and Christos Papatheodorou (eds), 2006, 416 pp

ROBYN EVERSOLE, JOHN-ANDREW MCNEISH
AND ALBERTO D. CIMADAMORE | editors

Indigenous peoples and poverty

an international perspective

CROP
International Studies
in Poverty Research

Zed Books
LONDON | NEW YORK

Indigenous peoples and poverty: an international perspective was first published by Zed Books Ltd, 7 Cynthia Street, London N1 9JF, UK and Room 400, 175 Fifth Avenue, New York, NY 10010, USA in 2005

www.zedbooks.co.uk

CROP International Studies in Poverty Research

Cover designed by Andrew Corbett
Set in Arnhem and Futura Bold by Ewan Smith, London
Printed and bound in Malta by Gutenberg Ltd

Distributed in the USA exclusively by Palgrave Macmillan, a division of St Martin's Press, LLC, 175 Fifth Avenue, New York, NY 10010.

A catalogue record for this book is available from the British Library.
US CIP data are available from the Library of Congress.

ISBN 1 84277 678 9 hb
ISBN 1 84277 679 7 pb

Contents

Tables and maps

Tables

Maps

1 | Introduction: indigenous peoples and poverty

JOHN-ANDREW MCNEISH AND
ROBYN EVERSOLE

Why write about indigenous peoples and poverty?

In recent years poverty has moved to the centre of international development policy. 'Development' itself has failed to provide answers to human suffering and disadvantage, or to fulfil its broad promise to make poor people better off, eventually. Gone are the days of easy assumptions that industrial development, or technological progress, or cooperative economic activity, or enterprise development will automatically mend what is lacking when people are poor. Now the focus is upon that *lack* itself – defining it, measuring it, and sometimes even venturing to ask directly: What can actually be done about poverty?

Encouragingly, there appears to be a growing international consensus that poverty – and doing something about poverty – is the key development issue (Maxwell 2003). The UNDP has placed the eradication of poverty at the top of its list of Millennium Development Goals (MDGs). Concurrently, the World Bank has published the *Voices of the Poor* report and hosts the online site *Poverty Net*. More importantly, the Bank and the International Monetary Fund have made the national production of Poverty Reduction Strategy Papers (PRSPs) a condition of debt relief. The chorus of voices worldwide giving attention to poverty suggests that there is a real will to do something about it. Yet this rhetoric can easily lead on to dangerous ground. Suddenly, it seems, *poverty* is a concrete thing that can be identified, measured and fought. And *the poor* too easily become a category of people, homogenous in their poverty, awaiting outsiders' efforts to assist them.

Who are 'the poor' anyway? Indicators and methods for measuring poverty attempt to offer an answer – to assess who is 'in' and who is 'out' of this particular group. There is of course no such group. Being 'poor' is simply a conceptual category, a category one may place oneself in, or be placed in by others: one's neighbours, one's government, or people on the other side of the world. Someone may end up in this category, *poor*, for extremely diverse and shifting reasons, in an enormous variety of contexts, based on vastly different experiences and indicators: from the inability to pay the rent, to the impossibility of sponsoring a village festival, to the inaccessibility of schools for one's children. Given the huge variety of experiences the term encompasses, how can we even begin to talk about poverty?

Yet talking about poverty is useful, because these conversations call attention to patterns, and in doing so, they offer a lens for analysis. Where is poverty – however defined – always more prevalent? In what kinds of situations, in what places, in what roles, are people around the world most likely to be poor? Clearly, there are patterns. Once a pattern is recognized, it is possible to analyse it: to follow it back to source, to understand why that pattern exists. If there is observable disadvantage for a group of people, there are sure to be reasons behind it. Unearthing the reasons – discovering what creates a situation of disadvantage – is a solid first step towards understanding what can be done to reduce or eliminate poverty.

This book acknowledges and explores one key pattern of poverty: the fact that around the world, in vastly different cultures and settings, indigenous peoples are nearly always disadvantaged relative to their non-indigenous counterparts. Their material standard of living is lower; their risk of disease and early death is higher. Their educational opportunities are more limited, their political participation and voice more constrained, and the lifestyles and livelihoods they would choose are very often out of reach.

The United Nations estimates that there are at least 300 million people in the world who are indigenous – belonging to 5,000 indigenous groups in more than seventy countries (UN 2002). Not all the people in all these indigenous groups are poor. Many are not. But in country after country, region after region, the pattern repeats itself: people who are indigenous are much more likely to be poor than their non-indigenous counterparts. There is, in the terminology of Psacharopoulos and Patrinos (1994), a 'cost' to being indigenous. These authors' attempt to quantify disadvantage in Latin American countries showed how being indigenous regularly correlated to being below the poverty line, having less schooling and lower earnings. In Peru, for instance, they found that indigenous peoples were one and a half times as likely to be below the economic poverty line as non-indigenous Peruvians. And indigenous Peruvians were almost three times as likely to be extremely poor. In Guatemala, 38 per cent of all households were extremely poor – but the figure was 61 per cent for indigenous households (ibid.: xviii).

In an international consultation in 1999, the Director-General of the World Health Organization made the following observations about the status of indigenous peoples around the world:

> Life expectancy at birth is 10 to 20 years less for indigenous peoples than

for the rest of the population. Infant mortality is 1.5 to 3 times greater than the national average. Malnutrition and communicable diseases, such as malaria, yellow fever, dengue, cholera and tuberculosis, continue to affect a large proportion of the indigenous peoples around the world ... Indigenous peoples are over-represented among the world's poor. This does not mean only that they have low incomes ... indigenous people are less likely to live in safe or adequate housing, more likely to be denied access to safe water and sanitation, more likely to be malnourished ... (Brundtland 1999)

In most countries, indigenous peoples have less access to education than other groups, and they are often subjected to curricula designed for other cultural groups which ignore their own history, knowledge and values. Indigenous peoples also tend to have less access to national health systems and appropriate medical care, and may suffer nutritional problems when denied access to their traditional lands. Overall, according to a statement from the United Nations Working Group on Indigenous Populations, 'indigenous peoples worldwide continue by and large to be disadvantaged in every area of life' (Daes 2000). Martínez Cobo, in an earlier study of discrimination against indigenous peoples, reached a very similar conclusion: indigenous peoples were 'at the bottom of the socio-economic scale. They did not have the same opportunity for employment and the same access as other groups to public services and/or protection in the fields of health, living conditions, culture, religion and the administration of justice. They could not participate meaningfully in political life' (Martínez Cobo 1986, quoted in Daes 2000).

While data on indigenous disadvantage are available from some countries (though often not using definitions or formats that are comparable across countries), there is a general lack of reliable national-level data on indigenous peoples in many parts of the world; also, the accuracy of such data is sometimes disputed between government authorities and indigenous groups (PFII 2003). In many countries, reliable data with which to compare poverty indicators by ethnicity at the national level are simply not available (see, e.g., Plant 2002: 31; Damman this volume). Even in Australia, a committee headed by the prime minister recently concluded that 'the Australian Government lacks any meaningful data about Indigenous people, making it impossible to tell whether conditions are getting better or worse' (ABC 2003). Nevertheless, it is clear that 'in all major practical areas, Indigenous Australians are worse off than non-Indigenous Australians' (ibid.; cf. USDS 2002).

From wealthy countries to poor countries, from East to West, patterns of indigenous disadvantage persist. In India, for instance, about 8 per cent of citizens belong to scheduled tribes – and 80 per cent of these live below the poverty level (USDS 2002). Nor does the situation for indigenous peoples necessarily improve when they form the majority of national populations. In Bolivia, for instance, where indigenous peoples comprise over half the national population, and indigenous languages are now recognized as official national languages, we still find that between two-thirds and three-quarters of indigenous Bolivians are poor – they are much more likely to be poor than non-indigenous Bolivians (Psacharopoulos and Patrinos 1994: xviii, xix).

Reports from the various meetings of the United Nations Working Group on Indigenous Populations (WGIP) highlight that, for specific countries and areas, there are clear cases of indigenous peoples' disadvantage relative to non-indigenous people – including direct violations of human rights. Note, for instance, the following excerpts:

> A number of indigenous participants from, among other places, Australia, Canada, Guatemala, Cameroon, the Philippines and the United States of America reported that their Governments had failed to protect the rights of indigenous peoples and that human rights violations were taking place. They claimed that Governments and, in particular, military authorities were violating international human rights standards, inter alia through summary and arbitrary arrests and killings, use of violence, forced displacement of indigenous peoples and confiscation or denial of access to their communal and individual property.
>
> A number of indigenous observers from, among other places, Bangladesh, Ecuador, Indonesia, Nepal, New Zealand, Peru and the Russian Federation stressed the importance of the recognition of their right to land and control over natural resources. In this regard, activities of certain TNCs [transnational corporations] were considered detrimental to indigenous peoples.
>
> The issue of institutionalized discrimination against indigenous peoples was also seen as a reality in many countries. In this regard, references were made to the problems associated with administration of justice, including arbitrary detention, and access to social security and health care, including HIV/AIDS treatment for indigenous peoples. (UNHCR 2003: 7)

In many different parts of the world, across many different cultures, a pattern emerges in people's varied experiences of poverty. It is only one among many, but it may explain something very important. A clear pattern links indigenous peoples and poverty. What does this mean? Exploring this pattern, analysing it, can take us beyond facile assumptions about poverty and how to fight it. By asking the question *Why are indigenous peoples, despite all their diversity of cultures and contexts, disproportionately affected by poverty?* we begin a discussion that can illuminate the reasons for this pattern, and can then find strategies to address them.

Defining indigenous peoples

In the mid-1980s, the United Nations Sub-Commission on the Prevention of Discrimination and the Protection of Minorities commissioned a study into discrimination against indigenous peoples. The resulting five-volume report (1986) uses the following definition of indigenous peoples:

> Indigenous communities, peoples and nations are those which, having a historical continuity with pre-invasion and pre-colonial societies that developed on their territories, consider themselves distinct from other sectors of the society now prevailing in those territories, or parts of them. They form at present non-dominant sectors of society and are determined to preserve, develop and transmit to future generations their ancestral territories, and their ethnic identity, as the basis of their continued existence as peoples, in accordance with their own cultural patterns, social institutions and legal systems. (Martínez Cobo 1986)

This definition was accepted by an international gathering of indigenous peoples in July 1996; nevertheless, defining indigenous peoples is still problematic (WGIP 1996). Given the great diversity of the world's indigenous peoples, trying to include them all under a single definition is difficult, and any definition often contested. Even the process of establishing *any* definition at all of who is and who is not indigenous can itself be offensive to those tired of being defined and categorized by outsiders. *Self-identification*, many say, is at the heart of indigenous identity. In the United Nations Working Group meetings on the *Draft Declaration on the Rights of Indigenous Peoples*, the following concerns were expressed:

> In a statement on behalf of all the indigenous organizations participating, it was maintained that a definition of indigenous peoples was unnecessary and that to deny indigenous peoples the right to define themselves was to delimit their right of self-determination. It was claimed that the right of self-determination required that indigenous peoples define themselves without outside interference. They reiterated, together with several Governments, the need for a declaration with universal application. (CHR 1996: 7)

Definitions by their nature draw rigid lines, while identity can be more fluid – both for groups, and for the individuals who comprise them. Many people would prefer not to define indigenous peoples at all.

Yet while formal definitions may be problematic, the term does acknowledge clear commonalities of experience amongst diverse peoples – commonalities that have stimulated the formation of international organizations, alliances and working groups, and which require at least a name. The umbrella term *indigenous peoples*, as indicated by the definition above, highlights the important common characteristics that these many diverse peoples share: being original inhabitants of a land later colonized by others, and forming distinct, non-dominant sectors of society, with unique ethnic identities and cultural systems. Other commonalities, hinted at in the Martínez Cobo definition, include strong ties to land and territory; experiences or threats of dispossession from their ancestral territory; the experience of living under outside, culturally foreign governance and institutional structures; and the threat of assimilation into dominant sectors of society and loss of distinctive identity. The identifier *indigenous peoples* flags these kinds of basic similarities in peoples' histories and current identities.

Such peoples include the Aborigines or First Nations of Australia, New Zealand and North America; the hill tribes, ethnic minorities, ethnic nationalities, original inhabitants, scheduled tribes and other indigenous groups of Asia and the subcontinent; the indigenous *campesinos* ('peasants') or *indios* ('Indians') of Latin America; the indigenous peoples of Russia and Scandinavia; and even to some extent the tribal peoples or ethnic groups of Africa. Each category in turn contains great diversity, comprising many groups and sub-groups, distinguished by language or lineage or geographical area: a great complexity of ethnic identities. In the growing international indigenous discourse, these diverse groups are all brought together under a common banner of *indigenous peoples*.

Speaking of 'indigenous peoples' in the plural, rather than simply of 'indigenous people', recognizes this diversity. The Aymara and the Ojibwa, the San and the Guarani, are all peoples. Unlike *indigenous populations*, the term *indigenous peoples* recognizes that a shared identity, as a people, exists within each distinct group. Making 'peoples' plural also represents an effort to acknowledge the vast diversity contained within this umbrella term. It is an effort to avoid the danger of oversimplification, of indicating a stereotypical 'indigenousness'. When we speak of *indigenous peoples*, we recognize that we are dealing with no clearly defined group. Rather, we are placing under a single conceptual umbrella many different peoples. And even here, the variety of situations contained within this umbrella term can make generalizations difficult:

> The observer for Bangladesh [to the WGIP] said that it would be erroneous to look for indigenous people worldwide based on a Native American

stereotype. Recalling Commission resolution 1996/40 which referred to the diversity of the world's indigenous people, he said that their situation ranged from marginalization to mainstream, from non-recognition of traditional identity to recognition as a sovereign people, and that vulnerability and marginalization should not automatically be read into the indigenous model. (WGIP 1996)

Given the great complexity of both the historical circumstances and the current situations of ethnic groups around the world, there are many grey areas. For instance, most discussions of indigenous peoples – including the Martínez Cobo definition above – imply a minority population living within a numerically and politically dominant 'mainstream' culture. Yet in a country such as Bolivia indigenous peoples may be the majority and still marginalized. Or a majority ethnic group may define itself as indigenous and use this status to deny rights to smaller groups, as is sometimes the case in South-East Asia (see McCaskill and Rutherford this volume). McCaskill and Rutherford observe that the way in which national borders are drawn has affected the 'indigenous' status of mountain people, who have a long-standing presence in the *montaine* region of mainland South-East Asia – but not necessarily within the geographic boundaries of a present-day nation-state.

In places that have not experienced overseas colonization, definitions of 'indigenous' are less straightforward, as 'historical continuity with pre-invasion or pre-colonial societies' is more difficult to define or demonstrate. Overland (this volume) explains that in Russia, where indigenous groups have been incorporated by gradual territorial expansion rather than overseas colonization, the government defines the 'indigenousness' of an ethnic group rather arbitrarily – 'indigenous' groups are those that are small in size and earn subsistence livelihoods. The term itself, and the assumptions it houses, seem a poor fit for the circumstances of some ethnic groups. 'Indigenous peoples' often has the flavour of a borrowed term. It was designed to fit the experiences of the Americas, Australia and New Zealand, with their comparatively recent overseas colonization, and then adapted to other parts of the world that also have territorially rooted, culturally distinct and marginalized ethnic groups.

Indigenous captures this particular constellation of characteristics in a way that no other word does. Yet it also glosses over differences, and so it can become problematic. In Africa, which has also experienced overseas colonization, the term 'indigenous' is seldom used. Many native African peoples are not identified as indigenous peoples. Rather, indigenous peoples in Africa tend to be defined narrowly as those specific peoples that are non-dominant (vis-à-vis other ethnic groups) and have close ties to ancestral lands, including land-based livelihoods (hunting-gathering, herding) (Sylvain 2002: 1,075–6).[1] Non-dominance or marginalization, cultural distinctiveness and long-standing links to land are the key traits that the term 'indigenous peoples' captures. Yet these traits do not always appear together. Marginalized, culturally distinct groups do not all demonstrate 'indigenousness' (in the sense of territorial continuity and close links to land). Nor is long-standing territorial continuity necessarily accompanied by traits such as marginalization and cultural distinctiveness.

Such are the necessary considerations when attempting to write about indigenous peoples, and to trace the pattern linking indigenous peoples and poverty around the world. Yet despite a persistent tendency to stereotype, oversimplify and assume, the category *indigenous peoples* is none the less useful. It describes a pattern, a constellation of characteristics frequently seen together in different parts of the world. Perhaps more importantly, it also reflects real commonalities of interest among these diverse peoples themselves. These common interests have been the impetus for the emergence of a broad range of organizations and movements for indigenous peoples' rights, many of which are now active and visible on the international stage. Currently, several organizations of indigenous peoples have consultative status with the United Nations Economic and Social Council (ECOSOC), and hundreds of representatives of indigenous peoples and their organizations participate at international meetings of the United Nations (UNHCR 1997). Indigenous organizations may be specific to certain peoples (Inuit Circumpolar Conference, Asociación Centro Mapuche), certain geographic regions (South and Meso American Indian Rights Center, Asian Indigenous and Tribal Peoples Network), or they may be pan-indigenist organizations (Indigenous World Association, International Indian Treaty Council). These organizations' specific mandates and compositions vary, yet by adopting the language of *indigenous peoples* and *indigenous rights*, they recognize common interests and build alliances. As many scholars of social movements have shown, collective identity can be a strategic resource for indigenous peoples as they work for change (e.g. Selverston-Scher 2001; Brysk 2000).

The UN's Working Group on Indigenous Populations has been one of the most visible manifestations of international dialogue on the status and rights of indigenous peoples. This working group was established in 1982 and brings together delegates from around the world annually in Geneva. United Nations initiatives regarding indigenous peoples have generally originated in this working group (UNHCR 2003: 4). Beginning in 1985, this group began to develop a draft declaration on the rights of indigenous peoples, which is still undergoing negotiation and amendment. The 2003 session was attended by 871 participants representing thirty-two states, as well as UN bodies and a large number of non-governmental organizations (ibid.: 3), indicating the large international interest in issues affecting indigenous peoples, and the ability of the term itself to help create a common *indigenous* identity for diverse peoples around the world.

International indigenous movements are closely linked to broader human rights concerns shared by both indigenous and non-indigenous peoples. The banner 'indigenous peoples' has become a rallying point for those colonized, dispossessed and marginalized peoples who, by virtue of their long-standing presence in a given territory, are recognized by others to have a right to its resources. Yet it is not only the right to specific resources which is at stake, but also a right to self-determination – to live in one's own way, according to one's own culture. The question of indigenous peoples is thus really a sub-issue of a much larger question: that of *peoples*, of self-defined ethnic groupings determined to continue to live and work in their own particular way, with rights to a set of resources. *Indigenous peoples* specifically are those who, by virtue of their particular historical claims, are in the process of achieving an externally recognized right to peoplehood and territory. It was less than fifty years ago that ILO Convention 107 on Indigenous and Tribal Populations (1957) legally recognized indigenous peoples' claims to their ancestral territory. And even this document assumed that indigenous groups would eventually assimilate into national societies. Now, at the beginning of the twenty-first century, conflicts over rights to land and self-determination continue – and not only for indigenous peoples.

The world is full of peoples who are clamouring for rights, resources and recognition – or achieving these, sometimes at the expense of other peoples. Indigenous peoples are part of this wider context. Yet the identifier 'indigenous' also highlights an important difference, because those peoples that can convincingly sit under this banner enjoy two key advantages in their quest. First of all, indigenous peoples can present a clear moral argument for the reversal of past injustices. If a people has suffered from the incursions of an expanding state, if it has lost resources and self-determination as a result of unjust actions, is it not right that resources and self-determination should be restored? Second, indigenous peoples may gain a sympathetic hearing based on outsiders' perceptions of their unique and 'original' cultural status and their links to the land. Though often the subject of stereotyping, indigenous culture has also proved a source of fascination for anthropologists, students of indigenous art and music, and other interested outsiders appreciative of unique cultures, languages and knowledge systems. And, as long-standing occupants of ecosystems, indigenous peoples have a unique knowledge of their environment which is recognized to be of particular value (see, e.g., UNDP 2000; Alarcón-Cháires this volume).

Ultimately, 'indigenous peoples' is a fluid term, a useful term, and a term that has begun to develop important political currency. In the end, indigenous peoples define themselves, and there are no standard criteria; as one author has keenly observed, 'There is little agreement on precisely what constitutes an indigenous identity, how to measure it, and who truly has it' (Weaver 2001: 240). Yet the term 'indigenous peoples' flags a particular set of common interests which many diverse peoples share. These include a general desire to be recognized as culturally distinct, self-determining peoples, as well as more specific claims based on long-standing territorial continuity and, often, past dispossession. That dispossession, marginalization and discrimination have frequently been part of indigenous peoples' experience is indisputable. The language of indigenous peoples and indigenous rights names a category of common experience, and serves as a rallying cry for justice. It also opens a window of analysis into basic issues of development and poverty.

Poverty and policy

The attention given to poverty as a problem of development has never been greater than it is today. The now internationally agreed upon Millennium Development Goals (MDGs) set the halving of poverty by 2015 as number-one priority.[2] The reasons for the heightened level of international interest in the issue of poverty are complex and not easy to define. They relate to current poverty research, theory and development practice, as well as larger movements and pressures in global politics and economics. It is important to highlight here the global political and economic context because it reminds us that, although there appears to be a genuine shift towards creating policies that specifically target poverty in order to improve the circumstances of the poor (in contrast to general economic development), serious questions still have to be asked about the intentions and interests of the institutions and individuals involved in this global anti-poverty project. Furthermore, while attention to the particular plight of the indigenous poor and a focus on ethnicity have become accepted elements in the canon of poverty-reducing strategies, the resulting policies are still top heavy and contain unquestioned assumptions about development and who controls it. This should alert us to the fact that there is still some way to go before anti-poverty policies respond to local cultural complexity and diversity, or allow the actions, knowledge and strategies of indigenous peoples into the canon of 'good practice' (Øyen et al. 2002).

A new politics of poverty There have been tremendous academic advances made in the study of poverty in recent years. Research on poverty has moved beyond simple econometric measures towards an acceptance of multi-dimensional socio-economic perspectives on its conceptualization, formation and reduction (Spicker 2003). Whereas this opens up possibilities for better understanding of the term 'poverty' and the realities behind it, however, scholarly advances alone do not adequately explain poverty's renewed centrality in international development policy and debates. Rather, a series of circumstances has contributed to the renewed focus on poverty as a priority for development policy and practice. One is the end of the cold war and the gradual retreat from the logic of realpolitik[3] that dominated international politics for nearly four decades (Webster and Engberg-Pedersen 2002). Another is simply the sheer scale and extent of poverty in the world which, with the spread of democracy, as well as the presence of mass media and mass communication to raise public awareness and facilitate joint action, are not considered morally and politically acceptable. Both these causes are without doubt important in setting the scene for a renewed policy focus on poverty, but there are also other explanations that need to be taken into consideration.

For some analysts the new politics of poverty can be connected to the growing recognition that while economic growth may lead to a reduction in the number of people in economic poverty, it is not sufficient on its own to eradicate the social cause of poverty. There has also been a recognition that it is not sufficient to leave poverty reduction to the state alone, and that 'poverty reduction is not likely to take place in a sustained manner without the involvement of the poor' (ibid.). There is a growing acceptance in development practice that poverty reduction requires opportunities for the poor and organizations working on their behalf to exert an influence on political and economic processes. In taking this step, development specialists are recognizing the complexity and diversity of poverty. They are acknowledging that the particular conditions of impoverishment, and the needs and ambitions of poor people, can vary significantly.

Other analysts express their mistrust of the new politics of poverty, seeing it as a means to make market-driven development strategies more socially and ethically acceptable. The new politics of poverty is identified with what has been termed 'adjustment with a human face'. Here authors such as Escobar (1995) and Alvarez (1998) argue that 'social reform' and the 'war on poverty' are part of a strategy to legitimize an economic model and its associated reforms, by ensuring their political and social viability. The strategies of poverty reduction constitute pragmatic attempts to address poverty problems independent of, and disconnected from, the more general orientation towards economic change and global politics implied by the policies of adjustment (Escóbar de Pabón and Guaygua 2003: 18). This badly understood pragmatism conceives of people as mere receptors of benefits, rather than participants in development decision-making (McNeish 2002; Fernández 1989).

Though declaring an interest in improving social indicators, it can be argued that the new politics of poverty prioritizes economic growth and governmental stability over the real interests of poor people. Policies of poverty reduction can be understood to have come to the fore, not for the sake of the security of the poor but rather for that of the security of the prosperous. This emphasis is widely supported in the academic community[4] and reflected in policy-making at both the national and international levels. For example, in the Bolivian PRSP the preface states that 'poverty, inequality and social exclusion are the most severe problems that affect democracy and governability in Bolivia; consequently the maintenance of democracy demands prioritising these issues' (EBRP 2001: i). The UNDP has stated that poverty constitutes a danger in that it adds to social instability and could undermine the results of economic reforms (UNDP 1993).

New policies for poverty We now have some indication of the background to the renewed international interest in poverty. This not only explains current interest in anti-poverty policy but characterizes the political scene in which national and international policies and strategies for poverty reduction have been chosen and developed.

In the 1990s an acceptance grew of the need for a broader conceptual and methodological approach to the assessment of poverty. Although the dollar-a-day poverty line introduced in the 1990 *World Development Report* still serves as a basic yardstick with which to compare poverty levels across countries and over time, it has been criticized extensively. There is now wide acceptance of the need to take into account a much broader set of indicators to assess anti-poverty progress. This acceptance of a broader set of indicators has in turn had significance for indigenous peoples. The recognition of qualitative as well as quantitative anti-poverty indicators has created room within policy to take account of, and integrate, a multiplicity of social interests and demands.

The Millennium Development Goals (MDGs) focus on tangible dimensions of poverty that include human-development-based indicators such as literacy levels, levels of access to health services and access to basic services such as water and sanitation (Kanji 2003). Yet an even more profound shift than the widespread acceptance of such indicators by international organizations has been the integration of public participation into the mainstream of development practice. Acknowledging that local projects are far more successful when they take account of *stakeholders'* interests and knowledge,[5] in the 1980s non-governmental organizations (NGOs) and researchers started experimenting with different methods to integrate civil-society participation into the development process (Chambers 1997). By the early 1990s a large number of participatory techniques and practices[6] had been accepted as part of the standard practice of local development. As a result of their success, a process of *scaling-up* occurred whereby development practitioners in international organizations and national governments took participation into their standard vocabulary and policies (Holland and Blackburn 1998).[7] Indeed, in recent years the development community has made considerable efforts to add the *right to participation* to the terms proposed in their international rights-based approach (ibid.). For indigenous peoples, the concept of the right to participation is opening up the opportunity, at least in theory, to tailor development to their own interests and goals.

Concurrent with the developments in the area of participation, considerable academic debate has taken place around the concept and significance of *social capital* as a relevant concept for new anti-poverty policies. Social capital is generally understood to mean the social structures and networks necessary for sustaining collective action; the supposed normative contents of these structures,[8] as well as the outcome of the collective action achieved through them (Fine 1999). By expressing the interrelationship between local organizations and the state in quantifiable terms, social capital has had the effect of making social movements and the importance of social processes acceptable to the international donor community (Portes 1998; Woolcock 1998). The reports and literature of both the IMF[9] and the World Bank[10] now make repeated references to their aim of encouraging the growth and fulfilment of social capital in developing communities.

Beyond participation and social capital, in the last few years considerable advance has been made in rights-based approaches to development. In rights-based approaches, the International Human Rights framework of the United Nations has been utilized and expanded to define legal mechanisms to push national governments and the international community to take development seriously. Over the last year, the Office of the High Commissioner for Human Rights at the United Nations has been preparing draft guidelines for a 'Human Rights Approach to Poverty Reduction Strategies'. The Sector for the Social Sciences in UNESCO has recently been working with CROP/SIF on a draft document for 'Abolishing Poverty through the International Human Rights Framework' (UNESCO/CROP n.d.). One of the academic ideas that has been most persuasive to development practitioners and the international community is the idea of the 'right to development' (Aoed 2003) that has developed out of the work of Sen (1999). Although there is academic debate on its conceptualization (Alkire 2002) there is a growing acceptance by governments and the international system of an obligation to assist poor and marginalized individuals and their communities by developing the 'capabilities' they need to escape their condition. This capability approach is at present considered the central paradigm through which the international community, state institutions and the poor should work together for development and the *eradication* or *abolition* – rather than merely the *reduction* – of poverty. The most relevant and recent examples of this approach being taken on board by the international development community are the UNDP *Human Development Report* (2004) and the World Bank-funded Culture and Public Action Study (Rao and Walton 2004).

Persisting poverty of policy? There have clearly been improvements over the last decade in understanding poverty and developing anti-poverty policies. This process, however, and the resulting policy approaches, are certainly not without controversy.

Although supported by development practitioners and researchers on both the right and left of the political spectrum, the recent scaling-up of participation has polarized opinion. Sceptics highlight the way in which, despite the official rhetoric to the contrary, participation is often strictly managed and controlled by state mechanisms (Martínez 1996). They highlight the role of participation as 'sweetener' which takes public attention away from the conservative goals of the state (McNeish 2001). Rather than providing a sphere for democratic deliberation on public policy among autonomous civil-society organizations and the state, it has been demonstrated that state-sponsored participation gives specified groups the ability to take part in a prescribed methodology of participation in state-specified public policy matters (Van Cott 2000; Burkey 1991; Blackburn 1998). As well as having a common economic rationale, these prescribed methodologies are often heavily influenced by class and cultural prejudices. For indigenous communities this has meant that their locally defined development proposals, even when of economic value, are frequently dismissed as either impractical or wasteful by regional or national planners (McNeish 2001, 2002).

Similarly, important questions are being asked about the PRSP process. For many governmental and non-governmental donor organizations, the apparent change to a country-driven participatory process has been welcomed as heralding the international acceptance of a need for a more democratic, grass-roots-driven and targeted development. This optimism has not, however, been shared by all. For some sceptics PRSPs may be little more than 'old wine in new bottles' (Cling et al. 2000), the rediscovery of poverty being used as a way to disguise an economic model that produces poverty and corruption (Bendana 2002). Even among researchers who point to the improvement in language and practice created by the PRSPs, there is agreement that macroeconomic policy and poverty reduction remain two unconnected goals, each with their own contradictory policies and targets (May 2003). A body of research evidence demonstrates clearly that PRSP formation and conclusions remain governed by international policy and technocratic interests, with undeniable similarity between different nations' 'tailor-made' plans (Bendana 2002). For example, reports from Bolivia, Nicaragua, Uganda, Sri Lanka, Bangladesh, Pakistan and Cambodia all claim to demonstrate the extent to which citizens' participation in the PRSPs was purposely limited (McNeish 2002; Bendana 2002; Gariyo 2002; Bretton Woods Project 2003; NGO Forum Cambodia 2002).

Although contributing to development theory and practice, the concept of social capital has also been a subject of controversy. Academic debates rage not only about the persisting lack of clarity about the meaning and content of social capital as a concept (Coleman 1988; Putnam 1993; Harris and de Renzio 1997), but about the validity of this concept to both the social sciences and development practice (Molyneux 2002). Critics of the concept point to social capital theorists' over-reliance on formalized structures and networks. As a result, informal networks, as well as non-Western religious and cultural organization and leadership forms, are frequently left out of the social capital equation. By emphasizing formal and existing social structures and networks, the concept can appear static rather than transformative and may ignore the possibility of change by new actors or ideas (Tendler 1997). As such, some researchers highlight the dangers of it acting to further weaken the position and possibilities of already marginalized or weak groups, e.g. the poor, women and indigenous groups (Molyneux 2002).

Poverty policy and indigenous peoples These critiques of recent directions in development policy demonstrate that although improvements have been made, significant questions still need to be asked about the political context of development and the motivations of actors involved in poverty reduction at different levels. Indeed, this is all the more important when the target is the reduction of indigenous poverty, an area where questions of intention, prejudice and control are thrown into strong relief.

Inspired by the wider development practice of recent years, the World Bank and the Inter-American Development Bank (IDB) have unambiguously identified the reduction of extreme poverty facing indigenous peoples as among their foremost priorities (Plant 1998). The World Bank has become increasingly concerned to target indigenous communities with social funds. The first generation of social investment funds targeted the poorest municipalities, assuming that this would benefit all the poor, indigenous and non-indigenous alike. The results of the first projects pointed to the limits of poverty-targeting mechanisms, and to the need for special efforts to achieve greater participation by indigenous peoples, helping them to make their demands known. Thus, specific indigenous communities were targeted, and resources provided to assist them in developing their own proposals (ibid.). Similarly, the IDB has also highlighted the importance of indigenous community support mechanisms for designing and implementing sustainable bottom-up development projects (IDB 1997). At the country level, most IDB country documents now list the alleviation of indigenous poverty, or the more effective incorporation of indigenous peoples within national development models, highly among their strategic objectives (Plant 1998).

On the face of it, these attempts to target indigenous poverty reflect important changes in the development policies of these two influential institutions. Despite the stated intentions of these organizations to incorporate indigenous peoples within development planning, however, the questions of power and context remain largely unanswered. Without addressing the specificities of existing power structures or the premises of the international economy, policies towards indigenous peoples remain top-down, continue to treat indigenous peoples as isolated from national societies and economies, or fail to take indigenous peoples' own visions of survival and development seriously.

To some extent this flaw is made clear in a comparative report on World Bank and IDB policies on indigenous poverty. It states that:

> The World Bank's 1994 Indigenous Peoples and Poverty study was clearly a watershed, drawing widespread attention within this organization to the close correlation between indigenous identity and poverty. But much of the response has been to seek remedies within the framework of a self-development or ethno-development approach, based on empowerment of indigenous peoples within a local economy, rather than to examine and confront what may be seen as the structural causes of indigenous poverty. (ibid.: 33)

According to the IDB, their own approach is more 'open-ended', with no equivalent to the World Bank's operational directive that conditions policies and programmes at the national level. Although the IDB stresses taking full account of indigenous peoples' cultures and aspirations, however, and of their position in wider economic and political networks, some reservation must also be voiced in terms of the IDB's own approach to indigenous poverty. Although they are concerned with the issue of discrimination, there is still little reflection on their own role as self-defined stewards of indigenous development within the global economy. Although both these institutions claim support for the creation of new political 'spaces' for indigenous peoples' participation in politics and development, they also reserve the right to set strict checks and balances on the limits and character of their participation and visions for the future.

While seeking to have an impact on both policy-making and the academic understanding of indigenous poverty and development, this book does not claim to contain a solution to indigenous poverty. What it does offer is a comparative, cross-disciplinary and accessible understanding of the issue. The papers included in this volume not only describe the character of indigenous poverty, but also highlight the way in which possibilities and limitations for indigenous peoples to overcome poverty are shaped by existing and changing power structures and relationships in human society. As such, this book is not an attempt to be prescriptive, but rather to be aware of, and responsive to, the dynamics and complexities involved in understanding and addressing the issue of indigenous poverty.

In writing about how poverty affects indigenous peoples specifically, the intention is to underline both the differences and commonality of their experiences. We aim to demonstrate that differences and commonalities together form the realistic basis for the study of indigenous poverty, and can represent real opportunities for more effective poverty reduction strategies and policies. In this sense the book aims to contribute to both academic debates on indigenous peoples and poverty, and governments', international organizations' and NGOs' practical responses to poverty among indigenous peoples. Furthermore, by bringing together the experiences of diverse indigenous peoples in a comparative book, we also hope to offer indigenous peoples, organizations and activists some valuable practical insights from the experiences of others.

The story of this book

It is surely poignant that a book on the subject of poverty among indigenous peoples should be published immediately following the end of the International Decade for the World's Indigenous Peoples. While the closing of the International Decade serves as an important reminder of work still to be done and injustice unanswered, it is hoped that this book can suggest paths on which this work can move forward.

This book has an interesting and multi-stranded history. Its initial inspiration came in November 2001, when the Latin American Research Council (CLACSO) and the Comparative Research Programme on Poverty (CROP) co-organized an international conference entitled 'Indigenous Peoples and Poverty: Multi-disciplinary Approaches', working with the Faculty of Latin American Social Sciences (FLACSO) in Guatemala. The conference formed part of CLACSO and CROP's larger ongoing joint programme, 'Strengthening poverty research and academic support to poverty reduction programs in less developed countries and regions of Latin America and the Caribbean'.[11] The success of this international conference, and the strong engagement of its participants in discussions and debates on the issue of indigenous poverty, inspired the initial idea to assemble the conference papers and publish a book. In 2003 FLACSO drew on the inspiration of this conference to publish a book *El Rostro Indígena de la Pobreza*, focusing on indigenous poverty in Guatemala (Alvarez Aragón 2003). Yet the organizers also recognized the need to broaden the focus on indigenous poverty beyond the confines of most of the original conference papers, namely Central and South America.

At the same time as this conference was happening in Central America, a small research centre at Edith Cowan University in Western Australia was developing a strong relationship with members of a local indigenous community, as part of its regional development research programme. This small research centre suddenly found itself with a significant portfolio of indigenous research projects, and recognized the need to look further afield to place local issues and challenges in a larger context. International academic and practitioner literature offered important insights on various aspects of indigenous poverty, development, land rights, political organizations and so forth, yet there was little systematization of this knowledge in a way that addressed the basic question *Why are indigenous peoples so often poor, and what can be done about it?*

A research fellow at this centre had just completed an edited book on anti-poverty projects and non-governmental organizations (Eversole 2003). Interested in the question of indigenous poverty, and as an extension of her work with the research centre's local indigenous projects, she began drafting a book proposal for an international study of indigenous peoples and poverty. She then extended invitations to a select group of colleagues, working internationally, to prepare articles for this collection. The initial response was enthusiastic. At the same time, she was aware that CROP and CLASCO had recently held an international conference on a very similar topic, and so she approached Else Øyen, scientific director of CROP, to enquire as to the status of that project and whether a publication was being planned.

It soon became clear that this was an excellent opportunity for collaboration. The Australian manuscript, already in progress, could be combined with selected conference papers from the 2001 international conference to create a more in-depth book than either group could produce on its own. CROP and CLASCO each agreed to appoint a co-editor, and to lend their organizations' expertise and support to the project. Meanwhile, when the co-editor from Australia moved from Edith Cowan University to RMIT University (Victoria, Australia) in mid-2003, the project moved with her. The book was adopted as a project of RMIT University's Centre for Regional and Rural Development (CRRD). Thus, it became a three-way collaboration among CROP, CLASCO and CRRD – a collaboration based on three continents, and endeavouring to produce a book truly international in scope.

This book draws together contributors from more than ten countries, writing on the diverse – yet often surprisingly similar – experiences of indigenous peoples on five continents. It begins with a general introductory section on indigenous poverty and disadvantage around the world. This first section considers both quantifiable indicators of poverty – factors such as infant mortality, illiteracy rates, housing conditions, incomes and so forth – and less quantifiable aspects of poverty having to do with political voice, human rights and social exclusion. Part One thus lays the groundwork for the rest of the book by exploring particular patterns of disadvantage affecting indigenous peoples. Through specific studies from Mexico and Taiwan, as well as a comparative study from across the Americas, Part One demonstrates the very different international contexts in which indigenous peoples live, and the often surprising similarities in their situations when compared with those of non-indigenous peoples.

From there, the book moves on in Part Two to address the position of indigenous peoples in contemporary nation-states, with a focus on indigenous rights, citizenship and indigenous demands for self-determination. These chapters explore the relationships between indigenous peoples and nation-states in various countries around the world, within the broader context of globalized economies and international recognition of indigenous rights. Indra Overland reflects on the historical position of indigenous peoples in Russia, as well as the limitations of international aid in terms of reaching impoverished indigenous peoples who live in comparatively wealthy nations. Don McCaskill and Jeff Rutherford then discuss the situations of indigenous peoples in various countries of South-East Asia, within the context of national policies and global economies.

Part Two continues with Louise Humpage's insightful analysis of New Zealand anti-poverty policy for indigenous people, and the Māori's response. In this chapter, as well as the following chapter on two Colombian indigenous groups and their experiences of 'popular participation', it becomes clear that indigenous peoples have their own agendas, and that these agendas are often poorly understood and recognized even by those governments that claim to seek their participation and inclusion. The section's final chapter, by Stephen Cornell, explores indigenous demands for self-determination, offering a comparative study of four countries (Australia, New Zealand, Canada and the United States). Throughout Part Two, it becomes clear that understanding the relationships between indigenous peoples and nation-states is key to understanding indigenous poverty, and to uncovering the potential for change.

Part Three focuses specifically on indigenous peoples' own perspectives on development and poverty reduction, a theme that runs through the book as a whole. Here, a Latin American study by Pablo Alarcón-Cháires explores indigenous peoples' perspectives on the natural environment and development, offering various examples and suggestions as to how indigenous environmental knowledge and practice can contribute to poverty reduction for indigenous groups. This chapter is followed by an Australian case study describing an indigenous community members' own anti-poverty strategies in one Australian town. Part Three concludes with a reflection on the history, context and achievements of Sami anti-poverty strategies in the Nordic countries.

This book is structured to include a variety of voices and perspectives without sacrificing continuity and flow. The narrative thus begins by drawing attention to the pattern of indigenous poverty (Part One), then discusses its national and international contexts (Part Two) before moving on to the question of *development* – or doing something about poverty (Part Three). Each of these three sections opens with a short introductory chapter, which presents a conceptual background to the topic and the chapters that follow. The book's concluding chapter then draws together key themes from these three sections and reflects on their practical implications for poverty reduction among indigenous peoples. The aim is to create a convincing tapestry in which diverse stories and experiences are presented, key patterns explored, and conclusions drawn.

The strengths of this book lie in its international perspective, its focus on real-world cases, and its willingness to tackle, thoroughly and sensitively, one of the current 'big issues' in development and international policy. The book also has limitations. Because it has followed the contours of indigenous discourse internationally, it has sparse representation from some geographic areas, most notably the continent of Africa, where the terminology of 'indigenous peoples' is used less frequently. Even in other parts of the world, the book can offer only a small sampling of the great diversity of experiences of indigenous peoples. It does not attempt to profile all the indigenous groups of each region – impossible in anything short of a multi-volume encyclopaedia – and as a result, inevitably, valuable experiences and perspectives will be overlooked.

Drawing on contributions from a broad range of disciplines within and beyond the social sciences, this book is truly multi-disciplinary. As such, it has a further limitation in terms of not being able to deliver a common research methodology or common theory-set for the study of indigenous poverty. As the reader will see, the multi-disciplinarity of the contributions to the book also means that the presentation and language differ from chapter to chapter. These limitations aside, there is still a lot to be gained from a multi-disciplinary project of this kind, both in terms of contributing to a multi-dimensional understanding of poverty in general and in helping to provide a nuanced explanation of the complexities of indigenous poverty in particular. The decision to write about indigenous peoples and poverty has entailed choosing to ask difficult questions, and to invite a range of voices into the conversation. The authors of this book share a wide knowledge and a diversity of perspectives. Their insights, taken together, can illuminate a way forward to better understand – and act upon – the issue of poverty among indigenous peoples.

Notes

1 The International Labour Organization, in its Conventions 107 (1957) and 169 (1989), includes both 'tribal' and 'indigenous' people. 'Tribal' emphasizes distinctiveness from national cultures and a degree of self-rule, while 'indigenous' emphasizes descent and territorial links, as well as at least a certain level of cultural distinctiveness. Tribal peoples are those 'whose social, cultural and economic conditions distinguish them from other sections of the national community, and whose status is regulated wholly or partially by their own customs or traditions or by special laws or regulations'. Indigenous peoples are those 'who are regarded as indigenous on account of their descent from the populations which inhabited the country, or a geographical region to which the country belongs, at the time of conquest or colonisation or the establishment of present state boundaries and who, irrespective of their legal status, retain some or all of their own social, economic, cultural and political institutions' (Article 1, ILO Convention 169).

2 <http://www.undp.org/hdr2003/>

3 During the cold war development aid was steered pragmatically by the contrasting political interests and ideologies of the Soviet Union and the Western powers.

4 For example, '... if global poverty persists, the cost to the United States over the next decades will grow. Eliminating absolute poverty, therefore, is not just an ethical but an instrumental issue for US policymakers' (Sewell 2003).

5 In its World Development Report for 1990 the World Bank defined 'inadequate participation' as one of five reasons why aid projects had been ineffective. It concluded, 'Evidence supports the view that involving the poor in the design, implementation and evaluation of projects in a range of sectors would make aid more effective' (1990: 193).

6 For example, Rapid Rural Appraisal (RRA), Participatory Action Research (PAR) and Participatory Rural Appraisal (PRA). For a discussion of these methodologies, see Holland and Blackburn (1998).

7 Efforts at state-sponsored popular participation have also been tested in a number of countries throughout the developing world (Martínez 1996; Mohan 1996; Webster and Engberg-Pedersen 1992). These experiments are often combined with parallel efforts to decentralize government and encourage improved systems of governance and administration in urban and rural areas (Crook and Manor 1998).

8 Such as trustworthiness and reciprocal relations.

9 The IMF presently has 11,948 documents that discuss or mention social capital, <http://www.imf.org/>

10 <http://www.worldbank.org/poverty/scapital/>

11 This research and academic capacity-building programme is principally funded by the Norwegian Overseas Development Administration (NORAD).

References

ABC (Australian Broadcasting Corporation) (2003) 'Data ignores Indigenous people: PM's committee', ABC News Online, 13 November, <http://www.abc.net.au/ news/newsitems/s988016.htm>

Alkire, Sabina (2002) *Valuing Freedoms: Sen's Capability Approach and Poverty Reduction*, Oxford: Oxford University Press

Alvarez, S. (1998) 'La solidaridad privada e indiferencia pública: La nueva cara de la política social para los excluídos', Terceras Jornadas Internacionales: Estado y Sociedad: La reconstrucción de la esfera pública, Buenos Aires: Universidad de Buenos Aires, CEA

Alvarez Aragón, V. (2003) *El Rostro indígena de la pobreza*, Guatemala: FLACSO, Editorial de Ciencias Sociales

Aoed, A. (2003) 'The right to development as a basic human right', in L. Williams, A. Kjønstad and P. Robson (eds), *Law and Poverty: The Legal System and Poverty Reduction*, London and New York: CROP International Studies in Poverty Reduction/Zed Books

Bendana, A. (2002) 'Byebye poverty reduction strategy papers, and hello good governance', *Echoes*, 21, <http://www.wcc-coe.org/wcc/what/jpc/echoes/echoes-21-08.htm>

Blackburn, J. (ed.) (1998) *Who Changes? Institutionalizing Participation in*

Development (with J. Holland), London: Intermediate Technology Publications

Blackburn, J., C. Chambers and J. Gaventa (2000) 'Mainstreaming participation and development', OED Working Papers Series 10, Washington, DC: World Bank

Bretton Woods Project (2003) 'PRSP dangers exposed again', <http://www.brettonwoodsproject.org/topic/adjustment/index.shtml>

Brundtland, G. H. (1999) 'International consultation on the health of Indigenous Peoples', speech transcript, Geneva: World Health Organization, <http://www.who.int/director-general/speeches/1999>

Brysk, A. (2000) *From Tribal Village to Global Village: Indian Rights and International Relations in Latin America*, Stanford, CA: Stanford University Press

Burkey, I. (1991) *People's Power in Theory and Practice: The Resistance Council System in Uganda*, unpublished, Yale University

Chambers, R. (1997) *Whose Reality Counts? Putting the First Last*, London: Intermediate Technology

CHR (Commission on Human Rights of the United Nations) (1996) 'Report of the Working Group established in accordance with Commission on Human Rights resolution 1995/32 of 3 March 1995' (working group on the elaboration of a draft 'United Nations Declaration on the Rights of Indigenous Peoples'), 52nd session, Item 3 of the provisional agenda, E/CN.4/1996/84, 4 January, <http://www.unhchr.ch/indigenous/documents.htm>

Cling, J. P., M. Razafindrakoto and F. Roubaud (2000) 'The PRSP Initiative: old wine in new bottles?', paper presented at Annual Bank Conference on Development Economics, on <http://wbln0018.worldbank.org/ eurvp/web.nsf/Pages/Paper+by+Razafindrakoto/$File/RAZAFINDRAKOTO.PDF>

Coleman, J. S. (1988) 'Social capital in the creation of human-capital', *American Journal of Sociology*, 94: S95–S120 Suppl. S

Crook, R. C. and J. Manor (1998) *Democracy and Decentralisation in South Asia and West Africa: Participation, Accountability and Performance*, Cambridge: Cambridge University Press

Daes, E. I. (2000) 'Prevention of discrimination and protection of indigenous peoples and minorities', working paper on discrimination against indigenous peoples submitted by Mrs Erica-Irene Daes, chairperson-rapporteur of the Working Group on Indigenous Populations, in accordance with Sub-commission resolution 1999/20, Economic and Social Council, United Nations, 18 August, <http://ods-dds-ny.un.org/doc/UNDOC/GEN/G00/155/14/PDF/ G0015514.pdf?OpenElement>

EBRP (Estrategia Boliviana de Reducción de la Pobreza) (2001) Ministerio de Hacienda, La Paz: Bolivia

Escobar, A. (1995) *Encountering Development: The Making and Unmaking of the Third World*, Princeton, NJ: Princeton University Press

Escóbar de Pabón, S. and G. Guaygua (2003) *Estrategias familiares de trabajo, precariedad laboral y calidad de vida en el contexto de la Estrategia Boliviana de Reducción de la Pobreza*, unpublished paper

Eversole, R. (2003) *Here to Help, NGOs Combating Poverty in Latin America*, Armonk, NY, and London: M. E. Sharpe

Fernández, M. (1989) 'Las políticas sociales en el cono sur 1975–1985', in *Análisis de sus determinantes políticas y socioeconómicas*, Cuadernos del ILPES, 34, Santiago de Chile

Fine, B. (1999) 'The development state is dead – long live social capital?', *Development and Change*, 30(1): 1–19

Foucault, M. (1991) 'Governmentality', in G. Burchell, C. Gordon and P. Miller (eds), *The Foucault Effect: Studies in Governmentality*, London: Harvester Wheatsheaf

Gariyo, Z. (2002) 'The PRSP process in Uganda', Uganda Debt Network, <http://www.jubilee2000uk.org/jmipolicies/PRSPgariyobackground.htm>

Gonzalez, M. L. (1994) 'How many Indigenous People?', in G. Psacharopoulos and H. A. Patrinos (eds), *Indigenous People and Poverty in Latin America, an Empirical Analysis*, World Bank Regional and Sectoral Studies, Washington, DC: World Bank, <http://www-wds.worldbank.org/servlet/WDSContentServer/WDSP/IB/2000/02/23/000009265_3970311123315/Rendered/PDF/multi_page.pdf>

Harris, J. and P. de Renzio (1997) 'Policy arena: missing link or analytically missing? the concept of social capital', *Journal of International Development*, 9(7): 919–37

Holland, J. and J. Blackburn (1998) *Whose Voice? Participatory Research and Policy Change*, London: ITDG

IDB (1997) 'A strategy for poverty reduction', Washington, DC: Inter-American Development Bank, Social Programs Division

Kanji, N. (2003) 'Poverty assessments and project evaluation', unpublished chapter in *Approaching Poverty: A Poverty Reduction Manual for Practitioners*, SIDA/CROP

McNeish, J. (2001) 'Pueblo chico, infierno grande: globalization and the politics of participation in highland Bolivia', unpublished PhD thesis, University of London

— (2002) 'Globalisation and the reinvention of Andean tradition: the politics of community and ethnicity in highland Bolivia', *Journal of Peasant Studies*, 29 (3/4), London and New York: Frank Cass

Martínez, J. A. (1996) 'Municipios y participación popular en América Latina: Un modelo de desarrollo', La Paz: IAF/SEMILLA/CEBIAE

Martínez Cobo, J. (1986) 'Study of the problem of discrimination against indigenous populations', UN Sub-commission on the Prevention of Discrimination and the Protection of Minorities, UN Doc. E/CN.4/Sub.2/1986/7

Maxwell, S. (2003) 'Heaven or hubris: reflections on the new "New Poverty Agenda"', *Development Policy Review*, 21(1): 5–25

May, J. (2003) 'PRSPs: dismantling the anti-politics machine?', unpublished chapter in *Approaching Poverty: A Poverty Reduction Manual for Practitioners*, SIDA/CROP

Mohan, G. (1996) 'Neoliberalism and decentralised development planning in Ghana', *Third World Planning Review*, 18(4): 433–54

Molyneux, M. (2002) 'Gender and the silences of Social Capital: lessons from Latin America', *Development and Change*, 33(2): 167–88

Narayan, D. et al. (2000) 'Voices of the poor: can anyone hear us?', World Bank Documents, <http://wwww1.worldbank.org/prem/poverty/reports.htmcananyone>

NGO Forum Cambodia (2002) 'NGO comment on Cambodia's PRSP process', <http://www.ngoforum.org.kh/>

Øyen, E. et al. (2002) *Best Practices in Poverty Reduction: An Analytical Framework*, CROP International Studies on Poverty Research Series, London and New York: Zed Books

PFII (Permanent Forum on Indigenous Issues) (2003), second session, New York, 12–23 May, item 4 of the provisional agenda, joint paper on data collection and disaggregation by ethnicity, E/C.19/2003/4, <http://ods-dds-ny.un.org/doc/UNDOC/GEN/N03/276/77/ PDF/N0327677.pdf?OpenElement>

Plant, R. (1998) 'Issues in indigenous poverty and development', Washington, DC: IDB, <www.iadb.org/sds/doc/952eng.pdf>

— (2002) 'Indigenous peoples/ethnic minorities and poverty reduction', Regional Report, Regional and Sustainable Development Department, Asian Development Bank, Manila, Philippines, <http://www.adb.org/Documents/Reports/Indigenous_Peoples/ REG/indigenous_reg.pdf>

Portes, A. (1998) 'Social Capital: its origins and application in modern society', *Annual Review of Sociology*, 24: 1–24

Psacharopoulos, G. and H. A. Patrinos (1994) *Indigenous People and Poverty in Latin America, an empirical analysis*, World Bank Regional and Sectoral Studies, Washington, DC: World Bank, <http://www-wds.worldbank.org/servlet/WDSContentServer/WDSP/IB/2000/02/23/000009265_3970311123315/Rendered/PDF/multi_page.pdf>

Putnam, R. (1993) *Making Democracy Work: Civic Traditions in Modern Italy*, Princeton, NJ: Princeton University Press

Rao, V. and M. Walton (2004) *Culture and Public Action*, Stanford, CA: Stanford University Press

Selverston-Scher, M. (2001) *Ethnopolitics in Ecuador: Indigenous Rights and the Strengthening of Democracy*, Coral Gables, FL: North–South Center Press

Sen, A. (1999) *Development as Freedom*, New York: Knopf

Sewell, J. (2003) 'The realpolitik of poverty', in the Environmental Change and Security Project Report, Washington, DC: Woodrow Wilson International Center for Scholars

Spicker, P. (2003) 'Eleven definitions of poverty', unpublished chapter in *Approaching Poverty: A Poverty Reduction Manual for Practitioners*, SIDA/CROP

Sylvain, R. (2002) '"Land, water, and truth": San identity and global indigenism', *American Anthropologist*, 104(4): 1,074–85

Tendler, J. (1997) *Good Government in the Tropics*, Baltimore, MD: Johns Hopkins University Press

— (2002) 'First meeting of permanent forum high point of UN decade', United Nations, <http://www.un.org/rights/indigenous/ backgrounder1.htm>

UNDP (1993) *Human Development Report*, New York: United Nations Development Programme

— (2000) 'About indigenous peoples: frequently asked questions', <http://www.undp.org/csopp/CSO/NewFiles/ipaboutfaqs.html>

— (2004) *Human Development Report 2004, Cultural Liberty in Today's Diverse World*, New York: United Nations Development Programme

UNESCO/CROP (n.d.) 'Abolishing poverty through the International Human Rights Framework', unpublished consultancy report

UNHCR (1997) 'The rights of indigenous peoples', Fact Sheet No. 9 (Rev 1), Geneva: United Nations, <http://www.unhchr.ch/html/menu6 /2/fs9.htm>

— (2003) 'Prevention of discrimination and protection of indigenous peoples', Report of the Working Group on Indigenous Populations on its 21st session, Geneva: United Nations, <http://www.unhchr.ch/huridocda/huridoca.nsf/AllSymbols/ 5FF3562C094F43E2C1256D8A00316CE3/$File/G0315800.pdf?OpenElement>

USDS (US Department of State) (2002) 'Australia country reports on human rights practices – 2001', Bureau of Democracy, Human Rights, and Labor, <http://www.state.gov/g/drl/rls/hrrpt/2001/eap/>

Van Cott, D. L. (2000) *The Friendly Liquidation of the Past: The Politics of Diversity in Latin America*, Pittsburgh, PA: University of Pittsburgh Press

Weaver, H. N. (2001) 'Indigenous identity', *American Indian Quarterly*, 25(2): 240–55

Webster, N. and L. Engberg-Pedersen (2002) *In the Name of the Poor: Contesting Political Space for Poverty Reduction*, London and New York: Zed Books

WGIP (Working Group on Indigenous Populations) (1996) 'Discrimination against indigenous peoples', Report of the Working Group on Indigenous Populations on its 14th session, Geneva: United Nations, E/CN.4/Sub.2/1996/21, <http://www.unhchr.ch/Huridocda/Huridoca.nsf/TestFrame/f488deaaa4810a98802566ac00362df9?Opendocument>

Woolcock, M. (1998) 'Social capital and economic development: toward a theoretical synthesis and policy framework', *Theory and Society*, 27(2): 151–208

World Bank (1990) *World Development Report 1990*, New York: Oxford University Press

ONE | Indigenous poverty

2 | Overview – patterns of indigenous disadvantage worldwide

ROBYN EVERSOLE

This book begins with a simple observation: that there is a pattern linking indigenous peoples and poverty. This pattern emerges in many different contexts around the world, and it is woven of many different threads: economic, social and environmental; qualitative experiences of deprivation as well as quantitative lack. This international pattern of indigenous poverty is often thrown into relief by the contrasting colours of indigenous *wealth*: cultural wealth, environmental knowledge, social cohesion, sustainable economics. Poverty is clearly no innate characteristic of indigenous peoples. It is not something which indigenous peoples often *possess* or have a tendency to *be*. Rather, poverty is a pattern that results from human actions, set in particular historical, geographical, economic and social contexts. It is a pattern depicting relationships of disadvantage: poverty as a verb, not a noun; a process, rather than a static state. The pattern of poverty is continuously in the process of being woven – or unravelled to make something new.

Indigenous peoples in Latin America

Estimates vary, but the indigenous population of Latin America is something over 40 million. Indigenous peoples comprise nearly 10 per cent of the total Latin American population and are very diverse, speaking over four hundred different languages (Partridge and Uquillas 1996). These peoples include the descendants of complex civilizations such as the Maya, Aztec and Inca, as well as tribes of the forests and lowland plains, peoples such as the Yanomamo, Xavante, Miskito and Guarani. The indigenous peoples of Latin America live in a diverse range of settings, from tropical forest villages to mountain towns, and in the largest cities of the continent. They may be agriculturalists or hunter-gatherers, merchants or labourers, tradespeople or craftspeople or professionals. The largest indigenous populations are found in Bolivia, Peru, Ecuador, Guatemala and Mexico (Gonzalez 1994: 31). In these countries, indigenous culture has exercised a particularly strong influence on national culture, even as indigenous peoples themselves have experienced racism, marginalization, violence and pressures to assimilate.

Despite the widely varied contexts in which the indigenous peoples of

Latin America live, there is a clear pattern connecting indigenous peoples with poverty and disadvantage, from the highlands to the tropics. A study carried out in 1994 concluded that indigenous peoples in Latin America were more likely than any other group of a country's population to be poor, whether poverty was measured by income indicators, access to basic services such as water and sewage, educational attainment, literacy or housing quality (Psacharopoulous and Patrinos 1994). Recent research on the comparative conditions of indigenous and non-indigenous children in Latin America by Siri Damman (Chapter 5) indicates that indigenous children are more likely to die before one year of age than those of the general populations of the countries where they live, and are more likely to be stunted due to inadequate nutrition and health issues (parasites, disease). Another recent study by medical doctor Héctor Javier Sánchez-Pérez and his co-authors in Chiapas, Mexico (Chapter 3) finds similar patterns of disadvantage for indigenous women: this quantitative survey demonstrates that indigenous women tend to have lower educational attainment, live in more impoverished municipalities, and suffer from higher infant mortality rates.

These kinds of comparative studies, focusing on measurable economic and social indicators, provide a good base from which to talk about indigenous poverty. They make it possible to quantify some aspects of the relative disadvantage experienced by indigenous peoples vis-à-vis other groups, as well as the absolute impacts of this disadvantage on various aspects of people's lives. Reflecting on these studies, it is possible to argue convincingly that a clear pattern of disadvantage exists in which the indigenous peoples of Latin America are overall worse off than their non-indigenous counterparts. These studies also draw attention to some of the obvious and measurable forms this disadvantage takes (infant and child mortality, stunting, lack of services and opportunities, poor living conditions), making clear the unacceptability of current conditions and the need for change.

Yet these indicators do not paint a complete picture of poverty. Among indigenous peoples in Latin America, as elsewhere, there are aspects or 'dimensions' of poverty that are not easy to measure but are none the less a very real part of people's daily lives. For indigenous peoples in Latin America, these dimensions of poverty often take the form of racism – reinforced by deeply embedded assumptions about the inferiority of indigenous culture vis-à-vis European culture (see Regional Meeting 2001: 7–8) – accompanied by linguistic and cultural marginalization from the centres of commercial, intellectual and political power. Even where indigenous languages are recognized as national languages, bilingual education is promoted and indigenous cultures are acknowledged and even celebrated (though generally as a tourism resource), the practical obstacles that divide most indigenous people from opportunities are still vast. The dominant languages, institutions and cultural expectations in the countries of Latin America are still overwhelmingly non-indigenous. Those who cannot navigate comfortably within them are marginalized. And while the presence of significant indigenous political movements seeking change has allowed this marginalization to be articulated (Rojas 2003; Ticona Alejo 2000), it has not yet been eliminated.

Indigenous peoples in Asia

It is estimated that about 70 per cent of the world's indigenous peoples live in Asia (IFAD 2000/2001). Yet defining indigenous peoples is particularly problematic in this part of the world. As Barnes (1995) writes in the introduction to the excellent volume *Indigenous Peoples of Asia*, '"Indigenous peoples", a category that first came into existence as a reaction to the legacy of Western European colonialism, has proven especially problematic in postcolonial Asia, where many governments refuse to recognize the distinction sometimes advanced by dissident ethnic groups between indigenous and nonindigenous populations' (Barnes et al. 1995: 2).

The Philippines, where around 20 per cent of the total population is indigenous, is the only Asian country to have officially adopted the term 'indigenous peoples' (Vinding 2003a: 236). Nevertheless, Asian participation in international indigenous movements and forums is sizeable. And in 1992, the Asian Indigenous Peoples Pact was formed, bringing together the indigenous peoples of Asia in a joint quest for self-determination (Gray 1995: 44).

In Asia, which has experienced different waves of migration and a succession of colonial experiences, one ethnic group may have longer-standing claims than another without actually being the original inhabitants of an area (ibid.: 36–9). Thus, indigenous peoples are often defined as *prior* rather than *original* inhabitants (ibid.). For instance, many of the peoples of the Chittagong Hill Tracts in Bangladesh are not the original inhabitants of that region – only the Kuki peoples can make that claim – but they all pre-date recent efforts by the Bangladesh army to colonize the area through violent attacks on villages (ibid.: 39). As McCaskill and Rutherford indicate in Chapter 8, the indigenous peoples of Asia do not have the same well-defined, long-standing and recognized status as indigenous peoples in recently colonized areas such as North America, Australia or New Zealand. Nevertheless, the identifier *indigenous peoples* serves many groups in Asia to indicate their claims as prior inhabitants vis-à-vis later arrivals.

Indigenous poverty in Asia takes many forms. Gray (ibid.: 46–52) classifies the problems faced by the indigenous peoples of Asia in four categories: militarization; plundering of resources; forced relocation; and cultural genocide. Hill (1996) adds to this list the forced integration of indigenous peoples into market economies – giving the example of the Santals of north-central India – and bigotry/discrimination, such as that experienced by the Ainu in Japan and the original inhabitants of Taiwan and the Philippines. Examples for each of these categories can be found in the International Work Group for Indigenous Affairs (IWGIA) *Indigenous World* reports (e.g. Vinding 2003a) and the various reports to the UN's Working Group on Indigenous Populations. Nor are these problems particular to Asia; rather, as Gray (1995: 45) observes, they are remarkably similar to the experiences of indigenous peoples in other parts of the world. In Chapter 4, Scott Simon presents a case from Taiwan of land loss, indigenous activism and cultural appropriation which would look familiar to other indigenous peoples across the globe struggling with similar issues.

Basic economic and social indicators also tell a story of poverty and disadvantage for many Asian indigenous groups. In Vietnam, for instance, the poverty rates in regions where ethnic minorities are concentrated remained high in the 1990s (73 per cent in the northern highlands and 91 per cent in the central highlands), even as poverty rates for the country as a whole decreased from 58 to 37 per cent (ILO n.d.: 2). In Nepal, the Dalit, who comprise 20 per cent of the total population, own only 1 per cent of the arable land, and as many as 80 per cent live below the poverty line (ibid.: 2). In China, illiteracy rates are high among minority groups and 'lack of fuel for fires, insufficient clothing and shoes, several months' shortage of grain each year, and extreme scarcity of animal protein are common conditions' (Tapp 1995: 215). Simon (Chapter 4) describes the situation of indigenous peoples in Taiwan as 'the underside of a miracle'; the country's so-called economic miracle has left indigenous peoples with higher unemployment rates and lower average incomes than the general population, as well as uncertain access to land.

Indigenous peoples in Africa

Many ethnic groups in Africa pre-date the arrival of European colonizers yet do not identify themselves as indigenous peoples. Other terms such as 'tribes' or 'ethnic groups' are generally preferred. While 'indigenous' is used in southern Africa 'to distinguish the black majority from the European and Asian settler minorities', these are not indigenous peoples in the United Nations Working Group on Indigenous Populations' sense of non-dominant indigenous groups with distinct cultural and territorial identities (ILO 1999:

3). The groups who identify as indigenous peoples in this sense are more specific: generally pastoralists or hunter-gatherers, such as the Pygmies, Hadzabe, Maasai and Tuareg, who have been marginalized, relative to agriculturalists, in both colonial and post-independence eras (ibid.: 3).

Pastoral and hunter-gatherer groups across Africa often have similar experiences of marginalization. They are frequently in a state of partial integration (at the lowest level) into cash economies, and suffer dispossession from their traditional resources and pressure to abandon traditional lifestyles and livelihoods. Thus, for instance, the Nama and San people constitute some of the poorest of the poor in South Africa, dispossessed of their traditional lands, without access to traditional bush food, and stigmatized as a rural underclass fit only for menial labour (ibid.: 12–13). In Uganda, forcible eviction from their forests for a Nation Parks scheme moved many Twa Pygmies 'from a fairly independent existence to being landless, impoverished squatters, forced to survive by working for local farmers' (Vinding 2003a: 387). And in Ethiopia, the indigenous peoples (such as the Somali, Afar, Borena, Kereyu and Nuer) are estimated at about 5 million people, or 12 per cent of the country's population; they are mainly pastoralists and, according to the 2003 *Indigenous World* report, 'are subjected to the worst forms of political, economic and social marginalization and subjugation' as well as 'social, ethnic, religious, political and economic inequality'; for them, 'development' often involves confiscation of their grazing lands and forced sedentarization (ibid.: 358–9).

African indigenous peoples have generally been less involved in international indigenous movements than indigenous peoples of other parts of the world. For the first time in 1989, seven years after its founding, two indigenous representatives from Africa (both from Tanzania) attended the United Nations Working Group on Indigenous Populations (Parkipuny 1989). Since then, however, African involvement in international indigenous forums has increased. The Indigenous Peoples of Africa Co-ordinating Committee (IPACC), an advocacy network of indigenous peoples' organizations in Africa, was founded in 1996 by a group of organizations in attendance at the United Nations WGIP; this committee now has over seventy members.[1] Meanwhile, within Africa, groups such as the Amazigh cultural movement in various countries of North Africa are working for the recognition of the rights of particular indigenous groups. In 2001, the African Commission on Human and Peoples' Rights established a Working Group on the Rights of Indigenous People/Communities in Africa, marking the first time that this important African organization had dealt specifically with the issue of the human rights of indigenous peoples (IWGIA 2004).

Indigenous peoples in wealthy nations

For students of development accustomed to drawing sharp distinctions between the countries of the so-called North and those of the South – that is, between wealthy ('developed') and poor ('developing') nations – the similarities among indigenous peoples across these countries can be surprising. As Damman (Chapter 5) demonstrates in her study of indigenous children in the Americas, 'in rather wealthy countries such as Argentina, Chile, the USA, Canada and Brazil, one notes with interest that in spite of their relatively strong economy and small indigenous populations, the ratios [for infant mortality and stunting] remain approximately the same as in other parts of the Americas'. She notes that in Canada, Inuit children are 2.2 times more likely to die before one year of age as children in the general population; Métis and Canadian Indian children are 1.9 times more likely to die, and a similar trend exists in the United States.

A meeting of the indigenous peoples of Australia, New Zealand, Canada, Hawaii and the mainland United States in 2001[2] concluded that 'indigenous peoples by any social or economic indicator do not have equality with the members of the dominant societies where they live. They remain severely disadvantaged and marginalised' with discrimination 'deeply embedded in the social, political and economic fabric of these countries' which has become 'systematic and institutionalised' (Regional Meeting 2001). While living in wealthier countries may mean that the absolute poverty of indigenous peoples is lower, many still suffer relative poverty vis-à-vis the general populations in which they live.

Indigenous poverty in wealthy countries takes a variety of forms, some measurable and some not. Poverty indicators here may range from a greater incidence of ill health and unemployment to the loss of sacred sites to outside developers and the loss of language, cultural knowledge and social cohesion. As Cornell indicates in Chapter 11, reservation-based indigenous groups have some of the lowest income, employment, health, housing, education and other statistics in the United States. In New Zealand as well, Humpage observes in Chapter 9 that Māori as a group continue to demonstrate lower levels of educational attainment, employment, income, health and housing relative to non-Māori. In Australia, indigenous people overall have lower incomes, higher unemployment and incarceration rates, and much lower life expectancy than the non-indigenous population (see Chapter 14). And even in Norway, while the standard of living for the Sami is now nearly equal to that of other northern Scandinavian citizens, there are still experiences of racism, discrimination and threats to land rights (see Chapter 15).

Patterns of indigenous disadvantage

This introductory overview has attempted to highlight common patterns of indigenous poverty and disadvantage which criss-cross the globe. In vastly different contexts, indigenous peoples demonstrate surprisingly similar experiences of poverty in the form of land loss, income inadequacy, health challenges, social marginalization, violence, pressures to abandon traditional practices, and so forth. While the specific conditions and experiences of poverty of each indigenous group vary, many different groups often have surprisingly similar experiences. The categories of problems faced by indigenous peoples that Gray (1995) and Hill (1996) identify hold true not just in Asia but in many other places around the world. Militarization, plundering of resources, forced relocation, cultural genocide, the forced integration of indigenous peoples into market economies, and discrimination in everyday social life are not characteristic of the experience of all indigenous peoples or of all indigenous individuals, but they are sufficiently common to indicate a pattern. Around the world, indigenous peoples experience poverty – and they experience it in often surprisingly similar ways.

Drawing attention to indigenous poverty and disadvantage is not intended as an exercise in negativity. Rather, the purpose is to understand the characteristics of indigenous poverty, as a way to help understand poverty's causes – and potential solutions. Most notably, attention to the patterns of indigenous poverty and disadvantage worldwide reveals some key points:

1 As with all experiences of poverty, indigenous poverty is multi-dimensional, encompassing both measurable and non-measurable aspects of people's lives.
2 Indigenous poverty, specifically, is related to the cultural differences between dominant and non-dominant groups. Non-dominant indigenous peoples have cultures distinct from those of the dominant groups in the areas where they live. They tend to have different ways of doing things, different values, and even speak different languages. When dominant groups impose their culture (e.g. market capitalism, sedentary lifestyles) and destroy aspects of indigenous culture (e.g. access to land, language), poverty tends to increase.
3 Indigenous poverty is also related to racism. Indigenous peoples are often racially distinct from dominant cultures which have frequently branded them as inferior. Racist assumptions may be used by members of the dominant society to justify the appropriation of indigenous peoples' resources, as well as the exclusion of indigenous peoples from resources and opportunities available in the dominant culture.

4 Finally, indigenous poverty is related to social marginalization. Indigenous peoples are often defined as 'non-dominant', frequently colonized, peoples. Non-dominant peoples are those which, for a variety of reasons, are not in a powerful position vis-à-vis other groups. They may therefore find it difficult to exercise their influence or defend their interests. With growing indigenous rights movements, this situation is slowly changing. Yet around the world, appropriation of indigenous physical and cultural resources, militarization of indigenous territory and other such experiences can be attributed to indigenous groups having little social and political leverage with which to defend their rights and interests.

The chapters in Part I compare the situations of different indigenous peoples vis-à-vis the mainstream societies in which they live. Whether contrasting measurable indicators, as do Sánchez-Pérez and Damman, or exploring the less quantifiable social and political contexts of disadvantage, as does Simon, the authors in this section draw attention to the ways in which poverty affects indigenous peoples particularly. In doing so, they highlight aspects of the *process* of poverty (see Vinding 2003b) – poverty not as a noun but a verb, a process seated in social relationships. Clearly, it is in the interaction of people and institutions that conditions of poverty emerge. The conditions described here for indigenous peoples are the result not only of historical relationships and encounters, but also of current choices and actions. The active creation of poverty continues in our institutions and our relationships, with consequences not only for indigenous peoples, but for human society as a whole.

Notes

1 Information on the Indigenous Peoples of Africa Co-ordinating Committee (IPACC) is available from <http://www.ipacc.org.za/content.asp>

2 A regional meeting at the World Conference against Racism, Racial Discrimination, Xenophobia and Related Intolerance, Sydney, Australia, 20–22 February 2001.

References

Barnes, R. H., A. Gray and B. Kingsbury (eds) (1995) *Indigenous Peoples of Asia*, Ann Arbor, MI: Association for Asian Studies

Dogra (2000) 'Indigenous people helpless against land grabbers', Asia Times online, 2 June 2000, <http://www.atimes.com/>

Gonzalez, M. L. (1994) 'How many indigenous people?', in G. Psacharopoulous and H. A. Patrinos (eds), *Indigenous People and Poverty in Latin America, an Empirical Analysis*, Washington, DC: World Bank

Gray, A. (1995) 'The indigenous movement in Asia', in R. H. Barnes, A. Gray and B. Kingsbury (eds), *Indigenous Peoples of Asia*, Ann Arbor, MI: Association for Asian Studies

Hill, C. V. (1996) 'Indigenous peoples of Asia' (review), *Journal of Asian Studies*, 55(3): 700–1

IFAD (2000/2001) 'Rural poverty report 2000/2001', fact sheet: *The Rural Poor*, <http://www.ifad.org/media/pack/rpr/2.htm>

ILO (n.d.) fact sheet: *Discrimination At Work: Asia*

— (1999) 'Indigenous peoples of South Africa: current trends', report, Project for the Rights of Indigenous and Tribal Peoples, Geneva: International Labour Office

IWGIA (International Work Group for Indigenous Affairs) (2004) 'Indigenous peoples' rights and the African Commission', <http://www.iwgia.org/sw371.asp>

Parkipuny, M. (1989) 'The human rights situation of indigenous peoples in Africa', remarks to the 6th Session of the United Nations Working Group on Indigenous Populations in Geneva, Switzerland on 3 August 1989 <http://www.cwis.org/fwj /22/hra.htm>

Partridge, W. L. and J. E. Uquillas, with K. Johns (1996) 'Including the excluded: ethnodevelopment in Latin America', paper presented at the Annual World Bank Conference on Development in Latin America and the Caribbean, Bogotá, Colombia

Psacharopoulous, G. and H. A. Patrinos (1994) 'Indigenous people and poverty in Latin America: an empirical analysis', Washington, DC: World Bank

Regional Meeting (of Indigenous Peoples on the World Conference against Racism, Racial Discrimination, Xenophobia and Related Intolerance, Sydney, Australia, 20–22 February) (2001) 'Indigenous peoples and racism', report, Geneva

Rojas, R. (2003) 'Dirigentes indios de Latinoamérica llaman a preparar la toma del poder político', *La Jornada*, Mexico, 5 June

Sylvain, R. (2002) 'Land, water, and truth: San identity and global indigenism', *American Anthropologist*, 104(4): 1,074–85

Tapp, N. (1995) 'Minority nationality in China: policy and practice', in R. H. Barnes, A. Gray and B. Kingsbury (eds), *Indigenous Peoples of Asia*, Ann Arbor, MI: Association for Asian Studies

Ticona Alejo, E. (2000) 'Organización y liderazgo Aymara, 1979–1996 La Paz', Universidad de la Cordillera, AGRUCO

Vinding, D. (2003a) 'The indigenous world 2002–2003', Copenhagen: International Work Group for Indigenous Affairs (IWGIA), <http://www.iwgia.org/sw162.asp>

— (2003b) 'Poverty', editorial, *Indigenous Affairs*, 1

WGIP (Working Group on Indigenous Populations) (1995) 'Discrimination against indigenous peoples', report of the Working Group on Indigenous Populations on its 13th session, Geneva: United Nations, E/CN.4/Sub.2/1995/24, <http://ods-dds-ny.un.org/doc/UNDOC/GEN/G95/ 133/26/PDF/G9513326.pdf?OpenElement>

3 | The conditions of life and health for indigenous women in areas of high marginalization, Chiapas, Mexico

HÉCTOR JAVIER SÁNCHEZ-PÉREZ, GUADALUPE VARGAS MORALES AND JOSEP MARÍA JANSÁ

Several studies have demonstrated that Chiapas (with nearly 4 million inhabitants, based on the results of the last population census) is the most socio-economically marginalized state in Mexico (CONAPO 1998; INEGI 1990). Of Chiapas' over 20,000 communities, nine out of ten are considered to be high or very high socio-economic marginalization areas, even based on its own official statistics (CONAPO 1998). In addition to being one of the most socio-economically marginalized areas in Mexico, the state of Chiapas also evidences the worst demographic, health-related and health resource indicators in the country (Sánchez-Pérez et al. 1995; Sánchez-Pérez 1999).

As regards its health conditions, for instance, the 1991–95 infant mortality rate in the three most marginalized states of the country, Chiapas, Oaxaca and Guerrero – all of them situated in the south-east of Mexico – shows a ten-year lag compared to the country as a whole, but that rate turns into a twenty-year lag compared to other northern states (CONAPO 1998). In relative terms, the largest number of deaths and births with no healthcare services occurs in Chiapas. Based on health sector figures, at least one out of ten cases of cholera, and one out of three cases of malaria, occurs in Chiapas, and there are endemic areas of poverty-related diseases within the state (Health Secretariat, Pan American Health Organization 1995).

In this context, the above-mentioned conditions for women living in Chiapas are among the poorest in the country. For example, the illiteracy rate in Chiapas is 26 per cent (the highest in the country), as compared with 10.6 per cent in Mexico as a whole. In the case of women, the illiteracy rate in Chiapas is 33 per cent (against 13 per cent at national level). Additionally, Chiapas shows the highest birth rate in Mexico, the highest aggregate fertility rate and the lowest life expectancy for women (Sánchez-Pérez 1999).

Moreover, it should be noted that there are significant indigenous settlements in Chiapas. Of the sixty-two ethnically and linguistically recognized peoples in the country, people from at least forty different ethnic groups live in Chiapas, including groups such as Tzeltal, Tzotzil, Chol, Tojolabal, Zoque, Kanjobal, Mame, Chuj and Jacalteco. Based on the last population and household census count of 1995, there are 768,720 people living in Chiapas aged five or older who speak a native language (32 per cent of whom, at least, cannot speak Spanish). This means that at least one in four in the state is an indigenous inhabitant (INEGI 1996).[1]

Even though it is true that socio-economic marginalization within Mexico is greater among indigenous peoples than among non-indigenous groups, there are different levels of socio-economic marginalization within these indigenous groups. For example, the following features can be mentioned (CONAPO 1998):

- Whereas 58 per cent in the Mixteco group (central area of the country) live in municipalities rated as 'very highly marginalized', 93 per cent of the Tzeltal group live in such areas.
- The Tzeltal, Tzotzil and Tojolabal groups have the largest average number of children per woman in the country (over 4.1 children per woman).
- In 1995, the estimated infant mortality rate was 33 per 1,000 children born alive for Chontal-speakers, 40 for Chinantec and Zapotec groups, but 79 for the Tarahumara group, 81 for the Tzotzil group, and 87 for the Tojolabal group.

Despite these figures, however, there are almost no studies analysing the living and health conditions of indigenous and non-indigenous women in highly socio-economically marginalized areas in Chiapas. As a result, research has been conducted to analyse health conditions in highly and very highly socio-economically marginalized areas of the Border Region, one of the nine administrative regions into which the state of Chiapas is divided (Sánchez-Pérez et al. 1996). This paper includes the results of the analysis of the living and health conditions of indigenous women in that region.

Goals and work methodology

The core goal of this paper is to analyse the living and health conditions of indigenous women in highly and very highly socio-economically marginalized areas, focusing on the Border Region of Chiapas, Mexico. For this purpose, a survey was conducted in thirty-two localities (n=1,894 households) of the Border Region of Chiapas between March and October 1998. This region of nearly 425,000 inhabitants is located in the border area between Mexico and Guatemala and is one the poorest areas of Chiapas.

Of its twelve municipalities, two are deemed to be very highly marginalized, nine highly marginalized and one is regarded as having medium-level marginalization (CONAPO 1993). They have many Mayan (most of them of the Tojolabal group) and non-Mayan peasant (*campesino*) settlements.

The thirty-two localities under study were randomly selected based on two criteria for inclusion: the level of socio-economic marginalization (high or very high, as classified by the Consejo Nacional de Población) (ibid.), and how far the communities were from the nearest healthcare centre (<1 hour, or one or more hours) (Sánchez-Pérez et al. 2000, 2001; World Bank 1997). The selection of communities was based on the two municipalities rated as very highly marginalized in the region (CONAPO 1993), as well as a random selection of the nine highly marginalized municipalities. Then, field data provided by different governmental agencies (Secretariat of Health, Secretariat of Public Works, etc.) and various non-governmental organizations working in the region were used to prepare a list of communities in the selected municipalities based on how far they were from the nearest healthcare centre, sorted as per the World Bank's (1997) proposed approach for analysing access to healthcare centres – less than an hour; one or more hours. Of the 1,894 households selected for the study, survey data could be collected for 11,274 people in 1,878 households.

For the analysis of the living and health conditions of women in the area under study, only the data for people aged between fifteen and forty-nine were taken into account: totalling 2,558 women and 2,476 men. For study-related purposes, the population was classified as indigenous or non-indigenous, depending on whether or not they could speak a native language (CONAPO 1998, 1993), thus resulting in a total of 523 indigenous women and 487 indigenous men (mainly from the Tojolabal Mayan ethnic group) and 2,035 non-indigenous women and 1,987 non-indigenous men, i.e. of mixed race.

The following indicators were analysed: *Demographic Indicators.* 1.Aggregate Fertility Rate (AFR); 2. Pregnancy within two years prior to the study. *Socio-economic Indicators.* 1. Schooling; 2. Employment; 3. Social security; 4. Household indicators (household floor type, material used to cook food, water availability in the house, type of bathroom, lighting – electricity or solar energy – and available refrigerator); 5. Area of residence (urban/rural); and 6. Marginalization level of the municipality of residence (very high/high, as per CONAPO 1993). *Health-related Indicators.* 1. Morbidity observed within fifteen days prior to the study; 2. Self-assessment of health condition; 3. Pulmonary tuberculosis; 4. Result of last pregnancy (born alive, stillborn, aborted) and health-related problems during pregnancy and delivery; 5. Survival of the youngest child resulting from the last pregnancy (alive/dead); 6. History of dead children. *Use of and Access to Healthcare Services.* 1. Appropriate pre-natal healthcare (five or more consultations) and place of last pregnancy consultation within two years prior to the study; and 2. Delivery-related healthcare for last pregnancy: agent, place of delivery and whether a Caesarean section was performed or not.

The Aggregate Fertility Rate (AFR) was estimated using the Brass method, i.e. based on the data collected for children born alive, dead children born alive, and surviving children of mothers aged fifteen to forty-nine who reported having delivered one or more children born alive at the time the study was conducted. Pregnancy-related indicators were based on pregnant or not-pregnant status at the time the study was conducted and on pregnancy completion or non-completion within two years prior to the study.

For the morbidity observation category, a list of 'guiding symptoms' (Ochoa-Díaz et al. 1996) was read out at the selected households so that household members could tell whether they had observed any disease or not within fifteen days prior to the study. The diagnosis of pulmonary tuberculosis required an active search of coughing individuals among those aged fifteen or older within the health survey (Sánchez-Pérez et al. 2001). Individuals who reported cough symptoms for fifteen or more days were asked to provide sputum samples for bacilloscopes and cultures, which were processed pursuant to the regulations in force in Mexico (Balandrano et al. 1996).

Regarding pre-natal care and delivery-related healthcare, data about the last pregnancy completed within two years prior to the study were collected directly from women aged fifteen to forty-nine. Pre-natal care was deemed to be appropriate in the case of women reporting five or more consultations, pursuant to the official regulations in force in Mexico (Norma Oficial Mexicana 1995). Based on the answers provided by the interviewees, pregnancy results were classified as born alive, stillborn or abortion.

Results

The data collected by this study are shown by type of indicator.

Demographic indicators The age structure for the four groups under study was almost identical (the median was twenty-five years old and the average age was twenty-eight years old). The 1996 Aggregate Fertility Rate was 7.1 for non-indigenous women (NIW) and 8.1 for indigenous women (IW). Moreover, 27.4 per cent of NIW had completed a pregnancy within two years prior to the study, whereas 40.8 per cent of IW were in the same

TABLE 3.1 Socio-economic indicators analysed in men and women aged 15–49, according to indigenous/non-indigenous status, in areas of high and very high socio-economic marginalization in the Border Region of Chiapas, Mexico

Indicator	Indigenous women (n=523)	Non-indigenous women (2,035)	Indigenous men (487)	Non-indigenous men (1,989)
Schooling				
No schooling (%)[1]	50.1	16.0	28.7	8.7
1–3 years of schooling (%)	29.9	34.0	33.3	30.3
High school or higher (%)	2.1	12.4	9.7	16.8
Average (no. of schooling yrs)	0.7	1.5	1.2	1.7
Median (no. of schooling yrs)	0.0	2.0	1.0	2.0
Occupation (%)				
Agricultural jobs	67.3	17.4	80.7	79.0
Non-agricultural jobs	6.3	11.6	19.3	21.0
Household chores	26.4	71.0	0.0	0.0
No social security (%)[2]	97.9	96.1	95.9	96.5
Household condition (%)				
With earth floors	72.9	45.6	81.3	51.8
Firewood cooker	92.4	80.5	97.9	91.9
No water inside the house or solar energy	70.7	32.8	72.3	33.3
No electric power or solar energy	17.8	13.1	15.0	13.7
No refrigerator	95.8	81.7	96.5	83.7
No toilet or latrine	47.0	19.4	48.7	20.3
Area of residence (%)				
Urban	16.1	21.9	13.8	20.6
Rural	83.9	78.1	86.2	79.4
Level of poverty of the municipality of residence(%)[3]				
High	1.0	61.6	2.3	58.8
Very high	99.0	38.4	97.7	41.2

Notes: 1 All the indicators analysed bear statistically significant differences ($p<0.05$), unless otherwise stated. 2 Without statistically significant differences among the four groups analysed. 3 According to the National Population Council classification (CONAPO 1993).

situation ($p<0.05$). In addition, 6.3 per cent of NIW were pregnant at the moment the study was conducted, while 9.1 per cent of IW were in the same situation ($p<0.05$).

TABLE 3.2 Health-related indicators analysed in men and women aged 15–49, according to indigenous/non-indigenous status, in areas of high and very high socio-economic marginalization in the Border Region of Chiapas, Mexico[1]

Indicator	Indigenous women (n=523)	Non-indigenous women (2,035)	Indigenous men (487)	Non-indigenous men (1,989)
With morbidity observation within 15 days prior to the study (%)	71.3	73.3	58.3	56.5
Health condition assessment at the moment the study was conducted (%)				
Good/very good	61.2	57.2	68.0	68.7
Regular	13.7	19.7	11.8	17.5
Bad/very bad	25.2	23.1	20.2	13.8
With pulmonary tuberculosis (rate per 100,000 in the group)	191.2	393.1	0.0	201.1
With health problems during the last pregnancy within two years prior to the study (%)[2, 3]	15.1	19.3	–	–
With health problems during the last delivery within two years prior to the study (%)[2, 4]	6.0	8.7	–	–
Result of the last pregnancy within two years prior to the study, abortion or stillborn (%)[2]	2.5	1.0	–	–
Children born alive within two years prior to the study but who had died when the study was conducted (%)[5]	4.1	1.2	–	–
Mortality rate in children aged two or less (per 1,000 children born alive)	41.2	11.96	–	–
With history of dead children (%)[6]	46.0	30.2	-	–

Notes: 1 All the indicators analysed bear statistically significant differences (p<0.05), unless otherwise stated. 2 Based on 199 IW pregnancies and 591 NIW pregnancies. 3 p=0.107. 4 p=0.151. 5 Based on 194 children born alive from IW and 585 from NIW. 6 Only in women with one or more children born alive: 385 IW and 1,360 NIW.

Socio-economic indicators Table 3.1 shows that for all the analysed indicators indigenous groups are more marginalized than non-indigenous groups. In the case of schooling, the underprivileged situation is more serious in indigenous women (IW) than in non-indigenous women (NIW) and non-indigenous men (NIM). Whereas 50 per cent of IW have zero years of schooling, only 8.7 per cent of NIM are in the same situation. Moreover, while only 2.1 per cent of IW reach high-school educational level or higher, 17 per cent of NIM reach this level.

Additionally, it should be noted that even though a greater proportion of IW and IM live in rural areas compared to their non-indigenous counterparts, the differences become far more significant when analysing the indigenous/non-indigenous status of people according to the marginalization level of the municipality where they are living. Whereas nearly 40 per cent of NIW and NIM are living in very highly marginalized areas in socio-economic terms, almost all the indigenous population (men and women) are living in this type of area.

Health-related indicators The proportion of people reporting a morbidity observation within fifteen days prior to the study was almost the same among IW and NIW (71 per cent and 73 per cent respectively). In addition, IM and NIM values were also very similar (58.3 and 56.5 per cent respectively), but lower than women's values ($p<0.05$). Regarding self-observation of health condition at the moment the study was conducted, 61.2 per cent of IW reported a 'good' or 'very good' health condition, 13.7 per cent a 'regular' health condition, and 25.2 per cent reported feeling 'bad' or 'very bad'. In the case of NIW those values were 57.2, 19.7 and 23 per cent respectively. In the case of (indigenous and non-indigenous) men, a greater tendency towards feeling 'good' or 'very good' was found in comparison with women ($p<0.05$). It is worth noting that in the case of NIM only 13.8 per cent reported feeling 'bad' or 'very bad'.

Pulmonary tuberculosis (PTB) was diagnosed more often among NIW, with a PTB prevalence of 3.93 per 1,000 women (eight PTB cases were spotted in this group), while IW accounted for 1.91 (with one case) and the value in NIM was 2.0 with the same denominator (four cases identified). No cases were identified in IM. The observed differences were not statistically significant.

As to the observation of health problems during the last pregnancy and delivery within two years prior to the study, there was a slightly greater observation of problems among NIW than among IW, which was not significant from a statistical point of view. Regarding the result of the last pregnancy, 2.5 per cent of pregnancies (out of 199 documented among

TABLE 3.3 Pre-natal controls and delivery care indicators for the last pregnancy within two years prior to the study in women aged 15–49, according to indigenous/non-indigenous status, in areas of high and very high socio-economic marginalization in the Border Region of Chiapas, Mexico

Indicator	Indigenous women (n=199)	Non-indigenous women (591)	p
Pre-natal controls (number of visits)			
Appropriate (5 or more) (%)	82.9	75.8	0.068
1–4 (%)	16.1	21.2	
Zero controls (%)	1.0	3.1	
Average (SD)	7.18 (3.38)	6.68 (3.61)	0.086
Pre-natal controls (start month)			
Average (SD)	3.38 (1.37)	3.32 (1.47)	0.629
Median	3.0	3.0	–
Start within the first three months (%)	64.6	65.7	0.709
Reasons for not attending 5 or more pre-natal controls (%)	(n=34)	(n=143)	0.785
No need	46.7	54.3	
Distance to health facilities	10.0	8.0	
Short of money	13.3	10.9	
Healthcare services assessed as poor-quality	13.3	9.4	
Other	16.7	17.3	
Pre-natal control agent (%)			
Midwife	69.0	55.0	0.001
Services at healthcare centre	30.0	39.5	
Private visit to a physician	1.0	5.2	
Non-sanitary	0.0	0.3	
Delivery agent			
Midwife	79.0	51.2	0.000
Services at healthcare centre	17.6	25.9	
Private visit to a physician	0.5	3.4	
Alone or with a family member (non-sanitary)	1.5	19.5	
Place of delivery (%)			
At home or at a relative's home	80.4	70.8	0.011
Midwife's home	4.5	3.4	
Services at healthcare centre	15.1	22.2	
Private visit to a physician	0.0	3.2	
Automobile	0.0	0.3	
Caesarean section (%)	2.0	7.2	0.008

IW within the two years prior to the study) ended in an abortion or in a stillborn baby, i.e., there were five stillborn babies. In the case of NIW, 1.0 per cent of pregnancies (six minors), out of 591, ended in an abortion or a stillborn baby ($p<0.05$). Additionally, 4.1 per cent ($n=8$) of the 194 babies born alive from IW had already died when the study was conducted, whereas only 1.2 per cent ($n=7$) of the 585 babies born alive from NIW had died when the study was conducted ($p<0.05$). These figures imply that the mortality rates in children aged two or less were 41.2 per 1,000 babies born alive from IW and 12.0 for children delivered by NIW. Such figures show that the mortality rate among children aged two or less is 3.4 times higher in IW than in NIW.

Finally, the indicator related to a history of dead children among women who had delivered at least one baby born alive showed that this occurred 1.5 times more often among IW than among NIW.

Use of and access to healthcare services The differences observed as regards the number of pre-natal consultations among IW and NIW remained at the statistical significance limit level. Five or more pre-natal consultations, however, and a lower number of women with zero consultations, were more often observed among IW than among NIW. No differences as to the month of pregnancy inception were observed among IW and NIW. The average number of consultations was 7.2 (standard deviation 3.4) for IW and 6.7 (standard deviation 3.6) for NIW. Approximately 65 per cent of women in both groups initiated their pre-natal consultations in the first three months of pregnancy. Statistically significant differences, however, were found in the health agent used for pre-natal consultations. Sixty-nine per cent of IW went to a midwife, whereas only 55 per cent of NIW did the same.

It is interesting to note that there were almost no differences as to the reasons given for not having a greater number of pre-natal consultations. Some of the reasons given were: consultations were considered to be unnecessary (nearly half of the women in both groups); a shortage of money to pay for healthcare services; the services were assessed as poor-quality; and the distance to healthcare centres.

There were also statistically significant differences in terms of the delivery agent. Among IW, 78.7 per cent were attended by midwives, another 14.7 per cent by a physician, 4.7 per cent by a health promoter or nurse, and 1.9 per cent were attended by a non-health-service agent (self or a family member). In the case of NIW, 51.1 per cent were attended by midwives, 24.3 per cent by physicians, 4.8 per cent by health promoters or nurses, and 19.8 per cent did not receive any kind of healthcare, i.e. almost one in five women in this group had no healthcare during pregnancy.

Finally, only 2 per cent of IW pregnancies ended in a Caesarean section while the percentage went up to 7.2 per cent for NIW.

Discussion of the results

The results obtained from the different health indicators studied in the region demonstrate the existence of worse health conditions, as a result of the prevailing socio-economic conditions, than those encountered by other studies elsewhere in Mexico and at the national level (there are very few existing data available on indigenous women living in areas of high marginalization). We can can highlight the following examples:

a) *Prevalence of morbidity acknowledged by individuals in the last fifteen days.* In the National Health Survey (SSA 1994b), there is a 10 per cent prevalence while in this study there was a 56 per cent prevalence.
b) *Proportion of people who consider their health to be 'bad/very bad'.* In the same national survey they discovered that 3.5 per cent of the country's population considered their health to be such. In our study, 14 per cent non-indigenous men perceived their health to be such, while among indigenous women (IW) the rate was 25 per cent.
c) *Proportion of women with a history of miscarriage.* In a study conducted with the peasant community in the Fraylesca de Chiapas region (Ochoa Díaz et al. 1999) it was found that 12 per cent of 'rich', 25 per cent of middle-class and 34 per cent of poor peasant women had experienced miscarriages. In this study, the percentages were 46 per cent among IW and 30 per cent among NIW.
d) *Proportion of people attended by medical services.* Chiapas is the Mexican state with the lowest medical service coverage (45 per cent compared to the national level of 86 per cent) (SSA 2001). In some of the regions without indigenous communities, such as Fraylesca, it has been documented at 32 per cent (Sánchez-Pérez et al. 1998). In our area of study, 25 per cent of NIW had a nearby medical unit in proximity, but only 15 per cent of IW had such units.

The results of this study indicate that, even in areas of high and very high socio-economic marginalization, poverty conditions and the worst health and living standards become more evident in indigenous groups than in non-indigenous groups. In general terms, both men and women are found to be in worse socio-economic conditions than their non-indigenous counterparts.

In this sense, a number of social inequalities are revealed by this study:

1 The socio-economic inequality (class-related inequality) suffered by indigenous and non-indigenous men and women in areas of high socio-economic marginalization in Chiapas compared to other socio-economic regions.
2 The inequality between indigenous men and women compared to their non-indigenous counterparts (ethnic inequality).
3 The condition of indigenous and non-indigenous women compared to indigenous and non-indigenous men (gender-based inequality).
4 The inequality between indigenous women and non-indigenous women due to poverty and the fact of being indigenous and a woman (class, ethnic and gender inequality).

There are two particularly striking aspects. On the one hand, there is the fact that indigenous women have significantly lower educational levels (which might be explained by the fact that indigenous women's education is mainly focused on household care, as well as by the poor educational condition of Chiapas, particularly in areas of high socio-economic marginalization). On the other hand, there is the fact that the indigenous/non-indigenous polarity in the locations under study grows in relation to the marginalization level of the municipalities they belong to, but the difference is much less marked between urban and rural municipalities, in a context where little more than ten communities in Chiapas (out of over 22,000 located in this state) have more than ten thousand inhabitants.

The following aspects may be noted as regards the analysed health-related conditions:

1 The increased disadvantages for indigenous women compared to their non-indigenous counterparts, as is shown by the lower likelihood of their completing their pregnancy by delivering a baby born alive (at least twice as low), the higher mortality rate for their children aged two or less (four times higher than in non-indigenous women), and an increased history of dead children.
2 Several factors explain the higher rate of pulmonary tuberculosis (PTB) in non-indigenous groups than in indigenous groups (both in men and women), for instance the quality and quantity problems in sputum samples taken for the diagnosis of PTB in indigenous groups (Sánchez-Pérez et al. 2002). In spite of having Spanish–Tojolabal translators and the fact that samples were obtained at the coughers' homes (Sánchez-Pérez et al. 2001, 2002), communication problems most probably prevented the collection of a greater number of better-quality samples. For example, no cases were found among indigenous men (IM) (n=487), whereas only one PTB case was found among indigenous women (IW)

(n=523). The finding of at least one more case, either in indigenous men or indigenous women, would have increased the prevalence levels to figures similar to those observed in non-indigenous groups. Another explanatory factor could be the insufficient number of individuals in the indigenous groups under study: data were collected from 523 IW and 487 IM, whereas the number of non-indigenous men (NIM) was nearly 2,000, as was the case for non-indigenous women (NIW).

3 Regarding self-observation of health problems, indigenous women did not see themselves as a group at greater risk compared to NIW, in spite of experiencing worse health conditions for particular indicators (result of last pregnancy, history of dead children, survival of last child). In contrast, the trend was that NIW considered that they were suffering more health problems than IW.

4 The morbidity rate observed within fifteen days prior to the survey showed almost the same prevalence in both groups. The variable that made a difference for this indicator among the four groups under study was not indigenous/non-indigenous status but the gender of the individuals. A higher morbidity prevalence was found among women than among men.

5 No clear trend was found among IW and NIW as regards self-observation of health condition at the moment the study was conducted. The differences observed under this indicator were also more related to the fact of being a man or a woman rather than to indigenous or non-indigenous status: a higher rate of 'good' or 'very good' self-observations was found among men than among women. Two aspects should be highlighted for this indicator: first, the best self-observations of health condition were found among NIM; second, there were some differences between IW and NIW. A higher rate of 'good' or 'very good' health self-observations was found among IW than among NIW. IW also accounted, however, for the highest rate of 'bad' or 'very bad' answers. In fact, while the NIM group accounted for the lowest proportion in this category, the IW group evidenced the greatest proportion.

6 NIW also reported being more prone to health problems during their last pregnancy and delivery than IW, in spite of the fact that, as mentioned before, stillborn cases and children born alive who died before they were two years old were more often found among IW. This is a very important issue because such a situation reflects a very low level of health risk awareness within this group of women, at significant variance with the health conditions found (according to the health indicators analysed in this study).

Based on the analysed indicators, at least three aspects should be highlighted as regards use of and access to healthcare services.

1 Pre-natal consultations among IW tended to be greater than among NIW, owing basically to the important role of midwives in the area under study. In this way, the lower frequency of midwife services among NIW largely explained the fact that one in five women (either because of distance to healthcare centres, lack of money or for some other reason) was not provided with healthcare services during delivery (this situation accounted for only 2 per cent of IW).
2 It is important to highlight the significant number of home deliveries (80 per cent among IW and 71 per cent among NIW) because they are performed under poor sanitary conditions in most cases, as has been documented by other studies (Sánchez-Pérez et al. 1998) and as indicated by the household indicators analysed (see Table 3.1).
3 Caesarean deliveries were 3.6 times higher among NIW than among IW (7 per cent versus 2 per cent respectively). In spite of this, the proportion of Caesarean sections in both groups did not approach the recommended 15–20 per cent under the official regulations in force for second- and third-level health facilities (SSA 1994a). In this sense, this variable seems to depend on factors that are not associated with obstetrical risk conditions in women, such as living in an urban or a rural area, the marginalization level of the municipality of residence, and accessibility (cultural, geographical, economic and transportational) to second- or third-level health facilities. Obviously, women who receive midwife care or those who do not have healthcare at all (i.e. those who are helped by family members or minister to themselves) have no chance of having a Caesarean section performed during delivery, whereas for women who attend health facilities this will depend on whether they go to a hospital or a first-level health facility, which in turn will largely depend, as mentioned before, on factors related to the accessibility of second-level healthcare, which is usually low in the area under study.

Conclusion

The living and health conditions of indigenous women are a serious socio-economic, ethical and health problem requiring action. The results of this study highlight the need to develop mechanisms that reduce the inequalities in soco-economic conditions, ethnicity and gender that affect these women. To make substantial improvements in the living and health conditions of indigenous people (taking into consideration particularly the situation of women) in the region under study, policies should thus aim at a dramatic reduction in, or elimination of, the factors contributing to inequality, poverty, exclusion and poor health conditions in this sector of the population. Special focus should be placed on issues such as the improvement of levels of investment and access to land, education levels, household conditions, and ensuring food-related safety. In order to improve health conditions, it is necessary to develop programmes beyond those focusing simply on reproductive health, including action to secure better quality, accessibility and management of health services in multicultural contexts (including knowledge of and respect for culture and customs, a basic knowledge of native languages on the part of the health facility staff providing the services, and so forth), as well as health-related education, to train women and build awareness so that they may identify health risks for themselves and for their children. In this context, it is important to support midwives, by means of training, reference systems and resources, and to improve hygiene and sanitary conditions under which home deliveries are performed (Sánchez-Pérez et al. 1998).

Note

1 According to the concepts defined by the Consejo Nacional de Población (CONAPO 1998), indigenous groups are 'characterized by cultural values, language and identity of their own, as well as by their social organization and their specific ways of establishing a relationship with Nature, organizing for work and being governed by rules and regulations derived from their customs'. Owing to the complex difficulties involved in analysing what is meant by indigenous or non-indigenous, however, in Mexico the indicator for this status is based on the fact of whether or not a native language can be spoken by the population aged five or older (INEGI 1990, 1996). CONAPO (1998) has recently presented a proposal to include the condition of a native language being spoken by the head of the household and/or husband/wife in Mexican households, so that living in a household whose head speaks a native language would be a sufficient condition for considering an individual indigenous, whether he/she can speak it or not.

References

Balandrano, S., F. G. Anzaldo, F. G. Peña and M. X. Betancourt (1996) *Manual de procedimientos de laboratorio INDRE/SAGAR: 18. Tuberculosis*, Mexico: Secretariat of Health, Secretariat of Agriculture, Cattle-Raising and Rural Development, Pan American Health Organization

CONAPO (Consejo Nacional de Población) (1993) *Indicadores socio-económicos e índice de marginación municipal, Mexico, 1990*

— (1998) *La situación demográfica de México 1998*, 2nd edn

Health Secretariat, Pan American Health Organization (1995) *Situación de salud en México. Indicadores básicos 1995*, Mexico: Health Secretariat, Pan American Health Organization

INEGI (Instituto Nacional de Estadística, Geografía e Informática) (1990) *XI censo general de población y vivienda 1990*

— (1996) *Chiapas: Conteo de población y vivienda 1995. Resultados definitivos. Tabulados básicos*

Norma Oficial Mexicana (para la atención de la mujer durante el embarazo, parto y puerperio y del recién nacido) (1995), Mexico: Diario Oficial de la Federación

Ochoa Díaz, H., H. J. Sánchez-Pérez and L. Martínez Guzmán (1996) 'Uso de un índice de bienestar social para la planificación de la salud a nivel municipal', *Salud Publica Mex*, 38: 257–67

Ochoa-Díaz, H., H. Sánchez-Pérez, M. Ruíz-Flores and M. Fuller (1999) 'Social inequalities and health in rural Chiapas, México: agricultural economy, nutrition, and child health in La Fraylesca Region', *Cad. Saúde Pública*, Rio de Janeiro, 15(2): 261–70

Sánchez-Pérez, H. J. (1999) *Tuberculosis pulmonar en zonas de alta marginación socio-económica de Chiapas, México: problemas y retos a superar. El caso de la Región Fronteriza*, PhD dissertation in Medicine (Public Health), Barcelona: Universidad Autónoma de Barcelona

Sánchez-Pérez, H. J., M. Martín-Mateo and J. M. Jansá (1996) *Necesidades de salud en zonas de alta y muy alta marginación socio-económica de Chiapas*, Barcelona: El Colegio de la Frontera Sur, Instituto Municipal de la Salud de Barcelona, Universidad Autónoma de Barcelona, Consejo Nacional de Ciencia y Tecnología (CONACYT)

Sánchez-Pérez, H. J., G. Morales-Vargas and J. D. Méndez-Sánchez (2000) 'Calidad bacteriológica para consumo humano en zonas de alta marginación socio-económica de Chiapas: ¿apta o no apta?', *Salud Pública Mex*, 42: 397–406

Sánchez-Pérez, H. J., J. A. Flores-Hernández, J. M. Jansá, J. A. Caylá and M. Martín-Mateo (2001) 'Pulmonary tuberculosis in areas of high levels of poverty in Chiapas', *International Journal of Epidemiology*, 30: 386–93

Sánchez-Pérez, H. J., M. Hernán, S. Hernández-Díaz, J.M. Jansá, D. Halerpin and A. Ascherio (2002) 'Detection of pulmonary tuberculosis in Chiapas', *Annals of Epidemiology*, 12(3): 166–72

Sánchez-Pérez, H. J., H. Ochoa-Díaz and O. R. Miranda (1995) 'La situación de salud en Chiapas: consideraciones para su análisis', in O. R. Miranda, C. Valqui (eds), *Chiapas: el regreso a la utopía*, Mexico: Editorial Comuna, Universidad Autónoma de Guerrero, pp. 63–80

Sánchez-Pérez, H. J., H. Ochoa-Díaz, A. Navarro, I. Giné and M. M. Martín (1998) 'La atención del parto en Chiapas, Mexico: ¿dónde y quién los atiende?', *Salud Publica Mex* 40: 494–502

SSA (Secretariat of Health) (1994a) *Norma Oficial Mexicana de los servicios de planificación familiar*, Mexico: Diario Oficial de la Federación, 30 May

— (1994b) *Encuesta Nacional de Salud II*

— (2001) *La salud y el sistema de atención. Chiapas. Condiciones de salud, nivel y distribución*, <http://www.ssa.gob.mx>

World Bank (1997) 'The state in a changing world', *World Development Report*, Washington, DC: Oxford University Press

4 | Scarred landscapes and tattooed faces: poverty, identity and land conflict in a Taiwanese indigenous community

SCOTT SIMON

How can you buy or sell the sky, the warmth of the land?
The idea is strange to us. – Chief Seattle

In recent years, the interlinked goals of poverty reduction, empowerment of poor communities and participatory development have all become key areas of concern in international development. Influenced in part by the ideas of Paulo Freire (1970), these approaches attempt to place the needs and perspectives of the poor at the heart of development analysis and planning. In this era of 'post-development' or 'alternative development',[1] even the avatars of progress at the World Bank have attempted to hear the 'voices of the poor' through ambitious 'participatory poverty assessments' involving over 60,000 poor men and women in sixty countries (Narayan 2000; Narayan et al. 2000b; Narayan and Petesch 2002).

Although projects such as Voices of the Poor are commendable, they remain incomplete to the extent that they tend to lump poor and indigenous communities in the same category. This paper contends that the economic needs of indigenous peoples, defined as peoples with distinct cultures in subordinate positions in colonial or post-colonial circumstances,[2] must be considered to be distinct from those of other poor communities, and special attention must be paid to how they became impoverished in the first place. With different starting places, indigenous communities need radically different strategies for the attainment of social justice and economic empowerment. Crucial questions are thus open to exploration in specific communities throughout the world: How has 'development' contributed to poverty and disempowerment in indigenous communities? How does indigenous identity contribute to strategies of poverty reduction and economic empowerment? The experience of Taiwan has many lessons to offer scholars of development and indigenous peoples.

Indigenous peoples in Taiwan: the underside of a miracle

Although Taiwan has long been touted as an economic 'miracle' to be emulated by other countries (e.g. Fei et al. 1979; Galenson 1979; Gold 1986;

Wade 1990; World Bank 1993), even the existence of the island nation's indigenous peoples, not to mention the disastrous effect of development on their communities, is still little known outside of Taiwan. Among Taiwan's population of 22 million, nearly 400,000 people (1.8 per cent of the total population), in eleven legally recognized tribes, are of Austronesian rather than Han ethnicity.[3] In Chinese, these peoples are now collectively referred to as *yuanzhumin*, or original inhabitants.

Taiwan's indigenous peoples belong to the Austronesian linguistic family, a language family extending from Madagascar to Easter Island and Hawaii, from Taiwan to New Zealand. A recent theory, based on linguistics and genetic anthropology, suggests that Taiwan may have been the starting point of the entire Austronesian dispersal throughout the Pacific and Indian Oceans after their arrival from south-east China over six thousand years ago (Bellwood et al. 1995). In recent years, there have been increasing numbers of ethnographic and historical studies of these ethnic groups in western languages (e.g. Blundell 2000; Brown 1996; Cauquelin 2003; Chen 1996; Hsu 1991; Ka 1995; Shepherd 1993; Zheng 1995). The political economic study of these groups has led to important findings on issues of representation (Ching 2000, 2001; Chiu 2000; Hsieh 1994, 1999; Ren 1998; Stainton 1999a), indigenous social movements (Allio 1998; Barnes et al. 1995; Chiu 1989; Munsterhjelm 2002; Stainton 1999b, 2002), ethnic relations (Nettleship 1976) and religious change (Brown 2003; Huang 1996). As with indigenous communities in North America, there is also an extensive literature on medical problems. Nevertheless, there is still relatively little on economic development in these communities, even in the Chinese-language literature, with the notable exception of one special issue of *Cultural Survival Quarterly* (Arrigo 2002a, 2002b; Simon 2002) and research on urban aboriginal unemployment (Chu 2000).

Like indigenous communities around the world, the *yuanzhumin* of Taiwan have long been excluded from the fruits of development. Although their presence on Taiwan pre-dates Han occupation by more than six thousand years – and in spite of the fact that the country's industrial infrastructure was built with their labour – they remain disenfranchised relative to the Han majority. In 2001, the indigenous unemployment rate of 9.24 per cent, was, for example, far greater than the general unemployment rate of 3.89 per cent (Executive Yuan Indigenous Peoples Council 2001: 28); 37 per cent did not have regular employment at all (ibid.: 16). The average income of aboriginal people has consistently remained considerably less than that of Han people. In 2001, it was only NT$24,000 (US$686) per month for working aboriginal people, compared to NT$35,600 (US$1,017) per month for the working Taiwanese population at large (ibid.: 17).[4]

Since Taiwan in general has a high level of self-employment (see Shieh 1992), and Han entrepreneurs are present in even remote indigenous communities, aboriginal individuals often identify economic control of their own communities as one of their biggest social problems. In conversations in the villages, they often attribute the problem to questions of control over land. In what reflects a degree of assimilation to Han economic norms, some aboriginal individuals complain about difficulties accessing credit because their land is legally recognized as aboriginal reserve land and cannot be used as collateral. If aboriginal reserve lands were actually providing sustainable livelihoods for their communities, those individuals might have less reason to protest.

Han-owned Taiwanese corporations are adept at getting access to aboriginal land, even for such destructive purposes as mining, cement production and the disposal of nuclear waste. The result is that most aboriginal people are alienated from their traditional hunting grounds and instead work in low-paid dangerous occupations such as that of cement factory workers; 16 per cent of aboriginal people are engaged in construction, as compared to 8.2 per cent of the general population (Executive Yuan Indigenous Peoples Council 2001: 38).

Hsiulin Township in eastern Taiwan's Hualien County is a paradigmatic example. It is a community where the Taiwanese corporation Asia Cement has gained access to indigenous lands through fraud and deception. A political economic history of the tribe is the best starting point for understanding what has happened in Hualien County.

Taiwan's Tayal tribe

There is strong local controversy about whether the population of Hsiulin Township should be classified as part of the Tayal tribe, or as a separate tribe known as Taroko or Sediq. For the purposes of the present article, I refer to local members as Taroko, but use the term Tayal in historical contexts to refer to the larger groupings of linguistically related communities.[5] The Tayal tribe, with a population of 61,597, is Taiwan's second-largest indigenous group.[6] Dispersed throughout the mountainous regions of Taipei, Taoyuan, Hsinchu, Miaoli, Taichung, Nantou and Hualien Counties, they also have the largest geographical range. Owing their uncompromising resistance to both Han Chinese and Japanese violations of their property rights in past centuries, as well as a strong warrior tradition of headhunting and both inter- and intra-tribal warfare (Mowna 1998: 211), they have earned the reputation of being 'fierce barbarians' (*xiong fan*). Their facial tattoos, which both men and women traditionally receive after successfully attaining maturity, were also perceived as a sign of fierceness by Han Chinese colonialists, since criminals in China at the time were sometimes branded on the face as a form of punishment.

Throughout the waves of Han Chinese immigration to Taiwan from the seventeenth to the late nineteenth centuries, the Tayal remained largely in charge of their own territories. During the period of Ch'ing administration (1683–1895), in fact, the island was divided into the western part, marked as territory of the *shoufan* (literally, 'cooked barbarians') on maps, and the eastern part, marked as land of the *shengfan* ('raw barbarians'). Han Chinese settlers and sinicized aborigines, ancestors of today's 'native Taiwanese', were allowed to settle and cultivate land on the western part (see Brown 1996; Pasternak 1972; Shepherd 1993). The non-assimilated aborigines maintained control of their own territories, and Han Chinese were forbidden to settle in their regions. Considering the headhunting customs of some of the tribes, moreover, the incoming Han Chinese were unlikely to make such an attempt.

Before their integration into the successive Japanese and Chinese (Republic of China) states, the Tayal lived in close-knit communities regulated by strong religious beliefs. They believed that all of nature belonged to the omnipresent spirit *rutux*. The universe was structured according to a moral order called *gaga*. Any violations of the moral order were perceived to bring misfortune upon both individuals and the entire community. Individuals who violated *gaga*, for example, would fail to catch wild boars while hunting, would fall easily on dangerous mountain slopes, and would be bitten more easily by mosquitoes. Major violations of *gaga*, including the breaking of sexual taboos, required certain rituals to restore order (Mowna 1998: 59).

The Tayal, as hunters and swidden cultivators, ruled over vast hunting lands. According to Hsiulin Township anthropologist Masaw Mowna, they had a complex system of property rights institutions. The Tayal, he said, 'think that *property is life*' (ibid.: 183, emphasis added). In pre-colonial times, Tayal property rights were divided into public property owned collectively by the tribe and private property belonging to families and individuals. Collectively owned property included hunting grounds, mountains, forests, waters, uncultivated lands, lands abandoned by the deceased, tribal pathways, animals and fish that lived within those territories, and other mountain products such as bees and honey. Private property included cultivated land, agricultural products and tools, bamboo groves, and private pathways (ibid.: 184–6).

Since property was considered to carry the souls of the ancestors and represented hope for future generations, the protection of property rights was regulated by the moral order of *gaga*. Even within the tribe, property rights could not be transferred from one family to another without religious rituals that included the sacrificial slaughter of pigs (ibid.: 187). Tribal property rights were also jealously guarded from incursion by enemy tribes and rigorously enforced.

It was only after the Japanese takeover of the island that the indigenous peoples of central and eastern Taiwan became integrated into a modern state system with new systems of property rights. That transition marked the end of Tayal control over their own territory, and began the process of cultural loss. During the Japanese colonial period (1895–1945), in order to take control of the island's forests, as well as mineral and other natural resources, the Japanese limited indigenous people to 'mountain reservations', cutting their traditional territory of 2 million hectares down to 24,000 hectares. In order to put down resistance from indigenous peoples, the Japanese launched a number of violent expeditions into aboriginal territory, something the Chinese had not managed to accomplish. In the 'Five-year Expedition' of 1910–14, over ten thousand Tayal people were killed. In order to assimilate indigenous peoples, the Japanese encouraged them to take Japanese names and forced children to learn Japanese in compulsory elementary school education.

The Tayal tribe was the last tribe to be brought under Japanese domination. By the 1920s, the Japanese had already built police stations, schools and health clinics in most aboriginal villages. Japanese administrators, police officers, military officials, business people and teachers worked all over the island, implementing new systems of social control and expropriating aboriginal resources. It was only a matter of time before violence broke out as a result of this violation of sacred *gaga* (Ukan 2002).

In what is now known as the Wushe Incident, a group of over three hundred Tayal warriors attacked Japanese who had gathered at a sports event in Wushe (now Nantou County) on 27 October 1930, killing 130 people. It took Japanese forces two months, and the deaths of 216 aboriginal people, to completely quell the following uprisings. In an event that still remains a part of Tayal collective memory today, the Japanese hired Amis aboriginal militia to behead 101 people and return them to the Japanese for bounty payments. Tayal people still discuss this incident as evidence of Tayal fierceness and an Amis tendency to collaborate with outside oppressors.[7]

The Japanese designated much of Taroko territory as state-owned forest, built up the timber industry, and forcibly relocated the Taroko to what is now Hsiulin Township at the foothills of the mountains. Their traditional hunting lands are now the Taroko National Park. Many of the hiking trails in that park were originally hewed into the rock walls of the gorge by the

Japanese in order to move artillery into the mountains and defeat the 'fierce' Taroko people.

After its defeat in Second World War, Japan renounced its rights to its colonies in Taiwan and Korea. In 1945, without consulting the island's population, Taiwan was given to the Republic of China (ROC) to be ruled by General Chiang Kai-shek and the Chinese Nationalist Party (Kuomintang, KMT). After the takeover of China by the Communist Party, the KMT retreated to Taiwan. For indigenous peoples and native Taiwanese, Taiwan's transfer to Chiang Kai-shek's Republic of China was just a change from one violent colonial regime to another (Chiu 1999). In order to consolidate its rule, the KMT government massacred over 20,000 people in the 'February 28th Incident' (see Simon 2002) and imprisoned countless dissidents, including indigenous people, in the forty years of martial law that followed.

Like their Japanese predecessors, the KMT implemented policies of assimilating indigenous people and reclaiming their lands. Indigenous people were required to take Chinese names, and learn Chinese in school. Household registration regulations were composed to forcefully assimilate indigenous people. Upon marriage to a Han Chinese man, for example, an indigenous woman would lose her indigenous legal status. But a Han woman who married an indigenous man would retain her Han Chinese status.

Following Japanese precedents, the new Chinese state relocated entire indigenous communities in order to make room for national parks, industrial zones and reservoirs; or simply to facilitate administration and social control. The government nationalized traditional territories, hunting grounds and ritual sites, and forbade the traditional activities of hunting, fishing and slash-and-burn agriculture. Most lands with development potential were quickly turned over to either the government or Chinese capitalists.

In 1968, the KMT state began registering indigenous territories as legally recognized Aboriginal Reserve Land. Although indigenous people had lived on Taiwan for thousands of years before the Chinese arrived, aboriginal families received usufruct rights *rather than legal ownership* under the new system. Usufruct rights, moreover, were granted only under the condition that crops were planted for ten years. This stipulation forced the indigenous people to assimilate Chinese patterns of settled cultivation, primarily for cash crops. Aboriginal land could not be sold or rented to outsiders. It had to be either cultivated or ceded to the government as state property. The latter condition eventually permitted Taiwanese corporations to gain control of indigenous land with state support.

Asia Cement in Hsiulin township

Asia Cement is one of the KMT-related corporations that came into being during the import substitution policies of the 1950s to provide plastics, artificial fibres, cement, glass and other upstream materials for Taiwan's new industrial producers (Wade 1990: 77). Incorporated in 1957 and first listed on the Taipei stock exchange in 1972, it has expanded to become Taiwan's largest cement supplier. The Hualien plant, in Hsiulin Township, has been one of its largest manufacturing centres.

In 1973, Asia Cement applied to rent land from the Hsiulin Township Office, and held its first 'consultative' meeting with Taroko people. As the 'consultative' meetings with First Nations peoples in North America so often do, this event resulted in the further loss of aboriginal land. Township officials encouraged Taroko farmers to rent their land, promising that Asia Cement would provide local employment, prevent the migration of young people to the cities, and bring economic development to the community. The original landowners received monetary compensation for the displaced crops – a mere fraction of the land's real-estate value – and the promise that the land would be returned to them after twenty years. Neither Asia Cement nor the township office made it clear to the poorly educated farmers that cement mining and production would render their land unfit for agriculture.

Since Taiwan was under martial law from 1947 to 1987, there was scarcely room for protest. The company did little to fulfil its promise of employing Taroko people. Although it had promised one job to each of the more than one hundred families ceding land, only thirty people were employed in manual occupations as labourers, drivers and machine operators. Many of them developed respiratory ailments from inhaling cement dust, and three have died of lung complications. During my field visit in 2002, one young man fell to his death in the cement factory.

In 1993, Asia Cement's leases were set to expire. When some of the original owners tried to reclaim their land, however, they found that their property rights had mysteriously disappeared. Asia Cement claimed that the owners had relinquished their rights to the property *in perpetuity*, and that the company had the legal documents to prove it. They argued that the land was state property, and that they were renting it legally from the township office. In 1973, there had been little room for protest. Now martial law had been lifted, however, and the Taroko people were ready to fight back.

Aboriginal identity: a new form of social capital

By 1993, moreover, the Taroko had already gained the social capital that comes with legal identity as indigenous peoples. They had, like many other groups in similar colonial and post-colonial circumstances (Hodgson 2002), joined transnational alliances and 'become' indigenous. By adopting the identity of *yuanzhumin*, a translation from the aboriginal meaning 'original inhabitants', they had positioned themselves as colonized peoples with internationally recognized rights to property and possessions, cultural practices and knowledge.

The movement did encounter resistance. One Taiwanese anthropologist of Chinese origin, who had built a career out of studying Austronesian cultures on Taiwan, even made a public declaration to the effect that Taiwan's Austronesians were not true aboriginals (*yuanzhumin*), but rather *xianzhumin*, or 'first inhabitants'. His argument was that since the Austronesians also arrived in Taiwan from elsewhere, and quite likely from what is now China, they were simply earlier arrivals and thus deserved no special rights not accorded to the Chinese majority.

In spite of such objections, the aboriginal movement gradually built up momentum in the 1980s. It marks its genesis with the foundation of *Gaoshan qing* (Mountain Greenery) newspaper in 1983, and the foundation of the Alliance of Taiwan Aborigines (ATA) in 1984. After martial law was lifted in 1987, the movement grew in strength and number. Several indigenous publications, including *Shan-hai* and *Nandao Shibao*, were started, as well as a number of NGOs, some supported by the Presbyterian Church. Since 1991, the ATA and other indigenous groups have been the only Taiwanese NGOs to be recognized by the United Nations, a status that gives indigenous interests in Taiwan significant clout (see Allio 1998). In 1996, the Executive Yuan set up the Indigenous Peoples Council, which has since taken a proactive stance on such issues as poverty, unemployment and land rights.[8]

The Taroko struggle to reclaim their lands from Asia Cement quickly became an important feature of this movement, owing largely to the initiative of one ambitious woman from the community. In 1993, fifty-eight-year-old Igung Shiban, a Taroko woman who had spent most of her life with her Japanese husband in Japan, returned to Hsiulin Township with her husband while he recuperated from a serious illness. When she returned home, she was surprised to find that her father's property had come under the control of Asia Cement. She did not believe that he had agreed to relinquish his family's land in perpetuity.

With the help of her husband, Igung Shiban organized the concerned farmers of the community into an NGO known as the Return our Land Self-Help Association. They began by petitioning the local government, and finished by taking the case to court. One lucky day for the Taroko people, township officials left a hearing in anger, leaving behind a stack of documents. As Igung Shiban looked through them, she found that they were filled with irregularities. Some were missing dates or official seals. Most suspicious of all, the signatures of many former owners who had supposedly ceded their land to the township government were in the same hand. During close to a year of research, she pulled out the agreements, one by one, from the township office files and showed them to the signatories to confirm whether or not they had actually signed them. It turned out that most of the signatures to the agreements to relinquish land rights were forgeries.

Asia Cement first resorted to intimidation and violence in attempts to stop her research. Shiban and her husband were physically attacked by hired gangsters twice, and her husband had his leg wounded, but they didn't give up. Fortunately, local environmental activist and National Legislator Bayan Dalur, an indigenous representative for the opposition Democratic Progressive Party (DPP), helped them pursue the case by providing access to government documents.

In 1997, Igung Shiban herself ran for office as township council representative as a DPP candidate. The KMT, however, nominated her brother's wife as their candidate in order to split the loyalties of her clan group. Asia Cement also threw their financial resources into the campaign, offering local people as much as NT$10,000 to vote for the KMT. In a community with high unemployment and low family incomes, the temptation was difficult to resist. Still, Shiban lost the election by only fifty votes, a result that demonstrated a strong base of support in the community.

Since then, Shiban has continued her struggle for her ancestral land in both the courts and through other official channels. In 1998, she sent a report on Taroko land struggles to the United Nations Working Group on Indigenous Populations (Shiban 1997). As a result she gained the support of some journalists; Taiwan's 'Super TV' even made a documentary film on the Taroko struggle (Biho 1999). Igung Shiban has been adept at adopting the discursive practices of the international indigenous movement. In her documentary, she said, 'We are just like Indians in North America, whose lands have been taken away from them.' Linking her movement to international indigenous and environmental movements, she even recited a Chinese translation of Chief Seattle's famous speech in the documentary.

In August 2000, the Taroko people finally won cultivation rights in court, owing partly to intense lobbying on their behalf from Yohani Isqaqavut, chair of the Executive Yuan Indigenous Peoples Council. On 4 September 2000, the Taroko people were able to enter their lands for the first time in twenty-seven years. They celebrated the event with a traditional ceremony in commemoration of their ancestors.

The struggle has not yet reached a conclusion. In March 2001, conflict broke out when Asia Cement sent foreign workers to prevent Taroko farmers from planting crops on the land. A journalist was injured in the violence that ensued. Taroko people have planted crops several times since then, but Asia Cement responded by removing the young plants from the ground during the night. The company is hoping that intimidation will prevent the Taroko people from cultivating the land, a precedent that will eventually be recognized as a legal abandonment of the property. In 2001, an article about the conflict appeared in the *Los Angeles Times* (Chu 2001), causing Asia Cement to react further against the Taroko people and their allies. I was prevented by company guards from taking photos of the Asia Cement plant from the public highway.

Appropriating Taroko 'identity': the tattooed faces of Asia Cement

During the time when Igung Shiban was attempting to link Taroko to land issues, other forces in the community tried to take the pressure off Asia Cement through the promotion of cultural identity by way of research on facial tattoos. Until the Japanese occupation, the Taroko people had the custom of receiving facial tattoos at adulthood. Once young women learned to weave and young men learned to hunt, they were given tattoos on their faces. Only those individuals with facial tattoos, it was believed, would be allowed to cross the Rainbow Bridge into Heaven after death. The Japanese and Chinese colonial administrations, however, forbade the custom and it fell out of practice. By the 1990s, the remaining population of elderly Taroko with facial tattoos was rapidly disappearing.

Igung Shiban's younger brother, Kimi Shiban, was an employee of Asia Cement. In 1993, as a township representative, he took an interest in facial tattoos and convinced the township government to collect data and photographs of eighty-two elderly men and women with tattoos. In 1995, he realized that more educational work needed to be done when his son came home from school and asked, 'Is it true that our ancestors were all gangsters covered with tattoos?' In what eventually became the Atayal Facial Tattoo Culture Studio just down the street from Asia Cement, Kimi Shiban conducted life-history interviews and collected photographs of over two hundred elders with facial tattoos. The youngest person he interviewed was eighty-two, and the oldest 105.

The result of the project was a travelling exhibition of photographs and other Taroko artefacts. With funding from Asia Cement, the exhibition was shown at the provincial government's Taiwan Museum in Taipei's New Park and widely publicized. Asia Cement was thus able to position itself in public discourse as the protector and preserver of Taroko culture rather than as a colonizing power that had illegally encroached on Taroko territory.

The incursion of Asia Cement into Hsiulin Township has clearly destroyed the natural environment, alienated aboriginal people from their lands, and torn apart the community. The experience of the Taroko people in Taiwan, however, has important lessons for indigenous people worldwide in terms of land, indigenous identity and empowerment. Asia Cement's support of research into aboriginal tattoos shows clearly the danger that attention to 'cultural survival' as identity can pose. Although Kimi Shiban may have been sincere in his desire to preserve memories of his grandmother's generation, his work was ultimately used to detract attention from the real material problems of the Taroko people and to mine social capital for Asia Cement.

Asia Cement has been able to use this, as well as local elections, to divide the Shiban clan and members of their community. The corporation emerges as the winner when the community is unable to unite against its common enemy. By providing employment, Asia Cement has even been able to present itself as Hsiulin Township's solution to poverty. As one cement worker said to me, 'The land is already ruined anyway. But Asia Cement gives us job opportunities. We may as well work for them and earn their money. We have families to raise.' He was cynical about both Igung Shiban, whom he described as a radical troublemaker, and her brother, whom he perceived as getting rich by collaborating with Asia Cement. Unfortunately, the Taroko of Hsiulin Township are not the only indigenous community that has been torn apart by 'development'.

Conclusion

In recent years, much attention has been paid to 'poverty' and 'empowerment' in communities similar to Hsiulin Township, with an eye towards greater participation of the poor in development. In their global study, the World Bank concluded that a strategy for improvement must include four critical elements: 1) starting with poor people's realities; 2) investing in the organizational capacity of the poor; 3) changing social norms; and 4) supporting development entrepreneurs (Narayan 2000: 274). These suggestions, however, are clearly insufficient for indigenous peoples.

A study of the Taroko experience shows that such suggestions have to be modified in significant ways in order to better reflect the needs of indigenous peoples. As Arturo Escobar so forcibly argued, 'development' as a discourse often masks or even justifies patterns of inequality and colonial domination. Even the construction of 'poverty' as a relative lack of money and material possessions compared to the rich justified the extension of modern institutions into much of the world to solve this newly created problem (Escobar 1995: 23). In Hsiulin Township, in fact, 'poverty', 'development', and even 'cultural survival' have all been used to justify the control of Asia Cement over Taroko lands and the continuing presence of the company in their community.

Real empowerment of indigenous people is needed in order to contest the hegemonic forces of colonial domination. According to the World Bank definition, empowerment is 'the expansion of assets and capabilities of poor people to participate in, negotiate with, influence, control, and hold accountable institutions that affect their lives' (Narayan 2002: xviii). The democratization of Taiwan has contributed more to empowerment of Taiwan's indigenous peoples than state guidance, or international agencies such as the World Bank.[9] It is above all the contribution of Taiwan's grassroots NGOs such as Igung Shiban's Return our Land Self-Help Association which has allowed Taiwan's indigenous communities to start from the reality of the poor. Igung Shiban, and others like her in other Taiwanese indigenous communities (see Wen 2000), is clearly a good example of a 'development entrepreneur'. She has, however, managed to point out the crux of the 'poverty' problem far more clearly than the World Bank and other international agencies.

For indigenous peoples, poverty is not merely a problem to be solved by development agencies or NGOs through aid, private enterprise development or other strategies. Rather than being the root illness in itself, poverty in indigenous communities is a *symptom of colonial loss*. Colonialism destroyed prior systems of property rights, social systems that contributed to more or less egalitarian communities, and traditional ways of subsistence. It is only with the loss of those institutions that indigenous peoples became impoverished communities susceptible to exploitation by companies such as Asia Cement.

Although specific policy recommendations need to be tailored to different national contexts, the empowerment of poor people in indigenous communities can be achieved through nothing less than compensation for the losses of colonialism. Since the root of indigenous poverty is loss of land to colonial domination, that reality must be addressed as the foundation of economic development in indigenous communities. If it is to be real, empowerment in Hsiulin Township and other indigenous communities around the world must begin with either the return of indigenous lands or full compensation for their loss. Anything less will be a mere stopgap measure with little chance of success.

Notes

1 This literature on empowerment-based development is vast. For further essays and bibliographic information, see Crush 1995; Friedmann 1992; Parfitt 2002; Parpart et al. 2002; Rahnema and Bawtree 1997.

2 For the purposes of this paper, I accept the definition of indigenous peoples from José's Martínez Cobo's 1986 UN report on indigenous peoples:

> Indigenous communities, peoples and nations are those which have a historical continuity with pre-invasion and pre-colonial societies that developed on their territories, consider themselves distinct from other sectors of societies now prevailing in those territories, or parts of them. They form at present non-dominant sectors of society and are determined to preserve, develop, and transmit to future generations their ancestral territories, and their ethnic identity, as the basis of their continued existence as peoples, in accordance with their own cultural patterns, social institutions and legal systems. (Cobo 1986, cited in Hodgson 2002: 1,039)

3 'Han' here refers collectively to the three ethnic groups in Taiwan with roots in mainland China, usually referred to as Mainlanders, 'Native' Taiwanese and Hakka. As an ethnic marker for the dominant ethnic groups as distinct from indigenous people, it is more often used in indigenous communities than in urban settings.

4 US$1 = NT$35.

5 Alternative spellings for Tayal, sometimes seen in the ethnographic literature, are Atayal and Dayan.

6 The 28,000 members of the Taroko tribe in Hualien County are included in this figure. The Taiwanese government does not recognize them as a separate tribe.

7 Seeing me talk to an Amis man in a restaurant, one Taroko elder once warned me against making Amis friends. He used the Wushe Incident to prove 'their' untrustworthiness. Friendships and even intermarriage between the two groups, however, do occur in spite of mutual animosity.

8 As Taiwan seeks a national identity distinct from China, the small nation has finally become aware of indigenous issues and placed them at the forefront of the national agenda. In 1997, legal rights for indigenous peoples were finally included in the ROC constitution. In 2000, the Democratic Progressive Party elected Chen Shui-bian president and promised to affirm indigenous rights. By 2001, the government was considering the establishment of autonomous regions in areas of high Austronesian population in order to better protect indigenous rights. Such policies should not be viewed as Machiavellian moves to gain more space for Taiwan in the international arena; they are more accurately understood as responses to political pressure from grass-roots social movements.

9 Owing to pressure from China, Taiwan has not been permitted to join the United Nations and most affiliated international organizations such as the World Bank and the IMF.

References

Allio, F. (1998) 'The Austronesian peoples of Taiwan: building a political platform for themselves', *China Perspectives*, 18: 52–60

Arrigo, L. G. (2002a) 'A minority within a minority: cultural survival on Taiwan's orchid island', *Cultural Survival Quarterly*, 26(2): 56–61

— (2002b) 'In the Name of Progress', *Cultural Survival Quarterly*, 26(2): 70

Barnes, R. H., A. Gray and B. Kingsbury (eds) (1995) 'Alliance of Taiwan Aborigines', Report of the Human Rights Situation of Taiwan's Indigenous Peoples, in *Indigenous Peoples of Asia*, Ann Arbor: Association of Asian Studies, pp. 357–72

Bellwood, P., J. Fox and D. Tyron (eds) (1995) *The Austronesians: Historical and Comparative Perspectives*, Canberra: Australian National University

Biho, M. (dir.) (1999) *Land in Her Heart: Chun-chou Tien on the Offensive*, Taipei: Super TV (in Chinese)

Blundell, D. (ed.) (2000) *Austronesian Taiwan: Linguistics, Ethnology, and Prehistory*, Berkeley, CA: Phoebe Hearst Museum of Anthropology

Brown, M. (1996) *Negotiating Ethnicities in China and Taiwan*, Berkeley, CA: Institute of East Asian Studies

— (2003) 'The cultural impact of gendered social roles and ethnicity: changing religious practices in Taiwan', *Journal of Anthropological Research*, 59(1): 47–67

Cauquelin, J. (2003) *Aborigines of Taiwan: The Puyuma from Headhunting to the Modern World*, London: Routledge Curzon

Chang, T. P. (1999) *Invisible Land: History, Theory and Action in the Taroko Tribe's Movement to Oppose Asia Cement and Return our Land*, MA thesis, National Dong Hwa University Graduate Institute of Ethnic Relations and Culture, Hualien

Chen, C. K. (1996) 'From aborigines to landed proprietors: Taiwan aboriginal land rights, 1690–1850', in G. Hershatter et al. (eds), *Remapping China: Fissures in Historical Terrain*, Stanford, CA: Stanford University Press, pp. 130–42

Ching, L. T. S. (2000) 'Savage construction and civility making: the Musha incident and aboriginal representations in colonial Taiwan', *Positions: East Asia Cultures Critique*, 8(3): 795–818

— (2001) *Becoming 'Japanese': Colonial Taiwan and the Politics of Identity Formation*, Berkeley: University of California Press

Chiu, F. Y. L. (1989) 'Taiwan's aborigines and their struggle towards radical democracy', in D. Kumar and S. Kadirgamar (eds), *Ethnicity: Identity, Conflict and Crisis*, Hong Kong: Arena Press, pp. 143–54

— (1999) 'Nationalist anthropology in Taiwan 1945–1996: a reflexive survey', in J. Van Bremen and A. Shimizu (eds), *Anthropology and Colonialism in Asia and Oceania*, Richmond: Curzon Press

— (2000) 'Suborientalism and the subimperialist predicament: aboriginal discourse and the poverty of state-nation imagery', *Positions* 8 (1): 101–49

Chu, H. (2001) 'The tale of Taiwan's aborigines', *LA Times*, 1 June, p. A1

Chu, J. J. (2000) 'From incorporation to exclusion: the employment experience of Taiwanese urban aborigines', *China Quarterly*, 164: 1,025–43

Cobo, J. M. (1986) *The Study of the Problem of Discrimination against Indigenous Populations*, vols 1–5, United Nations Document E/CN.4/Sub.2/1986/7, New York: United Nations

Crush, J. (ed.) (1995) *Power of Development*, London: Routledge

Escobar, A. (1995) *Encountering Development: The Making and Unmaking of the Third World*, Princeton, NJ: Princeton University Press

Executive Yuan Indigenous Peoples Council (2001) *Report of 2001 Survey on Employment Conditions of Taiwanese Indigenous Peoples*, Taipei: Executive Yuan (in Chinese)

Fei, J. C. H., G. Ranis and S. W. Y. Kuo (1979) *Growth with Equity: The Taiwan Case*, New York: Oxford University Press

Freire, P. (1970) *Pedagogy of the Oppressed*, New York: Herder and Herder

Friedmann, J. (1992) *Empowerment: The Politics of Alternative Development*, Oxford: Blackwell

Galenson, W. (1979) *Economic Growth and Structural Change in Taiwan: The Postwar Experience of the Republic of China*, Ithaca, NY: Cornell University Press

Gold, T. (1986) *State and Society in the Taiwan Miracle*, Armonk, NY: M. E. Sharpe

Hodgson, D. (2002) 'Introduction: comparative perspectives on the indigenous rights movement in Africa and the Americas', *American Anthropologist*, 104(4): 1,037–49

Hsieh, S. C. (1994) 'From Shanbao to Yuanzhumin: Taiwanese Aborigines in transition', in M. Rubenstein (ed.), *The Other Taiwan: 1945 to the Present*, Armonk, NY: M. E. Sharpe, pp. 404–19

— (1999) 'Representing Aborigines: modelling Taiwan's mountain culture', in K. Yoshino (ed.), *Consuming Ethnicity and Nationalism: Asian Experiences*, Honolulu: University of Hawaii Press, pp. 89–110

Hsu, M. T. (1991) 'Culture, self, and adaptation: the psychological anthropology of two Malayo-Polynesian groups in Taiwan', Taipei: Academia Sinica Institute of Ethnology

Huang, S. W. (1996) 'The politics of conversion: the case of an aboriginal Formosan village', *Anthropos*, 91(4–6): 425–39

Ka, C. M. (1995) *Japanese Colonialism in Taiwan: Land Tenure, Development, and Dependency, 1895–1945*, Boulder, CO: Westview Press

Mowna, M. (1998) *Social Organization of the Tayal Tribe*, Hualien: Tzu Chi University Research Centre on Aboriginal Health (in Chinese)

Munsterhjelm, M. (2002) 'The first nations of Taiwan: a special report on Taiwan's indigenous peoples', *Cultural Survival Quarterly*, 26(2): 52–5

Narayan, D. (ed.) (2000) *Voices of the Poor: Can Anyone Hear Us?*, Washington, DC: World Bank

— (ed.) (2002) *Empowerment and Poverty Reduction: A Sourcebook*, Washington, DC: World Bank

Narayan, D., R. Chambers, M. K. Shah and P. Petesch (eds) (2000) *Voices of the Poor: Crying Out for Change*, Washington, DC: World Bank

Narayan, D. and P. Petesch (eds) (2002) *Voices of the Poor: From Many Lands*, Washington, DC: World Bank

Nettleship, M. (1976) 'Chinese–Aborigine relations on Taiwan: the Jin-ai Atayal as a descriptive case study', *Journal of Asian Affairs*, 1(2): 6–12

Parfitt, T. (2002) *The End of Development? Modernity, Post-Modernity and Development*, London: Pluto Press

Parpart, J., S. Rai and K. Staudt (eds) (2002) *Rethinking Empowerment: Gender and Development in a Global/Local World*, London: Routledge

Pasternak, B. (1972) *Kinship and Community in Two Chinese Villages*, Stanford, CA: Stanford University Press

Rahnema, M. and V. Bawtree (1997) *The Post-Development Reader*, London: Zed Books

Ren, H. (1998) 'The displacement and museum representation of aboriginal cultures in Taiwan', *Positions*, 6(2): 323–44

Shepherd, J. (1993) *Statecraft and Political Economy on the Taiwan Frontier, 1600–1800*, Stanford, CA: Stanford University Press

Shiban, I. (1997) 'Report to the United Nations Working Group on Indigenous Populations: our experience of the incursion of cement companies onto the land of the Taroko people, Hwalien, Taiwan', unpublished report

Shieh, G. S. (1992) *'Boss' Island: The Subcontracting Network and Micro-entrepreneurship in Taiwan's Development*, New York: Peter Lang

Simon, S. (2002) 'The underside of a miracle: industrialization, land, and Taiwan's indigenous peoples', *Cultural Survival Quarterly*, 26(2): 66–9

Stainton, M. (1999a) 'The politics of Taiwan aboriginal origins', in M. Rubinstein (ed.), *Taiwan: A New History*, Armonk, NY: M. E. Sharpe, pp. 27–44

— (1999b) 'Aboriginal self-government: Taiwan's uncompleted agenda', in M. Rubinstein (ed.), *Taiwan: A New History*, Armonk, NY: M. E. Sharpe, pp. 419–35

— (2002) 'Presbyterians and the aboriginal revitalization movement in Taiwan', *Cultural Survival Quarterly*, 26(2): 63–5

Ukan, W. (2002) 'The Wushe Incident viewed from Sediq traditional religion: a Sediq perspective', in C. F. Shih, S. C. Hsu and B. Tali (eds), *From Compromise to Self-Rule: Rebuilding the History of Taiwan's Indigenous Peoples*, Taipei: Avanguard Publishing Company (in Chinese), pp. 271–304

Wade, R. (1990) *Governing the Market: Economic Theory and the Role of Government in East Asian Industrialization*, Princeton, NJ: Princeton University Press

Wen, L. (2000) 'Colonialism, gender and work: a voice from the people of the lily and the leopard', *Anthropology of Work Review*, XXI(3): 24–7

World Bank (1993) 'The East Asian miracle: economic growth and public policy', Washington, DC: World Bank

Zheng, C. (1995) *Les Austronésiens de Taïwan: à travers les sources chinoises*, Paris: l'Harmattan

5 | Nutritional vulnerability in indigenous children of the Americas – a human rights issue

SIRI DAMMAN

During the 2003 session of the UN Permanent Forum on Indigenous Issues, it was pointed out that very little comprehensive information exists on the situation of indigenous peoples. The forum thus recommended that UN bodies provide more information on indigenous peoples' situation and living conditions, with a particular focus on children and youth (UN 2003).

According to a World Bank-sponsored compilation of available data from Latin America, indigenous peoples are prone to be poor and to experience overlapping fields of vulnerability (World Bank 1994). Another international study suggests that indigenous peoples are also vulnerable with regards to health (Alderete 1998). They not only tend to lack basic necessities, but also formal education, equal opportunities and political influence (UNDP 2000). Various international organizations and conferences have added indigenous peoples to the list of vulnerable groups[1] worthy of particular attention in regard to health, nutrition and development (PAHO 1994; WHO 2001; WSC 1990; FAO/WHO 1992; WSSD 1995; WFS 1996). As various international initiatives seek to address social inequalities – such as the World Health Organization's goal of 'health for all within 2000' and the more recent 'equity in health' – they have focused attention on vulnerable groups that for various reasons do not benefit equally from mainstream developments. On a parallel track, during the past fifteen years the UN human rights system has made substantial efforts to spell out the content and implications of specific economic and social rights, including non-discrimination with regard to food and health.[2]

It is rather intriguing that indigenous peoples[3] (hereafter IP), a highly diverse group of peoples, genetically very different with a wide variety of lifestyles, from all over the world, should be more vulnerable than others. It is also interesting to note that, in spite of a widespread consensus on their vulnerability, there is a general lack of systematic cross-national indicator-by-indicator analyses.

A rights-based approach to development, with its focus on non-discrimination, respect, equity, accountability, transparency and participation, might be of particular value to vulnerable groups, and to IP in particular. States have the potential either to undermine or to secure the enjoyment of the right to adequate food and the right to health, but according to international human rights standards, they have both a moral and legal responsibility to ensure these rights within their borders. An underlying assumption of this chapter is that one may detect a state's true dedication to Economic, Social and Cultural Rights (ESCR), including the right to food and to health and social justice, through the way it deals with the IP living within its borders. In a best-case scenario, IP are not marginalized, and enjoy their human rights, including the right to food and to health, on equal terms. If their nutrition and health indicators were the same as, or approaching, the country average, this would mirror the commitment of the state to indigenous peoples' rights. If, on the other hand, the gap between indigenous and non-indigenous indicators is large or increasing, this indicates a society where different groups have unequal access to vital resources.

In this study the author sets out to explore, although limiting herself to the American continent,[4] whether conclusions can be drawn about indigenous vulnerability on the basis of two indicators: infant mortality rate (IMR)[5] and stunting (height/age) in children. The nutrition-related indicators are carefully chosen according to the availability of data and their additional function as proxy indicators of socio-economic status and poverty (WHO 2001). Overall, Latin America is doing quite well in comparison to Africa and Asia in regard to stunting (PAHO 2002) and IMR. As this study will show, however, regional and national averages may conceal wide internal variances.[6] The results provide the starting point for the second part of the study – a discussion of the practical implications of the findings, from a human rights perspective.

Land tends to represent the basis for income and, in many cases, food, livelihood and economic survival for IP. The land, with all the animals and plants that live and grow there, represents their traditions, culture and spirituality, and by living on and using the resources of the land, they reinforce their identity as peoples. Land rights are therefore essential for IP. Historically, states have typically disregarded traditional land rights and indigenous peoples' collective use of land. This has been to the advantage both of the state itself and of commercial and other interests.

Indigenous peoples are typically caught up in a rapid acculturation, or rather deculturation, process, often accelerated by the confiscation of indigenous land. IP living in rural areas of the Americas, making a living in the traditional way, tend to experience deteriorating access to harvested traditional food resources. In the Arctic, traditional foods are contaminated by heavy metals and other toxins (AMAP 1997). Besides potentially harmful dietary and lifestyle changes, indigenous communities are also prone to poverty, and all it implies for living conditions: joblessness, high rates of suicide, substance abuse, violence, and social and cultural disintegration (IWGIA 1999; MRGI 1977).

In both developing and developed countries, IP seem particularly prone to suffer and die from diseases and conditions that in principle are easy to cure, including infectious diseases of the respiratory and digestive system, and chronic conditions due to nutritional deficiencies (Alderete 1998). Furthermore, children who were undernourished during their first years of life are more prone to become obese and to suffer from so-called lifestyle diseases, such as elevated blood pressure, type 2 diabetes and coronary heart diseases (CHD) later in life. Thus, indigenous children are more prone to be diabetic, obese and suffer heart conditions as grown-ups. So what we see is a 'double burden' of disease; in one and the same population, high levels of so-called poverty-related diseases exist side by side with diseases that until recently were associated with wealth and an affluent sedentary lifestyle.

The situation is called the 'nutrition transition', and is linked to rapid Westernization of traditional diets and lifestyle. The rise in lifestyle-related diseases is particularly strong in developing countries, including Latin America (Bermudez and Tucker 2003). This is a scary scenario, since the health budgets in these countries tend to be overburdened as it is (WHO 2003). In developed countries, obesity, diabetes and CHD are particularly evident among the poorer population groups, among whom one tends to find the indigenous communities. These people's diets are changing at an alarming pace towards one rich in refined flour, sugar and saturated fat, and their activity levels also tend to be changing from an active to a sedentary lifestyle (Kuhnlein and Receveur 1996; PAHO 2002). Not surprisingly, obesity in indigenous children is found to be on the rise in both wealthy and developing countries (Albala et al. 2002; Nakano 2003).

IP are often said to be 'genetically small'. Research by Habicht et al., however, showed that child stature at seven years differed substantially between the highest and lowest socio-economic levels, and that children from the same socio-economic class on different continents tended to present more similarities than differences between ethnic groups (Habicht et al. 1974). Thus, chronic malnutrition in early life leads to reduced body stature, so a person who is chronically malnourished during the first years of life will not reach the height he or she was genetically programmed for. Interestingly, it is shown that the average height of a population changes over time, which implies that height is a consequence of living conditions. While the height of Mayans in Central America has actually gone down by almost 12 centimetres during the last twenty centuries (McCullough 1982), children of Maya mothers who migrated to the USA are significantly taller than those in a comparable age group in Guatemala (Bogin et al. 2002).

Large proportions of the IP in South America live in mountainous areas, sometimes at 3,000 metres or more, and are often found to be small. It has been suggested that people living at high altitudes do not grow to be as tall as those living at lower levels owing to a supposed physiological effect of altitude on growth (Stinson 1980). Later studies, however, indicate that the effect that was attributed to altitude is negligible or small. The humble living conditions and food insecurity caused by short agricultural seasons in the mountainous areas are more likely causal factors (Bustos et al. 2001; Greksa et al. 1985).

Thus, the high levels of stunting generally found in the indigenous peoples of the Andean region and in Mesoamerica should be interpreted as reflective of resource constraints and poverty. Poor growth is due to a combination of food insecurity and poor diets, frequent infections and the inability of caretakers to provide the children with adequate care (Bustos et al. 2001). Even if many are self-sufficient in regard to food and basic necessities, curable infectious diseases often take a more serious turn in IP, since they tend not to benefit equally from the services of public healthcare. One reason for this is geographical, since IP often live in geographically marginalized areas, where health services are scarce and scattered. Furthermore, even if a health post is in the vicinity, if people do not have any savings, healthcare and medicines may still be inaccessible. The marginal areas are often also the ones with the least economic potential. Besides the issues of economic and geographical availability, authors also mention culturally based distrust and prejudices, discrimination and communication problems due to language or cultural differences as reasons for low health service attendance (PAHO 2002).

What does a human rights approach have to offer?

A human-rights-based approach to development starts from the ethical imperative that everyone is entitled to a certain standard of living. It provides a non-discriminatory and 'human-centred' vision of development. For obvious reasons, good health cannot be provided and ensured by a state, nor can states provide protection against every possible cause of human ill health. Consequently, the right to health must be understood as a right to the enjoyment of a variety of facilities, goods, services and conditions necessary for the realization of the highest attainable standard of health (UN/ECOSOC 2000a, 2000b).

As peoples without their own states, IP cannot become formal members of the United Nations. This has not stopped IP from providing a space for themselves, however, and quite successfully presenting their concerns both within and outside the explicit human rights context of the UN. Since the 1990s, Economic, Social and Cultural Rights (ESCR) have gained increasing influence within international development organizations. IP are the explicit subjects of two international human rights instruments, the ILO Convention No. 107 on Indigenous and Tribal Populations (hereafter ILO 107), and the ILO Convention No. 169 concerning Indigenous and Tribal Peoples in Independent Countries (hereafter ILO 169). ILO 169 was introduced in 1989 and was more to the liking of IP than was the assimilationist perspective of the earlier ILO 107; ILO 169 presents the idea that indigenous cultures and lifestyles, history, languages, religions, values and resources should be safeguarded through legally based protective measures. ILO 169 also opens the way for a certain degree of self-determination for indigenous communities (ILO 1989). Within the Americas, ILO 169 has been ratified by Argentina, Bolivia, Brazil, Colombia, Costa Rica, Dominica, Ecuador, Guatemala, Honduras, Mexico, Paraguay, Peru and Venezuela (ILO 2003), while Canada and the USA have still not ratified it (see Table 5.2 below).

On the surface, the differences between rights-based and conventional 'basic needs' approaches to food and nutrition may appear subtle. On further inspection, however, the differences are fundamental. The 'basic needs' approach defines beneficiaries and their needs, but the potential beneficiaries have no active claim to ensure that their needs will be met, and there is no duty or binding obligation on behalf of anyone to meet these needs. As such, basic needs approaches are based on policy decisions and economic and other considerations, and are voluntary. On the other hand, being based in law, the human rights approach to economic, social and cultural rights and to development substitutes for the 'political will approach', whereby the state is free to choose whether or not to act, a system based on legal imperatives, duties, obligations, and the monitoring of state performance. By emphasizing state responsibilities, beneficiaries are recognized as active subjects and 'claim-holders' who should be consulted and allowed to participate in decision-making and implementation. Duties or obligations are established, and those having the responsibility to act should be clearly defined (the 'duty-bearers') (UNDP 2000).

The concepts of claim-holders and duty-bearers set the stage for increased accountability. This is key both to improved target group influence and increased effectiveness of action. As such, potential 'value added' can flow from the application of a rights-based approach (Kracht 1997). Democratic processes, at both central and local levels, will be strengthened, and programmes are likely to become more sustainable, through the emphasis on accountability in decision-making and implementation. Increased accountability, consultation, inclusion and empowerment of beneficiaries would facilitate the identification of benchmarks and indicators to evaluate processes and results (UNDP 2000).[7]

Human rights treaties are legally binding on states, and are not therefore aspirations – unlike recommendations from global summits and conferences. The ethical and juridical aspects become all the more important in a world dominated by the ideology of 'free trade', which places an unprecedented emphasis on the rights and interests of companies, while threatening to marginalize large population groups. A human-rights-based approach obliges states to regulate national actors in the interests of rights-holders, and to challenge the trends leading to a weakened state. Human rights are, at least in theory, superimposed on all other international agreements. If the world community decides to give human rights more priority, the human rights system might very well provide a stronghold against international processes leading to an increased gap between rich and poor.

Infant mortality and stunting among indigenous children of the Americas

IMR and stunting as indicators of poverty In developing countries, more than 40 per cent of all children are stunted,[8] and over 50 per cent of all child deaths are directly or indirectly due to malnutrition (UNICEF 2000). Growth assessment (measuring prevalence of stunting/chronic malnutrition) is at the moment the best measure of the health and nutritional status of children, because stunting is caused by disease and inadequate food intake in a combined effect on child growth.

Stunting and infant mortality rates (IMR) are relatively well correlated. Both function as proxy indicators of poverty, reflecting the general socio-economic conditions in a society. What distinguishes them is that stunting is particularly sensitive to the general socio-economic conditions, including food insecurity, disease load, sanitary conditions and general poverty, while IMR better reflect the availability and accessibility of general health services, including birth attendance (PAHO 2002). This paper considers both IMR and stunting as poverty indicators. It does not attempt to correlate these with other measures of poverty, such as income levels or human development ranking, owing primarily to the paucity of such data for specific indigenous groups.

Comparing non-standardized data materials Comparative studies examining indigenous health systematically, indicator by indicator, are practically non-existent. Reasons for this may be the tendency not to consider ethnicity as an important variable for building models of inequity – a reflection of certain national ideologies, or of the methodological problems involved (ibid.: vol. 1, p. 100). Surely, methodological problems should not be underestimated. Currently, the methodological standards are poorly harmonized – for instance, when comparing studies on indigenous health, one finds that indigenous individuals are identified according to different criteria[9] – and few countries gather and analyse vital and health service statistics by ethnicity (PAHO 1998). Data-sets are more commonly disaggregated by gender, urban/rural location, or by region (see Table 5.1). The availability of region-specific data does open up the possibility of using geographic area as a substitute for ethnicity, given that IP are often located in well-defined geographical areas ('proxy area', Table 5.1).[10]

Findings Country averages from the relevant age group in the national health surveys were used as reference values; indigenous data were divided by the respective national average to express a ratio (indigenous value/national average). Comparing indigenous data with national averages was the best option available, since comparable data on 'non-indigenous' IMR and stunting tend not to be available.

The results show that all available ratios (indigenous/national average) on infant mortality and stunting in Table 5.1 are higher than 1. This indicates that indigenous children of the Americas are more prone to die before one year of age and to be stunted than the general population in the same country. Where the IMR is high, the proportion of stunting is high too, underlining the interconnectedness between the two.

As observed in the table, in some countries there is a relatively small difference between indigenous values and the country average, while in others the indigenous values are two to three times higher or more. In Canada the Inuit children are 2.2 times and Métis and Canadian Indians 1.9 times more likely to die before one year of age. In the USA, the same trend exists.

The data-set on Guatemala is disaggregated both by ethnicity, degree of urbanization and by socio-economic level; this opens up the possibility of further insights. The national IMR is 45/1,000, the indigenous IMR 56/1,000, and the *ladino* ('non-indigenous') value is 44/1,000. The ratio (indigenous/national) is small (1.2), but must be seen in connection with Guatemala's large indigenous population (66 per cent), which influences the country average. If one compares the indigenous IMR to the *ladino* value, the ratio increases to 1.3.

Forty-seven per cent of Guatemala's children are stunted, 67 per cent of the indigenous children and 34 per cent of the *ladinos*. Owing to the large number of stunted indigenous children, and the high proportion of

TABLE 5.1a Infant mortality rate (IMR) in indigenous children of the Americas, compared to average values in their countries

Country	Indig. pop. as % of total[1]	Medical doctors per 10,000 inhabitants[2]	Year referred to	IMR[3] nationally (× 1,000)	Ratio: indigenous value/national average		
					Nat. value ind.	Proxy area	Small studies
Bolivia	71	3.2	1998	67		1.9	
Guatemala	66	9.0	1999	45	1.2	1.3	
Peru	47	10.4	1996	43		1.5	2.6–3.6
Ecuador	43	13.2	1999	30		1.8–2.1	
Belize	19	7.4	1996	26		1.2	
Honduras	15	8.3	1995	36			
Mexico	14	15.6	1995	29	1.9		3.0
Chile	8	13.0	1999	10.1		Up to 4.1	
El Salvador	7	11.8	1998	35			
Panama	6	12.1	1999	21.3		1.8	
Nicaragua	5	6.2	2000	45.2			
Suriname	6	5.0	1999	29			
Guyana	6	1.8	1998	23			
Paraguay	3	4.1	1992	36	3.0		1.9–5.1
Colombia	2	9.3	1993	32.1			2.0
Venezuela	2	19.3	1995	23.1		1.4–1.6	
Argentina	1	26.8	2001	17.6		1.2	
Costa Rica	1	15.0	2000	10.2			
Brazil	.2	14.4	1998	33			
Canada	1	22.9	1996	7	1.9–2.2	3.1	
USA	.65	27.9	1998/96	7.2	1.6		

Notes: 1 PAHO (1998), citing Inter-American Development Bank, preliminary project for the creation of the Development Fund for Indigenous Peoples of Latin America and the Caribbean, Washington, DC, 1991; Instituto Indigenista Interamericano, Data Bank, Mexico, 1992, in PAHO/WHO, SILOS-34, 1993. 2 PAHO (2002), vol. 1, p. 381, table 'Ratio of doctors, nurses ...'). 3 Probability of dying between birth and exactly one year of age expressed per 1,000 live births (UNICEF 2000).

TABLE 5.1b Chronic malnutrition (CM) in indigenous children of the Americas, compared to average values in their countries

Country	Indig. pop. as % of total	Medical doctors per 10,000 inhabitants[2]	Year referred to	CM[1] nationally	Ratio: indigenous value/national average		
					Nat. value ind.	Proxy area	Small studies
Bolivia	71	3.2	1998	26.8		1.8	
Guatemala	66	9.0	1999	47	1.4		
Peru	47	10.4	2000	25.4		1.2/1.4	
Ecuador	43	13.2	1998	26.4		1.7	
Belize	19	7.4	1996	15		2.6	
Honduras	15	8.3	1992	36.3			1.9
Mexico	14	15.6	1996	33.9	1.7	1.3–1.4	1.8
Chile	8	13.0	2002	1.5		1.4	1.8
El Salvador	7	11.8	1998	23.3		1.3	
Panama	6	12.1	1997	14.4	3.5	1.6	
Nicaragua	5	6.2	2001	20.2		1.1–1.7	
Suriname	6	5.0					
Guyana	6	1.8	1997	10			1.7–1.9
Paraguay	3	4.1	1997–98	10.9			
Colombia	2	9.3	2000	13.5			
Venezuela	2	19.3	2000	12.8		2–2.2	
Argentina	1	26.8	1995–96	12.4		1.3	
Costa Rica	1	15.0	1992			2.7/2.2	
Brazil	.2	14.4	1988/90	15.4			3.6
Canada	1	22.9					
USA	.65	27.9					

Note: 1 Percentage of stunting/chronic malnutrition, moderate and severe, below minus 2 standard deviations from median height for reference population (UNICEF 2000).

the population that is indigenous, the 'indigenous/national average' ratio is 1.4. When indigenous children are compared to *ladinos*, however, the ratio increases to 1.97, showing more marked indigenous disadvantage. The data reveal that stunting is associated with a strong socio-economic gradient, and affects only 18 per cent of the richest, 52 per cent of those on an intermediate level, and 61 per cent of the poorest. A similar gradient is seen between big towns (29 per cent), smaller towns (41 per cent), and rural areas (57 per cent) (Castillo and Bixby 2001). Thus, indigenous children tend to be poor, stunted and live in rural areas in Guatemala, while *ladino* children are more likely to be better off, grow according to their genetic potential, and to live in bigger towns. The infant mortality ratio is smaller than that for stunting, indicating that health services are better distributed than wealth in Guatemala.

The data from Mexico, Chile and several other countries show that the IMR and stunting in smaller communities might differ quite substantially from the situation in areas that are predominantly indigenous, and from the national average for indigenous peoples. The data-set on stunting from Bolivia is interesting material for a longitudinal analysis of the health gap between an indigenous-dominated geographic area and the country average. In 1988–90 the stunting ratio between the predominantly indigenous area of Potosí and the country average was 1.25 (44.0/35.0), while in 1996 it was 1.4 (40.3/29.1), and in 1998 up to 1.8 (47.4/26.8). We see that in Potosí the rate of stunting is not changing much, while improvements are taking place on the national level. Further inspection of the data reveals that the urban centres experience impressive improvements, while the stunting rates in the rural areas are relatively unchanged.

To sum up, Table 5.1 indicates that:

- National averages may disguise substantial variations between regions and ethnic groups.
- The difference between indigenous communities within the same country may be substantial.
- Countries and regions of the Americas with big indigenous populations show the highest rates of IMR and stunting. The problems seem most serious in the Andean region, in the jungle areas of South America, and in Central America.
- Indigenous children from the Americas are more vulnerable to IMR and stunting than the average population in those countries.
- In comparatively wealthy countries such as Argentina, Chile, the USA, Canada and Brazil, one notes with interest that in spite of their relatively strong economy and small indigenous populations, the ratios remain approximately the same as in other parts of the Americas.

Seen in its wider context, Table 5.1 suggests that a socio-economic divide exists between indigenous and non-indigenous peoples all over the Americas, and that IP, more than the population at large, are subject to risk factors compromising their nutritional health and their probability of surviving childhood. Infant mortality is closely linked to stunting, but pre-natal care and the presence of trained birth attendants influence mortality rates substantially.

A key question is to what extent the health needs of indigenous peoples differ from the needs of the poor in general. The 'all American' pattern of indigenous vulnerability is explained in the Pan American Health Organization publication *Health in the Americas*, which links indigenous vulnerability to poverty, discrimination and the lack of culturally sensitive and participatory healthcare approaches (PAHO 2002). While poor people in general may experience discrimination, indigenous peoples in addition are prone to suffer from cultural insensitivity, language barriers and general communication barriers based on differences in thinking about health and illness, causes of disease, ways of curing, what constitutes 'human well-being', and so forth.

Individual states' efforts to address indigenous health issues seem rather whimsical and unfocused, and have to a large degree been characterized by a top-down 'one size fits all' approach (ibid.). As shown in Table 5.1, the results are not terribly impressive so far. New approaches are in the making, however, and the ongoing pan-American health reform initiative (ibid.) may help tune health and development policies to local realities through participation and partnership. Such approaches would take into consideration the fact that health services should be adapted to different circumstances and needs, and probably be much more conducive to indigenous health (Victoria et al. 2003). Furthermore, the current international and national focus on indigenous health, human rights and state obligations may trigger a new determination to address indigenous health issues more effectively.

States and their health- and food-related human rights obligations

The human rights system provides approaches and concepts that should be of particular use to indigenous peoples. First of all, the key principles of the right to health, including availability, accessibility, acceptability and quality, have been spelled out by the United Nations Committee on the International Covenant of Economic, Social and Cultural Rights (hereafter ICESCR) in its General Comment on the right to health (GC14), which clarifies the health-related obligations of the state (UN/ECOSOC 2000a). Second, state obligations to respect, protect and fulfil people's right to food (Eide 1987; UN/ECOSOC 1999) accentuate the right to conditions whereby people may feed themselves through their own efforts, and get assistance where that is no longer possible. Third, the human rights principle of non-discrimination, combined with affirmative action and protective measures, highlights the need for social justice and at times positive discrimination and special treatment to achieve equitable results. Finally, the principles of accountability, transparency, people's participation and decentralization[11] (also found in the concept 'good governance') can potentially provide guidance on how to govern in a way that is conducive to human well-being and human-rights-based development.

The right to adequate food and to the highest attainable standard of health A rights-based approach to food and health, and development as such, is inseparable from social justice, and requires the adoption of appropriate economic, environmental and social policies at both national and international levels, oriented to the eradication of poverty and the fulfilment of human rights for all (UN/ECOSOC 1999). The state can create and sustain/perpetuate poverty, but it can also do a lot to eliminate and prevent it. Through ratifying the relevant human rights treaties, states have taken on direct obligations. In Table 5.2 the reader will find a list of various human rights instruments that include paragraphs on the right to health or the right to food, and an overview of the ratification status of various states of the Americas. These human rights instruments include the right to health or the right to food as integral parts of human well-being and an adequate standard of living, highlighting the solid position that these rights have today.

In regard to the right to health, states have a core obligation to ensure equitable distribution of all health facilities, especially for vulnerable or marginalized groups (UN/ECOSOC 1999; UN/ECOSOC 2000a, 2000b). State parties to the Covenant on Economic, Social and Cultural Rights should adopt and implement national strategies and plans of action to ensure equitable distribution, and, based on epidemiological evidence, indicators and benchmarks, and give particular attention to all vulnerable or marginalized groups.

The General Comment 14 (UN/ECOSOC 2000a) addresses the concerns for equity in health under the following key principles:

- AVAILABILITY – there have to be enough functioning public health and healthcare facilities, goods and services, as well as programmes, to make them available to all.
- ACCESSIBILITY – health facilities, goods and services have to be accessible to everyone without discrimination. Accessibility has four

overlapping dimensions: non-discrimination (access for all, including vulnerable and poor segments of society), physical accessibility for all, economical accessibility (affordability), and information accessibility (linguistically appropriate formats).

- ACCEPTABILITY – health services must be culturally appropriate.
- QUALITY – health facilities, goods and services must be scientifically and medically appropriate and of good quality. This requires, *inter alia*, skilled medical personnel, scientifically approved and unexpired drugs and hospital equipment, safe and potable water, adequate sanitation, and conducive provider attitudes. In theory, health services should be of the same quality, whether the patient is poor or rich, rural or urban, indigenous or non-indigenous.

Regarding fulfilling the right to adequate food, the state's key role has been quite extensively explored (Eide 1987; Oshaug et al. 1994; UN/ECOSOC 1999); it includes respecting what people already do and protecting them against harm imposed on them by others. State obligations build first and foremost on respect for and protection of the food-acquiring and coping strategies the population use. When needed, the state must also proactively engage in facilitating and strengthening people in their efforts to maintain a livelihood and thus food security. Finally, whenever individuals or groups are unable, for reasons beyond their control, to enjoy the right to adequate food by the means at their disposal, states have the obligation to fulfil (provide) that right directly (Eide 1987; Oshaug et al. 1994). Thus, the right to food is a right to a set of conditions that make one able to feed oneself (and one's dependants) in dignity.

According to the General Comment 12 (UN/ECOSOC 1999), '... specially disadvantaged groups may need special attention and sometimes priority consideration with respect to accessibility of food. A particular vulnerability is that of many indigenous population groups whose access to their ancestral lands may be threatened.' In order to examine whether state parties honour their obligations in regard to food and health, one may, first, examine nutrition and health statistics on marginalized and vulnerable groups, and, second, state policy towards these groups.

Affirmative action and protective measures related to health It is established that everyone has the same right to health, without distinction of any kind. Few would dispute, however, that there is a tendency for the rural health services in poor areas to be less equipped, and to have fewer trained and competent staff. In regard to vulnerable groups, such as indigenous peoples, one also needs instruments for affirmative action. In many cases

TABLE 5.2 Ratification status of states of the Americas

State party	ICESCR[1]	ICCPR[2]	CERD[3]	CRC[4]	CEDAW[5]	ILO 169[6]	ACHR[7]	AP-ACHR[8]	Accept jurisdiction of Int-Am Court of HR[9]	Rights of indigenous peoples acknowledged in constitution[10]	Right to food in national constitution[11]
Argentina	1986	1986	1968	1994	1985	2000	1984	–	Yes	Yes	No
Belize	–	1996	2001	1990	1990	–	–	–	No		No
Bolivia	1982	1982	1970	1990	1990	1991	1979	–	Yes	Yes	Yes
Brazil	1992	1992	1968	1990	1984	2002	1992	1996	No	Yes	Yes
Canada	1976	1976	1970	1991	1981	–	–	–	No	Yes	No
Chile	1972	1972	1971	1990	1989	–	1990	–	Yes	Yes	No
Colombia	1969	1969	1981	1991	1982	1991	1973	1997	Yes	Yes	Yes
Costa Rica	1968	1968	1967	1990	1986	1993	1970	1999	Yes		No
Ecuador	1969	1969	1966	1990	1981	1998	1977	1993	Yes	Yes	Yes
El Salvador	1979	1979	1992	1990	1981	–	1978	1995	Yes		No
Guatemala	1988	1988	1983	1990	1982	1996	1978	2000	Yes	Yes	Yes
Guinea	1978	1978	1977	1990	1982	–	–	–	No		No
Guyana	1977	1977	1977	1991	1980	–	–	–	No		No
Honduras	1961	1981	2002	1990	1983	1995	1977	–	Yes	Yes	No
Mexico	1981	1981	1975	1990	1981	1990	1981	1996	No	Yes	No
Nicaragua	1980	1980	1978	1990	1981	–	1979	–	Yes	Yes	Yes
Panama	1977	1977	1967	1990	1981	–	1978	1992	Yes	Yes	No

	1	2	3	4	5	6	7	8	9	10	11
Paraguay	1992	1992	2003	1990	1987	1993	1989	1997	Yes	Yes	Yes
Peru	1978	1978	1971	1998	1982	1994	1978	1995	Yes	Yes	No
Suriname	1976	1976	1984	1993	1993	–	1987	1990	Yes		No
USA	–	1977	1994	–	–	–	–	–	No	Yes	No
Uruguay	1970	1970	1968	1990	1981	–	1985	1995	Yes		No
Venezuela	1978	1978	1967	1990	1983	2002	1977	–	Yes	Yes	No

Notes: 1 International Covenant on Economic, Social and Cultural Rights. 2 International Covenant on Civil and Political Rights. 3 Convention on the Elimination of Racial Discrimination. 4 Convention on the Rights of the Child. 5 Convention on the Elimination of Discrimination Against Women. 6 Convention No. 169 on the Rights of Indigenous and Tribal Peoples in Independent Countries (ILO). 7 American Convention on Human Rights (Pact San José, Costa Rica). 8 Additional Protocol to the American Convention on Human Rights in the Area of Economic, Social and Cultural Rights (Protocol of San Salvador). 9 Countries that have accepted the compulsory jurisdiction of the Inter-American Court of Human Rights. 10 Countries that include the rights of indigenous peoples in their constitution. 11 Countries that mention the right to food in their constitution.

the most vulnerable groups are lagging so far behind on health indicators that, to be able to reach the level of the rest of the population, compensatory measures or 'positive discrimination' are needed for a limited period of time, until the differences in nutritional health are eliminated. Affirmative action might be needed in cases where indigenous areas or services have been underfunded for a long time. Both the United Nations Committee on Economic, Social and Cultural Rights' General Comments on food and health, and ILO Convention 169, give such provisions.

For indigenous peoples, as in gender research, the difference between equality and equity is quite marked. The point is not for women and men – or indigenous and non-indigenous individuals – to be the same, but for them to achieve equity, that is, to eliminate unjust differences while allowing, respecting and even facilitating the 'differences that make the difference'. Thus, the goal is not only to have the state improve the outreach of conventional health services, but, with equity in mind, to comprehend that indigenous communities might need processes and models other than the conventional ones in order to achieve nutritional health and well-being. ILO Convention 169 states that the state parties are 'obliged to assist the members of the peoples concerned to eliminate socio-economic gaps that may exist between indigenous and other members of the national community, in a manner compatible with their aspirations and ways of life'.

When patient and healer belong to different health cultures, lack of common concepts may lead to confusion and lack of trust (Sachs 1987). Thus, health facilities, goods and services must be culturally appropriate. In the Americas, health personnel tend to be recruited predominantly from the latino/mestizo/white middle class, and tend not to speak indigenous languages. Cultural differences increase the likelihood of professional errors and patients are more likely to disregard the diagnosis given and choose not to follow up on medication if they don't understand or agree with the medical doctor's judgement. IP often use other models to explain symptoms and diseases, and different strategies to restore health.

Health-related protective measures would have to be tuned to the specific culture and needs of the individual indigenous community. Drawing on experiences from Canada, New Zealand and Australia, it appears that the way to achieve sustainable results in regard to indigenous health is through participatory approaches, capacity-building, and openness and responsiveness to cultural needs within the health services (Victoria et al. 2003; BMJ 2003). This implies that indigenous communities should be part of the decision-making process. General Comment 14 (para. 27) elaborates upon indigenous health issues, and takes on an equitable, participatory and culturally sensitive approach to health.[12]

Transparency, accountability, people's participation and decentralization Transparency and accountability are key principles for a sound participatory and democratic development process. Free access to information and clear lines of responsibility allow for discussions about the appropriateness of means and goals, interaction between all interest groups, and adjustments and corrections of policies and action.

When providing services for culturally or socially distinct groups it is particularly crucial to consult with the intended users. Such an approach is more likely to create sustainable and welcomed results, in addition to being an exercise in good governance, and in accordance with human rights principles. ILO Convention 169 (art. 25) addresses the importance of health services being community based and appropriate to local conditions, as an alternative to merely expanding the coverage of Western-style health services in a top-down manner.[13]

IP often maintain their culture's medical knowledge, using it in parallel to the Western medical system. In some areas traditional healers might be the only option available, as in some areas of Bolivia, Guatemala, Mexico, Peru and Ecuador (PAHO 1998, 2002). Allowing for community-based health services with indigenous staff or a higher availability of culturally 'bilingual'/sensitive health practitioners might help not only with verbal communication across languages but also with the translation of medical ideas and 'world views' between two (or more) cultures. In most countries, however, IP are poorly represented within the health services. According to ILO 169 (arts 26 and 27), indigenous youth should be actively recruited to medical schools and other health education and health work, including active involvement in curriculum development.

Rights: via political decisions or legal mechanisms

On the regional level, attitudes seem to be in close accordance with a human rights approach, and highly conducive to improved indigenous health. In the Summit of the Americas Plan of Action (Miami, Florida, 1994), signed by thirty-four heads of state, Equitable Access to Basic Health Services was defined as a key part of 'Eradicating Poverty and Discrimination in Our Hemisphere'. Nevertheless, despite impressive gains in the hemisphere, limitations on health service access and quality have resulted in persistently high child and maternal mortality, particularly among the rural poor and indigenous groups.

Increased accountability both at the national and at the international level might greatly support efforts towards an effective and equitable development process. The state must also play its part, however. To analyse whether a state has the intention of honouring its obligations in regard to indigenous peoples' right to health, one may consider their human rights treaty ratification record, their constitution, their laws and policies. Yet even if laws are good, there might be a lack of political will, and violators may be able to act with impunity, leading to little progress 'on the ground'. One must therefore expand the analysis to explore to what extent obligations are followed up in practical terms. This includes whether the principles of transparency, accountability and participation are observed, to what extent responsibilities are clarified, and whether funding and other resources are provided. In case of resource constraints, the state should call for assistance from the international community.

Government decisions may crucially impact on the food and health situation of the population. Governments are squeezed, however, between the interests of market forces and economic actors and those of the poor. Civil society can help create a counter-force to the negative consequences of economic globalization. Civil society groups can 'remind' politicians that in a democratic society they are representatives of the people, and keep them cognizant of their obligations. And if a strong international consensus can be built, international human rights obligations might be a forceful argument in pushing for debt relief or non-payment of debt, freeing up resources for states to fund improvements in health and food access.

The international human rights system is perhaps even more crucial to IP than to other groups. First, their natural resources are so attractive to the state and other actors that outside pressure may be needed for indigenous land to be demarcated and their land rights and ownership respected, in law and in fact. Second, IP might need outside support for their claims to equal rights to state services, and special rights to protect them against threats to their values and way of life. The human rights system offers provisions and mechanisms protecting IP from having to abandon their cultures, identities and lifestyles in order to obtain their share of a society's welfare and development. The international human rights system is often more sympathetic to indigenous claims than the national laws. This gives indigenous organizations and individuals a tool in the struggle against laws and state policies that do not respect their rights.

Conclusion

This study opens the way for further investigations into why indigenous peoples in all countries in the Americas have a higher prevalence of stunting, and are more prone to die in infancy, than other people in the countries where they live. The findings indicate that the indigenous children of the Americas are more disadvantaged than the average child in these countries. There is little reason to believe that health is determined by ethnicity, and one would assume that if everyone's right to food and to health had been observed, regardless of the ethnicity or economic status of the individual, this health gap would probably not exist.

There is good reason to assume that IP, owing both to their cultural distinctness and the discrimination they are prone to suffer, would benefit from policies regarding them as distinct from the poor in general, and granting them culturally acceptable services, affirmative action and special rights, within a framework of participation and respect. Owing to their culture, IP may have distinct goals, world-views and strategies, not necessarily consonant with mainstream ideas.

State parties to the International Covenant of Economic, Social and Cultural Rights report to the UN Committee on ESCR, providing data disaggregated for vulnerable groups. In nutrition and health policy-making targeting IP, states would benefit from disaggregating national health data in regard to ethnicity. This would reveal if, in what way and for what reasons IP are vulnerable. It might assist if specific data on indigenous peoples were available from international development agencies. Trends within human development are reported annually in publications such as the World Bank's *World Development Report*, UNDP's *Human Development Report*, WHO's *World Health Report* and UNICEF's *State of the World's Children*. It would be timely for a concerned body, in line with the Permanent Forum on Indigenous Issues' recommendations, to produce and regularly update information on the state of IP's health and work towards solving the methodological problems involved.

It might at times take a substantial amount of courage for a nation to investigate ethnic health differences, owing to the possible tensions that such a focus might create. Revealing discrimination and neglect of certain groups might be seen as a 'political' issue, too sensitive to address. Several countries in the Americas, however, have already adopted an open and positive attitude to looking into the health problems of IP. In doing so, they have made a move towards identifying causal factors and reducing the health gaps.

The international human rights system may eventually be given the full authority needed to function as a fully fledged monitoring and recourse mechanism. Even under present circumstances, however, the moral imperative of international human rights monitoring is not to be underestimated. The decisions of human rights commissions, committees or courts, on top of international political pressure, may push countries into complying with their obligations.

For the same reasons, IP may have a lot to gain from using forums open to them in the UN, such as the Working Group on Indigenous Populations, the Permanent Forum for Indigenous Issues, the Social Forum, and treaty bodies and international conferences, thus indirectly putting pressure on their governments. The moral imperative of rights-based language is also helpful for civil-society NGOs and associations of rights-holders claiming political, civil, economic, social and cultural justice. 'Public display' of health statistics is a useful approach. States tend to try to avoid accusations and complaints of human rights abuses and violations, and might stretch their political will and funding further to avoid it.

Ultimately, a human rights approach can provide useful strategies and principles for advocates of social justice, including those advocating equitable access to nutrition and health. Such an approach, with both moral and legal weight, will provide a useful framework within which to close existing health gaps for indigenous peoples, if states are willing to give it the backing it deserves.

Notes

1 Depending on the issue in question, vulnerability might be associated with certain age groups, such as pregnant women, children under five years of age or the elderly, by gender, by mental or physical conditions or handicaps, pregnancy or by sexual orientation. Analyses of health in relation to geography (e.g. urban/rural), economy (socio-economic strata and health) or race or ethnicity help add new insights related to determinants of health and ill health.

2 From General Comment no. 14 on the right to the highest attainable standard of health (UN/ECOSOC 2000a):

> *Core obligations* 43. ... States parties have a core obligation to ensure the satisfaction of, at the very least, minimum essential levels of each of the rights enunciated in the Covenant, including essential primary health care. ... these core obligations include at least the following obligations:
>
> a) To ensure the right of access to health facilities, goods and services on a non-discriminatory basis, especially for vulnerable or marginalized groups;
>
> b) To ensure access to the minimum essential food which is nutritionally adequate and safe, to ensure freedom from hunger to everyone;
>
> c) To ensure access to basic shelter, housing and sanitation, and an adequate supply of safe and potable water;
>
> d) To provide essential drugs, as from time to time defined under the WHO Action Programme on Essential Drugs;
>
> e) To ensure equitable distribution of all health facilities, goods and services;
>
> f) To adopt and implement a national public health strategy and plan of action, on the basis of epidemiological evidence, addressing the health concerns of the whole population; the strategy and plan of action shall be devised, and periodically reviewed, on the basis of a participatory and transparent process; they shall include methods, such as right to health indicators and benchmarks, by which progress can be closely monitored;

the process by which the strategy and plan of action are devised, as well as their content, shall give particular attention to all vulnerable or marginalized groups.

3 The term indigenous peoples is not defined, on request of indigenous peoples themselves. The countries who have ratified ILO Convention 169 (1989), however, will relate to the following description, found in Article 1(b) of the convention: 'Peoples in independent countries who are regarded as indigenous on account of their descent from the populations which inhabited the country, or a geographical region to which the country belongs, at the time of conquest or colonisation or the establishment of present State boundaries and who, irrespective of their legal status, retain some or all of their own social, economic, cultural and political institutions. According to the Article 2(c), self-identification as indigenous or tribal shall be regarded as a fundamental criterion for determining the groups to which the provisions of this Convention apply.'

4 Although this presentation deals specifically with indigenous children in the Americas, the observations and suggestions in regard to state obligations will probably have some relevance in regard to indigenous peoples in other parts of the world, as well as in regard to other marginalized groups.

5 The probability of dying between birth and exactly one year of age expressed per 1,000 live births (UNICEF 2000).

6 Some countries, such as Canada and the USA, do not collect national data on stunting any more, since stunting is not considered to be a problem; yet disadvantaged minorities within the country might still be stunted.

7 A recent forum is taking this up. The Sub-commission on Human Rights, concerned with the need for a new social architecture to complement the financial architecture, has been instrumental in establishing the Social Forum (UN/ECOSOC). This forum on economic, social and cultural rights will meet at the UN in Geneva for two days every year, and discuss themes such as poverty and human rights; the effect of international trade, finance and economic policies on income distribution; and equality and non-discrimination at the national and international levels and in regard to vulnerable groups, including indigenous peoples. It remains to be seen what influence this forum will have.

8 Stunting/chronic malnutrition, moderate and severe – defined as below minus 2 standard deviations from median height for reference population.

9 Criteria such as name, language, place of birth, skin colour, dress and community affiliation have been used (PAHO 2002). From a human rights perspective, self-identification is opted for (ILO Convention 16). Using secondary and tertiary sources of information, the author has not made any independent choice of definition, but has accepted the inclusion criteria used by the author(s) of each study.

10 Where the national surveys were segregated by regions only, the region(s) with the highest indigenous proportion were identified by using the *World Directory of Minorities* (MRGI 1997), PAHO publications (*Health in the Americas*) or similar sources. The author also included smaller studies on indigenous communities (see 'Small studies' in Table 5.1). These

smaller studies, however, might not be representative of the situation of all indigenous peoples in a country, and could lead both to underestimations and overestimations of the situation at large.

11 General Comment no. 12 (para. 23): 'The formulation and implementation of national strategies for the right to food requires full compliance with the principles of accountability, transparency, people's participation, decentralization, legislative capacity and the independence of the judiciary. Good governance is essential to the realization of all human rights, including the elimination of poverty and ensuring a satisfactory livelihood for all' (UN/ECOSOC 1999).

12 'The Committee considers that IP have the right to specific measures to improve their access to health services and care. These health services should be culturally appropriate, taking into account traditional preventive care, healing practices and medicines. States should provide resources for IP to design, deliver and control such services so that they may enjoy the highest attainable standard of physical and mental health. The vital medicinal plants, animals and minerals necessary to the full enjoyment of health of IP should also be protected. The Committee notes that, in indigenous communities, the health of the individual is often linked to the health of the society as a whole and has a collective dimension. In this respect, the Committee considers that development-related activities that lead to the displacement of IP against their will from their traditional territories and environment, denying them their sources of nutrition and breaking their symbiotic relationship with their lands, has a deleterious effect on their health' (UN/ECOSOC 2000a).

13 ILO 169 Art. 25 (ILO 1989):

1. Governments shall ensure that adequate health services are made available to the peoples concerned, or shall provide them with resources to allow them to design and deliver such services under their own responsibility and control, so that they may enjoy the highest attainable standard of physical and mental health.

2. Health services shall, to the extent possible, be community-based. These services shall be planned and administered in cooperation with the peoples concerned and take into account their economic, geographic, social and cultural conditions as well as their traditional preventive care, healing practices and medicines.

3. The health care system shall give preference to the training and employment of local community health workers, and focus on primary health care while maintaining strong links with other levels of health care services.

4. The provision of such health services shall be coordinated with other social, economic and cultural measures in the country.

References

Albala, C., F. Vio, J. Kain and R. Uauy (2002) 'Nutrition transition in Chile: determinants and consequences', *Public Health Nutr.*, 5(1A): 123–8

Alderete, E. (1998) *The Health of Indigenous Peoples*, Geneva: World Health Organization

AMAP (1997) 'Forurensningen I Arktis: Tilstandsrapport om det arktiske miljøet', Arctic Monitoring and Assessment Programme, Oslo, <http://www.grida.no/amap>

Bermudez, O. I. and K. L. Tucker (2003) 'Trends in dietary patterns of Latin American populations', *Cad Saude Publica*, 19, suppl. 1: S87–99

BMJ (*British Medical Journal*) (2003), 327: 403–47

Bogin, B., P. Smith, A. B. Orden, M. I. Varela Silva and J. Loucky (2002) 'Rapid change in height and body proportions of Maya American children', *Am. J. Human Biol.*, 14(6): 753–61

Bossuyt, M. (2000) 'Comprehensive examination of the thematic issues relating to racial discrimination. The concept and practice of affirmative action', preliminary report submitted by M. Bossuyt, Special Rapporteur, in accordance with sub-commission resolution 1998/5, United Nations Commission on Human Rights, Sub-commission on the Promotion and Protection of Human Rights, Document E/CN.4/Sub.2/2000/11, 19 June

Burger, J. (1991) 'Gaia atlas over de første folk', Copenhagen: Mellomfolkeligt samvirke

Bustos, P., H. Amigo, S. R. Munoz and R. Martorall (2001) 'Growth in indigenous and nonindigenous Chilean schoolchildren from 3 poverty strata', *Am. J. Public Health*, 91(10): 1,645–9

Castillo, R. M. and L. R. Bixby (2001) 'Equidad y salud materno-infantil en Guatemala, 1987–1999', Investigaciones en Salud Pública, Documentos Téchnicos, Proyecto ELAC 34, Washington, DC: Coordinación de Investigaciones División de Salud y Sesarollo Humano and Organización Panamericana de la Salud

Eide, A. (1987) 'The right to adequate food as a human right', Special Report, UN Studies in Human Rights, No. 1, New York and Geneva: United Nations

FAO/WHO (1992) 'World Declaration on Nutrition', Rome: ICN, FAO, WHO

Greksa, L. P., H. Spielvogel and E. Caceres (1985) 'Effect of altitude on the physical growth of upper-class children of European ancestry', *Ann. Human Biology*, 12(3): 225–32

Habicht, J. P., R. Martorell, C. Yarbrough, R. Malina and R. Klein (1974) 'Height and weight standards for preschool children: how different are ethnic differences in growth potential?' *Lancet*, 1: 611–14

ILO (1989) 'Indigenous and Tribal Peoples in Independent Countries', International Labour Organization Convention (no. 169), <http://www.unhchr.ch/html/menu3/b/62.htm>

— (2003) 'List of ratifications of International Labour Conventions', International Labour Organization Convention (no. 169) <http://webfusion.ilo.org/public/db/standards/normes/appl/>

IWGIA (1999) 'The indigenous world 1998–99', Copenhagen: International Working Group on Indigenous Affairs

Kracht, U. (1997) 'The right to adequate food: its contents and realization', issues paper prepared for consideration by the UN Committee on Economic, Social and Cultural Rights at its 'Day of General Discussion', 1 December

Kuhnlein, H. V. and O. Receveur (1996) 'Dietary change and traditional food systems of indigenous peoples', *Ann. Rev. Nutr.*, 16: 417–42

McCullough, J. M. (1982) 'Secular trends for stature in adult male Yucotec Maya to 1968', *Am. J. Phys. Anthropol.*, 58(2): 221–5

MRGI (1997) *World Directory on Minorities*, Madrid: Minority Rights Group International

Nakano, T. (2003), personal communication, Montreal: Centre for Indigenous Peoples' Nutrition and Environment (CINE)

Oshaug, A., W. B. Eide and A. Eide (1994) 'Human rights: a normative basis for food and nutrition-relevant policies', *Food Policy*, 19(6): 491–516

PAHO (1994) *Health Conditions in the Americas*, 2 vols, Washington, DC: Pan American Health Organization

— (1998) *Health in the Americas*, 2 vols, Washington, DC: Pan American Health Organization

— (2002) *Health in the Americas*, Scientific and Technical Publication no. 587, Washington, DC: Pan American Health Organization

Sachs, L. (1987) *Medicinsk Antropologi*, Stockholm: Lieber

Stinson, S. (1980) 'The physical growth of high altitude Bolivian Aymara children', *Am. J. Phys. Anthropol.*, 52(3): 377–85

UN (1948) 'Universal Declaration of Human Rights', New York: United Nations, <http://www.unhchr.ch/udhr/index.htm>

— (1966a) 'International Covenant on Economic, Social and Cultural Rights', New York: United Nations, <http://www.unhchr.ch/html/menu3/b/a_cescr.htm>

— (1989) 'Convention on the Rights of the Child', New York: United Nations, <http://www.unhchr.ch/html/menu3/b/k2crc.htm>

— (1994) 'Draft United Nations declaration on the rights of indigenous peoples', Document no. E/CN.4/SUB.2/RES/1994/45, <http://www.unhchr.ch/huridocda/huridoca.nsf/(Symbol)/E.CN.4.SUB.2.RES.1994.45.En?OpenDocument>

— (2003) 'Permanent Forum on Indigenous Issues', report on the second session (12–23 May), Economic and Social Council, Official Records, Supplement no. 23 (E/2003/43E/C.19/2003/22)

UNDP (2000) *Human Development Report 2000*, United Nations Development Programme, New York: Oxford University Press

UN/ECOSOC (1999) 'General comment no. 12 – the right to adequate food' (art. 11 of the ICESCR), E/C.12/1999/5, E/C.12/1999/5, <http://www.unhchr.ch/tbs/doc.nsf/(symbol)/E.C.12.1999.5,+CESCR+General+comment+12.En?OpenDocument>

— (2000a) 'General comment no. 14 – the right to the highest attainable standard of health' (art. 12 of the ICESCR), E/C12/2000/4

— (2000b) 'The right to food', Resolution 2000/10, E/CN.4/RES/2000/10, <http://www.unhchr.ch/html/menu2/7/b/mfood.htm>

— (2002) 'General Comment no. 15 – the right to water' (arts 11 and 12 of the ICESCR), E/C.12/2002/11, 26 November, <http://www.unhchr.ch/html/menu2/6/gc15.doc>

UNICEF (2000) *The State of the World's Children*, New York: Oxford University Press

Victoria, C. G., A. Wagstaff, J. A. Scellenberg, D. Gwatkin, M. Claeson, J. P. Habicht (2003) 'Applying an equity lens to child health and mortality: more of the same is not enough', *Lancet*, 19(362) [9379]): 233–41

WFS (World Food Summit) (1996) 'Declaration on World Food Security and World Food Summit Plan of Action', Commitment 7, Rome

WHO (World Health Organization) (2001) 'International Decade of the World's Indigenous People', Report by the Secretariat, 54th WHO World Health Assembly

— (2003) 'Shaping the Future', World Health Report, Geneva: WHO

World Bank (1994) 'Indigenous people and poverty in Latin America', in G. Psacharopoulis. O. Harry and P. Anthony (eds) *World Bank Regional and Sectorial Studies*, Washington, DC: The World Bank

WSC (World Summit for Children) (1990) 'World Declaration on the Survival, Protection and Development of Children', <http://www.unicef.org/wsc/plan.htm>

WSSD (World Summit for Social Development) (1995) 'Copenhagen Declaration on Social Development', Report of the World Summit for Social Development, A/CONF.166/9, 19 April

TWO | Indigenous peoples in nation-states: rights, citizenship and self-determination

6 | Overview – the right to self-determination

JOHN-ANDREW MCNEISH AND ROBYN EVERSOLE

Important advances have been made in the United Nations International Decade of the World's Indigenous Peoples. One of the most crucial has been the drafting of a Declaration on the Rights of Indigenous Peoples. This draft declaration, prepared by the UN Working Group on Indigenous Populations, proclaims the right of indigenous peoples to self-determination and to the full enjoyment of all human rights recognized in the UN Charter and international human rights law (Trask 1993: 281). In 2002 significant moves were made towards this draft's ratification, and a Permanent UN Forum for Indigenous Issues met for the first time. The United Nations Commission on Human Rights has also appointed a Special Rapporteur on the Human Rights and Fundamental Freedoms of Indigenous People. The rapporteur's functions include 'to gather, request, receive and exchange information and communications from all relevant sources, including Governments, indigenous people themselves and their communities and organizations, on violations of their human rights and fundamental freedoms'. Finally, the UNDP's recently released *Human Development Report* for 2004 makes a clear case not only for the respect of cultural diversity, but for 'cultural liberty', i.e. 'the capability of people to live and be what they choose, with adequate opportunity to consider other options' (UNDP 2004: 4).

These events mark the world community's growing recognition and acceptance of responsibility for the particular problems, interests and aspirations of indigenous peoples. In turn, the growing legal acceptability of indigenous rights discourses around the world has had significant impact on national legislation and the local treatment of indigenous peoples (Jentoft et al. 2003: 2–4). Such growing international recognition of indigenous peoples' rights has, for instance, justified landmark national court rulings in favour of indigenous peoples. It has also provided important support for the many indigenous peoples around the world that are attempting to negotiate their status within nation-states. International recognition of indigenous rights has given these groups a common language, while providing access to international forums where their perspectives and needs can be heard. Meanwhile, with the globalization of standards of governance, government administrations throughout the world are forced to acknowledge and formally legislate for the integration of such rights into national law.

The international indigenous rights movement therefore has a lot to celebrate at the end of the Decade of the World's Indigenous Peoples. Despite this, most indigenous activists recognize that there is still a lot of work to do in order to secure full recognition of both the common and special rights of indigenous peoples. Despite the extent to which human rights discourse has proved fruitful for indigenous rights movements, the UN system also has limitations in terms of fully responding to their claims and providing the kinds of remedies they seek (Engle Merry 1997). Specifically, while the globalization of standards of governance has meant that many prejudicial rules and constraints have been removed at the national and local levels, many of the exclusionary weaknesses of the international economic and political order still remain largely unquestioned.

For instance, as Overland will demonstrate in this section, persisting political boundaries mean that there are serious imbalances in the spread of assistance given by the international donor system. The result is that indigenous poor in so-called 'middle income' countries are largely ignored. This indicates the need to reconsider policy divisions based on historic economic differences, or outdated political conflicts.[1] Moreover, it indicates the need for critical analysis of, and changes to, the liberal and largely economic rationality of the international system on which human and indigenous rights both rely and operate.

This section focuses on the relationships between indigenous peoples and nation-states in an international context where indigenous rights are increasingly recognized, and yet are limited by liberal conceptualizations of citizenship and citizens' rights. This section argues, specifically, that an understanding of the issue of *indigenous self-determination* is key to reforming current debates on rights and unlocking the persisting deadlock in relationships between nation-states and indigenous peoples. The theme of self-determination emerges over and over in the chapters that follow as central to the question of indigenous poverty. These chapters raise important points about how states' attitudes towards indigenous peoples have repercussions on the opportunities and rights that are available to the latter. They assist us to unearth both the roots of indigenous disadvantage and the building-blocks of change.

The limits of liberalism

Many anthropologists have failed to give their support to indigenous rights and human rights discourses because these discourses are historically rooted in Western legal tradition and grew out of its particular social conditions (ibid.). They argue that the global spread of human rights discourse is similar in many ways to the imperialist introduction of legal orders from the West to the rest. This is not the argument we mean to make here. Indeed, we recognize that as a result of long-term globalization, 'there are no longer cultures for which the legal regimes of the West are totally alien or irrelevant', and thus it would seem foolish to believe that human rights discourse remains the exclusive property and domain of the West (ibid.: 29). Clearly, 'as various societies mobilise Western law in their demands for human rights, they reinterpret and transform Western law in accordance with their own local legal conceptions' (ibid.).

As long as cultures are seen as integrated, cohesive, bounded and more or less static, it is easy to perceive human rights as an intrusive, alien discourse. If, however, cultures are understood as 'complex repertoires of systems of meanings extracted from myriad sources and reinterpreted through local understandings and interests', this understanding 'provides a more fluid way of considering how human rights might be incorporated into local cultural practices and understandings' (ibid.: 30). The universalist/relativist debate distracts from an understanding of human rights in practice: examining local political struggles that mobilize rights language in particular situations.

Thus, the argument we want to make here is not against the international transference of legal ideas about rights. The issue is not one of transference or of reception, but more one of questioning what is being transferred and the existing limits placed by the international system on its local interpretation. We therefore do not mean to argue against the pursuit of a politics of rights, but to argue in line with Gledhill (1997) against settling for a politics of rights premised solely on liberal political institutions that embody various kinds of regulatory power.

While the system of international rights creates inclusive possibilities for some, its reliance on the goodwill of nation-states and international organizations that have long been established within the limits of liberal democracy results in the exclusion of others bearing demands and needs considered to be beyond the bounds of established discourse. Furthermore, because of the dominance of liberal democracy and the links that have formed between it and international capitalism, it is increasingly difficult for alternative forms of economic organization and ownership to find official sanction.

Despite the fact that local indigenous populations are more than able to make sense of Western/international legal ideas and find means to interpret and apply them for their own benefit, the premising of rights on liberal political institutions creates as many limits to indigenous rights campaigns as openings. The foundation of international rights discourse on an acceptance and enforcement of individual liberal citizenship means that more radical communal claims such as cultural identity, common land or 'strategic exclusion' (Chapter 9, this volume) cannot be officially justified. In this sense, while Western legal forms offer a powerful language in which to make claims against nation-states, their liberal formations also channel and constrain the kinds of wrongs enunciated and the remedies demanded. Indeed, this helps to explain how Western legal forms can operate as an indispensable force of emancipation at one moment of history – for example, the American Civil Rights movement – but become at another time a regulatory discourse, a means of obstructing or co-opting more radical political demands, or simply the most hollow of empty promises (ibid.).

The liberal foundations of current rights discourses and institutions are also responsible for placing limitations on policy aimed at development and poverty reduction. The range of social policy on offer from governments and political parties around the world has now narrowed considerably. Welfare assistance from the state, in those countries where it was available, is no longer considered an immediate and universal 'basic right'. The state speaking in the name of 'society' now argues that (normalized) families have private responsibilities towards individuals which should not be transferred to society at large, and that local 'communities' must shoulder more of the burden of care for the poor and incapacitated in their midst. The role of the state has been circumscribed to the elimination of the structural causes of individuals' 'lack of capability' to function as normal citizens – where 'normalcy' not only expresses prosperity, but also forms of life and behaviour that are part of 'a hegemonic (and class-based) "comprehensive conception of the good"' (ibid.: 177–8).

As policies focus on the importance of individual self-realization,[2] the poor, both indigenous and non-indigenous, are accused of living 'without thought for the future'. Their lack of ability to plan for the future (indicated by their continuing to have large families, failing to have their citizenship papers in order, or failing to buy into the security that the market can offer) is judged as exacerbating the fiscal problems of the late capitalist state and is used to reinforce the moral stigmatization not only of poverty but also of social difference. Here, the morality of living a responsible life has become equated with the secular obligation of citizenship and with the character of national belonging, or nationalism.

The consequences of this are often contradictory. The liberal insistence on individual obligation forms the basis for a discourse on rights where indigenous peoples and minorities are to be defended, and yet it can become an excuse for a concurrent condemnation of these peoples' ways of life. For example, as McCaskill and Rutherford describe for South-

East Asia, although cultural diversity is now often celebrated as part of national identity, many traditional practices are at the same time deemed manifestations of primitive and inferior cultures in need of the benefits of state-led modernization.

Rethinking the basis of indigenous rights

Indigenous peoples generally define themselves as *different* from the mainstream national societies in which they live. This difference is the characteristic often stressed in attempts to define what is meant by 'indigenous peoples'; they are 'distinct from other sectors of the society now prevailing in those territories' (Martínez Cobo 1986) with 'distinct cultural and territorial identities' (ILO 1999: 3). This difference is generally the basis of indigenous peoples' demands for self-determination and particular rights. Yet how different are indigenous peoples, really – and what does this difference mean in the context of the modern nation-state?

Nation-states are, after all, groupings of citizens – individuals. At the same time, it is perfectly common for these individuals to join together, in groups of common interest, to exercise their influence and make demands on nation-states. With the exception of totalitarian regimes, this is an expected pattern of relationship between the state and its citizens: certainly in a democracy, and even in patronage-based governance. Political parties, lobby groups, geographic communities and a broad range of organizations and institutions will attempt to influence national policy and practice whenever possible, and capture resources for themselves and their constituencies. This can be considered part of the institutional structure of the modern nation-state – the way things are done. Indigenous voices enter the chorus as one more interest group amid many.

But are they? For, as their argument goes, the indigenous contingent is *different*. They emphasize that they are *peoples*. That is, indigenousness is not simply a characteristic of particular citizens: such as being female, or under age eighteen, or a supporter of labour rights. Rather, indigenous identity posits an alternative citizenship arrangement – that of belonging to an indigenous group – which precedes, and often pre-dates, citizenship in the modern nation-state. The accuracy of this claim can often be defended with reference to historical population movements (see McCaskill and Rutherford in Chapter 8). Nevertheless, this is a worrisome concept for nation-states, whose very logic is based on the assumption that its citizens are individuals who *belong*, in the sense of both identity and answerability, to that nation-state. This is the liberal concept of citizenship. The term 'indigenous peoples', conversely, implies sovereignty: that as peoples, they can be the direct subjects of international law without the intermediation of nation-states (CHR 1996: 9). Thus, indigenous *peoples* have the potential to stand outside this state–citizen relationship and even to place their loyalties and their interests elsewhere.

It is not surprising that conflicts emerge when a group sees itself as an indigenous people while its governing state sees it as an interest group comprised of state citizens. If these groups are peoples in their own right, then the very basis of the legitimacy of state authority over them can be called into question. Indeed, over the years, various peoples have separated from nation-states and formed their own nations – seldom a painless process. Nevertheless, most indigenous groups do not aim to separate themselves from state membership or state authority. Few aim to secede from nation-states. Rather, as Louise Humpage describes in Chapter 9 for the Māori, the goal is most often characterized as self-determination – self-determination that is carried out *within* the borders of existing nation-states.

Yet what does it mean to be a self-determining people within an existing nation-state? The concept seems contradictory. Within an existing nation-state, aspects of national identity are obviously still retained to some degree. So is a recognition of state authority. Yet a self-determining indigenous people would also be assumed to have significant power to control their own affairs. Claims for self-determination may, for instance, involve indigenous peoples redesigning and taking more control over their own governing institutions and decision-making processes, rather than leaving these in the hands of state bureaucrats. Cornell describes such a process in the United States in Chapter 11. Self-determination may also mean having a guaranteed right to land and its protection from outside interests (Gray 1995: 54). Self-determination may even mean the establishment of autonomous regions or districts within nation-states, as has been the case in some parts of India (ibid.), or the presence of representative indigenous bodies within national governments, such as the Sami parliaments (see Chapter 15).

The idea of self-determining peoples within nation-states presses at – and beyond – liberal concepts of the nation-state. Yet *self-determination* is now the articulated goal of many indigenous peoples around the world. Gray (ibid.) has characterized self-determination as 'the converse of colonization', and emphasized that 'it is not a specific alternative but an open concept'. Yet how can a group be self-determining and still subject to a nation-state? What can such a relationship look like?

Peoples and collective rights

The rights of indigenous peoples are now being recognized on an international stage. Yet as we have seen, there are tensions between an international, liberal legal framework that is designed to protect the rights of the individual, and the emphasis that indigenous peoples place on *collective* rights. The rights of indigenous peoples are by definition rights that pertain to collectivities (peoples), not simply to indigenous individuals. Yet national and international legal institutions, with their liberal roots, are often ill equipped to deal with the defence of collective rights. And for nation-states, the recognition of collective rights steps outside the usual state–citizen relationship. When indigenous peoples ask that their collective rights, as peoples, be recognized, this initiates a new kind of relationship with the nation-state.

Structuring this relationship is a challenge for states. While a state may be accustomed to creating policies and laws to recognize the rights of collective groups of citizens (for example, women, the disabled, the elderly), these are essentially interest groups, not peoples. When dealing with most categories of citizens and their demands, the state can still easily assume that these individuals' primary loyalty of citizenship is to the state itself. It is thus unlikely to meet much resistance when the new laws and policies contain this assumption, and are declared and enforced through the existing institutions of the state, according to the state's own ways of doing things.

Not so, however, when creating laws and policies for indigenous peoples. Here, as the chapters in this section highlight, states' homogenizing solutions to indigenous people's problems not only meet with cries of protest, but also tend to generate ineffective results. The reasons for this are, again, tied to indigenous people's *difference* from other citizens. Their first loyalty of citizenship is often to a collectivity (tribe, sub-tribe, etc.). A direct citizen–state relationship that bypasses the authority of the indigenous collectivity is problematic and may lack authority. Indeed, policies that promote such a direct relationship, bypassing indigenous institutions, are generally understood as inimical to indigenous self-determination.

Indigenous people are also different from other citizens in terms of their culture, and this impacts on a state's ability to create appropriate policies and laws for them. Martínez Cobo (1986) highlights the fact that indigenous people have their 'own cultural patterns, social institutions, and legal systems'. While in some cases these may be in disarray owing to their experiences of colonization and/or partial assimilation into dominant societies, sufficient differences still persist. These differences create considerable dissonance between what members of the mainstream culture think indigenous people want or need and how they should go about achieving it, and indigenous people's own values and organizational principles. Dealing with indigenous institutions puts indigenous individuals on familiar turf;

dealing with state institutions, on the other hand, can be a very foreign experience. A recognition of collective rights not only acknowledges the legitimacy of indigenous institutions, but also of the cultural bridging role that they play.

Thus, for indigenous self-determination to be possible within the boundaries of the modern nation-state, it is necessary for nation-states to be willing to recognize and deal with indigenous collectivities. Yet working with indigenous collectivities is not an easy shift for states to make. It entails moving beyond the concept of the individual citizen with direct responsibilities to the state, and instead granting these indigenous collectivities significant decision-making powers – even when these decisions may conflict with state interests. There are further complications in terms of the practicalities of working with indigenous collectivities, particularly given that the nature of representation is often contested within indigenous groups themselves. As Cornell points out in Chapter 11, given the post-colonial disarray of many indigenous institutions and governance arrangements, determining what level of indigenous collectivity is appropriate, legitimate and capable of governance is not always easy in practice. Who determines whether a given indigenous collectivity is representative and legitimate? If representation is contested within indigenous groups, how are alternate indigenous views and agendas accommodated? As it stands, private interests can easily foment division by sponsoring one community faction over another and selectively 'consulting' those sympathetic to their own interests. Clearly there are challenges; as Chapter 9 (on New Zealand) and 10 (on Colombia) make clear, the mere act of recognizing collectivities does not necessarily mean that more pro-indigenous policies are created.

Furthermore, for contemporary nation-states the challenge of representation and consultation is not confined to their dealings with indigenous peoples. Indigenous quests for self-determination echo a larger set of issues which have been raised by a range of communities both indigenous and non-indigenous. They are familiar issues in the literature of community development and grass-roots development (see, e.g., Ife 2002; Coirolo et al. 2001; Annis and Hakim 1988), and in the contemporary rhetoric of groups from rural villages to urban ethnic groups: *'Respect us as a community', 'Respect our institutions and culture', 'Don't impose top-down state solutions', 'Allow us to make our own choices about our future'*. As modern nation-states choose how to deal with the chorus of voices seeking greater or lesser levels of self-determination, they face the opportunity to empower citizens – and also the fear of losing control. While indigenous peoples' claims for difference, and consequent demands for self-determination, may be more strongly justified culturally and historically than those of mainstream communities or new migrants, indigenous peoples are pursuing an issue that affects us all: how much choice do we, in our communities, have about state decisions that affect us?

Conclusion

In challenging a central principle in liberal democracy – i.e. that rights are ultimately enjoyed by individuals who remain equal under the law, but may be assigned special rights as individuals in a certain category – the movement for indigenous rights represents a powerful test of what liberal societies and the international system can offer 'minorities'. Under the present understandings and conditions of liberal democracy, this is a challenge that, despite its ethical basis, unfortunately continues to result in contradiction, intolerance and sometimes oppression. Great advances have been made in securing rights for indigenous peoples over the last decade, but the liberal discourse and institutions of the rights system create limits to, as well as possibilities for, future cultural diversity. For these barriers to be removed and further improvements to be made, it is therefore necessary for the basis of the international rights system to be radically reformed, and for indigenous claims for self-determination to be properly studied and addressed.

We aim to demonstrate that self-determination is not simply a political issue. As the chapters in this section argue, this quest is directly related to the issue of indigenous poverty. This is an important point, because states very often draw a distinction between the political claims of indigenous people and their socio-economic needs. States may highlight the need to do something about indigenous poverty, without seeing that this has anything to do with indigenous political claims for self-determination. Yet the chapters in this section suggest strongly that the reason state anti-poverty programmes have often failed is precisely that they have not taken the need for self-determination into account.

Nation-states concerned about reducing indigenous poverty need to realize that, despite their good intentions, their own state-run socio-economic policies are unlikely to offer solutions – regardless of how well crafted or tuned to best practice they are. Rather, states concerned with the needs of their indigenous citizens need to take into account indigenous people's declared *difference*, and specifically the implications of this for governance arrangements affecting indigenous peoples. The 'political' question of self-determination emerges as centrally important to the socio-economic challenge of poverty reduction for indigenous peoples. Humpage develops this theme further, while Stephen Cornell demonstrates that greater self-determination among indigenous people in the USA has led to important socio-economic poverty reduction.

By stressing self-determination and local control of decision-making, we do not mean to downplay the vital role of the state. The state has a clear role to play in reducing indigenous poverty – not only in developing a willingness to negotiate and work with indigenous collectivities, but also in a key form of direct policy action. Specifically, the state is in the position to redistribute national resources in a way that will address the historical and structural inequalities that produce indigenous poverty. Overall, the evidence presented in these chapters suggests that there is clear potential for indigenous self-determination that does not undermine state authority, but rather expands the state's flexibility through negotiated relationships with indigenous collectivities.

Notes

1 E.g. the Soviet Union.

2 See the Introduction for a fuller discussion of the issue of self-realization in an era of advanced liberalism.

References

Annis, S. and P. Hakim (1988) *Direct to the Poor, Grassroots Development in Latin America*, Boulder, CO and London: Lynne Rienner

Brown, W. (1995) *States of Injury: Power and Freedom in Late Modernity*, Princeton, NJ: Princeton University Press

CHR (Commission on Human Rights of the United Nations) (1996) 'Report of the Working Group established in accordance with Commission on Human Rights resolution 1995/32 of 3 March 1995', E/CN.4/1996/84, 52nd session, 4 January, Item 3 of the provisional agenda

Coirolo, L., K. McLean, M. Mokoli, A. Ryan, P. Shah and M. Williams (2001) 'Community based rural development: reducing poverty from the ground up', Rural Strategy Discussion Paper 6, Washington, DC: World Bank

Engle Merry, S. (1997) 'Legal pluralism and transnational culture: the Kaho'okolokolonui Kanaka Maoli tribunal, Hawai'i, 1993', in R. A. Wilson (ed.), *Human Rights Culture and Context*, London: Pluto Press

Gledhill, J. (1997) 'Liberalism, socio-economic rights and the politics of identity: from moral economy to indigenous rights', in R. A. Wilson (ed.), *Human Rights Culture and Context,* London: Pluto Press

Gray, A. (1995) 'The indigenous movement in Asia', in R. H. Barnes, A. Gray and B. Kingsbury (eds), *Indigenous Peoples of Asia*, Ann Arbor, MI: Association for Asian Studies, pp. 33–58

Hale, C. (1994) 'Between Che Guevara and the Pachamama: mestizos, Indian and identity politics in the anti-quincentenary campaign', *Critique of Anthropology*, 14(1): 9–39

Hart, H. (1964) *Law, Liberty and Morality,* Oxford: Oxford University Press

Holmes, S. and C. Sunstein (1999) *The Cost of Rights: Why Liberty Depends on Taxes*, New York: W. W. Norton and Co.

Ife, J. (2002) *Community Development: Community-based Alternatives in an Age of Globalization*, 2nd edn, Frenchs Forest, NSW: Pearson Education Australia

ILO (1999) 'Indigenous peoples of South Africa: current trends', report on Project for the Rights of Indigenous and Tribal Peoples, Geneva: International Labour Organization

Jentoft, S., H. Minde and R. Nilsen (2003) *Indigenous Peoples: Resource Management and Global Rights*, Netherlands: Eburon Delft

Martínez Cobo, J. (1986) 'Study of the problem of discrimination against indigenous populations', UN Sub-commission on the Prevention of Discrimination and the Protection of Minorities, UN Doc. E/CN.4/Sub.2/1986/

Trask, H.-K. (1993) *From a Native Daughter: Colonialism and Sovereignty in Hawai'i*, Monroe, ME: Common Courage Press

UNDP (2004) *Human Development Report 2004, Cultural Liberty in Today's Diverse World*, New York: United Nations Development Programme

7 | Poverty and international aid among Russia's indigenous peoples

INDRA OVERLAND

Russia is the world's largest country. Its population includes numerous indigenous peoples with unique languages, cultures and lifestyles – as well as claims to the largest indigenous territories in the world. At the same time, these peoples are poorer than most developing-country populations and are excluded from international aid flows.

This chapter begins by explaining who the indigenous peoples in Russia are. It then examines the background in Soviet policy for their current situation, and surveys the social, economic and medical problems of these groups today. The final part of the chapter focuses on why there is so little international aid to alleviate poverty among Russia's indigenous peoples, and what possibilities exist for increasing the amount of aid.

Indigenous peoples in the Russian Federation

The Russian Federation officially recognizes forty-five ethnic groups in its territory as indigenous peoples.[1] They live in all ten time zones of mainland Russia, from the Saami on the Kola Peninsula in the north-western corner of the country, to the Chukchi on Chukotka in the far north-east.

In Russia they are formally referred to as *malochislennye korennye narody* – literally 'numerically small indigenous peoples'.[2] In order to be classified as 'indigenous' in Russia, a people must not number more than 50,000. This somewhat arbitrary demographic limit reflects the difference between the Russian context and that in the Americas and Oceania. On those continents, indigenousness is relatively easily linked to the distinction between pre-colonial ethnic groups and those who arrived later. In an empire built on continuous land-based expansion such as Russia, such a distinction becomes less clear. The outer perimeter of the Russian empire expanded gradually over such a long period that the distinction between newcomers and latecomers is difficult to identify today. Consequently, indigenousness in Russia is more closely linked to subsistence livelihoods and population numbers than it is in countries with a history as overseas colonies.[3]

This means that several ethnic groups that have clearly been subjected to colonization by the Russians, but who number far more than 50,000, are not recognized as indigenous peoples within Russia, even though they

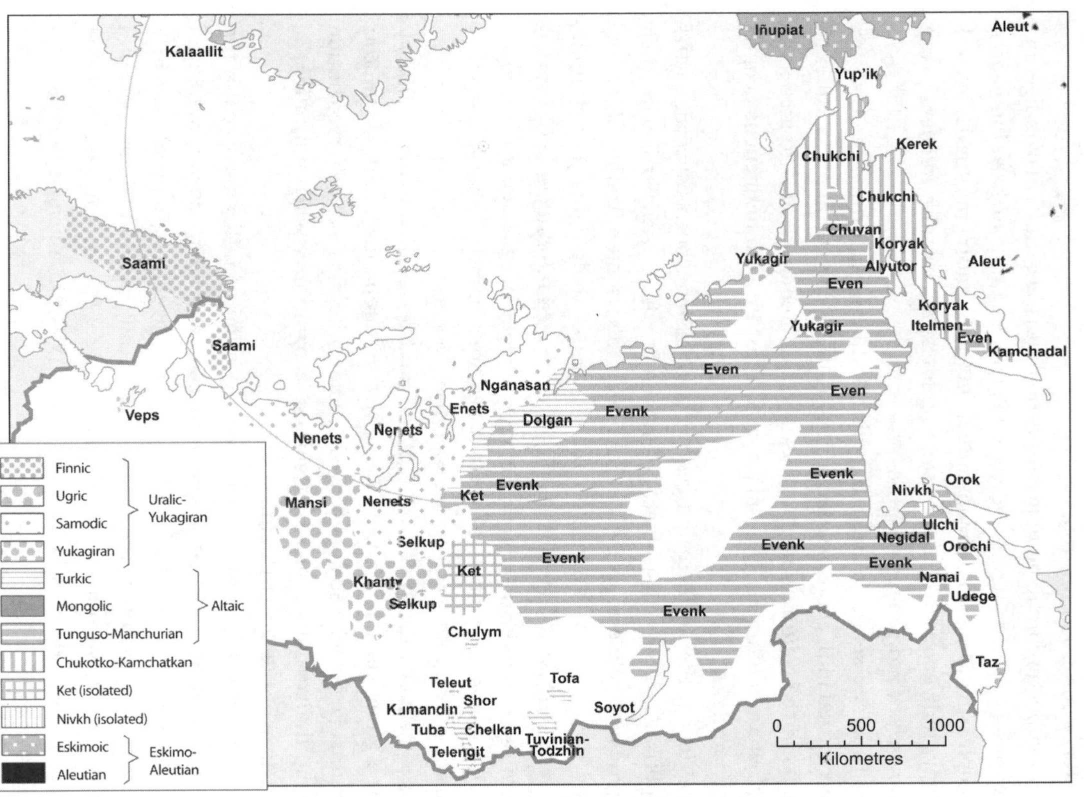

FIGURE 7.1 Indigenous peoples of Russia

might be so in an international context. The Komi of north-west European Russia and the Yakut of eastern Siberia are examples of such groups.

Recognizing that the official Russian definition of indigenous peoples is related to circumstances peculiar to the Russian context, this chapter will follow that categorization rather than the broader definition set out in ILO Convention No. 169.

Another important point in connection with the definition of indigenous peoples is that the terms 'indigenous peoples' and 'Northern indigenous peoples' are often used synonymously in the literature on Russia. Accordingly, 'indigenous peoples' as used in this chapter will also frequently refer to *northern* indigenous peoples.

There are several reasons for this. First, at least forty of the forty-five recognized indigenous peoples of Russia live in the northern and Siberian parts of the country, with lifestyles and livelihoods adapted to arctic and sub-arctic conditions. Thus, in practice, most Russian indigenous peoples are 'northern'.

Second, the northern indigenous peoples have been especially active politically, often using objects of material culture associated with their arctic livelihoods as symbols in both their inward mobilization of identity and their outward struggle for recognition of their rights. For example, several of these indigenous peoples are engaged in reindeer herding: they have used reindeer, reindeer sledges, lassos and garments made from reindeer fur as symbols of their indigenous identity. This has made it easier for a group such as the Saami of the Kola Peninsula to cultivate an indigenous identity. On the other hand it has also made it difficult for a group such as the Veps – who live in Karelia just south of the Kola Peninsula, but who do not engage in reindeer herding – to gain recognition as an indigenous people. They gained recognition as such only after the collapse of the Soviet Union.

The third reason for the frequent equation of indigenous peoples in Russia with the northern indigenous peoples is that, during the Soviet period, the latter were the only recognized indigenous groups in the USSR. At that time, the official term was 'numerically small indigenous peoples of the North, Siberia and the Far East', a concept introduced into Soviet legislation by decrees in 1925 and 1926 (Vakhtin 1994: 31; Kiselev and Kiseleva 1979: 20).

Soviet indigenous policy

In order to understand the origins of poverty among the Russian indigenous peoples, it is necessary to look briefly at Soviet policy towards them. These groups were deemed to have been particularly oppressed under the tsar, and their culture was judged to be especially backward. Thus, it was felt, their development warranted extra attention and assistance in order to enable them to catch up with the 'advanced nations' of the Soviet Union. According to Anatoliy Skachko, one of the people mainly responsible for the initial formulation of Soviet indigenous policy:

> if the whole of the USSR, in the words of comrade Stalin, needs ten years to run the course of development that took Western Europe fifty to a hundred years, then the small peoples of the north, in order to catch up with the advanced nations of the USSR, must, during the same ten years, cover the road of development that took the Russian people one thousand years to cover, for even one thousand years ago the cultural level of the Kievan Rus' was higher than that of the present-day small peoples of the north. (quoted in Slezkine 1994: 220)

Initially, the most important aspects of Soviet indigenous policy were collectivization and the replacement of 'nomadism as a way of life' with 'production nomadism' (Kuoljok 1985: 126; Vitebsky 1992: 223). In Soviet theory, the subsistence economies of the indigenous peoples were seen as embodying internal contradictions, for example between reindeer breeding and hunting in the tundra, or between reindeer breeding and fishing in the taiga (Slezkine 1994: 204). These practices were thought to result in inefficiency because they stretched sparse labour across vast expanses and diverging activities. The various central Soviet organs responsible for the indigenous peoples saw it as their task to help them overcome this situation by reorganizing them into progressively larger units, where the men would work in specialized brigades dedicated to single economic pursuits, i.e. production nomadism (Kuoljok 1985: 119; Vitebsky 1992: 223). Meanwhile the women and children were kept in the villages, the women engaged in gainful salaried employment as teachers, secretaries or accountants, and the children living in boarding schools.

In the earliest stage of collectivization, small groups of workers called *artels* were the main collective units.[4] During the first years after the revolution, there was pressure on the owners of large herds to join the collectives, and attempts to persuade nomadic groups to settle down around these units. The impact of these developments on the lives of the indigenous peoples, however, remained limited. Most people continued to work within units that corresponded to their old kin-based structures.

In the 1930s the *artels* were replaced by *kolkhozes* (collective farms, from *kollektivnoye khozyaystvo*). This process was accompanied by the intensified persecution of 'bourgeois elements'. In addition to 'rationalizing' the subsistence economy, collectivization was also intended to eradicate the injustices between the poor and the rich, between the owners of the means of production and the dispossessed. Among reindeer-herding peoples, for example, the most easily measured unit of wealth was reindeer. If 'kulaks' in the rest of the USSR were people who owned land and engaged in production for the open market, then among the reindeer herders they were those who possessed large herds. And those who had few or no reindeer of their own were 'oppressed proletarians' – whether or not they thought so themselves.

The persecution of successful reindeer herders struck at the very heart of herding society. It was a society based on the efforts and skills of individual herders and families in building up large herds, with assistance from relatives, young trainee herders and labour paid in kind. The removal of those who were most successful meant the removal of those who were most talented.

The Second World War and the years immediately following were a quiet period for the indigenous peoples in terms of governmental reforms. By the late 1950s, however, Soviet indigenous policy had regained its vigour and ambition. In 1957, a decree was issued concerning 'means for the further development of the economy and culture of the Northern Peoples', recommending the intensification and expansion of industrial and agricultural projects (Kiseleva 1994: 75). What followed was the policy of *ukrupneniye* (enlargement, amalgamation), in which some *kolkhozes* were fused into greater *sovkhozes* (Soviet farms, state farms, from *sovetskoye khozyaystvo*) (Vitebsky 1992: 232).

In comparison to the *kolkhozes*, the *sovkhozes* were larger, more industrial and mechanized. They relied on more varied economic activities and were state-owned enterprises run by appointed officials and salaried employees (Slezkine 1994: 212; Konstantinov 1996: 17). In the *kolkhozes* the employees were paid according to the profits of their *kolkhoz*, and were freer to dispose of the funds of the *kolkhoz* and determine their own working hours (Beach 1992: 119). In the *sovkhozes*, the state guaranteed their income, but also exercised greater control – increasingly through non-indigenous management personnel.

In connection with the replacement of the *kolkhozes* by *sovkhozes*, small villages were eradicated and the inhabitants transferred to large *sovkhoz* villages where they often became an ethnic minority (Sokolova 1994: 52). Those who were resettled were usually given little or no prior warning, and funds transferred to the local authorities to cover the cost of relocation were often embezzled or used to cover other expenses. For many individuals the result was considerable hardship (Antonova 1988: 171).

New Soviet boarding schools were an important part of the collectivization process. First established in the 1920s, they were reformed and greatly expanded in the 1950s (Utvik 1985: 52; Kiselev and Kiseleva 1979: 127). The task of the schools was to provide care and education, but also to turn out little Soviets (Slezkine 1994: 237). In order to become 'Soviet', the children had to assimilate a different lifestyle and detach themselves from the traditional livelihoods that their fathers were still engaged in, and from the care of their mothers, who were now busy serving the Soviet state. 'What followed was a cultural revolution of the most basic kind. The native children had to relearn how to eat, sit, sleep, talk, dress, and be sick, as well as to assimilate a totally new view of the world and their place in it' (ibid.: 241).

The result of Soviet policy was that many indigenous men continued to herd reindeer, hunt and fish, moving around in the tundra according to the seasons as they had done before, while the women and children were drawn into new Soviet structures. In the long term, this undermined the relationships that had constituted the fabric of the indigenous communities – between men and women, between parents and their children and between the communities and their historical territories.

On the other hand, it should be borne in mind that in many cases Soviet policy was misguided rather than intentionally destructive, paternalistic rather than consciously oppressive. It also included a range of support mechanisms that became integral to indigenous communities, in fields such as medical care, education and agricultural subsidies.

In several respects Soviet indigenous policy was similar to Western policies during the same period. For example, Danish resettlement programmes on Greenland bore a striking resemblance to the Soviet policy of *ukrupneniye* (enlargement). Thus, it is important to see the faults of Soviet indigenous policy as part of the wider conflict between the modern nation-state and industrialization on the one hand, and indigenous peoples in general on the other.

Poverty among the Russian indigenous peoples

When the Soviet Union collapsed, the positive aspects of its policies – the various support mechanisms and subsidies for indigenous peoples – also collapsed. The negative effects of its oppressive policies also lingered on, however. The combination of these two developments resulted in an overall worsening of the situation for the indigenous peoples.

Unfortunately, few reliable and comprehensive data on the socio-economic situation of the combined indigenous population are currently available.[5] This is in itself an obstacle to bringing about an improvement of their situation (Abryutina and Goldman 2003: 11). One important statistic that does exist is their average life expectancy. During the 1990s, various commentators reported that it was estimated to be around forty-four years of age (e.g. Sulyandziga 1998: 9; Agitaev 1999: 7). Recently the federal authorities have published an official estimate of forty-nine years, which is considered to be more accurate (Russian Government 2003). According to the vice-president responsible for health issues in the Russian Association of Indigenous Peoples of the North, the average life expectancy for some of the peoples still remains as low as thirty-seven years (Abrutina 2002: 170). In contrast, the average life expectancy for the rest of the country's population is sixty-six years (World Bank 2004: 110).

Owing to the lack of comprehensive data on the entire indigenous population in Russia, to better understand the situation it is necessary to refer to the situation of specific peoples and regions. One important source of information is letters from members of various indigenous peoples lamenting the fate of their people or village. Such letters are addressed to the authorities in their region or in the Russian Federation as a whole. They have been published in periodicals such as the *ANSIPRA Bulletin*, *Zhivaya Arktika* (Living Arctic) and *Severnye Prostory* (Northern Expanses). Although the evidence they provide is generally anecdotal, there is so much of it that it suggests a good overall picture of the current destitution among the Russian indigenous peoples. For example, ninety-five inhabitants of the indigenous village of Andryushkino in the republic of Sakha in far eastern Russia wrote the following in a letter to Sakha politicians and bureaucrats:

> Fresh vegetables – potatoes, cabbage, onions, garlic have long been out of sale in our village, to say nothing of fruit ... All there is to buy at the local Kolymtorg grocer's store is bread. Of all cereals one can buy semolina only at the village trading post with pasta pale as ashes into the bargain. There has been no rice, millet, buckwheat or oatmeal on sale for six months. Instead, there are cans and tins, many of them with expired dates. There has been no baby food for three or four years, nor any clothing and footwear for children. (Andryushkino Villagers 2002: 31)

Indigenous peoples struggle with a range of basic economic problems; among them unemployment is a particular problem. Many indigenous villages have an unemployment rate of over 60 per cent, and the average among indigenous peoples has been estimated to lie somewhere between 40 and 50 per cent (Agitaev 2002: 152–4; cf. Afanasjeva 2002: 140).

The main reasons for this high unemployment and other economic problems are rampant poaching, the collapse of management and subsidies, and a lack of access to markets. During the Soviet period, the country was isolated from world energy markets, and all types of fuel were heavily subsidized. With the emergence of Russia as the world's second-largest oil exporter, domestic fuel prices have also risen steeply, with the result that remote indigenous villages have been cut off from both supplies and markets. Poaching – sometimes by non-indigenous people, sometimes by unemployed indigenous people – has had a devastating effect on reindeer herds, as well as on game and fish stocks. For example, in the Evenki Autonomous Okrug in central Siberia the number of domesticated reindeer fell from 24,000 to under 2,000 between 1992 and 2002 (Pankagir 2002: 34).

Many indigenous peoples also struggle with social problems, especially suicide and violence. There are three to four times as many suicides among the indigenous peoples compared to the Russian average. In 1995, for example, there were 145 suicides per 100,000 inhabitants on Chukotka (the part of Russia that stretches out towards Alaska), while the Russian and US averages for the same year were respectively thirty-eight and twelve (Abrutina 2002: 170; cf. Agitaev 1999: 7).[6] Among the Saami, 30 per cent of deaths are due to unnatural causes, and more than half of those deaths are suicides (Afanasjeva 2002: 139). There are twenty-five times as many stabbings per capita among the indigenous peoples as among the general Russian population (RAIPON 2001: 7).

Finally, there are severe medical problems among the Russian indigenous peoples, in particular tuberculosis and alcoholism (which can also be counted as a social problem). In the Khanty-Mansi Autonomous Okrug in western Siberia, an average of forty people out of 100,000 die annually from tuberculosis, and in the Yamal-Nenets Okrug the figure is eighty-seven – whereas for Russia as a whole it is ten (Agitaev 1999: 7). The emerging HIV epidemic in Russia also poses a particular threat to indigenous peoples, who are very poorly informed about modes of contagion, and whose small and tightly knit communities are particularly vulnerable once a few locals have contracted HIV. The indigenous peoples are also susceptible to various other ailments. For example, in some indigenous communities 85 per cent of the inhabitants are infected with opisthorhosis (liver fluke infection) (RAIPON 2001: 7).

As a result of these social, economic and medical problems, the birth rate fell by 34 per cent and mortality grew by 42 per cent among the Russian indigenous peoples during the 1990s (Agitaev 1999: 8). The outcome has been a severe demographic crisis.

Poverty alleviation among the Russian indigenous peoples

Apart from the collapse of many state functions, the post-Soviet period has brought many changes in governmental policy towards the Russian indigenous peoples. Among the developments that have met loudest protest was the shutting down of the Committee on the North (Goskomsever) in 2001. The committee had been an important institution during most of the Soviet period and had constituted a united apparatus for the formation of Soviet indigenous policy. Although the committee had frequently been criticized, at least it provided a clear target for criticism and it was clear where lobbying efforts should be focused.

When the committee was shut down, responsibility for indigenous policy was split between the Ministry of Trade and Economic Development and the Ministry of Federal, Ethnic and Migration Policy. This did not bode well for the coherence of Russia's indigenous policy. The choice of the Ministry of Trade and Economic Development as the administrative body for the most important indigenous issues was also seen as an indication that they would now have less priority than economic development and the extraction of natural resources, which were the chief responsibilities of the ministry. When the Ministry of Federal, Ethnic and Migration Policy was later disbanded, this led to a further destabilization of indigenous policy.

Among the more positive changes during the post-Soviet period have been the formulation of three consecutive federal programmes in support of the socio-economic development of the northern indigenous peoples and the passing of three key laws on indigenous policy (Kharyuchi 2002: 41; Russian Government 1999, 2000a and 2003).[7] The three laws are:

- on the Guarantees of the Rights of Small Indigenous Peoples of the Russian Federation;
- on the General Principles of the Organization of Communities of the Small Indigenous Peoples of the North, Siberia and the Far East of the Russian Federation;
- on the Territories of Traditional Nature Use of the Small Indigenous Peoples of the North, Siberia and the Far East of the Russian Federation

The first of the laws is a broad statement on the intentions of the Russian state towards indigenous peoples. It echoes international standards, but has few practical consequences for indigenous peoples. The second law regulates the formation of indigenous communities of different types as recognized legal bodies. Like the first law, it does not have major financial or practical consequences for the indigenous peoples, but it has a potential impact on their social organization. The third law is the most important of the three. It outlines the formation of Territories of Traditional Nature Use (*territorii traditsionnogo prirodopolzovaniya* – generally referred to as TTPs). A TTP is a type of nature reserve where local indigenous peoples have special rights. Such reserves have major implications for land ownership and control over natural resources, protecting indigenous interests from those of the state and corporations engaged in the extraction of natural resources.

The problem with these improvements in the legal framework and policy is that the financial resources and administrative capacity to implement them have been lacking. To date, all applications for TTPs under the third and most important of the federal laws have been rejected – owing partly to a lack of clarity about the exact procedure for their formation, partly because they threaten other and more powerful actors such as the oil companies.

Another example of the difficulties of implementing post-Soviet indigenous policy is provided by the federal target programme Economic and Social Development of the Indigenous Peoples of the North towards 2011. While it includes proposals for the establishment of trading stations, slaughtering and processing plants, it fails to spell out what the trading stations will trade in and what the processing plants are to process (Abryutina and Goldman 2003: 11).

The virtually constant financial crisis of the Russian state in the post-Soviet period, in particular after the crash in 1998, has greatly weakened the state's ability to provide support for indigenous peoples. Its capacity for support has been further weakened by the embezzlement at various levels of administration of the funds that have been designated for the indigenous peoples. The improved finances since Vladimir Putin came to power have still not trickled down to the indigenous peoples, and the long-term effect at the local level of the clampdown on corruption remains to be seen.

In light of the dire situation of the indigenous peoples in Russia and the difficulties of the Russian government in improving their situation, foreign actors have found it necessary to step into the void. For example, when a Russian delegation went to the Economic Forum in Geneva to discuss the development of the Russian north, it was not the Russian government but foreign organizations which invited representatives of Russia's indigenous peoples to come along (Murashko and Sulyandziga 2002: 3).

Several foreign governments and aid agencies have involved themselves in the affairs of the Russian indigenous peoples – in particular the Danish Environmental Protection Agency and the Canadian Agency for International Development (Køhler 2001: 6). This involvement could, however, potentially be far greater. Current rules on Official Development Aid (ODA) are the main obstacle to its increase. For many donor countries, ODA is a contest for prestige in which they compete to give most, relative to the size of their gross national product (GNP). It is a long-standing UN aim that donor countries should spend the equivalent of 0.7 per cent of their GNP on ODA, and in several countries it is an official objective to increase ODA. At present, however, the resultant flows of ODA are not available to Russian indigenous peoples – because Russia is not officially classified as an ODA recipient state.

The Russian indigenous peoples and ODA eligibility

ODA is a technical-administrative term used to describe the highest and most official form of international aid. Aid flows are categorized as 'ODA' according to a list of recipient states maintained by the Organization for Economic Cooperation and Development (OECD). The underlying idea is that ODA should be strictly limited to benevolent and constructive support to poor countries. Originally it was intended to cover only support for long-term development in the world's very poorest countries. Over the past decades, however, it has been expanded to include other types of aid as well, in particular short-term humanitarian aid and the maintenance of Global Public Goods (discussed below).[8]

When the Soviet Union disintegrated, there was a debate about which of the post-Soviet states should receive ODA. It was decided that only the countries in Central Asia and the south Caucasus should be eligible. Assistance to the rest of the former Soviet Union was to be counted not as ODA but as Official Aid (OA). Thus the list of aid recipient states was divided into two main parts: countries eligible for ODA, and countries eligible for OA only.

OA may sound similar to ODA, but its status is fundamentally different. It cannot be included in the sum that is measured as a percentage of a donor country's GNP and used to compete for prestige as a generous donor. Thus, regardless of how much OA a donor state gives to Russia, or other states in the European part of the former Soviet Union, these sums are not considered the most benevolent form of development aid. Such assistance does not strengthen the prestige of the donor state in the same way that ODA does. This has functioned as a brake on Western aid to Russia. Although the country has received sizeable amounts of aid for nuclear safety and other areas of direct environmental or geopolitical benefit to the donor states, other areas lacking such significance have been neglected. One such area is the Russian indigenous peoples.

It is not clear exactly why Russia and the other European post-Soviet states were not included in the list of countries eligible to receive ODA. Bureaucrats in the donor countries tend to believe that it was because Russia was too wealthy and developed to deserve ODA, and that there was a desire not to inflate ODA beyond its original purpose of helping the very poorest countries. Other factors were also involved, including Russian sensitivities about being labelled as a poor country in need of help. These sensitivities might be particularly acute owing to Russia's history as a major global power and a donor of development aid in its own right. The issue is further complicated by the fact that most ODA recipient countries are former colonies of western European states, a relationship with which many Russians would be reluctant to be associated.

In addition to the list of ODA recipient states, there is also a list of international organizations through which ODA can be channelled. In principle the aid must still end up in the designated ODA recipient states, but on this point there is considerable confusion within the aid system. One high-ranking representative of the UNDP's Moscow office claimed that the funding it receives is counted as ODA. The OECD, however, replied by e-mail to this author that such flows were not to be counted as ODA.

There are at least two arguments as to why Russia's indigenous peoples might in principle qualify for ODA. First, although Russia as a whole is not among the poorest and most needy countries in the world, its indigenous peoples are far worse off than the populations of many countries currently receiving ODA. In light of the lack of comprehensive data on the income of the Russian indigenous peoples, it is possible to use their average life expectancy as a proxy indicator. At forty-nine years, it is lower than that of most countries on the ODA recipient list (Russian Government 2003).[9] Even in the low-income countries, which make up the poorest group of ODA recipients, average life expectancy is about fifty-nine years. Several countries on the ODA recipient list have life expectancies that are relatively high by any standard – for example, Brazil (sixty-eight years), Saudi Arabia (seventy-three years) and Turkey (seventy years) (World Bank 2003: 234–5).

Even some of the very poorest countries in the world have longer average life expectancies than the Russian indigenous peoples, for example, Bangladesh (sixty-one years), Cambodia (fifty-four years) and Eritrea (fifty-two years) (ibid.: 234–5). Since there is a strong correlation between average life expectancy and income, this indicates that Russia's indigenous peoples are worse off than many ODA recipient-state populations.

Second, even the situation of Russia as a whole does not provide a clear-cut argument for excluding the country from the list of ODA recipients. The widespread notion that the classification of ODA and OA recipient states is based on objective criteria is erroneous. In 2001 Russia's gross national income (GNI) per capita was US$1,750 (ibid.: 235). A number of countries had higher GNIs per capita than Russia, and were nevertheless included in the list of ODA recipients – for example, Brazil (US$3,060), Costa Rica (US$3,950), Croatia (US$4,550), Malaysia (US$3,640), Saudi Arabia (US$7,230) and Uruguay (US$5,670). It is also worth pointing out that some of these countries have significant indigenous populations. The result is that the indigenous peoples in Russia are at a particular disadvantage in relation to indigenous peoples in the rest of the world.

Factors relevant to extending ODA to the Russian indigenous peoples

Aid officials in the OECD countries tend to perceive the ODA rules as too rigid to allow for the extension of aid to the Russian indigenous peoples or indeed anybody else in Russia. Nevertheless, there are several factors that might facilitate such a change.

First, when ODA to South Africa was resumed after the end of apartheid, there were worries that this might benefit the wealthy white population. It was therefore stipulated that ODA should be targeted specifically at the black population, referred to as the 'Black Communities of South Africa' in OECD documents. This is one of the very few instances of a specific social group being singled out for ODA, and might constitute a precedent for qualifying specific social groups, rather than states, for ODA.

Second, Canada, Denmark, Norway, Sweden and the USA have all shown particular interest in the Russian indigenous peoples – owing not least to the existence of northern indigenous peoples on their own territories. All these countries are among the foremost donors in terms of gross ODA contributions. In addition, Denmark, Norway and Sweden have been the three biggest donors in relation to their own GNP during the past two decades. This means that the countries that rank highest in the competition for prestige as ODA donors are among those that have already shown an interest in Russian indigenous peoples. That may help to facilitate the linkage of Russian indigenous peoples and ODA.

Third, the very same countries that have shown an interest in Russian indigenous peoples also have general aid policies oriented towards the least developed countries (LDCs). At first sight, that might seem to make it less likely that they would want to devote ODA to indigenous peoples in Russia, since Russia is not among the LDCs. They have, however, made exceptions to their focus on the LDCs as far as indigenous peoples are concerned. Norwegian ODA, for example, generally goes to the poorest countries in Africa, but makes an exception for middle-income countries such as Guatemala and Nicaragua, where it focuses specifically on aid to indigenous peoples. In this respect, several of the main potential donors already have aid policies that might benefit Russian indigenous peoples once they manage to gain access to ODA in general.

Fourth, various non-state actors are gradually increasing their influence in organizations such as the UN. One could argue that a differentiation of the rules for ODA beyond categorization by recipient state would be in line with general trends elsewhere in the multilateral system.

Finally, ODA has increasingly come to include financing for Global Public Goods (GPGs). This term refers to matters, such as the environment and global health, that are important for mankind as a whole (Raffer 1998: 3). At least 15 per cent of ODA already goes to GPGs (Martens 2001: 8).

It could be argued that the diversity of the world's cultural heritage is one of the most important of all GPGs. Indigenous cultures are a particularly valuable, sensitive and endangered part of this heritage. The languages of the Russian indigenous peoples belong to disparate language groups, including the Finnic, Ugric and Paleo-Asiatic groups. Some of these tongues – for example, Yukagir – are so unique that it is difficult to categorize them in any of the world's known language groups. The various indigenous peoples of Russia also practise a wide range of sustainable livelihoods, including salmon fishing, sea mammal hunting, reindeer herding, moose hunting and berry and mushroom gathering.

Some of the Russian indigenous peoples are on the verge of extinction, along with their languages and ways of life. Groups such as the Aleut, Orok, Negidals, Yukagir, Ket, Enets, Nganasan and Tofalar are all set to disappear during the coming decades.[10] There are only an estimated 1,300 people left who identify themselves as Nganasan, 600 Aleut and 2,000 Sakhalin Nivkh. Groups such as the Ain, Vod, Kamasinets, Kerek, Omok and Yug have already disappeared in the course of the past three decades. Unless something is done, the ancient cultures of a large part of the earth – an area spanning ten time zones – will become extinct, and humankind will lose part of its cultural heritage. Surely, then, the culture of the Russian indigenous peoples is a GPG that should be covered by ODA like other GPGs, such as biodiversity and oceanic fish stocks.

Conclusions

Soviet indigenous policy, like the policies of many other industrial nations, tore apart the fabric of the country's indigenous communities – dissociating indigenous men and women, and indigenous parents and their children. The long-term result was weak and traumatized communities that were ill equipped to confront the crisis brought on by the collapse of the Soviet Union. They have continued to suffer from a range of social, economic and medical problems – especially unemployment, tuberculosis and suicide.

The Russian Federation has attempted to develop a new indigenous policy in line with international standards, but has lacked the resources and capacity for proper implementation. Some international actors have made an effort to step in and help the Russian indigenous peoples, but their involvement is limited by the rules on ODA – which exclude aid to Russia.

The numerous positive factors discussed in this chapter indicate that it may be possible to open up ODA to the Russian indigenous peoples. There is also an entirely different way of looking at this whole issue. If Russia is in fact such a wealthy and developed country that it does not belong on the list of ODA recipients, then it should take the responsibility for the welfare of its own indigenous peoples. In other words, Russia's absence from the list could be used to put pressure on the Russian government to improve its performance on indigenous issues.

Glossary

artel – a small, voluntary association of individuals who come together for a limited or indefinite period for the purpose of performing an economic activity. From the Tatar words *orta* (community) and *ortak* (common)

Goskomsever – from *Gosudarstvennyy komitet Severa*, Committee on the North

kolkhoz – short for *kollektivnoye khozyaystvo*, collective farm

malochislennye korennye narody – numerically small indigenous peoples

severnye prostory – northern expanses

sovkhoz – short for *sovetskoye khozyaystvo*, Soviet farm, state farm

territoriya traditsionnogo prirodopolzovaniya – territory of traditional nature use, a type of nature reserve with special rights for indigenous peoples

ukrupneniye – the enlargement and amalgamation of population centres and units of production (in the context of Soviet indigenous policy)

zhivaya arktika – living Arctic

Notes

1 For a list of the forty-five peoples, see Russian Government (2000b). Several ethnic groups in the southern republic of Dagestan that should probably also be recognized as indigenous peoples are not included in this list. The federal authorities have chosen to leave the definition of 'indigenous peoples' in Dagestan up to the Dagestani authorities, who have postponed the matter indefinitely. The reason for this procrastination is the extreme ethnic diversity of the mountainous republic, and the ethnic tensions that might arise if certain groups were categorized as 'indigenous' and others not.

2 For translations of Russian terms, see also the glossary at the end of the chapter.

3 In Africa, despite a history of overseas colonization, the distinction between indigenous peoples and other black Africans raises issues similar to those in Russia. For a discussion of the difficulties of defining indigenous peoples in Africa, see Saugestad (2000, 2002).

4 For varying and partly contradictory definitions of *artels*, see Kuoljok (1985: 109) and Schindler (1992: 56).

5 It is expected that better data on the situation of the indigenous peoples

will become available when the delayed results of the 2002 Russian census are published. During the Soviet period such censuses were carried out every ten years, but that taken in 2002 was the first since 1989.

6 Another estimate gives a rate of suicides of 65 per 100,000 inhabitants among the general Russian population in 1995 (RAIPON 2001: 7).

7 The three federal programmes are *Kompleksnyy plan meropriyatiy Mezhdunarodnogo desyatiletiya korennykh narodov 1994–2004* (Complex Plan of Measures in Connection with the International Decade of Indigenous Peoples 1994–2004); *Federalnaya tselevaya programma ekonomicheskogo i sotsialnogo razvitiya korennykh malochislennykh narodov Severa do 2000 goda* (Federal Earmarked Programme on the Economic and Social Development of the Indigenous Small Peoples of the North until 2000); *Federalnaya tselevaya programma ekonomicheskogo i sotsialnogo razvitiya korennykh malochislennykh narodov Severa do 2011 goda* (Federal Earmarked Programme on the Economic and Social Development of the Indigenous Small Peoples of the North until 2011).

8 Such broadening of ODA has been criticized by some commentators and donor countries as weakening efforts to support long-term development and diverting resources from the world's most needy countries (OECD 1998: 18; Martens 2001: 2). With the original, narrower definition, total ODA in 1994 would have been 0.2 per cent of the gross national product of all the member states of the OECD's Development Assistance Committee, rather than the 0.3 per cent that was recorded (Raffer 1998: 7).

9 Note that this is the new official figure released by the federal authorities. Previously an estimated average life expectancy of forty-four years had often been quoted (e.g. Sulyandziga 1998: 9). Average life expectancy for men among some of the indigenous peoples is in the low forties.

10 The Aleut live on the Aleutian Islands in the north-eastern part of the Pacific Ocean, the Orok on Sakhalin Island off Russia's Pacific coast, the Negidals on the Pacific coast near Sakhalin, the Yukagir in north-eastern Siberia, the Ket and Enets in the north-western part of central Siberia, the Nganasan in northern central and western Siberia, and the Tofalar south of the Ural mountains. For an overview of endangered and extinct indigenous languages in Russia, see <http://odur.let.rug.nl/~bergmann/russia/languages_endangered.htm>

References

Abrutina, L. (2002) 'Health and employment in the Arctic: the indigenous peoples of Russia's north and their access to health care' in T. Køhler and K. Wessendorf (eds) *Towards a New Millenium: Ten Years of the Indigenous Movement in Russia*, Copenhagen: IWGIA, pp. 164–79

Abryutina, L. and H. Goldman (2003) 'State policy and the health of indigenous peoples of the Russian north', *ANSIPRA Bulletin*, 9: 11–12

Afanasjeva, N. (2002) 'The socio-economic and legal situation of the Saami in the Murmanskaya oblast – an appeal to take urgent measures', in T. Køhler and K. Wessendorf (eds), *Towards a New Millennium: Ten Years of the Indigenous Movement in Russia*, Copenhagen: IWGIA, pp. 138–44

Agitaev, Y. (1999) 'Sammit liderov narodov Akrticheskogo regiona', *Zhivaya Arktika*, 1: 6–9

— (2002) 'Problems of employment: the ethnic aspect', in T. Køhler and K. Wessendorf (eds), *Towards a New Millennium: Ten Years of the Indigenous Movement in Russia*, Copenhagen: IWGIA, pp. 150–63

Andryushkino Villagers (2002) 'Andryushkino villagers appeal', *ANSIPRA Bulletin*, 7: 31–2

Antonova, A. (1988) 'Letter to the authorities of the RSFSR. December, 1988', in A. Pika, J. Dahl and I. Larsen (eds), *Anxious North*, Copenhagen: IWGIA Document no. 8

Beach, H. (1992) 'Reindeer herding on the Kola Peninsula – report of a visit with Saami herders of Sovkhoz Tundra', in R. Kvist (ed.), *Readings in Saami History, Culture and Language III*, Umeå: Centre for Arctic Cultural Research, pp. 113–42

Kharyuchi, S. (2002) 'Our life and future are in our hands', in T. Køhler and K. Wessendorf (eds), *Towards a New Millennium: Ten Years of the Indigenous Movement in Russia*, Copenhagen: IWGIA, pp. 34–48

Kiselev, A. A. and T. A. Kiseleva (1979) *Sovetskiye saamy: istoriya, ekonomika, kultura*, Murmansk: Murmanskoye knizhnoye izdatel'stvo

Kiseleva, T. A. (1994) 'Vliyaniye sotsialno-eknomicheskikh faktorov na razvitiye olenevodstva kolskogo poluostrova v 1900–1980–e gody', in L. N. Podyelskaya (ed.), *Voprosy istorii evropeyskogo Severa*, Petrozavodsk: Izdatel'stvo Petrozavodskogo Universiteta, pp. 72–7

Køhler, T. (2001) 'Danish support for the native north', *ANSIPRA Bulletin*, 6: 6

Konstantinov, Y. (1996) 'Field research on reindeer-herding on the Kola Peninsula: problems and challenges', *Acta Borealia*, 2: 53–68

Kuoljok, K. E. (1985) *The Revolution in the North: Soviet Ethnography and Nationality Policy*, Uppsala: Almqvist & Wiksell

Martens, J. (2001) *Rethinking the Relevance of ODA: Current Trends in the Debate on the Future of Official Development Assistance*, Bonn: World Economy, Ecology and Development Association

Murashko, O. and P. Sulyandziga (2002) 'Indigenous peoples of the north and the authorities in 2002', *ANSIPRA Bulletin*, 7: 3

OECD (1998) *Development Cooperation: Efforts and Policies of the Members of the Development Assistance Committee*, Paris: Organization for Economic Cooperation and Development

Pankagir, A. (2002) 'Problems of indigenous peoples of Evenkiya', *ANSIPRA Bulletin*, 7: 33–5

Raffer, K. (1998) *ODA and Global Public Goods: A Trend Analysis of Past and Present Spending Patterns*, New York: UNDP

RAIPON (2001) 'Accessible health care for indigenous peoples of the north in the Russian Federation: a strategy for survival', *ANSIPRA Bulletin*, 6: 7–9

Russian Government (1999) 'On the Guarantees of the Rights of Small Indigenous Peoples of the Russian Federation' [O garantiakh prav korennykh malochislennykh narodov Rossiyskoy Federatsii], federal law signed by President Yeltsin, 30 April

— (2000a) 'On the General Principles of the Organization of Communities of the Small Indigenous Peoples of the the North, Siberia and the Far East of the Russian Federation' [Ob obshchikh printsipakh organizatsii obshchin korennykh malochislennykh narodov Severa, Sibiri i Dal'nego Vostoka Rossiyskiy Federatsii], federal law signed by President Putin, 20 July

— (2000b) 'On the United Census of the Small Indigenous Peoples of the Russian Federation' [O yedinnom perechne korennykh malochiclennykh narodov Rossiyskoy Federatsii], Decree no. 255, 24 March

— (2001) 'On the Territories of Traditional Nature Use of the Small Indigenous Peoples of the North, Siberia and the Far East of the Russian Federation' [O territoriakh traditsionnogo prirodopol'zovaniya korennykh malochislennykh narodov Severa, Sibiri i Dal'nego Vostoka Rossiyskoy Federatsii], federal law signed by President Putin, 7 May

— (2003) 'On the Implementation of Measures in Connection with the International Decade of the Indigenous Peoples' [O khode relizatsii meropriyatiya Mezhdunarodnogo desyatiletiya korennykh narodov mira], Press Release no. 354, 6 March, Moscow: Russian Government

Saugestad, S. (2000) 'Dilemmas in Norwegian development assistance to indigenous peoples: a case study from Botswana', *Forum for Development Studies*, 27(2): 205–34

— (2002) 'Om avstanden mellom Geneve og Kalahari', *Norsk antropologisk tidsskrift*, 13(1–2): 22–33

Schindler, D. (1992) 'Russian hegemony and indigenous rights in Chukotka', *Inuit Studies*, 16(1–2): 51–74

Slezkine, Y. (1994) *Arctic Mirrors: Russia and the Small Peoples of the North*, Ithaca, NY: Cornell University Press

Sokolova, Z. P. (ed.) (1994) *Narody Severa i Sibiri v usloviyakh reform i demokraticheskikh preobrazavaniy*, Moscow: Institut etnologii i antropologii im. Miklukho-Maklaya

Sulyandziga, P. (1998) 'Speech given at the European Commission: indigenous peoples and sustainable development', *ANSIPRA Bulletin*, 1: 7–11

Utvik, U. (1985) *Kolasamene: Fra tsarens undersåtter til sovjetiske borgere*, Bergen: University of Bergen (masters thesis)

Vakhtin, N. (1994) 'The native peoples of the Russian far north', in Minority Rights Group (ed.), *Polar Peoples: Self-Determination and Development*, London: Minority Rights Publications, pp. 29–104

Vitebsky, P. (1992) 'Landscape and self-determination among the Eveny. The political environment of Siberian reindeer herders today', in E. Croll and D. Parkin (eds), *Bush Base: Forest Farm – Culture, Environment and Development*, London: Routledge, pp. 223–46

World Bank (2003) *World Development Report 2003*, Washington, DC: World Bank

World Bank (2004) *World Development Indicators 2004*, Washington, DC: Routledge.

8 | Indigenous peoples of South-East Asia: poverty, identity and resistance

DON McCASKILL AND JEFF RUTHERFORD

This chapter will examine the situation of the indigenous peoples of South-East Asia, focusing on Thailand, Lao PDR, Vietnam, Burma (Myanmar), Cambodia and Yunnan province in south-west China.[1] The indigenous peoples in these countries are among the poorest, most isolated and most marginalized in the world.[2] At the same time forces of globalization, development, regionalism and nationalism have reached into the most remote areas and have resulted in significant economic, political and cultural changes. Globalization in this context refers to increasing connectedness and economic integration of regions and states characterized by the broad processes of rapid modernization, liberalization and advances in technology. These forces result in significant intensification of cross-border trade, international investment, migration, information and ideas and interactions among states. These complex and sometimes contradictory processes have the potential for both positive and negative consequences for the indigenous people of the region. Globalization can lead to a 'fixing' or 'closing' of ethnic boundaries and affirmation of old identities as a response of indigenous peoples to rapid social change and assimilation forces. Conversely, it also contributes to a 'flux' or 'flow' of identity as indigenous people attempt to respond to their changing conditions as they are increasingly integrated into the nation-state. Globalization, therefore, appears to contribute to the formation of new identity boundaries as much as the reaffirmation of old ones (Meyer and Geschiere 2003).

On the one hand, globalization can lead to more opportunities for economic development with increased liberalization as nations in the region move from planned, centralized, state-controlled, subsistence economies to market economies characterized by deregulation, privatization, individualism and decentralization. It can be argued that decentralized economic policies and decision-making structures can result in increased local empowerment. Furthermore, some have suggested that globalization brings a shift in emphasis from universalism to particularism, as governments begin to recognize the significant cultural diversity within their borders, while indigenous groups become more aware of issues in common with similar groups in other locations and begin to assert their collective rights (Long

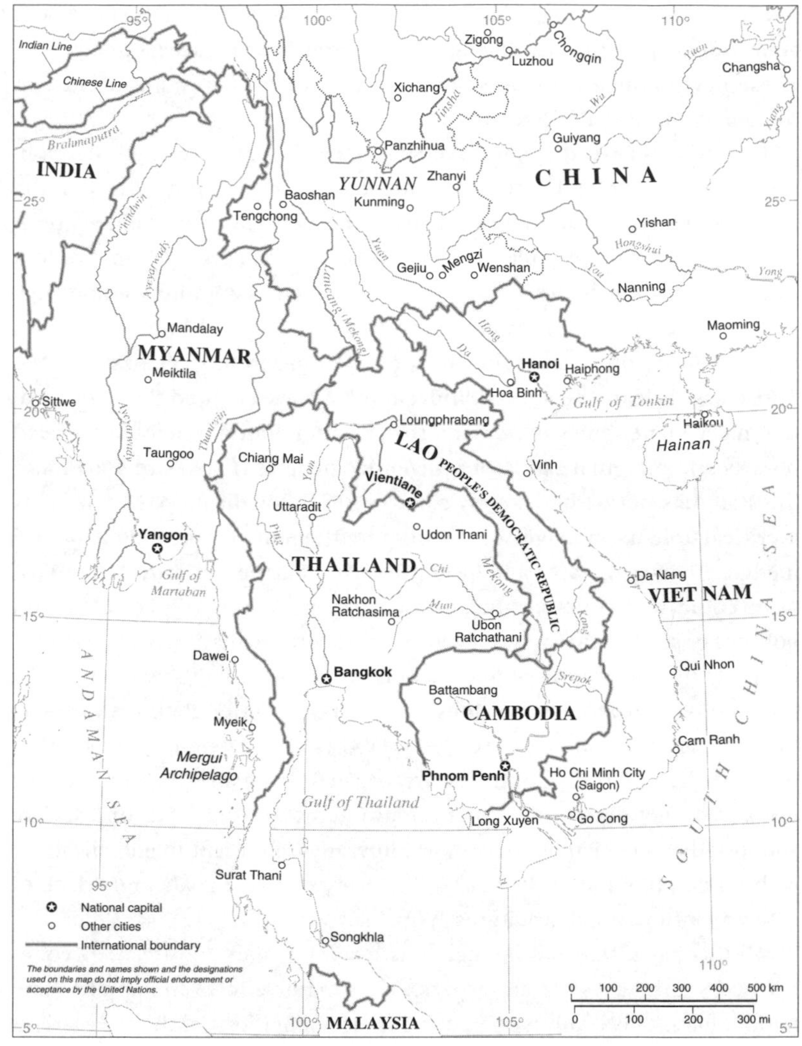

FIGURE 8.1 Mainland South-East Asia

1996). Increasingly, the concepts of multiculturalism and cosmopolitism are being used to characterize contemporary states. New social and political identities and movements based on transnational ideas of citizenship are emerging (ibid.). And ethnic nationalism is a force firmly established in all states of the region.

Finally, development strategies in all South-East Asian countries have emphasized poverty reduction as a central goal, with the recognition that indigenous peoples are among the poorest groups. Thus significant efforts have been made to increase local community infrastructure, transportation, educational opportunities, health facilities, tourism and access to markets. These development initiatives have, in some cases, led to an increase in the quality of life of indigenous peoples.

On the other hand, some have suggested that globalization, development, regionalism and nationalism are having a devastating effect on the indigenous peoples of South-East Asia. The rich and ruling elites are in a superior position to exploit the opportunities afforded by globalization, as there are few existing rules to govern the new economic relationships and because investment capital, access to markets and information and technology are often prerequisites for benefiting from globalization. The impacts will clearly be uneven. Indeed, many have claimed that globalization has widened the gap between the rich and poor and led to increased poverty and marginalization of indigenous peoples (Kaosa-ard 2003). And the state has not withered away as a result of globalization. It maintains a critical role as manager of development, agent of social control and mediator between global and local processes. Further, in most South-East Asian countries, economic liberalization does not necessarily correlate with political or social autonomy. Indeed, a central preoccupation of states in the region is the integration of minority groups into the nation as defined by the dominant group. Ruling elites are loath to describe their countries as multicultural or recognize the collective rights of indigenous groups within their borders. Various strategies are utilized to ensure that indigenous peoples do not assert any degree of autonomy. In this, governments are supported by the ideology of classical liberalism inherent in globalization, with its emphasis on individual rights over collective goals and a lack of concern with particular cultures (Vincent 2002).

All this has significant implications for indigenous cultures. The countries of South-East Asia are experiencing major efforts to support state nationalism. This involves convincing their populations of the state's right to a monopoly on governance within a specific territory, and attempting to unite the people by creating a common culture, often implying efforts to homogenize the population. Pressures for assimilation of indigenous peoples, whose distinctive cultures and identities may pose an implicit threat to national unity, are frequently brought to bear. Thus, in many instances traditional indigenous cultures are in danger of disappearing. At the same time, in recent years, some countries have recognized the presence of the distinctive cultures in their midst and instituted policies and programmes to recognize those cultures. Often, however, these policies tend to view indigenous cultures as cultural assets for socio-economic development such as tourism and marketing handicrafts and rarely involve indigenous peoples in a meaningful role or take seriously indigenous knowledge or the non-material aspects of culture. Indeed, traditional practices are usually viewed as manifestations of primitive and inferior cultures which can benefit from the virtues of civilization and modernization.

People not only passively accept their situation, but also creatively respond to it. Indigenous peoples in South-East Asia possess a strong 'national' identity and group consciousness, stemming from their shared history, common culture, attachment to a territory, sense of separateness from other groups and, in some cases, assertion of the right to self-determination. Increasingly, indigenous peoples are developing adaptive strategies to resist state assimilation pressures and protect their identity, and they are beginning to engage in cultural politics in their attempt to retain their territory and way of life.

This chapter will discuss the implications of these complex and often contradictory phenomena on the indigenous peoples of South-East Asia by describing their situation in each country.

Indigenous peoples, the state and marginalization

The indigenous peoples who live in the upland forests of mainland South-East Asia were of little interest to lowland societies or state authorities until the decades following the Second World War. Political divergences among the region's states following the Chinese revolution and during the Indo-Chinese wars meant different experiences for indigenous peoples. In Yunnan, Vietnam and Lao PDR, insurgency and socialist nation-building made for intense interaction between lowland and upland spheres. Examples include northern Vietnamese and Chinese efforts to win the loyalties of upland peoples with state-led development and Lao PDR government attacks on Hmong insurgents in the wake of the 1975 communist victory. In Thailand, post-Second World War skyrocketing international demand for opiates, especially in the 1960s and 1970s, veered from state and market promotion of the trade to a multi-million-dollar state–international partnership to expunge it. In Burma, state violence, ethnic insurgency and drug production plagued indigenous societies for decades and they continue into the present.

The mainstream viewpoint of indigenous peoples can be a schizophrenic one. For example, in Thailand they are often demonized as disloyal, drug-dealing forest destroyers, dirty and wild and trapped in a primitive means of existence. At the same time, they are romanticized by some as rugged traditionalists free from the corrupting influences of modern society, living in harmony with nature and each other. This contradiction is exemplified by the forestry department's efforts to evict 'forest destroyers' while the tourism authority advertises the exotic customs and ecological wisdom of the very same people.

Today the frontiers of the region are hardly less penetrable than in days past, with myriad forest trails criss-crossing the mountainous 'borders', but the impact of state defence of territorial sovereignty and the concomitant role of citizenship cards, border police and nation-building policies have wrought great change in indigenous societies. State policies vis-à-vis indigenous peoples will be explored in this section.

Citizenship The issue of citizenship – and its converse, statelessness – can only be understood in a regional context. While the Chinese and Vietnamese can boast more inclusive citizenship policies (Sturgeon 1997: 132; Duong 2002: 3) – citizenship is not overtly or covertly linked to ethnic allegiance to the dominant society – they are not facing the immigration pressures of Thailand, which is and has long been a magnet for the region's most desperate people. After all, no one is fleeing oppression *into* Burma. No one is escaping war *into* Lao PDR. For centuries, and continuing into the present, chaos and lack of opportunity have driven both Han Chinese and ethnic minorities from China into the mountains of mainland South-East Asia. This in no way justifies the harsh treatment dealt to migrants. It does mean that the problem is only meaningfully addressed in a regional context.

Of course, this is of little consolation to Thailand's stateless residents. Perhaps half the 800,000 upland indigenous peoples in Thailand, most born there or settled for decades, are denied the basic rights of Thai citizens. With no citizenship cards they fall prey to a pass-law system depriving them of the right to move freely within the country. They are denied access to public goods such as education and quality healthcare. They are politically voiceless, with no say in local or national elections. Their employment opportunities are starkly limited, with the black economy offering the only flexibility, though with great danger. Statelessness leaves them at risk of a range of abuses by unscrupulous police and employers (Kammerer 1989; Vaddhanaphuti and Aquino 1999; Ekachai 2002).

At root, this problem reflects bigotry in Thai society. Indigenous peoples are viewed as being outside the orbit of the Thai polity. Ethno-linguistically foreign to mainstream Thai society, predominantly non-Buddhist and barred by terrain from practising wet rice production, uplanders are viewed not only as different, but as inferior. At best indigenous peoples are denigrated as primitive, rustic and backward. At worst, they are viewed as a national security threat (Asian Development Bank 2000). Many state officials hold this view, and the problem is intensified by two enduring legacies of the centralized Thai state: the idea of state officials as rulers rather than public servants and the concept of *gin meuang*, or 'eating' the polity (McVey 2000).

The idea of officials as rulers stems from the system of absolute monarchy, in existence for centuries until 1932, and the following decades of military rule in Thailand. State officers have been dispatched for more than a hundred years from Bangkok to exert central control over the population and ensure order and regular tax flows to the national treasury. Such a system did not encourage sensitivity to cultural or language differences. It 'intended instead to convey the majesty and distance of the State, reminding country folk that they were relatively uncivilized and therefore rightfully without power' (ibid.: 4). Even today, all officials above the sub-district level are part of a hierarchy with authority radiating from Bangkok. These officials were ever poorly paid by the state, and are poorly paid today. The understanding was that the national treasury could be spared expense by allowing the up-country officials to live off the land – that is, *gin meuang*. In earlier times this meant 'eating' the surplus extracted from the populace. Today it means a wide range of corrupt practices.

Bigotry, official arrogance and corruption are of course prevalent in the rest of South-East Asia, but the Marxist-Leninist traditions of China, Vietnam and Lao PDR demanded efforts to win the loyalty of the diverse 'nationalities'. For instance, in Vietnam all indigenous peoples are granted citizenship, but an 'ethnic hierarchy' exists based on evolutionary theory espoused by Vietnamese ethnologists. This positions the majority Kinh at the apex of the hierarchy, with wet-rice-growing and 'civilized' peoples such as ethnic Tai on the next rung, above shifting cultivators still in need of civilizing (Duong 2002: 4). Such a Stalinist ethnic hierarchy was formalized into a systematic and pseudo-scientific effort at classifying and documenting the ethnic milieu in China, Vietnam and Lao PDR. In China, more than four hundred potential groups identified on the basis of local distinctions were reduced to the officially recognized fifty-six ethnic nationalities (Keyes 2002: 37). Also in China, a system of autonomous regions exists that provides for nominal self-determination. There are 159 autonomous areas governed by the Minorities Regional Autonomy Law of 1984, including five autonomous regions, thirty prefectures, and 124 counties. There are also 1,500 autonomous townships (Jianchu and Salas 2003: 129). The term 'autonomous' should be treated sceptically, however. After all, Tibet is considered an 'autonomous' region, despite the persistence there of violent repression, large-scale Han immigration and official management of Tibetan culture. These systems of classification and autonomy, furthermore, have wilfully ignored the true diversity of indigenous populations.

Cultural groups with no affinity with each other have been lumped into the same ethnic categories. Autonomous regions providing limited self-rule to a locally dominant indigenous group subsume many smaller groups, or people of a larger group dispersed throughout a large area. While China has recognized that problems exist for the 'minorities within minorities' in these autonomous areas, the demands for recognition continue (ibid.).

Despite the limitations of this statist approach to relations with the indigenous peoples, and the political limitations faced by most people in these still-authoritarian states, indigenous peoples enjoy citizenship and are free of the insecurity faced by many upland indigenous peoples in Thailand, who must live with the threat of deportation and denial of rights enjoyed by the rest of society. In Thailand, the structural racism of the citizenship system was most recently elaborated by the prime minister himself, who threatened revocation of citizenship of 'hill-tribe' peoples who are suspected of engaging in the drug trade. This threat was not extended to ethnic Thais convicted of the same crime.

Control and use of natural resources The protection and enhancement of upland indigenous cultures in South-East Asia are inextricably linked to land rights and sustainable farming. The indigenous peoples of South-East Asia are overwhelmingly agriculturists. While cultures and livelihood systems are dynamic and responsive to the array of external pressures exerted on them, they are ultimately grounded in the land. The diverse livelihood portfolios of indigenous peoples in the twenty-first century certainly include economic integration, opportunities for off-farm employment and migration to the cities by some members of the communities. But loss of access to farmland is a fundamental threat to the cultural and economic survival of upland minorities, and this is where the true struggle lies.

Struggles over natural resources are another important intersection between the state and upland indigenous peoples. These take many forms, but most common among them are infrastructure development, especially dam construction, and state enclosure of forests. State claims on natural resources in the name of national economic development and the 'general good' supersede local claims of land rights and subsistence. In each country of the region mass relocations of indigenous peoples have been undertaken, are threatened in formal state plans or are implied in blueprints for future development. Examples of this include Chinese dams on the upper Mekong and tributaries, Vietnam's disastrous experiment on the Black River, Lao's Nam Theun dams and a much-contested Thai government wish-list of dams, underground canals, water diversion projects, cable cars and a proposed rapid-rail tunnel from Chiang Mai to Mae Hong Son

(Dore 2003; Hirsch 1996). The results of these big projects in terms of indigenous lives are too often landlessness, ecological scarcity, cultural dislocation and malnutrition. It must be noted that the dubious benefits of these mega-projects and the proven insincerity of officials in previous cases where relocated people were left to fend for themselves have done little to limit state hunger for more projects. The ultimate success or failure of the projects, of course, has no bearing on the substantial money to be made along the way from contracts and kickbacks.

While some donor hesitation has arisen – the Asian Development Bank (ADB) excepted – based on the failure and corruption of past projects, big infrastructure proposals in South-East Asia are never discarded. They are shelved in anticipation of a more conciliatory political or financial climate. Current Thai, Chinese and ADB cooperation with the Burmese authoritarian regime in the planned construction of dams on the Salween river, in areas where the Burmese generals have overseen ethnic cleansing of indigenous peoples, is a stark example of state venality and big finance intersecting with indigenous lives.

A more far-reaching pressure on indigenous peoples has been state enclosure of forests in the name of 'conservation' of natural resources. National parks and wildlife refuges are carved on to maps in imitation of North American conservation systems, but in areas populated for generations by indigenous peoples. Traditional systems of agriculture are derided as primitive and outlawed. Swidden agriculture is replaced with 'permanent' commercial agriculture and tree plantations. In Thailand and China, destructive state-sanctioned logging and incentives for monocropping were followed in the 1990s with logging bans and the expansion of parks and other 'conservation' areas. Given the fact that exceptions in 'conservation' regulations can be made for capital development such as dams and tourism facilities, in the interests of national development, while traditional indigenous farming is outlawed, we argue that rhetoric about 'conservation' in this context should be treated as a hypothesis rather than an assumption, and subjected to rigorous empirical evaluation. In any event, it is clear that logging bans in China and Thailand led timber industries in both countries to aggressively and rapaciously exploit the Burmese forests, with the connivance of the Burmese dictators, to the tragic detriment to indigenous peoples along the Burmese frontier.

In each country of the region, then, state authorities armed with the rhetoric, technology and institutions of nature conservation related to international standards inherent in globalization – 'protection', mapping and national parks, for example – have steadily moved to restrict and in some cases criminalize the land-use practices of upland farmers (Thoms

1996). State policies concerning 'slash-and-burn' agriculture vary across the region, but the common attitude is that shifting cultivation is uniformly backward and destructive and should be replaced with either permanent fields or orchards, or reforested for watershed protection or timber production. This fallacy of the superiority of fixed-field production over swidden cultivation, whether in ecological or social terms, is universally accepted by the states of the region, though with much variety of actual implementation dependent upon local negotiations between communities and officials in the field. The ecological and social impacts of this often self-serving 'ecological orthodoxy' on indigenous peoples are many.

In Thailand, for example, the majority of upland peoples reside on state land, with no legal title to their homes or farmland. Upland minorities, by definition, live in the mountains. Mountains, by legal definition in Thailand, are the property of the Royal Forest Department. While this has been true for more than a century, in recent decades the capacity and motivation of the state to establish real control over the northern mountains has markedly increased. This is manifested by the rapid expansion of national parks, wildlife sanctuaries and watershed areas, all nominally in the name of protection. Another aspect is the establishment of tree plantations, also nominally for watershed protection but notably using commercial timber species in single-stand plantations. Whether 'protection' describes the activities carried out in these areas enclosed by state authorities is a matter of debate; what is clear is that state intervention in the lives of mountain and forest dwellers has increased dramatically in recent years.

The state enclosure of forestland – much of it forest only in memory – results in various dimensions of livelihood insecurity for indigenous peoples. First, the threat of relocation is always present, if not imminent. Second, because of this threat long-term planning is impeded and hopes for future generations of villagers are difficult to visualize. Third, access to land is limited by forestry department maps, fences and armed rangers. Fourth, enclosure of forestland bars local access to their traditional 'supermarket', the source of nutrition for generations of forest peoples. A study of a Karen village in Thailand's northern forest, for example, found that most (53 per cent) of the food consumed is gathered daily from the forest (40 per cent) or grown by the people themselves (13 per cent) in their rotational or paddy fields (Carrier 2002). Fifth, enclosure threatens the perpetuation of local knowledge and culture. As the 'schoolyard' is fenced off, young people are unable to learn from their elders and precious knowledge of biodiversity and medicinal uses of forest plants is lost for ever. Finally, traditional land-use practices are criminalized.

The term shifting cultivation, known pejoratively as 'slash-and-burn', encapsulates a diversity of traditional land-use practices ranging from the destructive to the ecologically sustainable. Forest laws usually do not discriminate between such practices. Because they all involve the clearing of trees, they are illegal. Cutting trees and burning the remains, even when done on plots of land that have been cleared and regenerated countless times by generations of farmers, is punishable by law. This limits land available to farmers, resulting in a choice between food insecurity or conversion to chemical agriculture. Alternatives limited to starvation and eventual environmental despoliation hardly hold out hope for perpetual tenure in the mountains.

The importance of forests for society at large – and the dangers of fire – has to be balanced with the livelihood and cultural needs of indigenous peoples. The intransigence of forestry departments and other organs of the state, however, precludes innovative adaptations to a convergence of problems and opportunities facing mountain peoples such as population growth, market demand for forest products, and environmental degradation. Potential components of sustainable adaptation are taken off the negotiating table, even when they offer real prospects for a sustainable future (for example, organic farming, community-based tourism, improving forest fallows with marketable plant species such as rattan and tea, and replacing fire with the use of green manures).

Population relocation State plans to resettle segments of national populations vary across the region, ranging from carrots in Lao such as State schools and clinics to the stick of ethnic cleansing in Burma. Relocation has been carried out in the name of national security, economic development and environmental protection, depending on the era and imperatives of the state. It is interesting to note that in Thailand and Lao PDR, upland indigenous populations are seen as a threat to the environment and thus ideally relocated to the valleys. In Vietnam, the sparse settlement of the uplands (for very good ecological reasons, as it turns out) was seen by the state as a safety valve for the overcrowded lowlands. In both cases, the complexity and diversity of indigenous relations with the land were ignored or stereotyped and the coercive tools of the state brought to bear.

In Thailand, the dearth of available arable valley land in which to relocate upland peoples vastly complicated these plans, and past relocations have often been to other upland areas, though ones with much less congenial environmental conditions. In any event, planning and practice generally diverge, with the understanding that a heavy-handed relocation policy would result in increased conflict and perhaps armed struggle. State experiences with ethnic insurgency are still quite vivid. The complexity of Thailand's elite politics also complicates plans by some agencies. Most recently, in 2002 army plans to relocate all border villages in the name of national security were torpedoed by the queen's birthday observation that the plan might not be the best idea.

In Vietnam, pressures on upland cultivators to leave their forest homes also exist, but are aggravated by a relentless state policy of relieving population pressures in the densely settled Red River valley and other majority-Kinh areas with incentives to relocate into the Central Highlands. While indigenous peoples are still demonized as primitive forest destroyers, it is recognized that state timber operations and the lowland settlers' ignorance of mountain agriculture are far more to blame for environmental problems in Vietnam (Salemink 1997). In Lao PDR, relocation is the answer to conflict between indigenous shifting cultivators and state forestry. The export of timber and timber products is still a major industry in landlocked Lao PDR, ranking as the primary source of foreign exchange in 1998. Thus the livelihood interests of indigenous peoples are at odds with the profits of a powerful elite, with predictable results (Pholsena 2002: 7). The Lao PDR model of 'bringing the people to development' differs from experiences in China and Thailand (in the latter because of the obvious failures of this model). In China and Thailand, considerable efforts have been made to set up schools and clinics in remote mountain areas (see below). In Lao PDR, the state tries to bring upland indigenous peoples closer to roads, markets and schools through relocation.

Assimilationist policies All the countries of the region have expended effort and funds to assimilate the indigenous peoples living in their mountain frontier, though with significant differences in capacity, tactics and results. In Yunnan, for example, the indigenous peoples have had long and sometimes intimate contact with the dominant Han Chinese. The pre-modern policy of Han frontier administrators was to progressively bring peripheral peoples within the orbit of Chinese civilization, then playing off the 'cooked' peoples against the 'raw' (Keyes 2002). This 'inclusivist' approach meant that if outsiders could learn the language and the literary classics, they could become Chinese (Sturgeon 1997). Following the communist victory in 1949, and employing an inclusivist policy of incorporating 'national minorities' within the socialist state, the Communist Party was capable of mobilizing people and resources from around the country and deploying them to the frontier in the name of national development. Conversely, the natural resources of Yunnan were exploited for national development. More recently, development policies have eyed Yunnan as the gateway to South-East Asia and as a tourist haven boasting rich biological and cultural diversity. All this attention by the Chinese state has not been uniformly welcomed, however. Communist Party dictates about superstition and feudal customs, especially when enforced by zealous Red Guards in the 1960s, and decentralization in the 1990s to powerful local-level entrepreneur-politicians, are two examples of pressures on indigenous cultures to change. Both tourism and infrastructure development benefits have tended to accrue to Han investors and migrant labourers, as well, with the costs – relocation, land alienation and environmental degradation among them – disproportionately borne by the indigenous peoples.

In Thailand, assimilation efforts were greatly facilitated by a vast inflow of capital from foreign sources in an effort to end opium production in the 1970s and 1980s. At the peak period of development during the 1980s, there were a total of 168 agencies from thirty-one government departments and forty-nine international donors and NGOs working in the mountains (Ganjanapan 1996). Much of that attention has shifted since to the recently accessible countries of former socialist Indo-China, but its legacy in Thailand has been intensified by state penetration of the uplands. A vast road network was created throughout the uplands, bringing with it schools, clinics and agricultural extension centres, the most influential being a range of Royal Projects specializing in fruits, vegetables or ornamentals for market. Television and other information technology such as the video player and cellular telephone link once isolated villages to the lures of advertising and the fantastical world of the Bangkok elite.

In the case of education, there is evidence that bringing schools to the uplands has been an assimilation project from the beginning. A statement from the Thai Department of Public Welfare confirms this, saying, 'Education for tribal people should be implemented in a distinctive way, which differs from general lowland primary schools ... It is not only for tribal people to read and write, but also to have them loyal to the government' (Leepreecha 2001: 143). One of the impacts of the national education project was to devalue minority languages, which were banned in school areas. Leepreecha writes that in Border Patrol Police schools in the 1970s students were taught to report on fellow students who used the forbidden language, and violators were made to run laps around the school or were beaten on their hands. While such punishment is on the wane, the denigration of minority languages continues. Leepreecha argues that an example of this is the increasingly common practice among many Hmong of using Thai-language kinship terms instead of Hmong ones.

While in the socialist countries pseudo-religious reverence of state and party were inculcated into the indigenous peoples, in Burma and Thailand Buddhism is identified with nationalism. As with all things, the

Burmese experience has been extreme, with Christian schools nationalized, indigenous religions denigrated and Muslim villagers forced to build pagodas. The state and mainstream perception in Thailand is that to be Thai is to be Buddhist. Leepreecha writes that the Buddhist religion, as one of the state's technologies of power, has been employed in the 'Thai-ization' assimilation project of the state. Thammacarik, a Buddhist mission project, was deployed in the 1960s into the uplands. A collaborative effort of the Buddhist Sangha and the Division of Tribal Public Welfare of the Department of Public Welfare, the project sent Buddhist monks into the hills and encouraged indigenous peoples to enter lowland monasteries (ibid.: 169).[3] Despite this, Leepreecha argues that conversion to Buddhism has had a minimal impact on Hmong culture, largely because of Thai Buddhism's long history of harmonious coexistence with animist beliefs. Conversion to Christianity, on the other hand – often originally as a means to gain powerful friends (foreign missionaries) as a counterbalance to state interference – has had a much greater impact on indigenous culture and identity (ibid.: 180).

Indigenous peoples and globalization

The meaning of 'globalization' is much contested. In the words of Thai scholar Nidhi Aeusrivongse, 'globalization does not have only a one-sided meaning, namely the economic integration of various countries under the rules set by globally hegemonic organizations acting under the supervision of the Western powers. It also means the integration of information available to people worldwide through the dispersal of the information system. The result has been the creation of social organizations at the international level that are connected as networks in a way never experienced before. Such development is usually termed civil society globalization or globalization from below' (Aeusrivongse 2003: 48). We would add that the dispersal of information – for instance, in the forms of corporate advertising and soap operas championing elite culture – is too often uni-directional, with little opportunity for articulation of indigenous perspectives.

For the purposes of the discussion of indigenous peoples and poverty, this chapter will consider globalization from both the top-down and bottom-up perspectives. Globalization from the top, or what might be called the most recent phase of imperialism, involves the rapid penetration of both market and state into once peripheral areas. While this penetration brings great change, it should be emphasized that marginalization is a persistent element of the change. The advent of chemical agriculture, 'ecotourism' and cellular communication, for instance, creates profits and facilitates communications, but not in equal measures for all. These interventions from the outside also bring with them debt, sickness, social stratification and the social construction of needs and desires. While state agencies and the mass media champion this external penetration of backward or 'poor' areas as modernization and progress, its impact raises questions about the very cultural survival of indigenous communities.

An important aspect of the impact of capitalist penetration is the commodification of nearly everything. Land, labour and the fruits of this combination – cash crops – replace production for subsistence and the barter economy. Off-farm and seasonal migration draw people into the cities to sell their labour in the service industries. The lure of fast money in the ubiquitous drug and sex trades draws many into the black economy, with dire results measured in addiction, HIV-AIDS, imprisonment and violence. The expansion of tourism, especially hill-tribe trekking, means indigenous clothing, ornaments, ceremonies and households all now have a value measured in dollars, baht or yuan, etc. The commodification of indigenous lives will now be explored in more detail.

Commercial agriculture Conflicts over natural resources are an everyday aspect of life in the mountains of South-East Asia. The rapid and widespread conversion of land-use practices from largely subsistence production to market-oriented agriculture has increased the value of land and its products. Given the concurrent increases in population of the uplands – either from fertility rates or immigration – and state enclosure of forestland and prohibition of shifting cultivation, pressures on soil and water are intense and in many areas increasing. This has social and environmental ramifications for indigenous peoples.

Thailand's far more advanced integration with the global economy, including commercial agriculture for lowland consumption and export, can be viewed as a harbinger of things to come for the rest of the region, though Vietnam's disastrous experiment with coffee in the Central Highlands and Yunnan's problematic experience with rubber offer national examples that counsel wariness regarding unbridled adoption of cash cropping. In the rest of the region, the benefits of integration of upland crop production with international markets have proved elusive, as the destitute coffee farmers of the Central Highlands of Vietnam learned after following state dictates to plant millions of coffee trees only to find themselves vulnerable to a slump in global coffee prices. In fact, in many areas of mainland South-East Asia rough terrain and crude infrastructure cast doubt on the very possibility of real links between indigenous peoples and the global economy.

Not in Thailand. Longan growers sell their product to processors who dry the fruit for export to Greater China. Taiwanese tea producers set up dryers in remote villages. Flower growers scout out remote villages to produce seed. Temperate vegetables near the border with Burma find their way to Bangkok dinner tables. Stories of failure abound, it is true: market failure, indebtedness and death from chemicals ought to temper economists' zeal for a globalized world. The fact remains, however, that the upland economy of northern Thailand is increasingly tied to the world outside.

The experience in Thailand with commercial upland agriculture is that there are many winners, but far more losers. And many of the 'winners' – for example, urban investors in tangerine plantations or strawberry processors – are not indigenous peoples. To make matters worse, problems externalized by these 'winners' such as chemical contamination from pesticides or forest encroachment or violent exploitation are borne disproportionately by indigenous and often stateless peoples.

During the dry season in northern Thailand, strife can be found in literally every catchment area in the region. Significant increases in both upland and lowland dry-season farming are leading towards a crisis in water demand, though official attention and lowland propaganda focus exclusively on water supply and target upland indigenes as the villains for clearing forests. Despite some scholarly attention to what Andrew Walker calls 'ecological orthodoxy' – such as the idea that forests make rain – sustained research and conflict resolution measures are needed to study the relationships between forests, water and the rapid expansion of dry-season agriculture (see Alford 1992; McKinnon 1997; Enters 1995; Kaosa-ard 2000; Walker 2002).

Conflicts over resources have led to road blockades by lowland farmers, demonstrations by upland minorities at government offices and even mob action – allegedly with official sanction – against property of indigenous people. It is one of the many ironies of the Thai hills that these resource conflicts have their roots in state–foreign partnerships to end opium production in the north.

The shift to commercial agriculture, including the use of chemical inputs and hybrid seeds, raises concerns over ecological – and by extension, cultural – sustainability. Farmland in the uplands is often steep and the soil poor, and irrigation is limited or non-existent. Allowing a sufficient fallow period – at the very least five years and in the past sometimes up to fifteen years – could limit the worst excesses of soil erosion and ensure that soil fertility was not depleted beyond recovery. Multi-cropping helped limit pest populations and diversified the upland diet. Today, land available for farming is increasingly limited by the establishment of national parks and reforestation projects, while the demand for hill property by lowland resort developers and orchard growers, among many others, is growing. Thus the marginal upland farmer's fallow period is reduced beyond sustainable levels, and reliance on chemical fertilizers and pesticides increases for those who can afford them.

Localized examples of the failures of chemical agriculture can be found throughout the hills. Soil quality declines, farmer health is threatened, debt increases and the haphazard application of pesticides sometimes fails completely to stop the pests, resulting in crop failure. Experiences the world over warn that chemical agriculture will temporarily reward a relatively wealthy minority but will drive the poorest farmer off the land. In the ecologically vulnerable upland farms of northern Thailand, a key problem is a lack of options. Many farmers cannot even afford the chemicals that would give them a few more years of production on over-farmed soil. Those who can afford them can do so until debt or soil degradation revoke even this option.

In a paradoxical twist to the story, the energetic response of some communities to opium prohibition, most notably the Hmong, has led to a new phase of recrimination and possible state repression. By replacing shifting cultivation and opium with permanent fields and cash crops such as cabbage, which require chemical fertilizers and pesticides, upland farmers are attacked for polluting watersheds and selling contaminated crops in the market. Announcements by the Minister of Natural Resources and Environment that chemical inputs will be banned in upper watersheds could foretell a new round of criminalization of upland farming.

More attention needs to be paid to environmentally sound ways for upland peoples to chart a middle course between currently untenable traditional practices and total reliance on chemicals. Organic agriculture, including targeting and developing niche markets for this increasingly popular business, must be urgently furthered with a view to improving upland community health and food security, while simultaneously buttressing land rights claims. That is, the link between land rights and sustainable farming (including agroforestry in community forests) must be aggressively researched, articulated, propagated and developed. This is not just smart strategy; if environmentalist warnings about the dangers of chemical farming prove true, then many upland farmers could be approaching a critical threshold that would add to the already great pressures on their livelihoods.

Drugs The production, distribution and consumption of illicit drugs must be considered from regional and international perspectives. For example, precursor chemicals for the production of amphetamines originate far from the production platforms of South-East Asia in Burma and Lao PDR.

Markets for these drugs, too, are distant from the producers. Changes in one country often have severe repercussions for neighbouring countries. In Thailand, for instance, suppression of opium production led to ramped-up production of heroin in Burma, while the dramatic increase in Bangkok's appetite for speed facilitates production of this drug in Burma and Lao PDR.

While the analogy of the 'flood' is used ad nauseum in Thai newspaper accounts of the drug problem – 'ethnic Wa drug lords flooding Thailand with drugs' – just as Americans talk of South American cocaine 'flooding' the United States, we argue that a 'pump' analogy is more fitting. It is urban Thai demand for amphetamines, like US consumers' hunger for cocaine, which drives the drug trade. For the indigenous Wa or Lahu cultivators of opium or the conscripted labourer in an amphetamine factory in the desperate hills of Burma's Shan State, this trade is a deadly scourge. The bottom rung on the drug ladder is not enriched by the trade, but imprisoned by it. The terrorist collaboration of the Burmese military and narco-armies such as the United Wa State Army is fed by urban demand for drugs in Bangkok, Shanghai, Sydney and Los Angeles and facilitated by official corruption every step of the way. The people who grow and make the stuff are the principal victims of the multibillion-dollar global drug trade, while the petty dealers – too often alienated indigenous youth – are the principal victims of so-called 'wars' against drugs.

Drug trafficking in Thailand became a national preoccupation in the mid-1990s as the dynamics changed quickly from a trade in heroin that largely transited Thailand en route to foreign markets to a trade in amphetamines specifically targeting skyrocketing Thai demand, especially among Thai youth. The Thai government, in fact, sees the trans-border trade of speed as national security threat number one. Owing in large part to the international collaboration discussed above, opium cultivation in the north is a tiny shadow of the past. Production levels declined in Thailand from an estimated 48,500 kilograms in 1980 to 3,700 kilograms in 1999 (Renard 2001: 36). Critics, however, argue that production is booming just across the border in Burma and Lao PDR, and that unintended consequences have included an epidemic of heroin and amphetamine addiction in indigenous communities.

Total South-East Asian opium production, the bulk of it in Burma, increased about 2.5 times between 1987 and 1995 – though the late 1990s did see a sudden decrease, mainly accounted for by poor weather conditions. Comparisons in the latest figures show the disparity between the three so-called Golden Triangle countries. In terms of area under poppy cultivation, Thailand reported 1,600 hectares in 2000, while Burma showed 108,000 hectares and estimates for Lao PDR ran from 19,000 to 26,000 hectares. In global terms, Thailand accounted for just 0.2 per cent of the world's opium poppy fields, while Burma recorded 50 per cent and Lao PDR nearly 9 per cent. In production terms, estimates of opium cultivation in Thailand for 2000 were 4.3 tonnes, compared with 1,085 tonnes in Burma and 167 tonnes in Lao PDR. Again on a global scale, Thailand's contribution of opium was less than 1 per cent, while Burma's production accounted for 23 per cent of the world total and Lao PDR's 4 per cent. Percentages for heroin production are roughly similar (UNDCP n.d.).

Heroin distribution channels for international markets, a decade ago running primarily through Thailand, are now increasingly snaking through China and Vietnam instead. Yunnan has surpassed Thailand as a transit route for external markets and both countries, as well as India, are integral to the trade as suppliers of essential precursor chemicals such as ephedrine (China, India) and caffeine (Thailand). Given important changes in patterns of production, distribution and consumption of illicit drugs in Asia, and the reality on the ground in the Thai 'angle', the evocative label 'The Golden Triangle,' is today little more than a catchy phrase for tourism advertisements. Perhaps a new geometric–colour combination is required.

Both heroin and amphetamines businesses exist now in parallel in montane mainland South-East Asia, disproportionately ravaging upland communities even as the people themselves are pinpointed as the principal culprits. While both heroin and speed enrich many, especially in the upper echelons of society – it is argued that modern Chiang Mai was built on heroin proceeds – heroin has killed foreigners and speed is destroying kids in Bangkok and other cities. This has changed the Thai approach to drugs completely. It is the grave misfortune of indigenous communities that they are located along the trafficking routes of the opium grown in the Shan hills and the heroin and amphetamines processed in factories lining the Burmese side of the border. Many indigenous peoples are implicated in the trade, though playing bit parts as mules and small-time dealers in a drama including some of the region's most powerful people. It is common in indigenous villages to find families deprived of parents or youth who are serving long jail terms for transporting relatively small amounts of drugs, or parents who have lost teenage kids to drug-related or extra-judicial killings, while the kingpins live in mansions and amass ill-begotten wealth with impunity. For example, in a Hmong community (population approximately one thousand) that has been relocated from the mountains of northern Thailand to an area in the lowlands with poor agricultural land and few employment opportunities, more than sixty youths are incarcerated for drug trafficking, mostly in an effort to support their amphetamine addictions.[4] Still, the common perception is that it is the 'hill tribes' which are responsible for the scourge of drugs in Thai society.

Thailand saw a 1,000 per cent increase in amphetamine abuse between 1993 and 2001, according to the UNDCP. The rise from 260,000 users to 3 million in eight years – including a current estimate of 300,000 amphetamine-dependent people nationwide (UNDCP n.d.) – has been paralleled by a dramatic increase in law enforcement measures, notably including the role of the army, involving a proliferation of roadway check points, border patrols and the activation of a long-dormant death penalty for trafficking. Though the drug routes from speed factories on the Burmese border to Bangkok schoolyards involve many different people from all walks of life, it is generally indigenous peoples which are blamed for selling drugs. Too often, of course, this proves to be true, and the attendant combination of violence, health problems, imprisonment and law enforcement is tearing communities apart.

Recent efforts to reorganize the state drug suppression apparatus into a ramped-up 'war on drugs' are particularly worrying given Thailand's history of authoritarianism and military interference in politics. In early January 2003 it was announced that the government would create a new unit called the National Centre to Defeat Narcotics under Deputy Prime Minister Chavalit Yongchaiyudh. It is clearly driven by the national security mindset that Thai human rights commission staffer Taneeya Roonchaleurn argues is a especially virulent artefact of the cold war and one that inhibits the adoption of human rights thinking. The deputies of the new agency will be drawn from the National Security Council, the Internal Security Operations Command and the supreme command, with the unit's impetus being to achieve unity in a notoriously fractured state suppression effort. The unit will also include officials from the public health and education bureaucracies, but the primacy of the military in the new structure is clear from the fact that the regional army commanders will lead suppression efforts, subordinating provincial governors, who are under the Interior Ministry's chain of command. This arrangement threatens to undermine the stated goal of unity, with Interior already criticizing the preponderance of military men in the new agency. Even more troubling is a plan, also opposed by Interior, to create a special zone in which the northern border provinces with the most indigenous peoples – Chiang Mai, Chiang Rai, Mae Hong Son and Tak – would come under direct control of the Third Army.[5] In early 2003 Prime Minister Thaksin gave authorities three months (until 30 April 2003) to rid the country of drugs. Although no one really expected this goal to be met, the militarization of the drug problem and the resultant bloodbath – more than two thousand people were killed in three months of extra-judicial killings and drug lords neutralizing competitors and potential informants – meant that the rights and security of indigenous communities were even more rigorously violated by the state.

Urban migration Anthropologists studying upland indigenous peoples argue that the migration of village dwellers to the cities, for a variety of reasons, is a major component of the dramatic changes in the region's uplands. Buadaeng et al. studied migration into northern Thai cities by indigenous peoples in a 2002 study in Chiang Mai and Chiang Rai. According to their study, the number of ethnic migrants from the uplands increased from 2,500 in 1996 to almost 4,690 in 2001. They argued that several factors converged in the rapid increase. These were: 1) a scarcity of land for agriculture, the result of state forest enclosure and sale of farmland to urban land developers; 2) inability or unwillingness of some individuals to conform to village regulations or cultural traditions, including sanctions against drug addiction; 3) the desire for higher education, which can only be found in the cities; 4) aspirations of material improvement associated with urban life; and 5) the opening of trade routes between neighbouring countries, which facilitates illegal immigration (Buadaeng et al. 2002: 3–4).

The sort of life facing urban migrants from the hills ranges from the educational opportunities of boarding schools to the hell of the brothel. The study by Buadaeng et al. found that urban migrants were engaged in studying, wage labour (mainly construction sites, petrol stations and restaurants), the sex industry, small-scale trading and, in the case of many children, as homeless beggars and pedlars. The study concluded that while some migrants had succeeded, mainly as traders but also as NGO workers or government officials, life was grim for the majority. They faced exploitation by unscrupulous employers or state officials, were at high risk of drug abuse and transmission of HIV and earned far-below-average wages. Their work is often physically dangerous and under-regulated (ibid.: 28–9).

The scholars conducting this study called for more empirical research on the phenomenon of urban migration by indigenous peoples, with an emphasis on both success and failure stories. The current emphasis on ethnic peoples as rural subsistence farmers is missing a large part of the story of the changing lives of these people.

Tourism The tourism industry is one of the world's leading money-earners. In Thailand, it is the top earner of foreign currency. Much of the draw in the mountainous north has been 'hill-tribe trekking'. This industry has expanded to the rest of the region, with indigenous villages in Lao PDR and Vietnam added to the trail of the ethno-tourist circuit. In China, Yunnan is promoted as the 'Great Cultural Province' with its indigenous peoples the key draw. Other draws of the 'hill-tribe trekking' industry in the region have been drugs and sex, as well as a trade in indigenous heirlooms.

In Thailand, the growth of tourism has been dramatic in recent decades. In 1960, about 81,000 foreign tourists visited Thailand, earning the country about US$4.9 million. The number of visitors mushroomed to nearly 2 million in 1980 (earning US$442.5 million), 5.3 million in 1990 (US$2.75 billion) and 7.8 million in 1998, earning the country US$6.1 billion (Alpha Research Co. 2000). The industry affects the mountains and its people in four main ways. First, many tourists who visit the north engage in 'hill-tribe trekking', which involves visiting and often staying overnight in upland villages after walking through the forest or riding elephants to reach them (which today can be done much more conveniently, though less dramatically, by road). Second, selling handicrafts to tourists is an important source of income for poorer families. This is done either in the village, at markets along major mountain roads, or in tourist areas of cities such as Chiang Mai and Chiang Rai. Third, in the 1990s developers scrambled for land to build upscale tourist resorts in the mountains to serve both the boom in foreign tourism and the demand of urban Thais for an escape from the increasingly congested city. A fourth area of importance is tourism in national parks, with the current Thai government pressuring the national parks department to become a profit-generating entity.

With the exception of the state's role in providing amenities for tourists at national parks, and the Tourism Authority of Thailand's spending on advertising and promotions for upscale tourism, state institutions play a minimal role in tourism in the north. The private sector, especially small- and medium-sized enterprises, leads the way. Forsyth differentiates between regulated and non-regulated tourism, with the former restricted spatially to places such as national parks. In that sense, most tourism in northern Thailand and neighbouring countries is of the non-regulated type, growing 'without the spatial and administrative restrictions that exist in a park "environment"' (Forsyth 1995). The record is mixed in terms of determining whether such tourism is a boon or a bane for the natural environment. Such activities may reduce environmental degradation by providing farmers with an alternative source of income to agriculture. They might relieve pressures on the land by both extracting labour from agriculture and providing money to purchase yield-enhancing and thus land-saving innovations such as fertilizers. On the other hand, as a society like Thailand develops economically and land is seen increasingly as an investment rather than a resource, another face of tourism is the resort industry, which has meant forest clearing and demands on scarce water resources. Such developments, including luxury resorts and golf courses, have 'encouraged a revolution in land ownership' because land used for tourism offers a higher rate of return than traditional agriculture (ibid.).

The number of adventure tourists walking the hills of the north twenty-odd years ago is unknown, but most reckon it was minuscule. Since then 'the industry has mushroomed' (Dearden 1993). Estimates of the number of trekkers vary, from Dearden's (1993) figure of 100,000 trekkers per year with a median trek length of three nights each, giving some 300,000 trekker nights per year in indigenous communities, to the Thai tourist police estimate of a high of more than 73,000 in 1995 (TDRI 1997). This does not include those who stop by roadside villages on bus tours through the mountains, which would likely constitute the majority of foreign visitors to the north, who are 'mainly attracted by the colorful ethnic minorities who are marketed as remote and exotic "tribes" living pre-industrial lifestyles' (Forsyth 1995). Forest trekking, rafting, elephant riding and, less today than a decade ago, opium smoking are among the various attractions. According to TDRI, in 1997 the average trek price was 1,200 baht, of which villagers received an average of 20 baht.[6] Chiang Mai is still the trekking headquarters for the region, with the main tourists strips lined with tour agencies advertising exotic getaways, but smaller centres have emerged in Chiang Rai, Mae Hong Son and Pai. In recent years, the attraction of the opening of formerly communist Indo-China has cut into the Thai trekking business.

Scholars debate the balance of pros and cons of the tourist industry as it expands throughout the mountains. In fact, 'expand' might not be the best term, because one dynamic of the trekking business is the tendency for tour operators to quit villages that attain too high an economic status – in part from tourism – and move on to find more 'authentic hill tribes' (Dearden 1993; Michaud 1997). Trekking, along with roads, electrification and communications technology, brings the outside world to the village. The resulting commodification of customs – villagers will sometimes put on shows and dances, for a fee – and hunger for material objects and the cash to purchase them is decried by many (see Michaud 1997), but trekking should be seen as just one of many forces of change in the uplands. Cash and the need for it are part and parcel of the shift to commercial agriculture, after all. As has already been noted, the returns from this business are far from evenly distributed. Those losing out in the changing indigenous village welcome off-farm sources of income.

While the number of national parks in Thailand nearly doubled between

1985 and 1995, the number of visitors tripled to 12 million per year by 1995 (Kaosa-ard and Wijukprasert 2000). The injustice of this is readily evident to indigenous peoples that have either been relocated or live with the threat of eviction every day, or have seen their traditional farmland placed off limits. As they watch busloads of well-heeled tourists or rowdy Thai students drive past, they may wonder at the logic of state forest 'conservation' policies.

Conclusion: identity, resistance and empowerment

Given the difficult situation for indigenous peoples in South-East Asia described above, it is a major challenge for them to protect their culture and identity and assert their rights. State concerns with nation-building and controlling frontiers, coupled with negative stereotypes and the desire to assimilate all populations within their borders, continue to plague indigenous peoples. Policies with such manifest goals as protection of biodiversity and the ecosystem, often supported by Western environmentalists, have resulted in the creation of numerous national parks and forest preserves in the region with supporting programmes to relocate indigenous peoples (who are viewed as threats to the environment) out of 'protected' highland areas and strict controls placed on activities inherent in the indigenous knowledge of the people. McNeely (1997) argues that the harshest programmes of restrictions on land use have targeted areas where indigenous peoples reside, and reports on extensive resettlement initiatives to remove indigenous peoples from protected areas, including an example of 550 Muong households being moved out of Cuc Phuong National Park in Vietnam.

Elements of globalization and modernization have come to characterize an increasingly large number of indigenous communities. TV aerials bristle in even seemingly remote villages, and in those communities that have been the most aggressive in the transition to cash cropping, satellite dishes are all the rave. In one Hmong village in Thailand studied by Kunstadter and Prapamontal (2001), motorcycles were universal and every other family owned a pick-up truck. TV sets, video players and cellular phones are now seen as essentials in many mountain communities.

This does not mean that poverty is not a crushing problem in most communities, however, as the largesse of economic development has not been equitably divided. This social differentiation of traditionally egalitarian societies is the subject of much academic criticism. Much of what was a culture intimately linked to the production of subsistence rice has now been commodified, with 'authentic hill-tribe dancing' performed for a fee and traditional ceremonies accompanied by photo-snapping Western tourists. Increasingly, off-farm employment in urban centres is important for many indigenous peoples, with working-age people travelling to Chiang Rai, Chiang Mai, Bangkok and even abroad to places such as Taiwan and Saudi Arabia seeking employment. The monetary remissions back to the village are not inconsiderable, though a less welcome import has been the arrival of HIV-AIDS. In all, most mountain villages of northern Thailand bear little resemblance to those of a generation ago.

Characterized by threats to indigenous knowledge and identity, poverty, powerlessness and marginalization, the forces of globalization, modernization and nationalization might appear to leave indigenous peoples little choice but to abandon their culture, migrate to urban centres, integrate into the lowest economic strata of society and eventually assimilate into the dominant group. Yet individuals not only passively accept their situation but also actively create and even resist it, even under the most oppressive of circumstances. In describing the effects of external forces, care must be taken not to reify the actions of the state and assume a uniformity of application or exaggerate their impact. Indigenous peoples cope with their situations and develop strategies to address issues and do so on the basis of local knowledge and within a particular cultural framework. This framework includes specific and shared beliefs, values, attitudes and behaviours that are appropriate to the group. And cultures and identities are adaptable. Aspects of cultures are preserved, transformed, sustained and revitalized as a result of both internal and external forces.

In addition, globalization and nationalism are not the homogeneous tyrannical forces they are often made out to be. Virtually all South-East Asian nations have moved from state-controlled centralized economic systems to one that is more market driven, decentralized and liberalized, which, in theory, allows for more freedom for local and regional initiatives and decision-making and increased autonomy in asserting collective aspirations. Long argues that globalization has not destroyed cultural, ethnic, economic and political diversity but rather has '... generated a whole new diversified pattern of responses at national, regional and local levels' (Long 1996). This includes the development of new social and political identities and movements based on diverse social commitments including ethnicity and locality.

Similarly, globalization is characterized by issues related to the nature of science, technology and knowledge in terms of how they shape the social relations and value orientations of diverse cultures. Specifically, so-called 'expert' and 'local' modes of knowledge encounter one another, with contrasting cultural and epistemological frameworks (ibid.). Increasingly there is a questioning of centralized, standard solutions to problems of development in favour of more flexible, localized and sustainable strategies which involve local people in meaningful decision-making roles in the 'development' of their communities (McCaskill 1997). *Indigenous knowledge* is now recognized as a viable concept within a larger paradigm of knowledge. The Karen in Thailand have utilized these processes to turn a liability into an asset as they attempt to legitimize their natural resource management system. They have effectively argued that what is termed 'slash-and-burn' agriculture by outsiders is, in fact, an effective and forest-conserving 'rotational farming system' based on indigenous knowledge practised for centuries (Trakarnsuphakorn 1997).

New networks of global communication and information are also affecting cultures and identities even in remote indigenous communities. The ability to transmit symbolic images across borders allows for individuals to compare themselves and their situation with others, communicate with indigenous groups in other countries and develop 'transnational' or 'cosmopolitan' notions of citizenship. These images and lines of communication can be utilized to organize, reinforce identities and further collective goals. The Hmong, for example, have effectively used communication tools such as the Internet and video to connect communities and organizations from around the world to reinforce identities and create new ones.

The question arises: how can indigenous peoples in South-East Asia sustain a viable individual and collective identity given the pressures they face? At the most fundamental level our identity is our understanding of who we are. It is formed and maintained through a social interaction with other individuals and collectivities. Identity is about meaning, which is the outcome of agreement or disagreement, convention and innovation, shared, and always to some extent negotiable (Jenkins 1996). On the one hand, we possess unique individual identities while on the other we share aspects of our identity with others as part of our collective identity. Indeed, we have multiple identities based on ethnicity, gender, nationality, social class, occupation, religion and so on. But an important aspect of our identity, especially for marginalized groups, is how others perceive us.

It has been pointed out that the social categorization of indigenous groups by members of the dominant society is frequently negative. Damaging negative stereotypes abound. It is not enough to assert one's identity, it must always be reinforced by others. And identity formation always involves power, the power of one group to establish its way of life as normative. Thus indigenous peoples are faced with the challenge of constructing an identity that balances positive group identification against the onslaught of negative categorizations by others. As discussed above, contradictory pressures by the state to assimilate indigenous peoples into the nation while at the same time withholding citizenship and threatening them with relocation from their homes have had the effect of marginalizing indigenous groups and maintaining them in a vulnerable situation.

A study of Hmong and Dan Lai communities in northern Vietnam discovered that many villagers now accept the negative stereotypes about their cultures that have long been prevalent among lowland Kinh (Cuc and Rambo 2001). In a Hmong village close to the Lao border, close to sixty individuals are currently in prison as a result of drug-related offences, primarily the result of supporting drug addictions.[7] There can be no doubt that, for many individuals, factors such as drugs, coupled with urban migration and state attempts to annihilate and commodify indigenous cultures, have had the effect of weakening aspects of indigenous cultural identity.

Nevertheless, increasing numbers of indigenous peoples are developing adaptive strategies, constructing internal processes in their communities while responding to the challenges and opportunities of external forces. For example, in 2002 the Hmong in Thailand organized a major ceremony to affirm their identity and attempt to reverse the negative images held by Thai society. It involved presenting the Thai royal family with a silver musical instrument symbolic of their culture as a gesture to signify that they were good citizens of Thailand, and not drug-smuggling forest destroyers. Hmong from around the world attended the ceremony as well as a significant number of lowland Thais. In other cases individuals are taking advantage of the economic opportunities of globalization and integrating into the regional economy. In the process they are attempting to create a new identity based on blending elements of ethnic and dominant group cultures. For example, a Hmong community located near a major Thai city has been able to take advantage of substantial income generated by tourism (supplemented by agriculture) to develop a significant improvement in their standard of living. They have also emphasized the importance of education and welcomed technological and infrastructure changes in their community. In short, they have viewed globalization as a positive opportunity.

This community in turn is utilizing its increased 'economic capital', higher levels of education and increased knowledge of Thai culture to elevate its status among Thais. Individuals reported that, while Thais looked down on them previously, now they enjoy a greater degree of acceptance and equality.[8] They suggested that while some aspects of traditional Hmong culture are disappearing (i.e. songs and stories) and others are changing (i.e. ceremonies) the fundamental nature of their culture (i.e. language, clans, world-view) remains strong. They conceive of their primary identity as Hmong and see their biculturalism in positive terms. Thus the forces of globalization, under some circumstances, can contribute to an improvement in economic circumstances and exposure to aspects of the dominant society while at the same time not resulting in the assimilation of indigenous people. Indigenous identities can be protected, maintained and enhanced.

To understand how these identity-protecting strategies function it is important to recognize that critical components of identity are developed during primary socialization. Children, in effect, 'take on' the world of those in charge of their upbringing. They identify with significant others and in the process the child becomes capable of identifying himself or acquiring a subjectively coherent identity (Berger and Luckmann 1967). In this process they internalize the beliefs, values, roles, language and behaviours that characterize their indigenous culture and social structure. Secondary socialization occurs when the individual encounters the institutions of the lager society. But secondary socialization must be superimposed on the already formed identity and the content is much less subjectively inevitable than the contents of primary socialization. When contradictory definitions of reality become a threat to an established identity, indigenous peoples must establish mechanisms to counter those threats.

An increasing number of indigenous peoples are rejecting the negative images attributed to them by dominant groups. They are asserting the indigenous collective identity learned during primary socialization through a number of adaptive strategies designed to legitimize their way of life and collective rights. In some cases they are reversing the direction of social categorization and turning derogation into dignity. For example, interviews in Karen villages in Thailand revealed that, while villagers were aware of the negative stereotypes of them held by lowland Thais, they effectively rebuffed them by articulating negative images of Thais. The Karen claimed a moral superiority by pointing out negative behavior they believed characterized Thai culture, such as excessive alcohol consumption, immoral sexual practices and disrespectful gender relations.[9]

In addition, indigenous organizations are playing an important role in resisting the negative influences of the state and increasingly addressing issues and asserting their collective rights. In Thailand, where the greatest freedom exists for the formation of such organizations, a number of indigenous associations such as the Inter-Mountain Peoples Education and Culture of Thailand (IMPECT), the Hmong Association of Thailand and the Akha Association have been operating for fifteen years. Their roles include conducting development projects in indigenous communities, organizing cultural and political events, advocating on behalf of members, and, in recent years, coordinating with indigenous groups in other parts of the world. With the passing of the new constitution in 1997 various forms of political protest have become possible and indigenous peoples have become active in organizing marches, sit-ins and demonstrations. Also notable in Thailand are the beginnings of a movement towards a recognition of the validity of indigenous cultures by state agencies. For example, at Rajapat University in Chiang Rai an ethnic studies programme has begun with a curriculum based on indigenous cultures.

Unfortunately, as described earlier, most states in South-East Asia prohibit the formation of indigenous organizations and do not allow any overt form of political protest. But even under the most oppressive circumstances, indigenous peoples find ways to resist external pressures and reaffirm their culture and identity. In Burma indigenous groups such as the Karen, Shan, Wa and Kachin have been waging a war against the ruling dictators for fifty years. Indeed, a paradox inherent in attempts to assimilate indigenous peoples is that these attempts may serve to strengthen identity. Indigenous identities tend to persist. They become critically important when threatened. The need for boundary maintenance becomes most important when the boundaries are under pressure. Contrary to expectations that indigenous identity would disappear because of the homogenizing effects of state nationalism, indigenous identity does not vanish, '... but instead emerges in a new, often more powerful and more clearly articulated form' (Eriksen 1993). Struggles of ethnic nationalism are inherent in all countries in South-East Asia.

Thus while the forces of globalization and nationalism discussed in this chapter are exerting intense pressures on indigenous peoples in South-East Asia, they are also affording new opportunities. Globalization can offer indigenous peoples new opportunities to assert their identities and create new ones. Meanwhile, there are examples of state agencies that support indigenous peoples and promote aspects of indigenous culture. For example, in Kunming China the Yunnan Nationalities University teaches numerous courses in indigenous cultures to a student body which is 80 per cent indigenous. It is clear that indigenous cultures and identities will not disappear. Indigenous identity is so fundamental to an individual's being that people are willing to die to ensure its survival. It is to be hoped that the states of South-East Asia will come to recognize the legitimate territorial, cultural and political rights of indigenous peoples as they attempt to balance construction of viable cultures and identities with integration into the nation-state.

Notes

1 Although Yunnan is not technically part of South-East Asia it has numerous indigenous groups in common with the other countries.

2 The term *indigenous peoples* as used in the South-East Asian context differs from the more common usage of the term in, for example, North America, Australia or New Zealand. In these nations indigenous peoples have been referred to as tribal peoples, Indians, native peoples, aboriginal peoples and, more recently, as First Nations. In this context the term refers to the original inhabitants who have lived in a territory from time immemorial, have been subjugated by colonial regimes, and by virtue of their occupation of a territory possess certain usufructory rights (rights of occupancy and usage) to the land. These rights are often codified in legal agreements such as treaties and legislation with corresponding special legal status. Subsequent attempts at assimilation through such draconian institutions as residential schools have resulted in serious social problems and severe cultural loss.

3 The primary goals of the Thammacarik Project are: 1) to propagate Buddhism among highlanders; 2) to improve their minds, provide them with basic education and health services and resolve emergency problems; 3) to convince highlanders to become Thai; and 4) to teach highlanders their moral and civic duties (Leepreecha 2001: 170).

4 McCaskill, interview with village headman, Chiang Rai, 2003.

5 As reported in the *Bangkok Post*, 11 January 2003, p. 1.

6 About 40 baht to the dollar at the time of writing.

7 McCaskill, interviews with Hmong villagers, Chiang Rai Province, 2003.

8 McCaskill, interviews with Hmong villagers, Chiang Mai Province, 2004.

9 McCaskill, interviews with Karen villagers, Chiang Mai, 2003.

References

Aeusrivongse, N. (2003) 'Comment on Ammar's chapter', in K. Mingsarn and J. Dore (eds), *Social Challenges for the Mekong Region*, Bangkok: White Lotus

Alford, D. (1992) 'Streamflow and sediment transport from mountain watersheds of the Chao Phraya Basin, northern Thailand: a reconnaissance study', *Mountain Research and Development*, 12(3)

Alpha Research Co. (2000) 'Thailand in figures, 1998–1999', Bangkok: Alpha Research

Asian Development Bank (2000) 'Health and education needs of ethnic minorities in the Greater Mekong sub-region', Thailand Country Report, June, ADB TA No. 5794–REG

Berger, P. and T. Luckmann (1967) *The Social Construction of Reality: A Treatise on the Sociology of Knowledge*, New York: Anchor Books

Buadaeng, K., P. Boonyasaranai and P. Leepreecha (2002) *A Study of the Socio-economic Vulnerability of Urban-based Tribal Peoples in Chiang Mai and Chiang Rai, Thailand*, Chiang Mai: Centre for Ethnic Studies and Development, Social Research Institute

Carrier, A. (2002) 'Food self-sufficiency in a realistic light: a study of Pgak'Yau village's food consumption patterns', research paper, Trent University Thailand Year Abroad Programme, Chiang Mai University

Cuc, L. T. and A. T. Rambo (eds) (2001) 'Bright peaks, dark valleys: a comparative analysis of environmental and social conditions and development trends in five communities in Vietnam's northern mountain region', Hanoi: National Political House

Dearden, P. (1993) 'Trekking in northern Thailand', London: 5th International Conference on Thai Studies/SOAS

Dien, K. (2002) *Population and Ethno-demography in Vietnam*, Chiang Mai: Silkworm Books

Dore, J. (2003) 'The governance of increasing Mekong regionalism', in K. Mingsarn and J. Dore (eds), *Social Challenges for the Mekong Region*, Bangkok: White Lotus

Duong, B. H. (2002) 'Ethnic minorities in Vietnam: current development and a closer look at the issue of education', report presented to the sub-regional seminar on Minority Rights: Cultural Diversity and Development in South-East Asia, Chiang Mai, 4–7 December

Ekachai, S. (2002) 'Fighting for a future', *Bangkok Post*, 9 July

Enters, T. (1995) 'The economics of land degradation and resource conservation in northern Thailand, challenging the assumptions', in R. Jonathan (ed.), *Counting the Costs: Economic Growth and Environmental Change in Thailand*, Singapore: Institute of South-East Asian Studies

Eriksen, T. H. (1993) *Ethnicity and Nationalism: Anthropological Perspectives*, London: Pluto Press

Forsyth, T. J. (1995) 'Non-regulated tourism as a form of environmental management in northern Thailand: the case of Pha Dua, Chiang Rai', in R. Jonathan (ed.), *Counting the Costs: Economic Growth and Environmental Change in Thailand*, Singapore: Institute of South-East Asian Studies

Gandi, L. (1998) *Postcolonial Theory: A Critical Introduction*, Edinburgh: Edinburgh University Press

Ganjanapan, A. (1996) 'The politics of environment in northern Thailand: ethnicity and highland development programmes', in P. Hirsch (ed.), *Seeing Forests for Trees: Environment and Environmentalism in Thailand*, Chiang Mai: Silkworm Books

Hirsch, P. (1996) 'Resource tenure, management and competition in three Thai watersheds', report presented at the 6th International Conference on Thai Studies, Chiang Mai, 14–17 October

Jenkins, R. (1996) *Social Identity*, London: Routledge

Jianchu, X. and M. Salas (2003) 'Moving the periphery to the centre: indigenous people, culture and knowledge in a changing Yunnan', in M. Kaosa-ard and J. Dore (eds), *Social Challenges for the Mekong Region*, Chiang Mai: Chiang Mai University

Kammerer, C. A. (1989) 'Territorial imperatives: Akha ethnic identity and Thailand's national integration', in J. McKinnon and B. Vienne (eds), *Hill Tribes Today: Problems in Change*, Bangkok: White Lotus

Kampe, K. (1997) 'Introduction: indigenous peoples of South-East Asia', in D. McCaskill and K. Kampe (eds), *Development or Domestication? Indigenous Peoples of South-East Asia*, Chiang Mai: Silkworm Books

Kaosa-ard, M. (2000) 'Thailand's natural resources and the environment beyond the year 2000', Occasional Paper no. 4, Chiang Mai University: Centre for Sustainable Development Studies, Faculty of Economics

— (2003) 'Poverty and Globalization', in K. Mingsarn and J. Dore (eds), *Social Challenges for the Mekong Region*, Chiang Mai: Chiang Mai University

Kaosa-ard, M. and P. Wijukprasert (2000) *The State of the Environment in Thailand: A Decade of Change*, Bangkok: Thailand Development Research Institute

Keyes, C. (2002) 'The peoples of Asia: science and politics in the classification of ethnic groups in Thailand, China and Vietnam', presented as the presidential address to the 54th annual meeting of the Association for Asian Studies, Washington, DC, 6 April

Kunstadter, P. and T. Prapamontol (2001) 'Changes in land use and environment in the northern Thai highlands', paper presented at the EUROSEAS Conference, School of Oriental and African Studies, London, 6 September

Lee, K. (2003) 'Social challenges for Lao PDR', in K. Mingsarn and J. Dore (eds), *Social Challenges for the Mekong Region*, Chiang Mai: Chiang Mai University

Leepreecha, P. (2001) *Kinship and Identity among Hmong in Thailand*, PhD dissertation, University of Washington

Lim Joo-Jock (1982) 'Territorial power domains, South-East Asia and China: the geo-strategy of an overarching massif', Singapore: Institute of South-East Asian Studies

Long, N. (1996) 'Globalization and localization: new challenges to rural research', in L. M. Henrietta (ed.), *The Future of Anthropological Knowledge*, New York: Routledge

McCaskill, D. (1997) 'From tribal peoples to ethnic minorities: the transformation of indigenous peoples', in D. McCaskill and K. Kampe (eds), *Development or Domestication? Indigenous Peoples of South-East Asia*, Chiang Mai: Silkworm Books

McKinnon, J. (1997) 'The forests of Thailand: strike up the ban?', in D. McCaskill and K. Kampe (eds), *Development or Domestication? Indigenous Peoples of South-East Asia*, Chiang Mai: Silkworm Books

McNeely, L. A. (1997) 'Mobilizing broader support for Asia's biodiversity: how civil society can contribute to protected area management', Gland, Switzerland: IUCN, ADB

McVey, R. (2000) *Money and Power in Provincial Thailand*, Singapore: ISEAS

Meyer, B. and P. Geschiere (2003) *Globalization and Identity: Dialectics of Flow and Closure*, Oxford: Blackwell

Michaud, J. (1997) 'A portrait of cultural resistance: the confinement of tourism in a Hmong village in Thailand', in M. Picard and R. E. Wood (eds), *Tourism, Ethnicity, and the State in Asian and Pacific Societies*, Honolulu: University of Hawaii

Pholsena, V. (2002) 'The dilemmas between development and cultural diversity: the case of Lao PDR', report presented to the sub-regional seminar on

Minority Rights: Cultural Diversity and Development in South-East Asia, Chiang Mai, 4–7 December

Renard, R. D. (2001) *Opium Reduction in Thailand, 1970–2000: A Thirty Year Journey*, Bangkok: United Nations Drug Control Programme

Salemink, O. (1997) 'The king of fire and Vietnamese ethnic policy in the Central Highlands', in D. McCaskill and K. Kampe (eds), *Development or Domestication? Indigenous Peoples of South-East Asia*, Chiang Mai: Silkworm Books

Sturgeon, J. (1997) 'Claiming and naming resources on the border of the state: Akha strategies in China and Thailand', *Asia Pacific Viewpoint*, 38(2)

TDRI (1997) *Study Project for the Management of the National Master Plan for Tourism*, Bangkok: Thailand Development Research Institute (in Thai)

Thoms, J. M. (1996) *Illegal Conservation: Two Case Studies of Conflict between Indigenous and State Natural Resource Management Paradigms*, MA thesis, Peterborough, Canada: Frost Centre for Canadian Heritage and Development Studies

Trakarnsuphakorn, P. (1997) 'The wisdom of the Karen in natural resource conservation', in D. McCaskill and K. Kampe (eds), *Development or Domestication? Indigenous Peoples of Southeast Asia*, Chiang Mai: Silkworm Books

UNDCP (n.d.) *Regional Profile for South-East Asia and the Pacific*, <www.undcp.un.or.th/ad/profile/regionalprofile.pdf>

Vaddhanaphuti, C. and K. Aquino (1999) 'Citizenship and forest policy in the north of Thailand', Presented at the 7th International Thai Studies Conference, Amsterdam, 6 July

Vincent, A. (2002) *Nationalism and Particularity*, Cambridge: Cambridge University Press

Walker, A. (2002) 'Forests and water in northern Thailand', *Chiang Mai University Journal*, 1(3)

9 | Tackling indigenous disadvantage in the twenty-first century: 'social inclusion' and Māori in New Zealand

LOUISE HUMPAGE

Influenced by a Third Way politics, the Labour-led coalition[1] elected to govern New Zealand in 1999 aimed to promote 'social inclusion' through a new 'social development' approach to social policy. Although yet to be articulated in any formal manner, this aim was reflected in a policy strategy called 'Closing the Gaps' which specifically targeted Māori, the indigenous peoples of New Zealand. The strategy was promoted in terms of 'self-determination' and the Treaty of Waitangi, but its title revealed that government policy for Māori continued to define the 'problem' in terms of Māori socio-economic disparity. It was thus concerned with the needs (and increasingly the obligations) of Māori as citizens, rather than their rights as indigenous peoples and treaty partners.

This comes as no surprise given that the concepts of social inclusion and exclusion may be regarded as contemporary manifestations of traditional social policy concerns with poverty, cultural deficit and social cohesion which have already proved problematic for Māori.[2] In supporting this contention, this chapter briefly outlines the traditional assumptions upon which Māori affairs policy has been founded, before exploring the Labour-led government's major achievement in the Māori affairs portfolio, the Closing the Gaps strategy. This discussion foregrounds an analysis of the 'improving effectiveness', 'capacity-building' and 'partnership' policy initiatives that were central to the strategy targeting Māori, as well as to a more general social development approach to social policy that reflected British understandings of social inclusion. It is argued that, owing to overlaps in the rhetoric that accompanied this social inclusion discourse and the language used by Māori calling for greater self-determination, the Closing the Gaps strategy gave the appearance of accounting for Māori understandings of the problem, which highlight the unequal power relations that exist between Māori and the state. In concluding that a social inclusion discourse makes no challenge to historical assumptions about Māori deficit and disparity, however, this chapter asserts that the Closing the Gaps strategy continued to marginalize alternative, indigenous-defined solutions. This is because the Labour-led government continued to consider many such solutions, which include forms of 'strategic exclusion' achieved through the development of parallel development mechanisms at the local, regional and national level, as irreconcilable with state authority and legitimacy.

These arguments are based on a qualitative analysis of government documents, including unpublished cabinet papers, policy statements, submissions on legislation, media releases and political speeches, covering the period 1999–2003.[3] Data collected from twenty-eight interviews undertaken between April and December 2001 with politicians, government sector officials, representatives of Māori organizations and well-known commentators on Māori affairs are also used in the chapter. These sources together provide the basis for a comprehensive overview of a policy strategy that promised a 'new era of partnership', yet in practice offered only a twenty-first-century twist on the conceptually poor policy foundations that have historically failed to successfully address Māori disadvantage.

The traditional parameters of Māori affairs policy

The relative socio-economic disadvantage that Māori experience has been the central focus of Māori affairs policy since the Second World War, when social policy concerns began to be incorporated into this portfolio. It is beyond the scope of this chapter to document the continuing poverty and disadvantage that Māori experience in New Zealand. Suffice to say there have been fluctuations and improvements in terms of absolute measures but, with the exception of Pacific peoples in some cases, Māori as a group continue to demonstrate lower levels of educational attainment, employment, income, health and housing relative to non-Māori[4] (see Te Puni Kōkiri 2000a; Ministry of Social Development 2003). Given that, in 2000, 15 per cent of New Zealanders identified themselves as Māori and this figure is expected to increase to approximately 22 per cent by 2051 (Te Puni Kōkiri 2000a: 13), the negative effects of Māori disadvantage continue to present a significant challenge for New Zealand governments.

In attempting to address the relative disadvantage of Māori, government policy has traditionally applied a needs-based discourse to Māori. This conceptualizes Māori as just one of many disadvantaged groups whose 'needs' can be met by activating equal citizenship rights. This needs-based discourse, which conceives indigenous culture as a major explanation for indigenous poverty and disparity, has legitimized state intervention into Māori communities under the pretence of 'helping' Māori peoples gain access to the kind of socio-economic status their non-Māori counterparts enjoy (see Fleras and Spoonley 1999).

Following the failure of policies of assimilation and integration to eliminate disparities between Māori and non-Māori, a more forward-looking, positive focus on Māori development was introduced in the mid-1980s (see Māori Economic Development Summit Conference 1984). In the context of increasing economic constraints and neo-liberal agendas, this attempted to refocus largely 'negative' spending (such as on imprisonment or unemployment) on 'positive' initiatives aiming to develop Māori capability to meet their own needs (Durie 1998: 6–9). Although promoted by the fourth Labour government (1984–90) with reference to 'devolution' and 'self-determination', no more than a principal–agent relationship of delegation was envisaged. Under National Party-led governments during the 1990s, this rhetoric was largely abandoned, but large numbers of Māori providers were contracted to provide 'culturally sensitive' social services and emphasis was placed on encouraging Māori into business.

Such government-defined Māori development initiatives none the less perpetuated the long-held interest in 'civilizing' and 'modernizing' Māori, even if this goal was increasingly articulated in terms of building their labour market skills and participation in the mainstream economy rather than cultural assimilation. This economic emphasis is not surprising for development as an academic activity has been dominated by economists and focused on poverty, with rational organization and technological efficiency used as standards of 'progress' towards the values that Western liberalism privileges (see Hall and Midgley 1988; Verhelst 1990; Sardar 1999). Lacking a context-specific philosophy and a set of relevant indicators against which progress can be measured (Durie et al. 2002: 12), a reorientation towards Māori development thus did not seriously challenge government's preoccupation with 'closing the gaps' between Māori and non-Māori. In fact, addressing these gaps was the major goal behind Māori development policies during the 1990s, even if the initiatives implemented sometimes shared similarities with Māori proposals for greater self-determination at the local level.

Māori scholars and leaders critical of government policy agree that socio-economic disparities between Māori and non-Māori should be eliminated. But they question government's preoccupation with measuring Māori against a non-Māori standard. A Māori scholar and former policy adviser noted in an interview: 'I think a lot of Māori believe that ... we're on a journey to self-determination, but there's no sort of yardstick of that, you can't measure that against anybody else, it's about going from A to B ... rather than try to "close the gaps" between another sort of community and our community.'

In addition, government's focus on Māori disadvantage has diverted attention away from majority group *advantage*, allowing the structural factors (including colonization and ongoing systemic discrimination) that cause socio-economic disparities to go largely unaddressed. Although hardly unified by one voice, Māori have long argued that the solution requires renegotiation of the gaps in *power* that exist between Māori and the state, rather than simply putting a Band Aid on the socio-economic gaps that separate Māori and non-Māori.

This thinking was reflected in a recent study (ibid.: 38, 57) which consulted twenty-five Māori professionals about developing Māori-specific outcomes and indicators. Along with 'Māori well-being', '*tino rangatiratanga*' was the top outcome area mentioned by interview participants. Although literally meaning absolute chieftainship or full chiefly authority, *tino rangatiratanga* can be more broadly defined as the power to be self-determining (Fleras and Spoonley 1999: 27). Self-determination is a multi-dimensional concept and Māori individuals, tribal groups and non-tribal configurations have proposed a variety of means through which *tino rangatiratanga* might be expressed (see Melbourne 1995; Durie 1998).

There have been occasional calls for a separate Māori state (see Evans 1981; Awatere 1984), for example. But most Māori realize the impracticality of such a proposal given the high degree of familial and geographical integration between Māori and non-Māori. Many more proposals articulated by Māori recognize the benefits gained from being part of a single, larger state while at the same time proposing greater autonomy for Māori through parallel development mechanisms. These include a parallel Māori parliament, bicultural legislatures in the existing parliament and devolved authority across a range of jurisdictions, including health, welfare, economic development, law and education (see Mead 1997; Walker 1999; Winiata 2000). In addition to such expressions of self-determination at the level of national politics, the outcomes study also reflected the interest of many Māori in exercising *tino rangatiratanga* at the local levels of *iwi* (tribe), *hapū* (sub-tribe or clan) and whānau (extended family). While some Māori individuals prioritize one particular area, Durie et al. (2002: 18, my emphasis) stress that 'the whole notion of Māori development is underpinned by a widespread aspiration for control and self-management at local, regional, *and* national levels'.

New Zealand governments are now relatively comfortable with initiatives that allow Māori to exercise a degree of self-determination at the local and regional levels where it overlaps with broader agendas for minimizing the size and cost of the state. For instance, the entry of Māori organizations into social service provision, which may be regarded as a form of parallel development at the local or regional level, was supported because it enabled responsibility and accountability in these areas to be decentralized.

Proposals for greater self-determination at the national level, however, have been harder for governments to endorse. This is because they challenge the state's authority and absolute sovereignty by invoking the need for some form of power-sharing arrangement between the state and indigenous peoples.

The practices of governance without formal government are expanding, leading to 'indigenous governances' (forms of government that arise in and are endemic to the everyday lives of subjects, such as community organizations)[5] being increasingly utilized by governments to bring gains in terms of innovation, flexibility and cost efficiencies (O'Malley 1996: 313; Tully 1999: 178). Dean (1999: 149) suggests that such 'technologies of rule' have also distanced the processes of regulation from the forms or images of coercion. We may, therefore, regard the increasing incorporation of Māori personnel, culture and governances into the government's work as a means of shoring up the legitimacy of the state in light of Māori resistance to government policy and authority, as well as growing international acceptance of indigenous rights and cultural pluralism more generally. This has been particularly necessary given that the 1835 Declaration of Independence and Article 2 of the Māori-language version of the 1840 Treaty of Waitangi provide a strong moral and legal argument that Māori were recognized as distinct, sovereign peoples with the right to self-determination prior to colonization. New Zealand governments have resisted recognition of Māori self-determination at the *national* level, however, because this would discredit the assumptions that underlay colonial settlement, including the supposed civilizing mission and ethnic superiority of Europeans, and call into question the legitimacy of the former settler state and its citizens (Mulgan 1998: 179–80).

In responding to these potential threats to state legitimacy, National-led governments trod an ambivalent path during the 1990s. They increasingly acknowledged the state's role in Māori dispossession and endorsed the unique rights that Māori hold through the Treaty of Waitangi claims settlement process. Yet, at the same time, they failed to adequately endorse the relevance of indigenous and treaty rights to social policy (see Barrett and Connolly-Stone 1998). Māori development initiatives implemented by government consequently tended to marginalize proposals for a *Māori-centred* form of development to which Māori identity, culture and governance are integral. This is the case even though international and local commentary (e.g. Cornell and Kalt 1998; Loomis 2000a; Begay and Kalt 2002; Durie et al. 2002) suggests that, unless Māori development is closely aligned with Māori views and Māori aspirations for greater self-determination, the relative disparity that many Māori experience is unlikely to be resolved.

Māori affairs at the turn of the century: the Closing the Gaps strategy

The Labour Party's 1999 election campaign, which actively targeted Māori in an effort to regain support lost to the New Zealand First Party[6] in 1996, suggested that Labour had listened to Māori concerns about Māori affairs policy. Recognizing that the priority National-led governments had placed on treaty claims settlements during the 1990s failed to provide a long-term, holistic approach to the social problems that affected Māori, the Labour-led coalition government announced 'Closing the Gaps' as its flagship social policy strategy in June 2000.

The first major arm of this $243 million strategy attempted to 'improve the effectiveness of government performance for Māori' as part of a broader emphasis on the development of strategic, evidence-based social policy. 'Capacity-building' was a second arm of Closing the Gaps, which symbolized what Māori development meant for the Labour-led government at the turn of the century and offered Māori communities a chance to improve their long-term capabilities for preventing and solving issues for themselves. Alongside the effectiveness and capacity-building initiatives sat measures aiming to address issues of Māori representation and participation and thus put 'partnership' into practice. For example, the New Zealand Public Health and Disability (NZPHD) Act 2000 included three specific provisions relating to Māori.

In the first months of the Labour-led government's term, the Closing the Gaps (CTG) strategy was promoted with frequent reference to the Treaty of Waitangi, partnership and self-determination. This rhetoric suggested that the Labour-led coalition was keen to extend into social policy a rights-based discourse recognizing Māori claims to self-determination, as National-led governments had been loath to do. Nevertheless, it is argued that the CTG strategy provided no serious challenge to traditional, needs-based discourses of citizenship. The strategy's core project was social inclusion where the problem continued to be framed in terms of disparities between Māori and non-Māori.

This interest in social inclusion was influenced by a developing Third Way politics, in particular Tony Blair's New Labour government in Britain, which argued that the market alone could not meet the needs of citizens and that the state should invest in social development as a means for achieving social inclusion (see Maharey 2001a). The concepts social inclusion and exclusion hold the potential to look beyond just the distribution of resources to structural issues, including those manifesting themselves at the local, national and global levels (see Percy-Smith 2000; Peace 2001). A shift towards a focus on social development might thus be regarded as constructive, bringing some welcome innovations in terms of measuring social outcomes and thinking strategically about social policy issues (see Ministry of Social Development 2002a).

The goal of social inclusion was founded, however, on an assumption that the ideal, 'active' citizen is one who participates in self-management, free choice and personal responsibility (Rose 1999: 257–8). Those not participating in this kind of activity are defined as 'excluded' and in need of shaping, guiding and moulding so that they are capable of responsibly exercising their individual freedom and thus allowing government to 'rule from a distance'. Part of a broader shift towards a focus on what the Labour-led government called 'active citizenship', the three CTG initiatives under analysis in this chapter assisted in setting out the attributes and values of a person who truly 'belongs' and thus should be considered a 'real' citizen. This is because the initiatives together provided a technical means for managing the risk that Māori 'exclusion' posed to effective governance, in that each attempted to shape Māori conduct to suit the moral and political requirements for optimizing government performance and, as a consequence, enhance state legitimacy (Dean 1999: 165–8). A focus on social inclusion was thus an extension of traditional social policy concerns with poverty, cultural deficit and social cohesion described earlier.

In representing a first articulation of this general social policy framework[7] aiming to improve social inclusion through social development, the CTG strategy was clearly not driven by Māori perspectives and aspirations. A small number of initiatives specifically targeting Pacific peoples, a multidimensional population group that grew out of waves of migration from islands in the Pacific following the Second World War, were included under the Closing the Gaps umbrella. This indicated that Māori were regarded as just one of many disadvantaged targets of social policy and that the needs-based focus traditionally found in the Māori affairs arena remained intact. The strategy's key policy tools – improving effectiveness, capacity-building and partnership – were also applied in other portfolios across government, either at the same time or shortly following the introduction of CTG (see Ministry of Social Policy 2001).[8] As a result, it was easy for the Labour-led government to respond to a public backlash against the strategy's specific targeting of Māori[9] by rebranding it in the more general terms of 'reducing inequalities' from the end of 2000.

That the strategy's underlying philosophy was more generic than Māori-specific was not clear at the time because the goal of social inclusion was couched in the same language of self-determination and partnership that Māori use to articulate claims for greater autonomy. There is some overlap between these two projects, in that Māori agree that reducing socio-economic disparities between Māori and non-Māori should be a crucial goal for the government sector (Durie 2000: 418). Yet it can be argued that these disparities are *symptoms* of the unequal power relations that exist between Māori and the state, rather than the core problem itself. Thus, the CTG strategy, although initially appearing to be a significant response to ongoing inequalities in power between Māori and the state, continued to rely on generic social policy constructs that were conceptually incapable of fully accounting for either the causes of Māori disadvantage or the solutions proposed by Māori that call for greater self-determination.

'Improving the effectiveness of government performance for Māori' The CTG strategy's first arm placed an emphasis on improving the effectiveness of government performance for Māori. This appeared to be a natural starting point for the strategy. Māori had long argued that government policy had failed to solve the problem of relative disparity because it did not adequately account for either the diverse realities that Māori experience or their desires for greater self-determination. In addition, the newly elected Labour-led government found that expenditure on Māori programmes had increased but little evaluation had been undertaken to assess whether they were actually effective and achieved the outcomes intended. A February 2000 cabinet paper (Office of the Prime Minister 2000: 5) consequently noted: 'The lack of information is a major impediment to improving the provision of programmes and services and more effectively addressing the gaps.'

Anthony Giddens (1998: 74), Britain's Third Way intellectual figurehead, has suggested that '[to] retain or regain legitimacy, states without enemies have to elevate their administrative efficiency'. With an emphasis on 'what works', the Labour-led government aimed to make 'social investment' by implementing initiatives based on evidence about which government-led interventions can actually make a difference in improving outcomes (see Ministry of Social Development 2002b). This was seen as a way to gain greater accountability for policy outcomes and over government departments, as well as distance Labour from the excesses of neo-liberalism (an ideology that it had promoted in the mid-1980s) and restore public faith in government[10] (see Cabinet Committee on Closing the Gaps 2000; Clark 2002). Recent critiques of 'advanced liberalism' (see Dean 1999; Rose 1999) also suggest that being able to measure and count a problem is necessary to govern it. As a result, evaluation and auditing may be regarded as a central mechanism for governing at a distance through indigenous governances embedded within communities (Rose 1999: 155, 221).

Thus, although Māori were a specific target for this emphasis on government effectiveness, it was clearly part of a broader reorientation towards strategic, whole-of-government, evidence-based policy that reflected a Third Way politics more generally (see Maharey 2001b; Ministry of Social Policy 2001). The goal of improving government performance for Māori provoked an important shift in government sector thinking by encouraging departments to account for their Māori-related outcomes more than ever before. For example, the funding and authority of the Māori Development ministry, Te Puni Kōkiri, was increased to enable it to monitor the effectiveness of social policy programmes for Māori. In addition, government departments and their chief executives became more accountable for their delivery to Māori (and Pacific peoples) through quarterly and annual reporting mechanisms (see Cullen 2000). These initiatives went a considerable way to establishing the processes and systems necessary to measure outcomes so that it was possible to conclude whether improvement had occurred or not. Given the context of poor government sector capacity for strategic thinking, this in itself was a major achievement for the Labour-led coalition.

The implementation of the CTG effectiveness initiatives suffered, however, from poor planning and poor communication between different sectors of government. The Labour-led government also demonstrated a lack of willingness to engage with the complexities that measuring Māori disparity involved, even when Simon Chapple (2000), a Department of Labour economist, published a report critical of the 'ethnic' focus of the CTG strategy. While promoting a particular personal standpoint, Chapple correctly identified the tendency of government departments to predominantly use external indicators of comparison when analysing disparity issues, resulting in the diversity contained within the 'Māori' and 'non-Māori' groups being underestimated (see Durie 1998: 92). Instead of fully engaging with this dispute, the Labour-led coalition went on the defensive and, following further debate about this and other aspects of the policy strategy, abandoned the CTG slogan in an attempt to divert public attention from Māori issues (see Baehler 2002).

This raises questions as to the Labour-led government's level of commitment to pursuing improved outcomes for Māori when compared to improving the accountability and *cost*-effectiveness of programmes in social policy more generally. Certainly, several commentators (e.g. Elwood 2003; Marston and Watts 2003; Nutley et al. 2003) have highlighted the limitations of evidence-based policy if 'evidence' is perceived as a resource-rationing tool that is neutral and objective instead of politically driven. More fundamental, however, was the supposition that it was appropriate for government agencies to leave Māori communities largely out of the outcome definition, policy development and evaluation process of policy and programmes that aimed to benefit them.

Māori opinion was, of course, represented through Te Puni Kōkiri's contribution to the policy development process. Interview data also suggest that the Māori policy election manifesto (Labour Party 1999a) upon which the CTG strategy was loosely based had been developed by a collection of Māori Labour Party members over some years. But neither the effectiveness initiatives, nor the CTG strategy more generally, was initiated by or subject to widespread consultation with Māori communities. Associate Minister of Māori Affairs Tariana Turia suggested that the weaknesses created by this lack of Māori input had not been resolved as the Labour-led government embarked on a second term in 2002. Commenting on a recently released research report on the living standards of older Māori, Turia (2002: 2) stated:

> The report is intended to promote informed debate, and lead to evidence-based policy, 'on the situation of Māori (as tāngata whenua),[11] as well as non-Māori'. I think this is unlikely, because the research does not reflect tāngata whenua paradigms, or world views ...
>
> I believe mainstream social survey methods and statistical data are part of a colonial research paradigm that does not recognise the whānau dimension of Māori lifestyles. New research and evaluation methodologies are required, to fully capture the experience of tāngata whenua.

In the short term, any limitations relating to the effectiveness initiatives may have been the result of a desire to avoid further complicating the already difficult process of establishing an outcomes-based approach to the government sector's work or provoking any further backlash against the Labour-led government and Māori. It could be argued that this was only a *first* phase in the broader process of improving outcomes for Māori, with appropriate stakeholder values and input to be included as the government sector developed more experience and the outcomes-based approach became embedded in bureaucratic structures. Indeed, in 2002, Te Puni Kōkiri commissioned important research (Durie et al. 2002: 58) which produced 'Te Ngāhuru', a very complex, integrated and holistic Māori outcomes schema. This attempted to address the long-standing problem of supplementing generic outcome measures with Māori-focused outcomes that apply only to Māori and are not transferable to other populations (ibid.: 48).

Te Puni Kōkiri's (2003: 14) most recent 'Statement of Intent' certainly appeared to be influenced by the thinking behind this outcomes schema, but did not adopt the full range of outcomes it outlined. Focused on *whānau* development at the local level and defining its ultimate outcome in relation to social, economic and cultural development, Te Puni Kōkiri

(2003:1) still skirted the broader power inequalities between Māori and the state at the national level. The importance that Te Ngāhuru placed on *tino rangatiratanga*/autonomy, both as a determinant of positive outcomes for Māori and as an outcome itself, was thus not matched (Durie et al. 2002: 53). Three years following the introduction of the effectiveness initiatives, no significant challenge was made to the fundamental assumption that government departments would continue to be accountable to the political leadership of the day, rather than Māori themselves, for the effectiveness of their performance for Māori. This demonstrates the way in which indigenous discourses of resistance may be incorporated into government's work but reinterpreted or revised so that they do not threaten government agendas or authority.

Such an example emphasizes that Māori values and input should never be regarded as 'add-ons'. Rather, appropriate Māori involvement should be sought right from the initial stages of planning through to the implementation stages of any government initiative for Māori. There is growing Māori interest in a *Kaupapa Māori* (literally, Māori agendas) framework being applied in the policy context to achieve this goal. Developed out of Māori concerns regarding research, such a Māori-centred approach places heavy emphasis on 'being and acting Māori' as a critical part of the research enterprise, so that the *whole* research process reflects Māori attitudes and traditions (see Cunningham 1998; Smith 1999). Given the competing bureaucratic and political agendas that constrain policy development within mainstream institutions (including the Māori-focused Te Puni Kōkiri), it is unlikely that such a framework could be fully implemented without greater autonomy and control, potentially through parallel policy and/or political institutions.

In failing to offer this level of input and control, the effectiveness initiatives may have been 'effective' for the Labour-led government, in terms of tracking spending and temporarily managing the risk that Māori disadvantage presented. Certainly, increased attention to Māori outcomes offered the Labour-led government the tools to place Māori affairs funding under greater surveillance and control and, correspondingly, increased the likelihood of greater political manipulation. In remaining centred on government agendas regarding control and legitimacy, however, the effectiveness initiatives were not 'effective' at responding to Māori calls for greater opportunity to exercise self-determination over issues of specific concern to Māori. As the following discussion about capacity-building demonstrates, the Māori development arm of CTG also failed to realize this goal, despite rhetoric suggesting otherwise.

'Capacity-building' The concept of capacity-building has been a common component of development models advanced by indigenous peoples as a way to strengthen the ability of indigenous communities to exercise self-determination. Central to this indigenous interpretation of capacity-building has been the need to build the cultural, economic and *political* strength of indigenous peoples (see Loomis 2000a, 2000b). In New Zealand, the Labour-led coalition developed capacity-building initiatives across the government sector following the 1999 election, with specific funding ($113 million over four years) allocated to those targeting Māori (Horomia 2000: 1). Political rhetoric suggested that capacity-building was a response to Māori desires for self-determination and an improved relationship between Māori and the state (see Office of the Minister of Māori Affairs 2000a: 10). Indeed, Minister of Māori Affairs Parekura Horomia (2000: 1) rather grandly promoted capacity-building as a 'new era of partnership' in Māori development and as having 'the potential to reshape New Zealand as we know it' (Horomia cited in Te Puni Kōkiri 2000b: 1).

It is argued that the understanding of capacity-building adopted by the Labour-led government was rather more limited in its scope than that endorsed by indigenous peoples, for two related reasons. First, Māori capacity-building did not embody the level of financial and political autonomy central to indigenous models. By 2002, a significant $17.1 million had gone to 1,897 applicants, and this fact should not be overlooked, given the constraints of previous Māori affairs funding (Horomia and Turia 2002). But the 565 applications received in the first year requested a total of $34 million, when Te Puni Kōkiri had only *$9.2 million* to allocate.[12] As a result, many communities received only very small sums of money, perhaps $2,000 here or $5,000 there, out of what was described as a very complicated and demanding application process. The chief executive of a non-tribal Māori organization indicated that this meant: 'The amount of money they poured into it ... looked huge, but broken down it was nothing.' In addition, two prominent Māori leaders agreed that capacity-building mostly funded 'committees to sit around talking about capacity-building', with a lot less action at the level of Māori communities.

Receiving capacity-building funds also placed Māori communities under the regulation of the state in that they were required to meet substantial accountability and monitoring requirements (see Te Puni Kōkiri 2000c). Capacity-building funds thus remained dependent on the 'goodwill' of government and tied to its objectives, even if these did at times overlap with those of some Māori communities. It must be noted that a 'direct resourcing' initiative offered greater flexibility and a higher degree of autonomy. In 2001 the Labour-led coalition announced direct resourcing worth $15 million over three years as a means through which Māori communities could directly approach Te Puni Kōkiri with innovative solutions and apply for funding to develop them (Horomia and Turia 2001). Cabinet was slow in approving direct resourcing and, following changes in its planned implementation, it was deferred until 2002/03 (Te Puni Kōkiri 2002b: 60). The direct resourcing fund was also rather small once divided between a large number of organizations and over a three-year period, being described by one interview participant as more 'the ambulance at the foot of the cliff' than a great opportunity for autonomy and control.

In addition to these financial limitations, neither capacity-building nor direct resourcing offered the degree of political autonomy found in indigenous models of development. A Te Puni Kōkiri official indicated the agency was 'very much openly supporting and encouraging, strengthening the governance of Māori communities', but that references to 'political development' or '*tino rangatiratanga*' were avoided because they provoked resistance to Te Puni Kōkiri's work. For example, the Treasury (government's primary economic and financial adviser) reacted strongly to a paper from the Office of the Minister of Māori Affairs (2000b: 7) which suggested that capacity-building would fund 'political initiatives in [Māori] communities'. The Treasury recommended a greater emphasis on evaluation so that capacity-building funding could be monitored for effectiveness in achieving the goals of *government*. Within this context, capacity-building's core goal was thus conceived as improving the efficiency and effectiveness of government-funded social services delivered by Māori providers.

There is a second major reason why the coalition government's version of capacity-building could never have fully endorsed Māori self-determination, even with greater financial and political support. Founded upon a Third Way notion of 'community empowerment', it also suffered from conceptual limitations. As indicated earlier, capacity-building is one of the core policy solutions in the social inclusion repertoire. Minister of Social Services and Employment and Labour's key Third Way thinker Steve Maharey indicated in an interview that the notion of capacity-building reflects the trend for Third Way governments to be 'struggling away from being a traditional social-democratic party where the state is the mechanism for doing things to saying the state is a *facilitator* of people doing things for themselves'. Third Way governments have recognized that communities are sites of relevant knowledge regarding local needs and capability and have the flexibility to meet diverse needs and the motivation to mobilize resources and energy far beyond that which commercial self-interest and government regulation can achieve (Harris and Eichbaum 1999: 234–5). It has already been noted that governments have been interested in adopting indigenous governances that allow them to rule from a distance. As a consequence, they have looked to build the capacity of local communities so that they are empowered to solve local problems (see Clark 2000, 2001).

Māori capacity-building was driven by this same desire for community empowerment which underlay more general initiatives. Yet while there might be some overlap in the actual activities engaged in as a means to community empowerment and Māori self-determination, the philosophies behind the two outcomes are significantly different (see Jenkins and Jones 2000: 139). Servian (1996: 5–7, 12) has noted that the term 'empowerment' can be defined in numerous (often contradictory) ways, but it frequently refers to those in authority *giving power to* or *meeting the needs* of those who are *powerless*. Implying that communities are in deficit and need to have power invested in them to discourage social exclusion, the goal of empowerment thus complements the way in which Māori have traditionally been conceived by New Zealand governments as culturally lacking (see James 1999: 20).

Capacity-building is consequently an example of government giving Māori communities 'permission' to assume greater responsibilities and accountabilities for meeting their own needs, but only at a level that does not threaten the political status quo because it continues to define them simply as groups of disadvantaged citizens. The discourse of community empowerment may therefore have had its origins in a language of resistance and critique, but it was transformed into an expert discourse whereby government officials aimed to create a set of conditions requiring Māori communities to be active citizens and thus allow government to be more effective at meeting its *own* goals (see Rose 1999; Dean 1999).

This is in contrast with the notion of Māori self-determination, which assumes that Māori *already* hold power (as 'first peoples' and through Article 2 of the Māori-language treaty),[13] although their ability to exercise it has been diminished. As noted earlier, there is no one means through which *tino rangatiratanga* might be expressed. Calls for greater government recognition of this existing power through the transferral of authority and control over decision-making and resources are, however, widespread. This might potentially involve significant structural changes within existing institutional arrangements at the local, regional *and* national levels and is clearly quite a different outcome than that which the Labour-led government's Māori capacity-building initiative intended to achieve.

Loomis (2000a: 19) has argued that if capacity-building had truly been about *self-determined* development, Māori would have been encouraged to develop their own measures of success. These might have been along the lines of the Te Ngāhuru outcomes schema discussed earlier or a 'Tino

Rangatiratanga Index' developed by a graduate class at the School of Māori and Pacific Development at the University of Waikato, which identified seven criteria for self-determined indigenous governance and development[14] (ibid.: 38). Developed by Māori, both the schema and index position political autonomy at the local, regional and national levels as central to Māori development.

The Labour-led government's capacity-building initiative, however, was designed, regulated and monitored by government and subject to its political needs and interests (Te Puni Kōkiri 2000c: 2). For all the rhetoric concerning empowerment and self-determination, capacity-building made little significant movement towards greater self-determination for Māori except at the most basic, local level. Nor did it seriously attempt to make the government sector more accountable to Māori communities. As a result, Loomis (2000a: 22, emphasis in the original) noted at the time: 'Government's current capacity-building initiative seems to recognise the importance of Māori self-determination, but not the strategic difference between *government* reducing disparities and *Māori* achieving their own development through self-governance.' Driven by government's desire to reduce the risk of Māori disadvantage and the cost of governance through greater self-management by Māori at the community level, capacity-building did not endorse Māori self-determination at all levels of governance. The next section, concerned with 'partnership', supports the argument that negotiating a power-sharing arrangement where Māori could exercise greater self-governance was never on the agenda for the Labour-led government.

'Partnership' The term 'partnership' usually suggests a mutually supportive dialogue whereby power is shared between equals (Morton and Gibson 2003: 9). Certainly, indigenous peoples have tended to equate partnership with the development of power-sharing relationships that reflect the equal, sovereign status of both indigenous peoples and the state. Indigenous calls for partnership have thus commonly articulated a desire for indigenous peoples to assume decision-making power over all matters related to themselves, while engaging in dialogue with the state over matters of mutual interest. In being concerned with governance over all things indigenous, rather than simply indigenous participation or representation, partnership in this context is an outcome in its own right (see ibid.: 2).

In New Zealand, the term 'partnership' resonates with even deeper meaning because Māori have long argued that Article 2 of the Māori-language version of the Treaty of Waitangi indicates that Māori rights to self-determination were never extinguished and that the treaty was intended as the basis for an ongoing partnership between Māori and the state. New Zealand governments since the mid-1980s have increasingly accepted that, even though there may not have been a partnership as such at the original signing of the treaty, it seems clear that Māori signatories were keen to establish a working relationship with the British queen and her people (Durie 1991: 157). The question of how and to what degree such a partnership might be expressed remained under debate on the cusp of the twenty-first century. But political rhetoric prior to the 1999 election and in early promotion of the CTG strategy suggested that the newly elected government was willing to acknowledge that the unique relationship Māori have with the state should be reflected in social policy.

It is argued, however, that initiatives implemented as part of the CTG strategy were founded upon the more limited understanding of partnership employed by Third Way governments in their pursuit of social inclusion. In the context of social inclusion, partnership is defined as a functional means or process through which to achieve improved outcomes (greater social inclusion) and conflated with consultation and participation (see Morton and Gibson 2003). In this way, Labour-led government used the term partnership when referring to the government sector 'supporting stronger communities for the shaping and local co-ordination of the delivery of services' and 'greater community say in the design and delivery of policy and services' (Maharey 2000: 7; see Ministry of Social Policy 2001).

Although there was certainly talk about the treaty and the relationship that stemmed from its signing, the CTG strategy was founded upon this Third Way understanding of partnership rather than that articulated by Māori and other indigenous peoples. O'Malley (1996: 316–17) highlights the fact that in appropriating indigenous discourses to achieve the ends sought by governments, policy-makers often 'make sense' of such discourses by ignoring aspects that are 'incomprehensible', thinking of practices as if they were situated within a familiar rather than an 'alien' culture and assigning significance according to familiar rather than to 'alien' priorities. In the context of the CTG strategy, this resulted in partnership being interpreted so that government remained the 'senior partner' in the treaty relationship, deciding when and where the implementation of partnership might occur. In addition, while the Labour-led coalition recognized that Māori consultation and participation were desirable, there was no question that both processes would take place within mainstream, rather than parallel, institutions and mechanisms or that traditional notions of absolute sovereignty would remain unchanged.

Attempting to combine the 'gaps' focus of other CTG initiatives with a partnership framework built upon the principles of the Treaty of Waitangi, the New Zealand Public Health and Disability (NZPHD) Act 2000 illustrates such contentions. The act's prime purpose was to abolish the government-appointed Health Funding Authority established under a National-led government and replace it with twenty-one democratically elected District Health Boards (DHBs) that would govern the country's hospitals. Giddens (1998: 76) considers 'improving democracy' to be another form of risk management for ensuring legitimacy in 'states without enemies'. Certainly the Labour Party (1999b: 4) had vowed prior to the election to 'restore the [health] system's moral authority' by improving democracy in this area.

In addition, the Labour Party (1999a: 6) had promised 'fair' representation for Māori on statutory and other government agencies and advisory boards as a means with which to improve 'Māori participation in democracy'. As a result, the NZPHD Act made direct reference to the Treaty of Waitangi (a first in social policy legislation),[15] required every DHB to maintain partnership relationships with '*mana whenua*' (defined as people with customary authority over a particular area)[16] and guaranteed two DHB positions to Māori representatives. Promoted in terms of the treaty and of partnership, these legislative provisions suggested that significant power had been conceded to Māori.

In regarding participation as having a 'voice' or being represented within a decentralized administrative or management context as power, the Labour-led government appeared to regard power as if it could be measured and distributed by the state, rather than as a set of relations between groups in society (see Servian 1996; James 1999). Young (1990: 31–2) argues that because power is a relation, not a thing, it cannot be distributed. While exercise of power may sometimes depend on the possession of certain resources, the resources are not in themselves power. Rather, power consists of a relationship between the exercisers and those over whom power is being exercised. Regarding power as a commodity to be distributed misses the structural phenomena of the domination and oppression that Māori experience.

Thus, although the two guaranteed positions for Māori on each of the twenty-one DHBs, for example, were a significant measure, they failed to account for the fact that such representatives are unlikely to exercise significant power within a context that, in all other respects, reflects majority group values and norms. Māori 'participation in democracy' was constrained by what Tully (1999: 172) calls 'rules of recognition', which include the types of knowledge, standard forms of conduct and relations of power that govern negotiations between citizens and governments. In this case, such rules included acceptance of government's 'senior partner' status, with the Labour-led government retaining the power to appoint four members to the DHBs, two of whom would be Māori if none was elected (Office of the Minister of Health 2000: 1–3). As only four Māori members were successfully elected on to the twenty-one, eleven-person boards across the country in 2001, the coalition government consequently maintained considerable control over whom it approved (or disapproved) of as suitable for the DHB positions (Ministry of Health 2001).

Reference to the treaty – and thus the unique relationship that exists between Māori and the Crown – in the health legislation also did not radically modify government's long-running preoccupation with the relative disparity of Māori. The Labour-led coalition's interpretation of the treaty was one that prioritized Māori needs as citizens over their rights as treaty partners. This was possible because there are both English- and Māori-language versions of the Treaty of Waitangi, each consisting of three articles. Article 2 of the Māori-language treaty guaranteed Māori the continuing possession of '*tino rangatiratanga*' in balance with the '*kāwanatanga*' (governance) granted to the British Crown in Article 1. Article 2 is commonly interpreted by contemporary Māori to indicate that their rights to self-determination were not extinguished and that the signing chiefs expected to continue governing themselves, although they did cede to the British Crown the right to govern all present and future colonists. In the English-language treaty, however, the term '*kāwanatanga*' in Article 1 was translated as 'sovereignty'. This suggested that the British Crown alone held the power to govern, limiting the notion of *tino rangatiratanga* to a form of property rights. A third article, which was much the same in both the Māori- and English-language treaties, guaranteed Māori equal rights as British citizens.

It is Article 3 which was the focus of the Labour-led government's interest in the treaty within a social policy context. By positioning Māori as disadvantaged and excluded citizens rather than sovereign peoples, the government could be seen to be fulfilling its obligations as a treaty partner, while at the same demonstrating the limits of government's engagement with Māori. Ignored were Māori calls (see Hancock 1999) for greater control over Māori health (including funding, criteria, management and delivery of services), as well as greater accountability to Māori and further Māori involvement in developing tools of measurement and the benchmarks necessary to improve Māori health. As a result, Māori certainly achieved some important gains out of the implementation of a more functional, Third Way understanding of partnership, but the potential for a partnership based on a power-sharing relationship was not fulfilled.

In situating debate about Māori and social policy within a citizenship discourse (as correlated with Article 3), the Labour-led government opted for a similar position to that of its National-led predecessors in the 1990s.

It is argued, however, that the social inclusion discourse adopted by the Labour-led government made this position all the more troubling in the twenty-first century. The goal of social inclusion is to eliminate social exclusion, which is seen as an inherently negative outcome. While the policy focus has largely been on involuntary forms of exclusion that manifest themselves in poverty and marginalization, an underlying aim has also been to discourage *voluntary* exclusion. Work activity testing for welfare beneficiaries has been the most explicit attempt to combat such voluntary exclusion from the workforce (see Percy-Smith 2000: 20).

Initiatives aiming to improve participation in democracy have also attempted, however, to redress the withdrawal of more affluent groups from public institutions, such as education and health, and society more broadly. Indeed, Giddens (1998: 105) has noted that: 'Exclusion at the top is not only just as threatening for public space, or common solidarity, as exclusion at the bottom; it is causally linked to it and limiting the voluntary exclusion of the elites is central to creating a more inclusive society at the bottom.' For this reason, a key characteristic of what the Labour-led government called 'active citizenship' was the 'social participation' (through, for example, volunteerism or involvement in democratic processes) of all citizens.

Barry (1998: 2) indicates that we should be sceptical about the 'voluntary' nature of self-exclusion when withdrawal from mainstream participation occurs within the context of discrimination and inequality, which is certainly the case for indigenous peoples. The perception that any form of self-exclusion is inherently detrimental to society has enormous consequences for indigenous peoples wishing to gain greater levels of self-determination through parallel forms of development. As noted earlier, calls for a separatist exclusion that rests upon a breakaway Māori state have been rare, but many more proposals articulated by Maori recognize the benefits gained from being part of a single, larger state while at the same time proposing a form of strategic exclusion that allows greater autonomy for Māori through parallel development mechanisms.

The Labour-led government did not make any specific comments on such proposals. But in being based on a social development approach with social inclusion as its goal, its flagship CTG policy strategy worked from a conceptual framework which could not possibly conceive that a 'new era of partnership' might actually require the strategic exclusion of Māori from the mainstream.

Conclusion

This chapter has argued that the CTG strategy continued to conceive of relative Māori socio-economic disadvantage as the key problem for Māori affairs policy, with the solution being the integration of Māori and other disadvantaged groups into the mainstream labour market and society. An analysis of the CTG strategy and its three key initiatives – which aimed to improve the effectiveness of government performance for Māori, build Māori capacity and encourage partnership – certainly provided some important opportunities for Māori. But they were limited by conceptual weaknesses that were not altogether obvious, owing to overlaps in the language used by Māori to promote greater self-determination and that adopted by the Labour-led coalition to promote a social development approach to social policy.

It was this generic approach, aiming to improve social inclusion, which drove the CTG strategy. No matter how genuine the intentions of particular politicians or officials, the strategy's initiatives were conceptually incapable of addressing the unequal power relations between Māori and the state which cause and perpetuate socio-economic disparities. In failing to provide the conceptual space for a process of power-sharing within a common legal and governmental order, CTG did not fully account for the unique needs and rights of Māori as indigenous peoples and treaty partners. Instead, attempts to 'include' Māori encouraged integration of Māori 'difference' into mainstream institutions as a means to enhance social cohesion and maintain the legitimacy of the state. In the twenty-first century, this aim of integration was not driven by an open desire on the part of the coalition government to extinguish Māori culture; in fact, there was explicit support for its retention (see Labour Party 1999a). The common refrain that social inclusion and cohesion were necessary as an 'essential building block for a growing and innovative economy' (Clark 2002: 10) suggested that a kind of corporate assimilation, likely to enhance Māori integration into the mainstream labour market and the global economy, was a key pursuit.

This outcome demonstrates that social policy solutions for indigenous peoples such as Māori should not be founded on whatever conceptual discourse happens to be internationally popular at the time; the wholesale adoption of neo-liberal economic rationalism has already demonstrated this lesson in New Zealand, for the negative effects of deregulation, corporatization and privatization hit Māori disproportionately in comparison to non-Māori (see Te Puni Kōkiri 2002a). It is clear that there is a need for policy to pay serious attention, rather than mere lip-service, to the alternative discourses offered by indigenous peoples.

Over the years, Māori have refined one such discourse, based on the notion of '*tino rangatiratanga*', which reflects the specific historical and cultural context of New Zealand. This discourse embodies a range of proposals at the local, regional and national levels as diverse as Māori communities themselves. For instance, this chapter has highlighted the way in which Māori outcomes indicators which account for *tino rangatiratanga* could be applied in the current policy context. The implementation of a 'bulk-funded' model in the social service context would also allow Māori providers greater autonomy, while parallel institutions in particular policy areas and/or at the political level would offer Māori the level of input and control they have long sought in developing policy solutions for Māori problems. Underlying such diverse proposals is the assumption that greater Māori self-determination over all things Māori would improve the long-term well-being of Māori communities. Certainly, evidence provided in other chapters found in this volume indicates that greater indigenous self-determination may be the only real solution to the Labour-led government's self-defined goal of 'closing the gaps' in poverty and disadvantage that exist between Māori and non-Māori.

The CTG strategy none the less represented the latest example of government policy in New Zealand attempting to engulf and neutralize indigenous resistance by importing elements of an indigenous discourse into government. While at the same time disqualifying Māori self-determination from serious discussion, this act has also established sites of resistance within state rule. Continued Māori frustration with government policy consequently has the potential to cause instability *within* state institutions and processes (see O'Malley 1996). This chapter has demonstrated that a new interest in social inclusion did nothing to resolve this and other tensions and contradictions long evident in the Māori affairs policy portfolio.

Glossary of Māori words

hapū sub-tribe; clan

iwi tribal grouping; confederation

Kaupapa Māori Māori-centred research framework; literally, Māori agendas

kāwanatanga governance; trusteeship; the right to govern and make laws

mana whenua Māori people with customary authority over a particular area (as defined in the NZPHD Act 2000); literally, title, sovereignty (predicated on landholding) or customary rights over land

tāngata whenua 'people of the land'; local people; indigenous inhabitants

taonga property; treasure; treasured aspects of Māori society

Te Ngāhuru title of a Māori outcomes schema developed by Durie et al. (2002)

Te Puni Kōkiri Ministry of Māori Development

tino rangatiratanga absolute or highest chieftainship; full chiefly authority; sovereignty; the power to be self-determining

whānau extended family

Notes

1 Under New Zealand's Mixed Member Proportional (MMP) representation electoral system, the Labour Party had to form a coalition with the Alliance Party to gain the majority needed to govern the country. Alliance was Labour's coalition partner for the 1999–2002 period, which is the main focus of discussion, but following the August 2002 election a coalition was formed between Labour and the Progressive Party (established when Jim Anderton, then deputy prime minister, left Alliance). To provide consistency and to reflect the fact that the Labour–Progressive coalition was largely a continuation of the same administration, the term 'Labour-led' is used to refer to both coalitions. Similarly, 'National-led' is used to refer to all governments during the 1990s, although only the 1996–99 administration was a coalition government under MMP.

2 Depending on how they are defined, the concepts 'social inclusion' and 'exclusion' have the potential to go beyond these traditional social policy concerns to include broader, structural issues. It is argued that in the New Zealand context this potential was not fulfilled, however, with social exclusion often used interchangeably with poverty, socio-economic disadvantage and disparity, and with social inclusion frequently correlated with social well-being, social participation and social cohesion.

3 Particular focus, however, is placed on the Labour-led government's first parliamentary term (1999–2002) when plans for the Māori affairs policy portfolio were laid out.

4 There is, however, continuing debate as to how these disparity 'gaps' are best measured owing to disagreement about the way in which 'Māori' should be defined for such purposes (see Chapple 2000; Baehler 2002; Kukutai 2003).

5 'Indigenous' in this sense thus incorporates other groups besides those whom we refer to as 'indigenous peoples'.

6 Māori have traditionally tended to vote Labour, but this trend was radically altered in New Zealand's first election using MMP in 1996. The New Zealand First Party captured five Māori electorate seats and, given the choice of forming a coalition with either of the National or Labour parties, chose the former against most predictions.

7 The social development approach was not officially launched until a year after the Closing the Gaps strategy, but an interview with Steve Maharey, Minister of Social Services and Employment, suggests that it was under development from November 1999.

8 In fact, only thirty-nine of seventy-two initiatives placed under the Closing the Gaps umbrella title exclusively targeted Māori and Pacific peoples (Young 2000: A17), despite strong perceptions that it was a 'Māori' strategy.

9 This backlash, provoked by the political opposition, was fed by Chapple's (2000) report criticizing the Māori focus of some Closing the Gaps initiatives and by widespread debate about the Māori-specific provisions found in the NZPHD Act 2000.

10 Dean (1999: 169) argues, however, that while auditing and evaluation may be presented as techniques for restoring trust, they actually presuppose and contribute to a culture of mistrust.

11 Literally, 'people of the land', but this term is often used to refer to Māori as the local people or indigenous inhabitants of New Zealand.

12 A further $9.3 million was allocated in 2001/02 but this decreased to $8.6 million in 2002/03 (Te Puni Kōkiri 2002b: 80).

13 There are both English- and Māori-language versions of the Treaty of Waitangi, which provide inconsistent translations of the three articles contained within the document.

14 These were listed as: cultural identity, values and protocols; the people guide the development process and aims; governance, particularly decisions about the ownership and management of development, is under the ultimate control of the members of the tribe, nation, organization or community; the whole membership or community benefits equitably from the process and outcomes of development; the organization, tribe or community enjoys relative economic self-sufficiency instead of disadvantage and dependency; the tribe, nation or community owns or has access to the necessary resources for sustained development; all the tribe, nation or community's *tāonga* [treasures or treasured aspects of Māori society] and resources are known to them, their rights recognized, and processes in place to monitor, protect and/or utilize them for present and future generations (Loomis 2000a: 38).

15 References to the Treaty of Waitangi have been included in other types of legislation, most notably the State Owned Enterprises Act 1986.

16 Developed without consultation, this particular clause appeared to favour tribally based organizations over pan-Māori organizations and thus caused considerable debate within Māori communities.

References

Awatere, D. (1984) *Māori Sovereignty*, Auckland: Broadsheet

Baehler, K. (2002) 'Ethnicity-based research and politics: snapshots from the United States and New Zealand', *Social Policy Journal of New Zealand: Te Puna Whakaaro*, 18: 18–30

Barrett, M. and K. Connolly-Stone (1998) 'The Treaty of Waitangi and social policy', *Social Policy Journal of New Zealand: Te Puna Whakaaro*, 11: 29–47

Barry, B. (1998) 'Social exclusion, social isolation and the distribution of income', Discussion Paper CASE/12, London: Centre for Analysis of Social Exclusion

Begay, M. and J. Kalt (2002) 'Corporate and institutional strengthening for effective indigenous self-governance on the ground: policy lessons from American Indian nations', Indigenous Governance Conference, Australian National University, Canberra, 3–5 April

Cabinet Committee on Closing the Gaps (2000) 'Government performance for Māori: state sector reforms', GAP (00) 5 minute, 22 February

Chapple, S. (2000) 'Māori socio-economic disparity', paper for the Ministry of Social Policy, September

Clark, H. (2000) 'Address to the Economist Roundtable', Wellington, 10 August

— (2001) 'Building an innovative and dynamic economy', address to Auckland Chamber of Commerce Post-Budget Luncheon, Auckland, 25 May

— (2002) 'Implementing a progressive agenda after fifteen years of neo-liberalism: the New Zealand experience', address to London School of Economics, London, 22 February

Cornell, S. and J. Kalt (1998) *Sovereignty and Nation-building: The Development Challenge in Indian Country Today*, Harvard Project on American Indian Economic Development, John F. Kennedy School of Government, Cambridge: Harvard University

Cullen, M. (2000) 'Budget 2000: the speech', *New Zealand Herald*, 16 June, pp. D4–5

Cunningham, C. (1998) 'A framework for addressing Māori knowledge in research, science and technology', in Te Pūmanawa Hauora (ed.), *Proceedings of Te Oru Rangahau: Māori Research and Development Conference*, Palmerston North: Massey University, pp. 387–97

Dean, M. (1999) *Governmentality: Power and Rule in Modern Society*, London: Sage

Durie, E. (1991) 'The treaty in Māori history', in W. Renwick (ed.), *Sovereignty and Indigenous Rights: The Treaty of Waitangi in International Contexts*, Wellington: Victoria University Press, pp. 156–69

Durie, M. (1998) *Te Mana, Te Kāwanatanga: The Politics of Māori Self-determination*, Auckland: Oxford University Press

— (2000) 'A framework for considering constitutional change and the position of Māori in Aotearoa', in C. James (ed.), *Building the Constitution*, Wellington: Institute of Policy Studies, pp. 414–25

Durie, M., E. Fitzgerald, T. K. Kingi, S. McKinley and B. Stevenson (2002) 'Māori specific outcomes and indicators', a report prepared for Te Puni Kōkiri, School of Māori Studies, Palmerston North: Massey University

Elwood, D. (2003) 'From research to social policy and back again: translating scholarship into practice through the starry eyes of a sometimes scarred veteran', *Social Policy Journal of New Zealand*, 20: 6–28

Evans, R. (1981) 'Aftermath of Waitangi – building a national movement', *Newsletter*, Waitangi Action Committee, Otara, August

Fleras, A. and P. Spoonley (1999) *Recalling Aotearoa: Indigenous Politics and Ethnic Relations in New Zealand*, Auckland: Oxford University Press

Giddens, A. (1998) *The Third Way: The Renewal of Social Democracy*, Cambridge: Policy Press

Hall, A. and J. Midgley (1988) 'Introduction', in A. Hall and J. Midgley (eds), *Development Policies: Sociological Perspectives*, Manchester: Manchester University Press, pp. 1–9

Hancock, F. (ed.) (1999) *Māori Realities through Māori Eyes: Social and Economic Disparities between Māori and Non-Māori: Participant Contribution/Gifts to the Auckland and Wellington Futures Conferences*, James Hēnare Māori Research Centre, Auckland: University of Auckland

Harris, P. and C. Eichbaum (1999) 'Towards a post-Washington consensus', in S. Chatterjee, P. Conway, P. Dalziel, C. Eichbaum, P. Harris, B. Philpott and R. Shaw (eds), *The New Politics: A Third Way for New Zealand*, Palmerston North: Dunmore, pp. 221–41

Horomia, P. (2000) *Te Puni Kōkiri's Role in Capacity-building: A Key Measure in Closing the Gaps*, Wellington: Te Puni Kōkiri

Horomia, P. and T. Turia (2001) 'Direct resourcing whanau, hapu, iwi and Māori development', press release, 24 May

— (2002) 'Solid Māori development progress', press release on Budget 2002, 10 May

James, W. (1999) 'Empowering ambiguities', in A. Cheater (ed.), *The Anthropology of Power: Empowerment and Disempowerment in Changing Structures*, London: Routledge, pp. 13–27

Jenkins, K. and A. Jones (2000) 'Māori education policy: a state promise', in J. Marshall, E. Coxon, K. Jenkins and A. Jones (eds), *Politics, Policy, Pedagogy: Education in Aotearoa/New Zealand: An Introduction*, Palmerston North: Dunmore, pp. 139–54

Kukutai, T. (2003) 'The dynamics of ethnicity reporting', discussion paper prepared for Te Puni Kōkiri, Population Studies Centre, University of Waikato, January

Labour Party (1999a) *He Pūtahitanga Hōu: Labour on Māori Development*, pre-election policy document, 16 October

— (1999b) *Focus on Patients: Labour on Health*, pre-election policy document, October

Loomis, T. (2000a) 'Capacity-building and the new role of the state', paper presented in the New Zealand Treasury Guest Lecture Series, Wellington, 31 October

— (2000b) *Government's Role in Māori Development: Charting a New Direction?*, Working Paper no. 6, Department of Development Studies, School of Māori and Pacific Development, Hamilton: University of Waikato

Maharey, S. (2000) 'Making work pay: social justice and the renewed welfare state', presentation to the Institute of Policy Studies, Wellington, 11 December

— (2001a) 'Values and politics: some reflections on the new social democracy in a New Zealand context', comments made to a seminar hosted by the Foundation for Policy Initiatives, Auckland, 23 March

— (2001b) 'Conference opening: the long road to knowledge longitudinal research and social policy', address to the Ministry of Social Policy 2001 Seminar Series, Wellington, 5 April

Māori Economic Development Summit Conference (1984) *Māori Economic Development Summit Conference: Conference Background Papers*, Wellington: Māori Economic Development Summit Conference

Marston, G. and R. Watts (2003) 'Tampering with the evidence: a critical appraisal of evidence-based policy-making', *The Drawing Board: An Australian Review of Public Affairs*, 3(3): 143–63

Mead, S. (1997) *Landmarks, Bridges and Visions: Aspects of Māori Culture*, Wellington: Victoria University

Melbourne, H. (ed.) (1995) *Māori Sovereignty: The Māori Perspective*, Auckland: Hodder Moa Beckett

Ministry of Health (2001) 'DHBs: elected members', <http://www.moh.govt.nz/moh.nsf/>

Ministry of Social Development (2002a) *Annual Report 2001–2002*, Wellington: Ministry of Social Development

— (2002b) *Briefing to the Incoming Minister: Building Leadership for Social Development*, Wellington: Ministry of Social Development

—-(2003) *The Social Report: Indicators of Social Well-being in New Zealand*, Wellington: Ministry of Social Development

Ministry of Social Policy (2001) *The Social Development Approach*, Wellington: Ministry of Social Policy

Morton, M. and P. Gibson (2003) 'The rhetoric and practice of partnership: experiences in the context of disability', Connecting Policy Research and Practice, Social Policy Research and Evaluation Conference, 29–30 April, Ministry of Social Development, Wellington

Mulgan, R. (1998) 'Citizenship and legitimacy in post-colonial Australia', in N. Peterson and W. Sanders (eds), *Citizenship and Indigenous Australians: Changing Conceptions and Possibilities*, Cambridge: Cambridge University Press, pp. 179–95

Nutley, S., H. Davies and I. Walter (2003) 'Evidence-based policy and practice: cross-sector lessons from the United Kingdom', *Social Policy Journal of New Zealand*, 20: 29–48

Office of the Minister of Health (2000) 'Equitable representation for Māori on District Health Boards', memorandum to Cabinet Social Policy and Health Committee, released 1 August

Office of the Minister of Māori Affairs (2000a) 'Government performance for Māori', paper submitted to the Cabinet Business Committee and later referred to the Cabinet Committee on Closing the Gaps, GAP (00) 2, 31 January

— (2000b) 'Providing for capacity-building: the role of Te Puni Kōkiri, paper submitted to the Cabinet Committee on Closing the Gaps, GAP (00) 16, 3 April

Office of the Prime Minister (2000) 'Government performance for Māori: state sector reforms', paper submitted to the Cabinet Committee on Closing the Gaps, GAP (00) 5, 22 February

O'Malley, P. (1996) 'Indigenous governance', *Economy and Society*, 25(3): 310–26

Peace, R. (2001) 'Social exclusion: a concept in need of a definition?', *Social Policy Journal of New Zealand: Te Puna Whakaaro*, 16: 17–35

Percy-Smith, J. (2000) 'Introduction: the contours of social exclusion', in J. Percy-Smith (ed.), *Policy Responses to Social Exclusion: Towards Inclusion?*, Buckingham: Open University Press, pp. 1–21

Rose, N. (1999) *Powers of Freedom: Reframing Political Thought*, Cambridge: Cambridge University Press

Sardar, Z. (1999) 'Development and the locations of Eurocentrism', in R. Munck and D. O'Hearn (eds), *Critical Development Theory: Contributions to a New Paradigm*, London: Zed Books

Servian, R. (1996) *Theorising Empowerment: Individual Power and Community Care*, Bristol: Policy Press

Smith, L. T. (1999) *Decolonizing Methodologies: Research and Indigenous Peoples*, London/Dunedin: Zed Books/University of Otago Press

Te Puni Kōkiri (2000a) *Progress towards Closing Social and Economic Gaps between Māori and Non-Māori: A Report to the Minister of Māori Affairs*, Wellington: Te Puni Kōkiri

— (2000b) 'Minister: new policy can reshape our nation', *Te Puni Kōkiri Newsletter*, 59: 1

— (2000c) 'Te Puni Kōkiri's role in capacity-building', Wellington: Te Puni Kōkiri

— (2002a) *Māori in the New Zealand Economy*, 3rd edn, Wellington: Te Puni Kōkiri

— (2002b) *Annual Report of Te Puni Kōkiri (Ministry of Māori Development) for the year ended 30 June 2002*, Wellington: Te Puni Kōkiri

— (2003) *Statement of Intent, 1 July 2003*, Wellington: Te Puni Kōkiri

Tully, J. (1999) 'The agonic freedom of citizens', *Economy and Society*, 28(2): 161–82

Turia, T. (2002) 'Beehive Chat 21', online newsletter, Wellington, October, <http://www.beehive.govt.nz/ViewNewsletter.aspx?DocumentID=15235>

Verhelst, T. (1990) *No Life without Roots: Culture and Development*, trans. B. Cumming, London: Zed Books

Walker, R. (1999) 'Māori sovereignty, colonial and post-colonial discourses', in P. Havemann (ed.), *Indigenous Peoples' Rights in Australia, Canada and New Zealand*, Auckland: Oxford University Press, pp. 108–22

Winiata, W. (2000) 'How can or should the treaty be reflected in institutional design?', in C. James (ed.), *Building the Constitution*, Wellington: Institute of Policy Studies, pp. 205–6

Young, A. (2000) 'Cracks show in gaps policy', *New Zealand Herald*, 14 December, p. A17

Young, I. M. (1990) *Justice and the Politics of Difference*, Princeton, NJ: Princeton University Press

10 | Political participation and poverty in Colombian indigenous communities: the case of the Zenú and Mokaná peoples

A. CAROLINA BORDA NIÑO AND DARIO J. MEJÍA MONTALVO[1]

Through its political mobilization, the Colombian indigenous movement has contributed greatly to the recognition of cultural diversity in Colombia. The state's formal recognition of cultural diversity has been accompanied by policies aimed at ensuring the inclusion of ethnic groups within the social and economic life of national society. At the same time, however, these policies have been based on governmental administrative structures' own concepts and appraisals of indigenous peoples' social problems, interpreted from the standpoint of indigenous economic disadvantage. Policies targeting poverty are clear examples of this; their focus on economic issues fails to take into account the cultural characteristics of indigenous communities.

This chapter intends to address the relationship between poverty and ethnic and cultural diversity in Colombia. It starts by highlighting the definitions of poverty that have informed the creation and implementation of public policies to transform the living conditions of an indigenous population defined as 'poor'. It then considers how these understandings of poverty have influenced how poverty has been dealt with in Colombian public policy. It argues that, despite the ground-breaking recognition of ethnic diversity in the Colombian constitution of 1991, policies targeting poverty have not been informed by a perspective of ethnic diversity. Rather, the government targets general and abstract indicators of poverty within programmes with specific time frames and using efficiency criteria that are different from those of communities. Such policies demonstrate a lack of awareness that such actions alter the collective life and create resistance which generally leads to the failure of such programmes. In short, these anti-poverty approaches fail to take ethnic and cultural diversity into account.

Overall, it can be said that the political participation of indigenous peoples in Colombia has influenced the formal recognition of 'diversity', but not the implementation and execution of policies that are based on a perspective of ethnic diversity. When discussing the legal recognition of ethnic diversity, it is important to understand what, exactly, is being recognized and how; for instance, are indigenous groups recognized as *peoples* (with the autonomy which that implies) or as communities subject to state control? The experience of Colombia is particularly worthy of exploration, as its constitutional reform process of 1991 can be characterized as resulting in 'the most ambitious attempt of any Latin American state to implement legal pluralism' (Van Cott 2000). Here, indigenous organizations influenced the constitutional reform process in order to achieve significant ethnic autonomy (Van Cott 2001).

This chapter will consider the processes of identity construction, organization and political participation of two of Colombia's many indigenous ethnic groups, the Zenú and Mokaná, comparing and contrasting the experiences of these two groups. The different experiences of these groups, and their distinct priorities and strategies, underline the diversity among indigenous groups, as well as the importance of ethnic and political identity construction in addressing social issues. They also draw attention to the limitations in the way in which ethnic and cultural diversity is currently recognized by the Colombian state. The chapter's conclusion suggests the basic outlines of a new approach to addressing poverty in Colombia, one that is based on the recognition of rights to cultural diversity.

Poverty and ethnic diversity in Colombia

Poverty has been measured in Colombia using the NBI (*índice de necesidades básicas insatisfechas*, or unmet basic needs index), which classifies as 'poor' those people and households which have inadequate housing, access to services, school attendance, and so forth. Available statistics from 1997 demonstrate marked differences among regions or departments. Using these NBI indicators, the areas with the greatest incidence of poverty are: Chocó, Córdoba, Sucre, Nariño and Boyacá, where over 50 per cent of the population can be categorized as 'poor'; those with the lowest incidence of poverty are Bogotá and the departments of del Valle, Atlántico and the coffee region (Caldas, Quindio and Risaralda). In terms of the poverty line, Bogotá shows the lowest incidence of poverty (30 per cent of the population is below the poverty line), with the poorest departments of the country being Atlántico, Córdoba, Bolívar, Cesar, La Guajira, Magdalena, Sucre, Boyacá, Tolima, Cauca, Chocó and Nariño. An abject poverty line has also been set based on the estimate of the income required to buy a minimum basket of food for survival (biological approach).

In 1986, the concept of absolute poverty was introduced in Colombia, within a context of governance crisis and increasing escalation of armed conflicts. With its policies to fight poverty, the government aimed to demonstrate the continued presence of the state in areas regarded as 'marginal', including of course areas with indigenous populations. The aim was to solve the crisis of governance through the eradication of poverty, regardless of local needs or diverse conceptions of development.

Those people considered to be suffering from 'absolute poverty' were those who did not have the means to meet either their material needs for food, housing, protection and health, or their non-material needs for education and social integration. The notion of *social integration* was used to define those groups which did not participate in the economic development of the country, and who were expected to adapt and participate. In this case, homogenization was the premise of development and, consequently, difference was the hurdle to be removed.

Indigenous communities were considered to be different and disadvantaged sectors, a backward population that needed to be integrated into mainstream society. Indigenous peoples were not seen as a population whose active participation was necessary to create stability in the nation,[2] as could be argued from a perspective of ethnic diversity. At present, even with the overt recognition of diversity, and constitutional mechanisms permitting a degree of administrative autonomy for indigenous groups, the state's goal remains to reduce diversity to homogeneity. It is thanks only to the struggle of excluded groups that diversity has been recognized to any extent.

After the concept of absolute poverty was introduced in 1986, Colombian policies over the next four years (1986–90) pursued the recovery of excluded regions and their integration into national development visions. Specific programmes were designed to work with indigenous populations. In most cases, indigenous peoples were characterized as farming populations ('*campesinos*'), in need of updated production methods and more urbanized lifestyles. Indigenous peoples reacted strongly against this approach, arguing that it was not they who should readjust to the state, but rather the state which should adjust to them.

The Colombian constitution of 1991 emerged from a process of constitutional reform in which indigenous organizations had an influential role. It recognized the nation's multi-ethnic and multicultural nature, and with it, participatory democracy as the core of the new state of democratic openness. Subsequent governments established more differentiated policies towards ethnic groups as compared with previous years; indigenous communities were recognized, and specific resources were allotted to these communities (government transfers). These advances meant a greater possibility for participation in the government policy-making affecting these populations, but they also led to the subsiding of struggles for identity, reduced political participation in the economic arena, and the transformation of identity in both political and cultural arenas.

Indigenous groups are well aware of the consequences of this process for them. Indigenous movements have faced a crisis; yet despite this crisis, new forms of resistance and autonomous development alternatives have emerged. Their articulation has been developed in tandem with indigenous organizations from other countries.

Recognizing diversity in Colombia

In the 1970s, national unity in Colombia was based on the populist model of national integration (Gros 1997). In the 1980s, this model began to undergo a crisis, and the state proved unable to meet growing social demands. The transformations that took place during the 1980s and 1990s included changes in the education system, the increased politicization of the population, the weakening of traditional ideological references (resulting from a crisis of confidence in traditional political parties), urbanization, and increased drug dealing and corruption. Together these changes resulted in a governance crisis. Political instability and political violence forced constitutional reform to the centre of the political agenda, as a response to a crisis of national government legitimacy and popular demand for an open, participatory process of radical constitutional reform (Van Cott 2001).

During this period, a revival of social movements from different sectors took place; these included movements of farmers, women, workers and indigenous peoples. Indigenous peoples' movements were able to significantly influence the constitutional reform process, and even, through political pressure, achieved the establishment of special self-governing indigenous territories (Van Cott 2000). From the state's perspective, it became necessary to think of ways to institutionalize, accept and take possession of popular social movements, towards the goal of national unity and state stability. Indigenous 'participation' was thus encouraged and promoted in state policy, and cultural diversity[3] became worthy of protection by law. Here, the political exercise was for culture and its manifestations to be recognized by the state[4] so that a conflictive element (the ethnic movement) would be integrated into the supposed national society.

Against this backdrop, however, there also emerged a counter-dynamic favouring transformation (Gros 1997: 35, 37). First, the indigenous population's access to formal education helped to foster the training of new leaders with new perspectives for the indigenous movement. Second, there was an increasing involvement of players outside indigenous movements themselves, which for different reasons served to encourage the recovery of ethnic identity. An example of this would be the ADM-19 political party, which formed a political alliance with indigenous delegates to the constituent assembly in 1990 and supported the passing of controversial indigenous proposals (Van Cott 2001: 48). Finally, the international context proved to be increasingly favourable to the defence and promotion of cultural diversity, given the growth in indigenous peoples' movements and the increasing recognition of indigenous rights on the international stage. In the political constitution of 1991, Colombia was declared a multi-ethnic and multicultural nation. This has created and continues to create processes of organizational construction, transformation and identity redefinition among all Colombian indigenous peoples.

The case of the Zenú people

The Zenú indigenous people dwell in the northern Colombian departments of Córdoba and Sucre. In the 1970s, they began a process of recovering their ethnic identity, mainly through their struggle for the recovery of land. This population mobilization was made possible thanks to the influence of the Asociación Nacional de Usuarios Campesinos (ANUC), a farmers' organization in the region. Although starting out as an economic struggle for land ownership, in a relatively short period of time the possibilities for action were broadened owing to the influence of a growing national indigenous movement. Although this resulted in ideological and political battles within ANUC to define the meaning of the struggle, there was an agreement on the centrality of land as a common symbol.

From the early 1980s, the identification of this population as members of an indigenous community became widely accepted. This was articulated in terms of cultural traditions surviving from the territorial expropriation processes from the start of the twentieth century, and the existence of a royal document from the Spanish Crown dated 1770 which granted the Zenú people the ownership of the lands of the region. A major achievement of the movement has been the reorganization of the *resguardo* (an indigenous community and its specific corresponding territory) and the establishment of its own town council, by order of the Colombian Agrarian Reform Institute.[5]

The active participation of the Zenú in national indigenous meetings and the unification of pro-farming and pro-indigenous political trends were the starting point for a struggle to solve welfare problems related to health, education and transport. From reclaiming land, they went on to conduct road blockades, demonstrations in the municipalities seats, and occupation of state institutions. The problem of land became conceptualized, not merely as land, but as territory. Thus, more than just tangible property, land as territory became an artefact that concretely articulated unmet needs and demands.

The growth of the Zenú movement over the last decade has been significant. This can be seen in the growing number of Zenú municipal councils, of Zenú territories, and the member population. As a whole, the *resguardo* had only six minor town councils in 1983. By 1994, it had seventy, and by August 2001 the number of minor town councils had grown to 335. The Zenú population in the 1980s was unknown, but there were 33,106 in 1993; by 1995 this had grown to 49,818, and by 2001 there were approximately 70,000 members of the Zenú movement. Likewise, in 1983 the Zenú movement had territories in four municipalities; while by 2001 it had territories in twenty municipalities between Córdoba and Sucre departments (Jaramillo and Turbay Ceballos 1986).

While the indigenous struggle focused its efforts on the fight for territory, it also looked for a better allocation of the resources generated by local production. The movement thus made demands for better education, transport and communication, water services and decent housing, as well as fair working conditions.

The Zenú indigenous movement cannot be fully understood without taking into account the armed conflict in Colombia, which has affected it directly. In the late 1980s and early 1990s, a variety of different guerrilla groups, such as the Partido Revolucionario de los Trabajadores (PRT) (Workers' Revolutionary Party), the Ejército Popular de Liberación (EPL) (Popular Liberation Army), the Ejército de la Liberación Nacional (ELN) (National Liberation Army) and, to a lesser extent, the Fuerzas Revolucionarias de Colombia (FARC) (Colombian Revolutionary Forces), began to appear in Zenú territory. The Zenú movement has also been affected by the establishment of radical positions within the indigenous movement in the south-west of the country, particularly the emergence of a guerrilla movement, Manuel Quintín Lame (MQL), in the districts of Cauca, Tolima and Nariño.

After the constitutional reform process in the early 1990s and the introduction of Law 60, which regulates the distribution of the nation's fiscal resources, the indigenous *resguardos* were given a share in national resources. The state, however, imposed regulations that determined the allocation of economic resources. This created a fragmented panorama of policies aimed at reducing the marginality of the indigenous population, but which ultimately prevented an adequate treatment of poverty for the Zenús. The participation of the Zenú people in the definition of policies has been limited to meeting the development planning requirements of core institutions (the Departamento Nacional de Planeación, or National

Planning Department) in coordination with the state territorial institutions (municipalities).

The main development investments for the Zenú people have comprised training in public resources management, intensive cattle and agricultural pilot production programmes, the construction of facilities for rural schools and healthcare centres, and loans for individual or family productive activities. Unfortunately, it can now be demonstrated that neither the economic nor the social conditions of the population have changed much, despite the sizeable amounts of money invested in targeted poverty reduction programmes.

The case of the Mokaná people

The transformations brought about by the political constitution of 1991 led to processes of organizational change and identity redefinition for all the Colombian indigenous peoples. For the indigenous Mokaná people, this process began in 1998, and involved approximately 25,000 people. It attempted on the one hand to gain – through the creation of political-participation bodies for the indigenous population – recognition by the state at different levels. On the other hand, it aimed progressively to configure a self-defined indigenous identity, informed by both current experience and accumulated knowledge.

The Mokaná people were recognized officially by the state as an indigenous group in 1998. In 2001, this recognition was withdrawn by the Dirección de Asuntos Indígenas (DAI) (Ministry of the Interior), which argued for the need to carry out a new ethnographic study to determine the indigenous nature of the population, because previous recognition of this community (not people) had been informally granted without an official ethnographic study. This decision mirrors the general process used by the Colombian state to discourage the recognition of cultural diversity rights. It can be explained by the economic and governance cost which the progressive increase in cultural and ethnic diversity recognition represents for the state.

After recognition was withdrawn, the Mokaná people officially requested that an official ethnographic study be undertaken. The DAI was given a period of six months to conduct the study. The DAI, however, started from the presupposition that the Mokaná could not be considered an indigenous people. This was clear from the statements made by the director of the study, who took the Mokaná's lack of a distinctive language, housing pattern, clothing or religion as indicating that they did not have their own culture. In the official view, they were considered a group of farmers looking for economic resources who were attempting to take advantage of public pro-diversity policies. There was no consideration whatsoever of the fundamental basis of being indigenous: i.e. self-recognition, as stipulated both in the political constitution and in international agreements.

The period between the grant and the withdrawal of recognition corresponds to a stage of cultural and political redefinition by the Mokaná people. During this time they set new political goals, reorganized their leadership, redefined their political strategies, and developed new strategies for using culture as a way to secure proposed political objectives. The basis of identity lies in the political project it represents, creates and reproduces. Cultural identity bears a dialectic relation with political identity; that is, accepting certain institutionalized exercises of power (politics) determines the legitimate rules of community practice (culture). At the same time, the assimilation of everyday cultural practices determines the structure of a specific exercise of political power.

The political community of the Mokaná is formed from the relation between material needs and the way to meet these needs based on ethnic identity, i.e. the experience of ethnicity. Ethnicity specifically refers to the 'call to identity, the exaltation of community values, that is more evident as a means rather than as an end. It expresses the will to access new cultural assets, new technology, development, modernity' (Gros 1997: 27). It also embraces the field of political action, born of the instrumentalization of ethnic identity, and taking place parallel to a process of cultural identity development. The goal of this political action is positive discrimination by the state, namely the recognition of cultural diversity and of specific corresponding rights. In addition to the quest for positive discrimination, the issue of territory is a key aspect of Mokaná political identity. Overall, the Mokaná's outward-looking political structure is specifically geared to the relationship between state and indigenous organizations.

In terms of the inward-looking relationship between the indigenous organization and the indigenous population itself, the development of Mokaná political identity is essentially based on the material benefits that leaders can generate for the community. This creates a highly volatile identity. In this case, the constant political participation of the population at large is neither necessary nor possible.[6] The strengthening of the organization is, rather, undertaken in terms of training community leaders in the skills to negotiate with the state apparatus and its representatives, and the mobilization of the population as necessary.

This political structure leads to the constitution of a weak political identity among Mokaná community members. Political decisions of great importance for the organization are not made in a democratic way, or according to the traditional ways of most indigenous peoples in the country – where political decisions are in the hands of wise individuals. In the

Mokaná organization, the most important decisions (such as support for certain political candidates, or the design of strategies to create an ethnic identity, or the appointment and removal of officers within the department's main deliberative body) are controlled by the community leadership, in the form of various councils, which are actually structured as consultative rather than decision-making bodies.[7]

The political participation of indigenous peoples such as the Mokaná, in interaction with national policies for diversity in Colombia, has resulted in the creation of a political identity with two basic features: dispersion and volatility. Political identity is dispersed because individuals may belong to different political groups, groups that may even have contradictory goals. For instance, it is not uncommon for an individual to belong to a traditional political group in the region (which claims for itself the electoral support of its members) while also belonging to an indigenous organization, which claims for itself the electoral support of those identified as indigenous (Senate and House of Representatives). Political identity is volatile because leaders and reference organizations are constantly changing, i.e. according to the changes in alliances among leaders and organizations. These changes occur as a result of the symbolic assets and, above all, the material support they can offer.

For the Mokaná group, the process of reindigenization offered a way to address their central aspiration, which is to respond to the needs of people in the rural context. Thus, in the political field they prioritize the ability to influence the dynamics of resource allocation, to undertake social projects, and to mean something in the rural context, rather than focusing on the particular political orientation of a candidate or a political alliance. The Mokaná people challenge the concept of *indigenous* because they do not demonstrate all the characteristic traits of 'indigenous' as defined by the state. They do not have traditions and customs considered by the authorities to be distinctive from the surrounding non-indigenous peoples, they do not have their own language, they farm and do not gather, and they claim political rights instead of respect for their cultural identity. We are faced with societies undergoing transformations, in which what comprises 'indigenousness' is both dynamic and diverse. The concept of ethnicity is useful here in that it takes into account this diversity.

Towards a definition of poverty from the ethnic diversity perspective

Human poverty has a multi-dimensional and diverse nature. It is a socially defined category. Consequently, the way to address it varies according to each social situation.

It is important to highlight the fact that the term *indigenous* is itself homogenizing, concealing differences in the way in which reality is viewed and how social transformations are generated in order to ensure both cultural and material survival. Therefore, a government policy cannot have the same results even if applied to relatively similar contexts. In many cases, collective preferences do not permit the changing of traditions in order to achieve a supposed improvement in the standards of living for individuals. Moreover, people understand deprivation in different ways: each person and community has its own definition of the deprivations and disadvantages that affect their lives.

Processes aimed at recovering identity – such as those of the Mokaná people – and processes of accelerated transformation of ethnicity – such as those experienced by the Zenú people – are strongly influenced by the political and legal transformation of the Colombian state. The initiatives of these peoples focus on their demands for territory, self-determination, development and their distinctive cultural traditions. Public policy aimed at reducing poverty among indigenous peoples should not disregard the existing relations, positions, knowledge and strategies that have emerged from indigenous social movements and political organizing – that is, the area of inter-ethnic relations (Zambrano 2002: 30).

The demands for territory, and with it the capacity for self-determination as regards the distribution of resources and governance roles within each community, are commonplace in Colombian indigenous communities. Poverty is, from an indigenous perspective, the lack of rights to territory, since this is a necessary condition to guarantee autonomous development and to be able to implement policies that fit the conditions and expectations of each indigenous people. In most cases, community members feel they possess the right to territory, whether or not this right is legally recognized. This allows indigenous peoples to implement, even without state recognition, their own development and self-management strategies, for instance health and education projects, and the commercialization of goods they produce using traditional methods.

In general, we can say that for indigenous peoples poverty can be measured according to the degree of autonomy they have over their territory. From this standpoint, plentiful economic resources do not translate into wealth. This helps explain why some peoples reject state-crafted anti-poverty policies: because the indicators are not applicable to them, do not satisfy them, or fail to measure the standards of living they hope for. Rather than trust state institutions to decrease poverty, many believe that the state itself is the problem: that ethnic groups' conditions of 'poverty' have been imposed by state institutions as they systematically exclude diversity.

Conclusion

The relation between the state and indigenous peoples in Colombia can be seen as contradictory. Indigenous peoples reaffirm their character as peoples, in opposition to the ambiguous ways in which state institutions define them.[8] Understanding this is key. The concept of *people* implies the exercise of self-determination as outlined by international agreements such as the United Nations Agreement on Economic, Social, and Cultural Rights, and the Agreement on Civil and Political Rights. It implies the right to the free exercise of political rights and provision for socio-economic and cultural development, self-government, increased negotiation capacity and, above all, the ability to assume legal-political competences (Díaz Polanco 2001: 5). In Colombia, however, the different levels of government recognize indigenous groups only as *communities*, i.e. as culturally diverse populations that require differentiated policies to become part of the national society to which they historically belong. The traditional forms of government and authorities of the communities are recognized, but always subject to the constitutional and legal rules of the state.

The Colombian indigenous movement has reached a significant consensus in terms of generic demands for the recognition of their cultural diversity, and that this recognition implies special rights. Nevertheless, there are still internal differences over how to use diversity as an asset, and how to achieve development objectives. Although in the case of the Mokaná people we see that ethnic diversity strategies can involve communication and awareness of similar experiences (such as the Zenú's struggle and that of other communities), it is impossible to think of similar procedures, strategies and tactics for all Colombian indigenous groups. Ethnic diversity implies not only differences from the majority population, but also differences among and within indigenous communities.

The generic term 'peoples' – indiscriminately used here – can disguise substantial differences in different groups' identities and their political self-identification. The Zenú people have envisaged a particular struggle, no longer centred on land as property, but rather on territory as the representation and expression of needs, demands and the processes through which they seek these. They have consolidated this struggle by institutionalizing a political organization now recognized by the state.

The case of the Mokaná people is different. Their action is focused on claiming the right to be a people, aiming for self-development and the recovery of their identity. Their struggle for recognition is relatively new compared to that of the Zenú people, and they have remained aloof from one of the key drivers of political transformation in Colombian indigenous communities: government transfers. They neither want nor need them.

Their goals, rather, are directed towards internal strengthening (identity and political organization).

The Zenú people's experience of direct struggle, their political failures and organizational achievements are well known to the Mokaná, for whom they provide a reference point. It is also true, however, that despite the youth of their movement, the Mokaná have also become a political point of reference for the Zenú people and for many other Colombian indigenous peoples. This communication makes it possible to trace the particular and shared logics among the indigenous peoples of a given region. It is also essential to understand these peoples' shared experience, and their recent political repositioning, when considering poverty from an ethnic diversity perspective.

Notes

1 We are grateful for the comments and suggestions of Professor Carlos Vladimir Zambrano from the Political Science Department, Universidad Nacional de Colombia.

2 This conceptualization can be traced back to colonial times, when indigenous people were regarded as minors (owing to the legal implications of such status), or historical leftovers standing in the way of development.

3 According to the state: ' ... Culture, with its different expressions, is the foundation of nationality ... ' (Colombia political constitution 1991, sect. 70).

4 For instance, consider the following excerpt from a 2001 state speech which referred to the transfer of economic resources to indigenous peoples and spoke highly of ethno-educational programmes: 'In Colombia, the political constitution, the legal norms, and jurisprudence have established and recognised the rights of indigenous peoples within the framework of the ethnic and cultural diversity of the Nation' (Indigenous Affairs Directorate 1998: 8).

5 Instituto Colombiano de la Reforma Agraria – INCORA – Resolution 054, 21 September 1984.

6 '*Population analysis (...).* Many of the people recorded in the census [Mokaná indigenous people in the main area of the Atlantic District] do not take part in the activities of the *cabildo* or in meetings; they are not interested in the indigenous organization, they are not aware of and have not participated in the process and have only shown interest in accessing benefits guaranteed by the State for indigenous people as previously stated' (Indigenous Affairs Directorate 1998: 36).

7 As regards the councils, the by-laws of the Tubará Deliberative Body (the political organization of the indigenous people) state: 'They are coordinators which help in the process to strengthen and control our indigenous people (...). As Councils, their coordinators and members *do not have the nature of traditional authorities*, they will act as guides only in the issues within their scope and upon the request of any authority or by the assembly of authorities of the Mokaná people' (emphasis added).

8 'In Colombia, the political constitution, legal norms, and jurisprudence have established and recognised rights to the *indigenous peoples* within the framework of the ethnic and cultural diversity of the Nation' (Indigenous Affairs Directorate 1998: 3). In another fragment of the same text: 'According to the habits and customs of the *indigenous communities*, the State recognises the existence of political-administrative organisational forms, represented by traditional authorities and deliberative bodies (*Cabildos*), as special public authorities which perform the roles of social control and organisation in their communities.'

References

Díaz Polanco, H. (2001). 'La población indígena y sus escalas. Puntos para la reflexión', Seminario Internacional FLACSO/CLACSO/CROP, 'Poblaciones Indígenas y Pobreza', Antigua, Guatemala, November

Dirección General de Asuntos Indígenas (1998) 'Consolidado de resguardos constituidos por departamentos', Bogotá: Ministerio del Interior

Gros, C. (1997) 'Indigenismo y etnicidad: el desafío neoliberal', in M. V. Uribe (ed.), *Antropología en la modernidad*, Colombia: ICANH

Jaramillo Arbeláez, S. and S. Turbay Ceballos (1986) *La identidad cultural entre los indígenas de San Andrés de Sotavento – Córdoba, Colombia*, Monografía de grado, Universidad de Antioquia, Facultad de Ciencias Sociales, Departamento de Antropología, Medellín, Colombia

Van Cott, D. (2000) 'A political analysis of legal pluralism in Bolivia and Colombia', *Journal of Latin American Studies*, 32(1): 207–34

— (2001) 'Explaining ethnic autonomy regimes in Latin America', *Studies in Comparative International Development*, 35(4): 30–58

Zambrano, C. V. (2002) 'Transición nacional, reconfiguración de la diversidad y génesis del campo étnico. Aproximación a la promoción de la diversidad en la década 1991 – 2001', *Pensamiento jurídico*, 15: 13–36

Field documents

Dirección General de Asuntos Indígenas (Indigenous Affairs Directorate) (1998) 'Consolidado de resguardos constituidos por departamentos', Bogotá: Ministerio del Interior

Instituto Colombiano de la Reforma Agraria (INCORA) (2001) 'Resguardos constituidos en el Departamento de Córdoba' Bogotá: INCORA

Ministerio Del Interior (1991) 'Constitución política de Colombia', Bogotá

— (1998) Letter 5857 of 18 December, Bogotá

— (1999) Letter 2053 of 16 June, Bogotá

— (Dirección de Asuntos Indígenas) (2002) Resolution No. 034 of 23 April, Bogotá

— (2002) Resolution no. 078 of 2 July, Bogotá

— (2002) 'Estudio etnológico para determinar la existencia de una parcialidad indígena perteneciente al pueblo Mokaná en el Municipio de Tubará, Atlántico', Bogotá

— (2003) Letter 0008 of 7 January, Bogotá

Organización Nacional Indígena de Colombia (2000) Resolution no. 002 of 1 July, Bogotá

Presidencia de la República (2002) Letter 10948 of 3 December, Bogotá

Territorio Indígena Mokaná (1999–2000) Internal correspondence, Atlántico, Colombia

— (1999–2000) Internal organization documents, Atlántico

— (1999–2001) Minutes of general meetings of Galapa partiality, Atlántico

— (2000) Minutes of general meetings of Tubará partiality, Atlántico

— (2001) 'Evaluación procuradores', Atlántico

— (2001) 'Life plan evaluation. Political strategies. Adoption of political strategies', Atlántico

— (2001). Interviews (seven hours of recordings). Atlántico

Interviews

1. Digno Santiago Gerónimo, Indigenous Mokaná Governor, Bogotá, 15 September 2001
2. Digno Santiago Gerónimo, Indigenous Mokaná Governor, Tubará, Atlántico, 3 October 2001

11 | Indigenous peoples, poverty and self-determination in Australia, New Zealand, Canada and the United States

STEPHEN CORNELL

Australia, New Zealand, Canada and the United States are among the world's wealthiest nations.[1] It is an often noted irony – and an occasional source of embarrassment to the governments of these countries – that the indigenous peoples within their borders are in each case among their poorest citizens. The irony is either explained away or made all the greater, depending on your frame of mind, by the fact that the wealth of these countries has been built substantially on resources taken from these peoples, whose poverty – in the grand scheme of things – is a recent creation.

Although my interest is not in the sources of indigenous poverty but in how to overcome it, this poverty is the subject of this chapter. In what follows, I consider the comparability of indigenous peoples' situations in these countries, including the mismatch in all four cases between indigenous demands for self-determination and state programmes to address socio-economic disadvantage. I then summarize evidence from the United States that indigenous self-determination and self-government are essential bases for improving the socio-economic conditions of indigenous peoples, explore some of the issues raised by this evidence, and conclude with implications for policy-makers.

One might ask whether US evidence on indigenous poverty is relevant to the three other countries listed above. There is as yet little systematic research that addresses the point, and this chapter draws most directly on work carried out with American Indian nations in the United States. My colleagues[2] and I have done additional, but less comprehensive research, with First Nations in Canada and have had only preliminary discussions about governance and development issues with Māori and Aboriginal peoples in New Zealand and Australia.[3] Consequently, the conclusions I draw from non-US research are necessarily speculative. Nevertheless, they are worth exploring. In all four countries, indigenous poverty has been not only deep and widespread but persistent, defying policy prescriptions. Both indigenous peoples and the states that seek to address this problem face daunting challenges. What works in one country may hold lessons for others. At the very least, it may point research in productive directions.

Differences

Do the historical and cultural differences among these four countries and their indigenous peoples overwhelm the insights we might draw from any one of them? What grounds have we for thinking that what works in one might be relevant to the others?

Obviously the differences are substantial, both historically and today. For example, Britain recognized Māori sovereignty over the North Island of New Zealand early on and then, over the years, set out to extinguish it. In contrast, it gave no recognition to Aboriginal sovereignty – or even occupancy – in Australia. Warfare between indigenous groups and European settlers and states was frequent and at times prolonged in the United States and New Zealand, but much less common in Canada and Australia. Serial treaty-making took place in Canada and the United States, but was unknown in Australia, while treaty-making in New Zealand was limited to the Treaty of Waitangi in 1840 – itself quite a different enterprise from Canadian and US treaty-making (Pocock 2000) – which, despite the refusal of some Māori to sign it, was viewed by the Crown as establishing British sovereignty over the whole of the North Island.

Likewise, once European control had been established, the administration of indigenous affairs differed in numerous ways among these countries. In the United States, for example, relations with Indian nations have been under the exclusive control of the federal government, with individual states playing only a minor role. In Canada, on the other hand, despite the prominence of the federal government, the role of the provinces in relations with First Nations has been substantial, especially in recent years (Morse 1998). In Australia, the administration of Aboriginal affairs largely ignored 'tribal' boundaries and often fostered a mixing of peoples, while such boundaries eventually became the basis of the organization of relations with American Indians, and both treaty-making and the administration of Indian affairs in many cases rigidified group boundaries or introduced new ones. We could point to numerous other legal, political and organizational differences in the history of indigenous–settler relations in these four countries.

Today, numerous differences remain, from the details of indigenous relations with central governments to land rights, from demographics to socio-economic conditions. Neither the relative size of the indigenous land bases nor the officially recognized rights of indigenous peoples to land are the same in all four countries. Recognition of Native title and restoration of some land rights to Aboriginal Australians are very recent, while most American Indian nations have exercised at least some jurisdiction over reserved lands for decades and, in some cases, much longer, and some of those reserved lands are extensive. Many First Nations in Canada have some measure of control over reserved lands, but in nearly all such cases the lands are minuscule in extent, while Māori, having suffered massive land losses over the years, have been engaged in a major effort in recent decades to regain significant lands and resources.

In all four countries the indigenous populations are small, but not equally so. At the turn of the twentieth century, indigenous peoples made up approximately 1.5 per cent of the overall US population, just over 2 per cent of that of Australia, more than 4 per cent of that of Canada, but close to 15 per cent of the population of New Zealand.[4] Tribal or equivalent groups range widely in size from populations of under one hundred, found in each country, to the Navajo nation in the United States, more than a quarter of a million strong. More than half of the Indian population in the United States live in urban areas; an even higher percentage of Māori do. While many Aboriginal Australians likewise live in cities and towns, they are much more likely than American Indians or Māori to live in remote regions. Indigenous groups are among the poorest populations in each country, but there are significant differences in social and economic conditions. In Australia, for example, Aboriginal life expectancy at birth in 1991 was 59.6 years but was 70.5 years for New Zealand Māori and registered Indians in Canada and 73.5 years for American Indians and Alaska Natives in the United States (Beavon and Cooke 2001).[5]

Commonalities

Although there are clear differences there are, however, also substantial similarities among these four locations and the situations of their indigenous peoples. The following seem particularly important and grounds for comparative enquiry.

- All four are settler societies, states in which 'the predominant population arises from immigrants and the indigenous population has become a displaced minority' (Perry 1996: 167).
- All four contemporary societies are of predominantly British heritage. Not only did immigrants from Great Britain long dominate settler populations, but all four legal and political structures draw heavily on English political traditions and common law. All are predominantly English-speaking societies today.
- Furthermore, as Moran (2002: 1,015–16) points out, 'countries like the United States, Canada, New Zealand and Australia, despite important differences, are all structured by the fact that they are predominantly English-speaking settler cultures which have to a large extent supplanted indigenous peoples'.

- But this fact structures not only these countries; it profoundly structures the experience of their indigenous peoples as well. In all four, supplanting these peoples has entailed enormous indigenous resource losses, the eventual destruction of indigenous economies and a good deal of social organization, precipitous population declines, and subjection to tutelary and assimilationist policies antagonistic to indigenous cultures (for a summary of the record in three of the four, see Armitage 1995).
- In all four cases, this history had catastrophic and long-lasting effects on the original inhabitants. As noted above, indigenous populations in each of these societies are at or near the bottom of the scale of socio-economic welfare.
- Despite this record, the disruptions and displacements that have occurred in each of these societies have not resulted in the complete disappearance of indigenous peoples, either through warfare and disease or through assimilation. In each case, indigenous populations survive, many of them not simply as aggregations of individuals but as distinct communities concentrated on remnant lands that have been the keys to their survival and over which they exercise varying levels of control.
- Furthermore, in all four cases the indigenous populations – either as individuals or as communities – have long occupied legal positions that differ in critical ways from those of mainstream populations. These positions vary from country to country and have changed over time, but indigenous legal distinctions vis-à-vis the mainstream has been a prominent feature of each country's history. Among the issues debated in all four countries and not entirely resolved in any has been that of the rights of indigenous peoples to govern themselves in their own ways and to shape their relations with encompassing societies in ways of their own choosing – in short, rights to self-determination. These rights have been variously challenged, ignored, undermined, acknowledged or modestly supported over the years and across these cases, but as the twenty-first century gets under way, they remain at the very heart of indigenous concerns and of inter-group tensions in each case.

These commonalities suggest that comparative enquiry across these four countries is by no means misplaced. On the contrary, the mix of convergence and variance invites comparison: why have the patterns of inter-group relations and of indigenous political and economic development varied in the ways they have?

The present enquiry, while prompted in part by these commonalities, begins with a further pattern shared across these countries, but not included in the above list: the gap between indigenous political assertions and the responses of states.

Indigenous assertion and state response

Recently a senior official of the Canadian government remarked, in a private conversation, that the government of Canada was quite willing to address issues of equality involving indigenous peoples, but was fundamentally unwilling to address issues of difference.[6] This was hardly the first time such reluctance had surfaced in Canada. In 1969, in a famous 'White Paper', the government of Pierre Elliot Trudeau, in support of the idea that 'we are all Canadians' (Perry 1996: 150), sought to end any distinct political or legal status for Canada's Aboriginal peoples. Under the government plan, these peoples would differ from other Canadians, as Armitage (1995: 80) says, 'only in ethnic origin, not in law'. Nor was the Canadian government alone. Other central governments in these societies have also been reluctant to directly address certain indigenous agendas.

What are those agendas? They are diverse, of course, but in recent decades indigenous groups in all four countries have been engaged in both tribal and supra-tribal political work on behalf of self-determination and self-governance.[7] The core of their argument is about rights. From a Western perspective, the argument is rooted in an evolving, if contested, body of international law (see, e.g., Anaya 1996; Havemann 1999; Tully 2000); from an indigenous perspective, in the priority and continuity of indigenous ties to the land and in the personhood that is substantially derivative of those ties, of shared cultural practice and of collective memory. Both perspectives support the right of indigenous peoples to determine their own futures and control their own affairs.

More specifically, this means the right to shape the political order of which they are a part, from their relationship with encompassing societies to the institutions by which they govern themselves – including the laws to which they and others are subject in their own lands – and thereby to maximize their control over lands and resources, cultural and civil affairs, and the nature and quality of community life.[8] These peoples have seldom sought, in recent decades, complete separation from those encompassing societies. Instead, they have generally envisioned 'nations within' status (Fleras and Elliott 1992), or what Anaya (1996: 112) describes as 'on the one hand autonomy and on the other participatory engagement' in the encompassing whole, an arrangement in which indigenous peoples 'are appropriately viewed as simultaneously distinct from yet parts of larger units of social and political interaction' (see also Behrendt 2001; Sanders 2002).

The outcomes of their efforts have varied across these cases. Indigenous groups have won some battles in pursuit of these ends, leading to policy changes of various kinds, to expanded indigenous self-rule within limited policy domains, to an increased indigenous voice in certain political affairs, and to the return of some lands and other resources. Other battles, however, have been lost, and the most fundamental issues of status and rights remain, in all four cases, substantially unresolved.[9]

Central governments, on the other hand, as illustrated by the Canadian case, have been reluctant to engage with the issues that form the core of indigenous concerns. They have preferred to focus on the socio-economics of integration and typically have interpreted self-government as an administrative project in which indigenous populations are allowed to manage programmes designed – usually by central governments – to address social problems and economic marginality.

In Australia, for example, Smith (2002: 3) observes that 'in recent years self-determination ... has been rejected as an active federal government policy position'. According to Sanders (2002: 2), the current government 'has preferred to focus its rhetoric on "practical" matters such as "overcoming disadvantage" and achieving better "outcomes" for Indigenous people in areas like employment, housing and health, while seemingly studiously avoiding any reference to self-determination ... ' (see also Dodson and Pritchard 1998).

Similarly, recent government policy in New Zealand, while paying some lip-service to the idea of self-determination, has been concerned primarily with 'closing the gaps' and for a time even adopted this as its official policy slogan. 'Closing the Gaps', remarks Loomis (2000: 11), 'means improving mainstream government services and targeting funding to Māori provider groups. In effect, better State intervention.' According to Humpage (2002: 45–6), the thrust of Māori affairs policy 'has been the state's desire to maintain and protect its own legitimacy from potential threats, including Māori calls for self-determination focused on the establishment of autonomous institutions and shared governance arrangements at the national level'. She goes on to point out that 'distributive justice, needs and development discourses have been used to support this preference for confining Māori claims to the domestic, dependent rights of citizenship ... Each of these discourses defines the "problem" largely in terms of Māori socio-economic status' (see also Maaka and Fleras 2000).

The exception to this pattern would seem to be, superficially at least, the United States. In the mid-1970s, in response to a nationwide movement of Indian political activism and aggressive demands by Indian nations for greater self-government and increased control over lands and other resources, the US government adopted a policy commonly known as 'self-determination'. This policy, at least on paper, acknowledged the right of Indian nations to decide for themselves what was best for them.

The rhetoric of self-determination, however, outstripped the reality. Despite the name, this was not self-determination in the classic sense. The intent was not to give Indian nations the power to reshape the political order either within tribes or in their relations with the United States. What policy-makers had in mind was more modest: a shift from federal bureaucrats to tribal ones in administrative authority over federal socio-economic support programmes (see Barsh and Trosper 1975; Deloria and Lytle 1983; Esber 1992). In other words, the federal idea was to treat self-government as self-administration, turning tribal governments into adjuncts of the federal administrative apparatus. In the years since, most federal involvement in Indian affairs has been more concerned with addressing social problems than with building indigenous capacities for genuine self-rule. This trend has been supported by recent US court decisions that have severely curtailed tribal jurisdiction and undermined indigenous rights of self-government (Getches 2001; Wilkins 2002).

In sum, central governments have tended to respond to indigenous peoples in the same ways they have responded to immigrant and other minority populations: with egalitarian and assimilative policies that attempt to address indigenous disadvantage and facilitate integration into encompassing societies. In particular, the stark discrepancy between indigenous socio-economic indicators and those of the society at large has been a matter of recurrent policy concern, generating a diverse array of initiatives designed to bring indigenous indicators more in line with the mainstream.[10]

Thus there is a significant mismatch between the ambitions of indigenous peoples and the responses of states. States generally have been more willing to engage with socio-economic issues of equity and access than the political issues of self-determination and difference that often have mattered more to indigenous peoples.[11]

It is not difficult to understand why. As Fleras (1999: 188) remarks, 'At stake in the ethno-politics of indigeneity are fundamental challenges to the conventions and tacit assumptions that underpin the governance of White-settler dominions.' Indigenous self-determination challenges state concerns about societal cohesion and universality ('we are all the same'). In cases where indigenous peoples potentially control significant natural resources, it threatens the ability of the state to utilize those resources or facilitate their movement on to the market; and it generally undermines the state's ability to tightly control either what happens within its borders or the political order itself, forcing the state to consider – in at least some areas of political structure – a decision-making partnership. As a result, and as Humpage (2002: 85) points out in regard to New Zealand, central governments concerned with indigenous issues have moved towards a rhetoric of distributive justice, 'which focuses on the narrow interest of redistributing socio-economic goods', and a needs-based discussion that positions indigenous persons 'as disadvantaged citizens who need "help" in achieving a similar socio-economic status' to non-indigenous persons. In short, reluctant to address indigenous self-determination, states instead address indigenous poverty.

But what if the two are connected? What if self-determination is a necessary element in the struggle against poverty? In fact, there is compelling evidence from at least one case – American Indian nations in the United States – that these two sets of issues are related in practical and concrete terms.

Indigenous poverty and self-determination: the US case

The pattern of American Indian poverty The indigenous peoples of the United States – commonly known to themselves and others as American Indians or Native Americans – are among the country's poorest citizens. American Indian reservations, as the reserved lands belonging to Indian nations are called, include a number of America's poorest places, and reservation-based populations rank at the bottom, or near the bottom, of the scale of income, employment, health, housing, education and other indices of poverty (Henson et al. forthcoming).

Strikingly, however, this situation is not uniform across Indian nations. In the last quarter or so of the twentieth century, some Indian nations began doing significantly better than others, building sustainable economies that fitted their own strategies and criteria of economic success. Furthermore, this uneven pattern of economic performance is not easily explained by many of the usual economic factors such as natural resource endowments, educational attainment or location, which vary widely across the more successful of these nations. Nor is the pattern easily explained by internal colonialism or dependency. While their histories of interaction with the colonial power have varied, Indian nations in the United States, excluding Alaska, have been subject to a broadly similar regime of legal and political domination.[12] The regime readily accounts for their descent into poverty, but not for differential success in escaping poverty.

Explaining the pattern In the mid-1980s, the Harvard Project on American Indian Economic Development began a research effort designed to explain the emerging pattern of indigenous economic success. What was enabling some Indian nations to break away from the overall pattern of seemingly intractable poverty? What were the conditions for sustained economic development on American Indian reservations?

This research effort, continuing today through the Harvard Project and its sister organization, the Native Nations Institute for Leadership, Management, and Policy at the University of Arizona, has produced results with policy-significant implications. Across a sample of nearly seventy Indian nations, the most consistent predictors of sustainable economic development on reservations are not economic factors such as location, educational attainment or natural resource endowments but rather largely political ones. Three have proved particularly important.

- *Sovereignty or self-rule.* Indigenous peoples need to have genuine decision-making power in their own hands, from constitution-making to law-making to policy. The primary reason for this is accountability: it links decision-makers and the consequences of their decisions.
- *Capable governing institutions.* Indigenous peoples have to be able to exercise decision-making power effectively. Doing so requires institutional stability, depoliticized dispute resolution mechanisms such as tribal courts, depoliticized management of resources and enterprises, skilled administration, and other provisions. These create an environment of governmental action that is stable, fair, competent and reliable, shifting the focus of government towards nation-building and away from factional battles over resources.[13]
- *A congruence between formal governing institutions and indigenous political culture.* There has to be a match between the formal institutions of governance and prevailing ideas within the community or nation about how authority should be organized and exercised. This cultural match is the source of government's legitimacy with those being governed, and therefore a source of its effectiveness (see Lipset 1963). One of the handicaps facing American Indian nations has been the stark mismatch between indigenous social and political organization on the one hand and, on the other, an imposed overlay of governing institutions designed largely by the US government in the 1930s. This has tended to produce tribal governments that lack support with their own citizens, have difficulty getting things done, and easily become objects of political opportunism and factional conflict.

Where these three factors are in place, community assets – from natural resources to location to human capital – begin to pay off. Where they are missing, such assets are typically squandered or fail to yield their potential.

In short, it is the political factors which either limit or release the potential of economic and other assets.[14]

The meaning and role of self-rule The first of these factors – sovereignty or self-rule – is of critical interest to this discussion. Sovereignty or self-rule appears to be a necessary, but not sufficient, condition for sustainable development on indigenous lands.

I say 'sovereignty *or* self-rule' because of the ideas of exclusivity and indivisibility often attached to the term 'sovereignty'. The protection and expansion of 'tribal sovereignty' have long been central political objectives of American Indian nations, but the term has not necessarily implied separate statehood or absolute authority vested in Indian hands. On the contrary, its common usage in Indian politics has tended to accommodate the possibility of a shared or limited sovereignty, a usage that has roots in, among other places, the Marshall trilogy of US Supreme Court decisions in the 1820s and early 1830s that described Indian societies as domestic dependent nations that, none the less, remained distinct political communities and retained exclusive authority within their territories.[15] Within this usage, one can imagine a sovereignty that is flexible both in the degree and the scope of authority across institutional or policy domains and which is tailored to support a particular relationship between peoples or nations. In some domains it may be an exclusive sovereignty; in some, it may be shared. Sovereignty thus becomes a continuous as opposed to a dichotomous variable.[16]

This usage, however, is less common outside the United States, where sovereignty is often viewed in zero-sum terms: to the extent that 'we' have it, 'you' don't.[17] The term self-rule, on the other hand, appears to carry less definitional baggage.

In any case, the core question from a development viewpoint is simple and can be phrased in a number of ways: Who controls the primary relationships involved? Who is exercising decision-making power? Who is calling the shots within a given policy domain or set of decisions? Who's in charge? To the degree that the answer to such questions is the indigenous nation, this is an example of indigenous self-rule. To the degree that the answer is someone else, it is the absence of self-rule.

The US research noted above shows that as Indian nations expand the scope and degree of their own decision-making power, the chances of sustainable economic development rise. This is particularly so in certain domains such as constitutional authority, the design of governing institutions, law-making, the management of lands and resources, the organization of civil society, and the determination of strategies for community and economic development. In such areas, the likelihood of achieving sustainable development rises as power and authority are devolved to indigenous nations or communities, moving non-indigenous entities, including central governments, from decision-making to resource roles and freeing indigenous peoples to decide these things for themselves and by their own criteria.

Admittedly, the shift in jurisdictional power is in itself no guarantee of sustainable development; it merely makes such development possible. As the research results summarized above indicate, more is needed. Those nations making the decisions have to be capable of governing well. They have to put in place an institutional environment that their citizens support and which can encourage and sustain economic activity and community initiatives that fit their strategic objectives and opportunities. But self-rule itself remains essential. Jurisdiction that is not backed up by effective governing institutions will be unproductive, but a set of well-designed governing institutions that lack jurisdictional authority will be toothless. In either case, the result will be something other than sustainable development.

Why does self-rule play such a large role in producing these effects? There are several reasons. First, with self-rule, decision-making reflects indigenous agendas and knowledge, making it more likely that solutions to problems will be appropriate and informed and, therefore, viable. Second, it puts development resources in indigenous hands, allowing a more efficient use of those resources to meet indigenous objectives. Third, it fosters citizen engagement in economic and community development, something effectively discouraged – with the attendant human energy being wasted – when the nation lacks substantive power. Fourth – and most importantly – it shifts accountability. Devolution makes governmental decision-making accountable to those most directly affected. The decision-makers themselves pay the price of bad decisions and reap the benefits of good ones. Consequently, and allowing time for a learning curve, decision quality improves. For generations, authority over indigenous peoples not only in the USA but in Australia, New Zealand and Canada has rested with non-indigenous governments, which have seldom been held accountable to the indigenous peoples they have governed. This divorce between those with the authority to make decisions and those bearing the consequences of those decisions has resulted in an extraordinary and continuing record of central government policy failure in all four countries.

Self-determination as an anti-poverty policy As already noted, when the USA moved to the 'self-determination' policy, its intent was modest: to bring

Indian nations into the administration of federal programmes and quash Indian complaints about lack of input. But with the federal government on the defensive, and presented with a policy that paid at least lip-service to the idea of tribal control over tribal futures, many Indian nations moved quickly to assert self-governing powers, variously redesigning governing institutions previously designed by outsiders, taking over management of resources, retooling development strategies, and displacing federal decision-makers in an assortment of reservation matters. Some of these assertions were confrontational. Others unfolded incrementally as tribal leaders took the initiative in governmental reorganization and constitutional reform, searched for alternative funding sources through business enterprises, excluded federal representatives from decision processes, stopped asking permission before acting, and filled the governmental gaps left by inadequate, incompetent or paternalistic federal administration.

As they did so, those nations that also backed up their asserted powers with effective and culturally congruent governing institutions began to see significant results. Among these were reduced unemployment, reduced welfare rolls, the emergence of viable and diverse economic enterprises – both tribal and private – on reservation lands, more effective administration of social services and programmes, including those addressing language and cultural concerns, and improved management of natural resources. In case after case, such nations proved to be much better at running their own affairs and managing their own resources than federal administrators had ever been.[18]

The US government had inadvertently stumbled on the only policy that – in three-quarters of a century of federal attempts to improve socio-economic conditions on American Indian reservations – actually made significant progress against reservation poverty. While the United States may not have intended the 'self-determination' policy launched in the 1970s to include constitutional authority and expanded tribal jurisdiction, a number of Indian nations chose to interpret it that way and benefited enormously from doing so. Self-determination, it turned out, was an effective anti-poverty policy – the first ever in US relations with Indian nations.

The transferability of US results

The American Indian experience connects self-determination and self-governance with overcoming poverty. It argues that the way to attack socio-economic disadvantage among indigenous peoples is not primarily by organizing centrally designed programmes addressing poverty and its related social pathologies – although such programmes can provide tribes with needed resources and expertise – but instead by substantially expanding the jurisdictional authority of those nations and empowering them to develop capable governing institutions that in turn can support sustainable, self-determined economies and social programmes of their own design.

But how generalizable is the US case? Can it be extended to Australia, New Zealand and Canada? Could expanded jurisdiction and constitutional authority, backed up by effective and culturally congruent governing institutions, yield comparable results in indigenous economic and community well-being?

Only systematic research can answer such questions definitively,[19] but I see little theoretical basis for believing the US results are inapplicable to these other situations. Specific development outcomes obviously depend on other factors as well, however, and the translation of these results into practical policy initiatives in other countries will require careful consideration of specific indigenous situations. At least three issues appear to be important: the economic circumstances of various indigenous peoples; the problem of identifying appropriate units of collective authority; and the willingness of mainstream societies to tolerate difference and invest in indigenous capacities. I consider the first two of these here and the last in the concluding section of this chapter.

Economic circumstances Within-country variation in economic resources and opportunities obviously has major impacts on the development potential of indigenous peoples. To pick an obvious and extreme US example, Indian and Eskimo nations located in remote regions of Alaska or on very small land bases face narrower economic opportunity sets than those faced by Indian nations located near large metropolitan areas or on large land bases. Similarly, variation in human capital can affect the ability of indigenous peoples to take advantage of certain kinds of opportunities – or at least delay action in response to those opportunities while human capital investments are made.

Such variation is apparent in all four countries. Many First Nations in Canada have been left with minuscule land bases, or are located far from markets and transportation systems. Many Australian Aboriginal communities are remote. The circumstances of Māori peoples likewise vary across the country. Some groups have higher levels of education or labour force experience than others.

Such variation does not negate the US results; it is apparent in the USA as well. Self-determination, self-governance and appropriate and effective governing institutions create an environment in which sustainable development becomes possible, but the nature and extent of development and of its impact on the community depend on what each indigenous nation or people has to work with and on the specific decisions it makes. What the US case indicates is that economic assets – whatever they may be – are far more likely to be productive where indigenous nations have decision-making power and the institutional capacity to back it up.

The social unit of authority But where should decision-making power and institutional capacity be located? Self-determination and self-governance require subjects, in the grammatical sense: someone has to do the determining and governing. In which social units do the rights to self-determination reside? Within which social units should the institutions of self-governance be built? Who, in these processes, is the 'self'?

In all four countries, one of the most prominent results of a century or more of colonialism, land expropriation, ethnic cleansing, imposed population movements, assimilationist programmes and related settler-state policies has been the transformation of indigenous group boundaries, many of which were already porous and dynamic long before European contact. Some collectivities disappeared while others were mixed or fragmented; some boundaries were invented out of whole cloth while others were solidified out of pre-existing relationships.

While these processes were common in the United States, the particular form they have taken there has provided, in most cases, unusual clarity about the identity of the 'self'. Despite urbanization and intermarriage among American Indian groups, tribal societies have continued to exist and, in some cases, thrive on Indian reservations. While warfare, colonialism and assimilationist programmes came close to extinguishing the Indian land base, the remnant parcels, some of them substantial, have combined with the treaty process and the peculiarities of federal Indian administration to simplify and rigidify inter-group boundaries that had previously been more complex or fluid. Although this process often ignored indigenous perceptions, it unintentionally provided a foundation for tribal continuity and survival (Cornell 1988b).

Today, both as political units and as frameworks of collective identity, most Indian nations remain robust. The 'self' in self-governance has in most cases been apparent, embedded both in continuing social relations and cultural practice and in formal political relationships established by treaty between individual Indian nations and the United States. This clarifies where constitutional authority and jurisdiction should be vested and focuses the challenge of nation-building.[20]

The situation has been more variable in the other three countries. A recurring concern in Australia, for example, according to Bern and Dodds (2000: 163), 'is how indigenous self-government and representation should be structured, given the array of goals that self-government is supposed to meet, and the diversity of Aboriginal communities'. Much of the organizational structure of inter-group relations in Australia today is embedded in local or regional, federally funded, indigenous service organizations or in the national Aboriginal and Torres Strait Islander Commission (ATSIC). Sanders (2002) argues that both the service organizations and ATSIC represent indigenous interests, albeit different sets of interests and in different ways, but he also acknowledges that many local Aboriginal communities see neither service organizations nor an elected national body as adequately representing their concerns.

Bern and Dodds discuss the situation in the Northern Territory, where Aboriginal polity is constituted in three primary forms: land councils, local communities, and kinship/language groups. Only the last has traditional roots. Local communities 'are largely based on pastoral containment and/or government/mission institutions', while the land councils are products of federal statute (2000: 174). Only a few groups, particularly those with a geographical base or strong language ties, have been effective at organizing 'above the level of the local community' (ibid.: 175). David Martin argues that in much of Cape York 'few if any Indigenous community-wide political institutions exist, apart from the quasi-local government community councils instituted under State legislation, and regional bodies ...' (2001: 14). Many communities are products of enforced relocation to mission and government settlements; the councils that have emerged in these situations, he claims, have 'neither the political nor the moral authority' required for effective self-governance. Any new institutional order will require identifying – and perhaps rebuilding – 'clear centres of political authority' (ibid.: 17) in these communities: a difficult task. Meanwhile, Diane Smith (2002) and others argue for a 'regionally dispersed, layered' system of self-governance in which local communities are jurisdictional building blocks, aggregated for certain purposes into larger structures.

A different indigenous history in New Zealand has led to some similar issues. According to the Māori historian Ranginui Walker, prior to European incursions the *hapu*, sometimes described as a clan,[21] was 'the main political unit that controlled a defined stretch of tribal territory' (1990: 64). Angela Ballara (1998) has traced the historical processes that encouraged Māori to alter this political structure. Such structures are generally dynamic, but the European agenda shaped the process of change in particular ways. Negotiating over land, Europeans searched for and encouraged paramount chiefs at ever larger scales of social organization. Māori responded to land pressure in part by combining in larger units to defend their interests. Over time, both Europeans and Māori tended to construct Māori – for purposes of inter-group relations – in fewer and larger social groups. The result was to privilege *iwi* (conceived as peoples, tribes or confederations of *hapu*), over *hapu*. Formal government policy and the organization of social programmes have tended to continue the trend in recent years, leading to what Manuhuia Barcham (2000: 141) calls 'the iwi-isation of Māori society'.

But the situation is further complicated by continuing diversification. A majority of Māori now live in cities. Along with the more general integration of many Māori into New Zealand society, this has produced new sets of interests that do not easily combine into *hapu* or *iwi* constructions. Speaking of the Māori concept of *tino rangatiratanga*, a polysemous concept that combines ideas of, among other things, sovereignty, self-determination, autonomy, nationhood and chieftainship, Maaka and Fleras remark that 'for some, tino rangatiratanga resides within the hapu; for others, the iwi; for still others only Māori as a collectivity; and for yet others still, within the individual' (2000: 100). Under these conditions, what form should self-government take? (see Humpage, Chapter 9).

In Canada, as in the United States, a lengthy history of treaty-making, land loss and paternalistic federal administration has reshaped Aboriginal political relationships and group boundaries. Particularly under the Indian Act of 1876 and its subsequent amendments, the government of Canada recognized various groups of Aboriginal people as bands, recognized certain lands as reserved to those bands, replaced indigenous governmental forms and practices with imposed ones, and, on behalf of assimilationist goals, regulated numerous aspects of Aboriginal life. While some group identities and boundaries supported by federal recognition made sense, others appear to have been chosen at the whim of local administrators or to be simply the result of a dispersed geography.[22] Widely distributed peoples sharing culture and language were often broken up and isolated from each other in small numbers on tiny acreages. Their modest self-governing powers were exercised through imposed institutions that had 'no ... congruence with the cultural premises of aboriginal people' (Scott 1993: 322). Today, Canada's indigenous population is much smaller, in absolute numbers, than the Indian population of the United States, but it is divided into many more First Nations located on many more, and generally much smaller, reserves.

In the 1990s, one of the major concerns of Canada's Royal Commission on Aboriginal Peoples was the effect of this historically generated fragmentation on self-government. The commission concluded that some Aboriginal bands and communities were too small to effectively exercise self-governing powers. 'The problem', said the commission, 'is that the historical Aboriginal nations were undermined by disease, relocations and the full array of assimilationist government policies. They were fragmented into bands, reserves and small settlements. Only some operate as collectivities now. They will have to reconstruct themselves as nations' (Royal Commission on Aboriginal Peoples 1996: 26). It went on to suggest that the thousand or so Aboriginal settlements or reserve communities in Canada comprised only '60 to 80' such nations, based on bonds of culture and identity (ibid.: 25). While some Canadian First Nations would dispute those numbers and might see themselves differently, the underlying issue remains: at what level of the social order should institution-building appropriately occur? Should it be in bands, tribes, confederations of tribes, or in different entities in different situations?

These legacies of colonialism and paternalism will not be easy to overcome. In many cases, finding appropriate social units of authority will be complex and time-consuming, but the fact that such units are sometimes no longer obvious is not an argument against self-determination. On the contrary, it should sharpen the focus of both indigenous peoples and central governments on a critical first step in nation building.[23] In searching for such units, several things should be borne in mind. First, the outcome should be home-grown. Imposed units are likely to be failed units. Second, the effort will take time. Rebuilding a sense of nationhood requires not so much exhortation or deadlines as it does careful deliberation and broad community participation. Third, both indigenous leaders and central governments will have to wrestle with two requirements of such units: they have to have legitimacy with the people they are going to govern, and they have to provide an efficacious foundation for governance. Combining legitimacy and efficacy is one of the major challenges of nation-building.

Conclusion: policy implications

There is substantial evidence from the US case that indigenous self-determination has been a critical element in the effort by American Indian nations to improve their socio-economic conditions. While indigenous situations in Australia, New Zealand, Canada and the USA vary, certain commonalities encourage comparative enquiry and a search for transferable policy insights. They suggest that it would be a mistake for other governments to dismiss the US evidence.

The overall policy implications appear to be three. First, the refusal to come to grips with indigenous demands for self-determination cripples the effort – prominent in all four countries – to overcome indigenous poverty. The two are profoundly connected, and public policy has to take this into account.

Second, implementing indigenous self-determination and building self-governing capacities will require both innovation and a diversity of models. A one-size-fits-all approach within any one country – a common temptation for central governments concerned with administrative control and convenience – is bound to fail.[24] It will come to grief on both the varied cultural distinctiveness that indigenous peoples have struggled to preserve and on the social organizational diversity that each country's history has imposed on its indigenous peoples.

Third, the best way to avoid the one-size-fits-all recipe for failure is to let indigenous peoples decide for themselves who the appropriate self in self-governance is and how self-governing institutions should be structured – and to accept the variety of relationships and governance solutions that will surely result. This is what self-determination means. Furthermore, not only is outsider decision-making in this regard the antithesis of self-determination, but neither collective units nor governing institutions that are imposed by outside authorities are likely to command the respect or allegiance of the peoples on whom they are imposed – which means they will not work.

The question of *what will actually work* ought to be of some concern to central governments. Surely the rights of indigenous peoples to reshape the political order they have been forced into and to govern themselves in their own ways provides a substantial argument for self-determination. But what the US data show is that there is an economic argument for it as well, not only from the point of view of indigenous peoples but also from the point of view of central governments and mainstream societies. They, too, have something to gain.

Poverty, after all, is expensive. Its costs come in at least two forms. First, the attempt to alleviate indigenous poverty through social service provision is an expensive strategy, tending to consist of palliatives instead of cures and, therefore, to be never-ending. Second, poverty is expensive in terms of lost resources, trapping human beings in dependency instead of helping them contribute to their own and other societies. The US data are notable in this regard, indicating that self-determining indigenous nations not only are more likely to build economies that support their own peoples, but in the process also spin off significant benefits to non-indigenous communities through jobs, expanded vendor business, reduced welfare rolls, and the like. Economically, self-determination is a win-win proposition.

If central governments reject the rights-based argument for self-determination, one hopes their economic self-interest will lead them to reconsider. As my colleague Joseph Kalt and I have written elsewhere (Cornell and Kalt 1998), the US record is clear: if central governments wish to perpetuate indigenous poverty, its attendant ills and bitterness, and its high costs, the best way to do so is to undermine tribal sovereignty and self-determination. But if they want to overcome indigenous poverty and all that goes with it, then they should support tribal sovereignty and self-determination, and they should invest in helping indigenous peoples build the governing capacity to back up sovereign powers with effective governments of their own design.

Notes

1 For example, according to the United Nations Development Progamme's 2002 *World Development Report*, in 2000 Canada ranked third among countries of the world, Australia fifth, the USA sixth, and New Zealand nineteenth on the Human Development Index, which combines indicators of knowledge, individual longevity and the standard of living in each country (United Nations Development Programme 2003).

2 'Colleagues' in this context refers to the community of scholars, practitioners and students concerned with indigenous governance and development issues and affiliated with the Native Nations Institute at the University of Arizona and the Harvard Project on American Indian Economic Development at Harvard University.

3 Although some of us have served as advisers on research efforts in both countries.

4 The figure for the USA is from <http://www.census.gov/prod/2002pubs/c2kbr01-15.pdf>; for Australia, from <http://www.abs.gov.au/Ausstats/abs%40.nsf>; for Canada, from <http://www.ainc-inac.gc.ca/nr/wc/bdg2k3h_e.html>; for New Zealand, from <http://www.stats.govt.nz/domino/external/pasfull/pasfull.nsf/web/Media+Release+2001+Census+Snapshot+16+Iwi?open>. All were accessed in March 2003.

5 For additional information on indigenous poverty in these four countries, see Hunter (1999); Royal Commission on Aboriginal Peoples (1996); Durie (1998: ch. 4); Henson et al. (forthcoming).

6 Reported to me in Ottawa in January 2003 by the second party to the conversation. See also Salée (1995) for further discussion of this issue in Canada.

7 The range of such work is enormous in all four countries. Illustrations and accounts can be found in, among many other places, Walker (1990); Indigenous Constitutional Convention Secretariat (*c.* 1999); Smith (1993); Cornell (1988a); Nagel (1996).

8 Anaya (1996: 81) describes self-determination as consisting of 'two normative strains: First, in what may be called its *constitutive* aspect, self-determination requires that the governing institutional order be substantially the creation of processes guided by the will of the people, or peoples, governed. Second, in what may be called its *ongoing* aspect, self-determination requires that the governing institutional order, independently of the processes leading to its creation or alteration, be one under which people may live and develop freely on a continuous basis.'

9 The literature on indigenous status and rights in these societies is vast, but see, for example, Ivison et al. (2000); Ivison (2002, 2003); Arthur (2001); Sanders (2002); Nettheim et al. (2002); Fleras and Spoonley (1999); Durie (2000); Price (2001); Royal Commission on Aboriginal Peoples (1996); McNeil (1998); Mohawk Council of Akwesasne (2002); Getches (2001); Wilkins (2002); Cornell et al. (2002).

10 Such policies have had decidedly mixed results in all four countries. For example, while considerable progress has been made in some areas, such as certain aspects of indigenous health, much less has been made in terms of the more general phenomenon of indigenous poverty.

11 In drawing a distinction between indigenous assertions and state response, I do not mean to suggest that indigenous peoples have been uninterested in equity or in addressing the grim realities of poverty. But indigenous politics in all four countries have tended to be recognitive first and distributive second. While there are exceptions, particularly among urban populations, rights to land, recognition and self-government have tended to take priority over socio-economic issues. This has distinguished much indigenous politics from the more distributive politics of immigrant groups or other, non-indigenous minority populations.

12 On Alaska, see Case and Voluck (2002); Berger (1985); and Cornell and Kalt (2003).

13 The idea that governing institutions matter to economic performance and societal well-being is well-established. See, for example, North (1990); Oberschall (1990); Barro (1991); Ostrom (1992); Knack and Keefer (1995); Egnal (1996); and La Porta et al. (1997, 1998, 1999).

14 For these results, see in particular Cornell and Kalt (1992, 1995, 1997a, 1997b, 2000, 2003); also Krepps and Caves (1994); Jorgensen (2000a); Jorgensen and Taylor (2000); Jorgensen et al. (forthcoming); and Harvard Project on American Indian Economic Development (1999, 2000, 2003).

15 *Cherokee Nation* v. *Georgia*, 30 US (5 Pet.) 1 (1831); *Worcester* v. *Georgia*, 31 U.S. (6 Pet.) 515 (1832). See the discussion of these decisions in Deloria and Lytle (1983).

16 See the discussion of sovereignty in Maaka and Fleras (2000: 92–4) and of devolution in Smith (2002: 3–5).

17 See Tully (2000: 51), who describes this view as holding that 'either the dominant state exercises exclusive jurisdiction or the indigenous people do', with no middle ground. Labelling this as one of the 'underlying presumptions' that states use 'to legitimize the system of internal colonization', he notes that it ignores the possibility that 'jurisdiction can be shared'.

18 Cornell and Kalt (1992, 1998); Cornell et al. (1998); Jorgensen (1997, 2000b); Jorgensen and Taylor (2000); Krepps (1992); Krepps and Caves (1994); Wakeling et al. (2001); Harvard Project on American Indian Economic Development (1999, 2000, 2003).

19 Such research has begun in Canada and finds evidence of similar relationships. See Jorgensen et al. (forthcoming); also Chandler and Lalonde (1998); and Moore et al. (1990).

20 Exceptions to this overall pattern include peoples forced together on to reservations or into shared treaty-making and others fragmented by warfare, forced migration and other events. Both Alaska and California also include many small Native groups located on small land bases, limiting human capital pools and prompting debate about building joint institutions of larger scale and broader jurisdiction.

21 Walker (1990: 63–5) identifies three basic units of Māori society: the *whanau* is an extended family, the *hapu* is a descent group composed of related *whanau*, and the *iwi* is a descent group composed of related *hapu*. Ballara (1998: 161) describes *hapu* as 'politically independent corporate and social groups which also regarded themselves as categorically identified with a wider set of people'. Like Walker, she emphasizes the prominence of *hapu*, but she also notes that this tripartite organization is neither as rigid nor as static as a simple description might imply (ibid.: 17–19).

22 There are similar cases in the USA but, thanks in part to differences in the treaty process, they are less prevalent than in Canada.

23 A number of indigenous peoples have actively taken that step at different times, from the Ktunaxa-Kinbasket Tribal Council in Canada to the Yakama Nation in the United States. See, for example, Native Nations Institute for Leadership, Management, and Policy (2001) and Yakima Nation Review (1978).

24 For discussions of a recent effort by the Canadian government to adopt just such an approach, see Mohawk Council of Akwesasne (2002) and Cornell, Jorgensen and Kalt (2002).

References

Anaya, S. J. (1996) *Indigenous Peoples in International Law*, New York: Oxford University Press

Armitage, A. (1995) *Comparing the Policy of Aboriginal Assimilation: Australia, Canada, and New Zealand*, Vancouver: University of British Columbia Press

Arthur, W. S. (2001) 'Indigenous autonomy in Australia: some concepts, issues and examples', Discussion Paper no. 220/2001, Centre for Aboriginal Economic Policy Research, Australian National University

Ballara, A. (1998) *Iwi: The Dynamics of Māori Tribal Organization from c. 1769 to c. 1945*, Wellington: Victoria University Press

Barcham, M. (2000) '(De)constructing the politics of indigeneity', in D. Ivison, P. Patton and W. Sanders (eds), *Political Theory and the Rights of Indigenous Peoples*, Cambridge: Cambridge University Press, pp. 137–51

Barro, R. (1991) 'Economic growth in a cross section of countries', *Quarterly Journal of Economics*, 106: 407–43

Barsh, R. L. and R. L. Trosper (1975) 'Title I of the Indian Self-Determination and Education Assistance Act of 1975', *American Indian Law Review*, 3: 361–95

Beavon, D. and M. Cooke (2001) 'Measuring Aboriginal well-being in four countries: an application of the UNDP's Human Development Index to Canada, the United States, New Zealand, and Australia', presentation to the Population Association of America, Washington, DC, 29–31 March

Behrendt, L. (2001) 'Indigenous self-determination in the age of globalization', *Balayi: Culture, Law and Colonialism*, 3: 1–7

Berger, T. R. (1985) *Village Journey: The Report of the Alaska Native Review Commission*, New York: Hill and Wang

Bern, J. and S. Dodds (2000) 'On the plurality of interests: Aboriginal self-government and land rights', in D. Ivison, P. Patton and W. Sanders (eds), *Political Theory and the Rights of Indigenous Peoples*, Cambridge: Cambridge University Press, pp. 163–79

Case, D. and D. A. Voluck (2002) *Alaska Natives and American Laws*, 2nd edn, Fairbanks: University of Alaska Press

Chandler, M. J. and C. Lalonde (1998) 'Cultural continuity as a hedge against suicide in Canada's First Nations', *Journal of Transcultural Psychiatry*, 35: 191–219

Cornell, S. (1988a) *The Return of the Native: American Indian Political Resurgence*, New York: Oxford University Press

— (1988b) 'The transformations of tribe: organization and self-concept in Native American ethnicities', *Ethnic and Racial Studies*, 11(1): 27–47

Cornell, S. and J. P. Kalt (1992) 'Reloading the dice: improving the chances for economic development on American indian reservations', in S. Cornell and J. P. Kalt (eds), *What Can Tribes Do? Strategies and Institutions in American Indian Economic Development*, Los Angeles, CA: American Indian Studies Center, UCLA, pp. 1–59

— (1995) 'Where does economic development really come from? Constitutional rule among the contemporary Sioux and Apache', *Economic Inquiry*, 33 (July): 402–26

— (1997a) 'Cultural evolution and constitutional public choice: institutional diversity and economic performance on American indian reservations', in J. Lott (ed.), *Uncertainty and Evolution in Economics: Essays in Honour of Armen A. Alchian*, London and New York: Routledge, pp. 116–42

— (1997b) 'Successful economic development and heterogeneity of governmental form on American indian reservations', in M. S. Grindle (ed.), *Getting Good Government: Capacity Building in the Public Sectors of Developing Countries*, Cambridge, MA: Harvard Institute for International Development, pp. 257–96

— (1998) 'Sovereignty and nation-building: the development challenge in Indian country today', *American Indian Culture and Research Journal*, 22(3): 187–214

— (2000) 'Where's the glue: institutional and cultural foundations of American Indian economic development', *Journal of Socio-Economics*, 29: 443–70

— (2003) 'Alaska native self-governance and service delivery: what works?', Joint Occasional Papers in Native Affairs no. 2003–1, Native Nations Institute for Leadership, Management, and Policy, and Harvard Project on American Indian Economic Development, Tucson: Udall Center for Studies in Public Policy, University of Arizona

Cornell, S., M. Jorgensen and J. P. Kalt (2002) 'The First Nations Governance Act: implications of research findings from the United States and Canada', report to the Office of the British Columbia Regional Vice-Chief, Assembly of First Nations, Native Nations Institute for Leadership, Management, and Policy, University of Arizona

Cornell, S., J. P. Kalt, M. Krepps and J. Taylor (1998) 'American Indian gaming policy and its socio-economic effects', report to the National Gambling Impact Study Commission, July, Cambridge, MA: Economics Resource Group

Deloria, V. and C. M. Lytle (1983) *American Indians, American Justice*, Austin: University of Texas Press

Dodson, M. and S. Pritchard (1998) 'Recent developments in indigenous policy: the abandonment of self-determination?', *Indigenous Law Bulletin*, 4(15): 4–6

Durie, M. (1998) *Te Mana, Te Kāwanatanga: The Politics of Māori Self-Determination*, Auckland: Oxford University Press

— (2000) 'Contemporary Māori development: issues and broad directions', Working Paper no. 7/2000, Development Studies Programme, University of Waikato

Egnal, M. (1996) *Divergent Paths: How Culture and Institutions Have Shaped North American Growth*, New York: Oxford University Press

Esber, G. S. (1992) 'Shortcomings of the Indian self-determination policy', in G. Castile and R. Bee (eds), *State and Reservation: New Perspectives on Federal Indian Policy,* Tucson: University of Arizona Press, pp. 212–23

Fleras, A. (1999) 'Politicising indigeneity: ethno-politics in white settler dominions', in P. Havemann (ed.), *Indigenous Peoples' Rights in Australia, Canada, and New Zealand,* Auckland: Oxford University Press, pp. 187–234

Fleras, A. and J. L. Elliott (1992) *The 'Nations Within': Aboriginal–State Relations in Canada, the United States, and New Zealand*, Toronto: Oxford University Press

Fleras, A. and P. Spoonley (1999) *Recalling Aotearoa: Indigenous Politics and Ethnic Relations in New Zealand*, Auckland: Oxford University Press

Getches, D. H. (2001) 'Beyond Indian law: the Rehnquist court's pursuit of states' rights, color-blind justice and mainstream values', *Minnesota Law Review*, 86(2): 267–362

Harvard Project on American Indian Economic Development (1999) *Honoring Nations: Tribal Governance Success Stories, 1999*, Cambridge, MA: Harvard Project on American Indian Economic Development, Harvard University

— (2000) *Honoring Nations: Tribal Governance Success Stories, 2000*, Cambridge. MA: Harvard Project on American Indian Economic Development, Harvard University

— (2003) *Honoring Nations: Tribal Governance Success Stories, 2002*, Cambridge, MA: Harvard Project on American Indian Economic Development, Harvard University.

Havemann, P. (1999) 'Chronology two: twentieth-century public international law and indigenous peoples', in P. Havemann (ed.), *Indigenous Peoples' Rights in Australia, Canada, and New Zealand*, Auckland: Oxford University Press, pp. 18–21

Henson, E., J. B. Taylor, S. Beane, K. Bishop, S. S. Black, K. W. Grant, M. Jorgensen, J. King, A. J. Lee, H. Nelson and Y. Roubideaux (forthcoming) 'Native America at the New Millennium', in Harvard Project on American Indian Economic Development, *American Indian Research and Grants Assessment Project: A Report to the Ford Foundation*

Humpage, L. V. (2002) 'Closing the Gaps? The politics of Māori affairs policy', unpublished PhD dissertation, Massey University

Hunter, B. (1999) 'Three nations, not one: indigenous and other Australian poverty', Working Paper no. 1/1999, Centre for Aboriginal Economic Policy Research, Australian National University

Indigenous Constitutional Convention Secretariat (*c.* 1999) 'Indigenous Constitutional Strategy, Northern Territory', Indigenous Constitutional Convention Secretariat, Casuarina, Northern Territory, Australia

Ivison, D. (2002) *Postcolonial Liberalism*, Cambridge: Cambridge University Press

— (2003) 'The logic of aboriginal rights', *Ethnicities*, 3(3): 321–44

Ivison, D., P. Patton and W. Sanders (eds) (2000) *Political Theory and the Rights of Indigenous Peoples*, Cambridge: Cambridge University Press

Jorgensen, M. (1997) 'Governing government', unpublished ms, John F. Kennedy School of Government, Harvard University

— (2000a) 'Bringing the background forward: evidence from Indian country on the social and cultural determinants of economic development', unpublished PhD dissertation, John F. Kennedy School of Government, Harvard University

— (2000b) 'History's lesson for HUD and tribes', unpublished ms, John F. Kennedy School of Government, Harvard University

— (ed.) (forthcoming) *Resources for Nation Building: Governance, Development, and the Future of American Indian Nations*, Tucson: University of Arizona Press

Jorgensen, M. and J. Taylor (2000) 'Patterns of Indian enterprise success: a statistical analysis of tribal and individual Indian enterprise performance', report to the National Congress of American Indians, Cambridge: Harvard Project on American Indian Economic Development, John F. Kennedy School of Government, Harvard University

Jorgensen, M., R. Akee, C. Goodswimmer and S. C. Rainie (forthcoming) 'Understanding First Nations' development success: cross-site analysis of four First Nations in Treaty 8, Alberta', Native Nations Institute for Leadership, Management, and Policy, University of Arizona

Knack, S. and P. Keefer (1995) 'Institutions and economic performance: cross-country tests using alternative institutional measures', *Economics and Politics*, 7(3): 207–27

Krepps, M. B. (1992) 'Can tribes manage their own resources? The 638 program and American Indian forestry', in S. Cornell and J. P. Kalt (eds), *What Can Tribes Do? Strategies and Institutions in American Indian Economic Development*, Los Angeles, CA: American Indian Studies Center, UCLA, pp. 179–203

Krepps, M. B. and R. E. Caves (1994) 'Bureaucrats and Indians: principal-agent relations and efficient management of tribal forest resources', *Journal of Economic Behavior and Organization*, 24 (2): 133–51

La Porta, R., F. Lopez-de-Silanes, A. Shleifer and R. W. Vishney (1997) 'Legal determinants of external finance', *Journal of Finance*, 52(3): 1,131–50

— (1998) 'Law and Finance', *Journal of Political Economy*, 106 (December): 1,113–55

— (1999) 'The quality of government', *Journal of Law, Economics and Organization*, 15 (April): 222–79

Lipset, S. M. (1963) *Political Man: The Social Bases of Politics*, New York: Anchor

Loomis, T. (2000) 'Government's role in Māori development: charting a new direction?', Working Paper no. 6/2000, Development Studies Programme, University of Waikato

McNeil, K. (1998) *Defining Aboriginal Title in the 90's: Has the Supreme Court Finally Got It Right?*, Toronto: Robarts Centre for Canadian Studies, York University

Maaka, R. and A. Fleras (2000) 'Engaging with indigeneity: tino rangatiratanga in Aotearoa', in D. Ivison, P. Patton and W. Sanders (eds), *Political Theory and the Rights of Indigenous Peoples*, Cambridge: Cambridge University Press, pp. 89–109

Martin, D. F. (2001) 'Is welfare dependency "welfare poison"?', an assessment of Noel Pearson's proposals for Aboriginal welfare reform, Discussion Paper no. 213/2001, Centre for Aboriginal Economic Policy Research, Australian National University

Mohawk Council of Akwesasne (2002) *Nation Building Process: Setting Our Path for the Future*, Cornwall, Ontario: Mohawk Council of Akwesasne

Moore, M. A., H. Forbes and L. Henderson (1990) 'The provision of primary health care services under band control: the Montreal lake case', *Native Studies Review*, 6(1): 153–64

Moran, A. (2002) 'As Australia decolonizes: indigenizing settler nationalism and the challenges of settler/indigenous relations', *Ethnic and Racial Studies*, 25(2): 1,013–42

Morse, B. W. (1998) 'Two steps forward and one step back: the frustrating pace of building a new Aboriginal–Crown relationship in Canada', in C. P. Cohen (ed.), *The Human Rights of Indigenous Peoples*, Ardsley, New York: Transnational Publishers, pp. 303–56

Nagel, J. (1996) *American Indian Ethnic Renewal: Red Power and the Resurgence of Identity and Culture*, New York: Oxford University Press

Native Nations Institute for Leadership, Management, and Policy (2001) 'Ktunaxa/Kinbasket Tribal Council: final report on governmental organization and nation building', Udall Center for Studies in Public Policy, University of Arizona, Tucson

Nettheim, G., G. D. Meyers and D. Craig (2002) *Indigenous Peoples and Governance Structures: A Comparative Analysis of Land and Resource Management*

Rights, Canberra: Aboriginal Studies Press, Australian Institute of Aboriginal and Torres Strait Islander Studies

North, D. C. (1990) *Institutions, Institutional Change and Economic Performance*, Cambridge: Cambridge University Press

Oberschall, A. (1990) 'Incentives, governance, and development in Chinese collective agriculture', in M. Hechter, K.-D. Opp and R. Wippler (eds), *Social Institutions: Their Emergence, Maintenance and Effects*, New York: Aldine de Gruyter, pp. 265–89

Ostrom, E. (1992) *Crafting Institutions for Self-Governing Irrigation Systems*, San Francisco, CA: Institute for Contemporary Studies

Perry, R. J. (1996) *From Time Immemorial: Indigenous Peoples and State Systems*, Austin: University of Texas Press

Pocock, J. G. A. (2000) 'Waitangi as mystery of state: consequences of the ascription of federative capacity to the Māori', in D. Ivison, P. Patton and W. Sanders (eds), *Political Theory and the Rights of Indigenous Peoples*, Cambridge: Cambridge University Press, pp. 25–35

Price, R. T. (2001) 'New Zealand's interim treaty settlements and arrangements – building blocks of certainty', in British Columbia Treaty Commission, *Speaking Truth to Power: A Treaty Forum*, Law Commission of Canada, pp. 135–63

Royal Commission on Aboriginal Peoples (1996) *People to People, Nation to Nation: Highlights from the Report of the Royal Commission on Aboriginal Peoples*, Ottawa: Minister of Supply and Services

Salée, D. (1995) 'Identities in conflict: the Aboriginal question and the politics of recognition in Quebec', *Ethnic and Racial Studies*, 18(2): 277–314

Sanders, W. (2002) 'Towards an Indigenous order of Australian government: rethinking self-determination as Indigenous affairs policy', Discussion Paper no. 230/2002, Centre for Aboriginal Economic Policy Research, Australian National University

Scott, C. H. (1993) 'Custom, tradition, and the politics of culture: aboriginal self-government in Canada', in N. Dyck and J. B. Waldram (eds), *Anthropology, Public Policy and Native Peoples in Canada*, Montreal: McGill-Queen's University Press, pp. 311–33

Smith, D. (1993) *The Seventh Fire: The Struggle for Aboriginal Government*, Toronto: Key Porter Books

Smith, D. E. (2002) 'Jurisdictional devolution: towards an effective model for Indigenous community self-determination', Discussion Paper no. 233/2002, Centre for Aboriginal Economic Policy Research, Australian National University

Tully, J. (2000) 'The struggles of indigenous people for and of freedom', in D. Ivison, P. Patton and W. Sanders (eds), *Political Theory and the Rights of Indigenous Peoples*, Cambridge: Cambridge University Press, pp. 36–59

United Nations Development Programme (2003) *Human Development Report 2002: Deepening Democracy in a Fragmented World*, New York: United Nations Development Programme

Wakeling, S., M. Jorgensen, S. Michaelson and M. Begay (2001) *Policing on American Indian Reservations: A Report to the National Institute of Justice*, Washington, DC: National Institute of Justice, United States Department of Justice

Walker, R. (1990) *Ka Whawhai Tonu Matou: Struggle without End*, Auckland: Penguin

Wilkins, D. (2002) *American Indian Politics and the American Political System*, Lanham, MD: Rowman and Littlefield

Yakima Nation Review (1978) '1855 Yakima Treaty chronicles', *Yakima Nation Review*, 9(3): 23

THREE | Indigenous peoples' perspectives on development

12 | Overview: indigenous peoples' perspectives on poverty and development

JOHN-ANDREW MCNEISH

The integration of indigenous peoples into development planning is no longer a new idea. Both the special nature of indigenous poverty and the possible contribution that indigenous knowledge and technology can make to sustainable development have been recognized in international development circles since the late 1980s. This recognition has been influenced by the growing number of international agreements on indigenous rights, as well as the publication of the Brundtland Report and the later statements made at the conclusion of the Rio Summit in 1992, which have been particularly influential in underlining the importance of indigenous peoples in future development. Indigenous peoples are now hailed by academics, development specialists and politicians alike as the 'guardians of nature'. The Brundtland Report states:

> These communities are the repositories of vast accumulations of traditional knowledge and experience that link humanity with its ancient origins ... It is a terrible irony that as formal development reaches more deeply into rain forests, deserts and other isolated environments, it tends to destroy the only cultures that have proved able to thrive in these environments ... Hence the recognition of traditional rights must go hand in hand with measures to protect the local institutions that enforce responsibility in resource use. And this recognition must also give local communities a decisive voice in the decisions about resource use in their area. (Brundtland et al. 1987: 114–16)

As outlined earlier in this volume, many international development organizations, including the World Bank and the Inter-American Development Bank, have drafted policies and backed projects aimed at encouraging indigenous participation in development processes. They have sought to identify strategies and techniques that fit with their recent conversions to a doctrine of sustainable development. There is no doubt that the integration of indigenous peoples into development thinking is positive, not only in terms of its contribution to cultural preservation, but also as a move towards identifying more realistic and sensitive strategies for poverty reduction. This is an issue taken up again and explored in detail in the chapter by Alarcón-Cháires. While his detailing of alternatives could be further critically nuanced, this section of the book aims to argue that there is a considerable need to rethink the assumptions of many indigenous development policies if the mistakes of previous integrative policies (so clearly described by Humpage in the case of New Zealand) are not to be repeated.

Indigenous knowledge and development

There are now numerous well-known examples of the incredible knowledge indigenous peoples have of their local environment. This knowledge is now recognized as a valuable source of ideas about sustainable development and adaptation to both environmental and economic change. It is now well documented, for instance, that the Mardu desert people have an extensive vocabulary for cloud and rain types and other weather phenomena (Tonkinson 1991: 37). They are also experts in assessing the likelihood and possible consequences of rainfall in their territory. Another elaborate form of knowledge is encountered among the Kayapó, who classify over fifty different types of diarrhoea/dysentery, each one with its respective herbal treatment (Posey 1987: 24). The Shuar people of Ecuador's Amazonian lowlands, in turn, use 800 species of plants for medicine, food, animal fodder, fuel, construction, fishing and hunting supplies (Posey 2000: 188–9).

According to Posey (ibid.: 189–90) there are numerous categories of traditional knowledge among indigenous peoples 'which clearly have great potential for application in a wide range of sustainability strategies'. Tribal peoples conserve biological diversity, and in some cases provide other environmental benefits through, for example, soil and water conservation, soil fertility enhancement, the management of game fisheries and forest management. By planting 'forest gardens' and managing the regeneration of fallow bushland in ways that take advantage of natural processes and mimic the biodiversity of natural forests, the natives of the Amazon demonstrate ways of using resources within the land's carrying capacity. Similarly, much of the world's crop diversity is in the custody of farmers who follow age-old farming and land-use practices that conserve biodiversity and provide other benefits (ibid.: 189).

Anthropology and particularly economic anthropology have gathered together an important corpus of information about the logic and techniques of non-Western economic systems and, in doing so, have contributed to wider debates in development practice about these alternatives to top-down strategies (Korovkin 1998; Goldin 1996; Smith 1984). Now, recognizing the need for local participation in development planning and the value of people's existing techniques, many international development organizations have been involved in funding research and projects designed to further study, catalogue and find a place for different kinds of indigenous knowledge within development planning and policy. As the chapter by Eversole, Ridgeway and Mercer argues, however, this research has not been related closely enough with the preoccupations that indigenous people define for themselves. Despite some interest in better engagement with indigenous populations and their knowledge of the local environment, international development professionals and governments by and large remain focused on the development of anti-poverty programmes initiated, or at least funded, by outsiders. As a result indigenous peoples' own initiatives and strategies have remained largely invisible, except in cases where they can easily be capitalized on within existing external industries and markets, for example biotechnology, organic products, crafts, etc.

While there has been some discussion within academic circles of the possible contribution of indigenous ideas to sustainable development, or ethno-economics, this has not been reflected in development practice. The practical agents of development have done little more than show their appreciation of the aesthetic, practical environmental and simple technical prowess of indigenous peoples. Meanwhile, the philosophical implications of economic systems that are based on personal relations, and not the accumulative rationale of market economics, have not been considered deeply enough. The contrast between the ethical and political structure of the international economy and that of indigenous economic systems remains largely unmade, and thus the appropriateness of the former remains unquestioned. This in turn leaves the way open for the kinds of abuse of indigenous culture demonstrated in the chapter by Simon.

An ontological shift that can encompass different economic rationales is necessary to achieve a clear understanding of development options. Specifically, it has been demonstrated that while conventional Western economics deals with the theory of goods, and focuses on the subjective relationship between consumers and objects of desire, other kinds of economics (those of exotic societies) refer to the 'personal relations' between people that the exchange of things (gifts) in certain social contexts creates (Gregory 1982: 8). The outcome of a model of society as an adjunct to the market is, as Polanyi (1944: 57) so well demonstrated, that instead of the economy being embedded in social relations, 'social relations' are embedded in the economic system. The practical implication of this change is that social relations become dependent on economic relations, and therefore also subject to a tendency of fluctuation and impermanence. Although a shift to a more sustainable model is needed, as the chapter by Humpage highlights, national governments still appear incapable of relating to indigenous conceptions of development and poverty, or of the strongly related issues of the politics of rights and inclusion. It is worth underlining the fact that, as the chapter by Eversole, Ridgeway and Mercer makes clear, indigenous strategies for poverty reduction tie together environmental, social, economic and political issues.

The way in which indigenous peoples constitute their knowledge of the environment and manage it still lacks recognition and influence at the level of international development bureaucracies. Studies of ecological knowledge demonstrate that, as a matter of fact, ecological knowledge does not exist as a separate entity. It is not restricted to a simple compilation of data (Posey 2000: 188). Rather, it exists as an element of the totality of the individual's bonds to the land and all living things, and as a part of the logically unified order of humankind, other beings and nature; thus, it also has a spiritual and supernatural dimension (Cavalcanti 2002). Ecological knowledge is the outcome of a long learning process that involves an accumulation of information through systematic methods. Amazonian natives' knowledge of several aspects of the ecosystem such as medicinal plants, animal behaviour, climatic seasonality and forest and savannah management, for instance, attests to a diversity of knowledge 'that can contribute to new strategies for ecologically and socially sound development' (Posey 2000: 1). This does not happen by accident. For an understanding of nature to make sense and to offer results, it is necessary that the natives classify, order and systematize the data that daily experience gives them. Contrary to simple preconceptions, this ordering has a physical impact on the local environment as well as human relations with it. As Posey demonstrated, 'Many so-called "pristine" landscapes are in fact a *cultural landscape*, either created by humans or modified by human activity (such as natural forest management, cultivation and the use of fire). Indigenous peoples and a growing number of scientists believe that it is no longer acceptable simply to assume that just because landscapes and species appear to outsiders to be "natural" they are therefore "wild"' (Cavalcanti 2002: 48).

Indigenous participation in development

Although 'indigenous participation' has become accepted in development practice,[1] indigenous peoples' participation in development has been integrated without real agreement among the international development community, governments and indigenous peoples themselves as to what their right to participate in development really means. In order for the 'right to development' to be fulfilled, there needs to be more reflection on what is meant by creating 'capability' among disadvantaged populations. And indigenous participation in development needs to be examined in the light of wider political debates focusing on the nature of political participation within 'advanced liberalism'.

There are now numerous well-known 'good practice' examples of participation in development (Fung and Olin Wright 2003; Webster and Engberg-Pedersen 2001; Abers 2003; Chavez Miños 2002; Tendler 1997; Rubin 1997). Yet while these positive experiences have been picked up by many governments, international organizations and overseas development agencies as a vindication of and basis for their policies, there is nevertheless considerable multi-disciplinary research available to demonstrate that these good practice examples should be considered exceptions to the rule (Cooke and Kothari 2001; Mohan and Stokke 1999; Crook and Manor, 1998; Stiefel and Wolfe 1998; Martínez 1996). For example, Martínez writes that although programmes for popular participation help to maintain the stability of the governmental system, such programmes are usually 'designed without the participation of [constituency] interests, without their goodwill or agreement. Rarely do they [the government] take into account local calendars and rhythms, or even less the specific cultures of the population; as a rule they are plans and rules imposed and alien to the concrete processes which operate in reality' (Martínez 1996: 73). According to Stiefel and Wolfe: 'the few projects in which people's participation has been successfully introduced and pursued are almost without exception "accidents" … normally due to the special efforts of one or a few committed individuals in the organisation of the "target group", and are not the result of any planned guidance by the organisation' (1998: 226).

Using fear of 'waste', 'bad management' and 'corruption' as cause for intervention, popular participation and often-related decentralization processes are frequently used as a tool for the re-establishment of centralized control (Cooke and Kothari 2001). In the interests of national sovereignty and governability, strict rules and numerous checks and balances are introduced and enforced to make sure that popular participation happens in a controlled and closely monitored environment. In the process, local informal systems of thought, organization and authority are re-engineered to match official requirements (though these may be locally manipulated and/or resisted). Indeed, although the policy language used to introduce decentralization and popular participation programmes may talk of respect for local culture and organization, governments generally perceive a need to define a standardized system for the whole population, making such sensitivity difficult, if not impossible, in practice.[2] As Juan Gonzalez writes about Colombia, 'in spite of the political rhetoric used many times behind the discourse on participatory democracy and development in the country, it is the administrative approach that has become dominant' (2000: 3).

The appropriation of participatory development by international financial institutions, as a means to soften the impact of their economic activities, explains in large part why so many countries have in turn adopted participation as an element of their national development policy. Indeed, while financial institutions' appropriation of these development ideas explains why states' adoption of them is so widespread, it also provides some indication as to why present applications of popular participation differ so much from the way they are understood in radical non-governmental development parlance. Whereas earlier development theorists supported decentralization strategies as a means to redistribute power, the World Bank adopted them as a means to streamline and cut the costs of government administration (Cooke and Kothari 2001). Thus, although both development theorists and the World Bank supported participatory development as a means to encourage the self-sufficiency of local communities, there is a crucial difference in their thinking. It is important to underline that this difference in thinking explains to a large extent the way in which participation has been implemented in practice.

Other than financially supporting the design and implementation of participatory development and decentralization schemes, the bank was in no way interested in covering the cost of the work towards self-sufficiency. This work is to be shouldered by local communities themselves. At the root of the World Bank's policy towards participatory development and decentralization is an ideological assumption about the role and responsibility of individuals. Individual citizens are free to act in a society and market in which the state is omnipresent only to ensure that competition between these individuals is free and unhindered (Foucault 1991: 119). This is a notion quite different from the socialist and communitarian ideas of academics involved in debates about participatory development. Interestingly, the World Bank's understanding of self-sufficiency also appears to move towards an idea of disciplined liberal individualism favoured by neo-conservatives. Here, we witness 'the multiple responsibilization of individuals, families, households, and communities for their own risks' (Dean 1999: 165).

Through the practice of policy, the World Bank and governments who support it aim to create a new kind of subject, i.e. individuals who are self-sufficient and responsible for their own self-improvement (Shore and Wright 1997). Here the idea matches the analysis of 'advanced liberalism' made by Nikolas Rose in that the aim is 'to govern without governing *society*, that is to say, to govern through the regulated and accountable choices of autonomous agents – citizens, parents, employees, investors' (Rose 1999: 298). 'Poverty' for the new subject 'is represented not as a social problem, but as a new possibility for poor individuals to experience "empowerment" through the actualization of their own self-management' (Hyatt 1997: 219).

Under the logic of 'new public management', the state acts only to create the organizational conditions for its citizens' self-realization. In this new dispensation, experts no longer act as the direct functionaries of a 'social' state. Instead they act as competitive providers of information and knowledge – for example, risk assessments – that enable individuals and their communities to steer themselves. As Nikolas Rose writes:

> they tutor them in the techniques of self-government – as in the burgeoning of private consultancies and training operations. They provide the information that will allow the state, the consumer or other parties – such as regulatory agencies – to assess the performance of these quasi-autonomous agencies, and hence to govern themselves through evaluation and audit. They identify those individuals unable to self-govern, and either attempt to re-attach them – through employment training, welfare-to-work etc. – or to manage their exclusion – through incarceration, or the residualization of welfare. (1999: 147)

As a means to encourage self-governance and the management of 'risk' (Beck 1992), popular participation supports an idea of empowerment. This idea of empowerment has been hollowed out, or 'depoliticized', however, to establish something quite different from the idea of sharing power. Existing structures of power are ignored and empowerment understood mainly in the sense of having a place, a voice within an administrative or management system. 'Empowerment', as Wendy James writes:

> now seems to have little more body to it than responsibility delegated from above, or from the centre, to monitor others below or beyond one, for whose activities one has to be accountable. One seems to be 'empowered' to take a shred of management responsibility and decision-making, but the contemporary sense of the word does not seem to entail any direct control of resources or scope to join with others at the same level in the structure to pursue collective bargaining with the centre. (James 1999: 14)

Development on their own terms

Through their fight for self-determination, indigenous peoples are clearly not interested in having their futures managed by others. The following chapters demonstrate that the self-determination of indigenous peoples has more to do with the right to define future development on their own terms than it has to do with questioning the legitimacy of the nation-states in which they have found themselves. Many indigenous peoples have already discovered for themselves that to uncritically accept participation in development can result in the reduction of freedom, not its creation. This is even further reinforced by the top-down nature and often inflexible economic rationale of development policies and programmes. There is therefore a need for some caution by indigenous peoples and indigenous rights workers when offered a voice and place within national and international development plans. Serious questions have to be asked about the goals and premises of such offers.

Having said that, it is also clear that, with caution, serious advances can be made. The chapter by Hicks and Somby demonstrates that early recognition of the managerial intentions of elites, government and international organizations, as well as their ethical rhetoric and concerns, can provide political opportunities on which indigenous peoples can capitalize. The Sami in Norway, Sweden and Finland can attribute a large part of their success in fighting for their rights and autonomy to their abilities to use their respective governments' discourses on democracy to their own advantage in terms of expanding their economic, social, cultural and political rights. There are particular features and conditions (for example, economic wealth, traditions of social democracy, etc.) within these nations' histories that have undoubtedly created a favourable context for the Sami's efforts. Their different histories of negotiation with these governments, however, are none the less instructive in terms of highlighting common 'pressure' points on which different indigenous peoples can press to strengthen their campaigns for rights and against poverty. Indeed, given the extent of coverage now offered by human rights conventions and rights-based models of development there are parallel mechanisms available to help indigenous people work on these national 'pressure points' for change.

Notes

1 The term 'indigenous participation' has been used to refer both to the participation of indigenous peoples specifically and to the participation of local people in general.

2 Although with their emphasis on standardizing individual rights this is particularly the case in liberal democratic countries, it is even more the case in countries that still have authoritarian governments.

References

Abers, R. (2003) 'Reflections on what makes empowered participatory governance happen', in A. Fung and E. Olin Wright (eds), *Deepening Democracy: Institutional Innovations in Empowered Participatory Governance*, London: Verso

Beck, U. (1992) *The Politics of the Individual and Public Interests*, University of Essex: Department of Government

Brundtland, G. H. (et al.) (1987) 'Our common future', report of the World Commission on Environment and Development, Oxford: Oxford University Press

Cavalcanti, C. (2002) 'Economic thinking, traditional ecological knowledge and ethno-economics', *Current Sociology*, 50(1): 39–55

Chavez Miñoz (2002) 'Porte Alegre, Brazil: a new, sustainable model of participatory and democratic governance', unpublished paper presented at Local Politics and Democracy Conference, Centre for Development Studies, University of Oslo

Cooke, B and U. Kothari (2001) *Participation: The New Tyranny?* London and New York: Zed Books

Crook, R. C. and J. Manor (1998) *Democracy and Decentralisation in South Asia and West Africa*, Cambridge: Cambridge University Press

Dean, M. (1999) *Governmentality: Power and Rule in Modern Society*, London: Sage

Foucault, M. (1991) 'Governmentality', in G. Burchell, C. Gordon and P. Miller (eds), *The Foucault Effect: Studies in Governmentality*, London: Harvester Wheatsheaf

Fung, A. and E. Olin Wright (eds) (2003) *Deepening Democracy: Institutional Innovations in Empowered Participatory Governance*, London: Verso

Goldin, L. R. (1996) 'Economic mobility strategies among Guatemalan peasants: prospects and limits of nontraditional vegetable cash crops', *Human Organization*, 55(1): 99–100

Gonzalez, J. M. (2000) 'State-led experiments in participatory development in Colombia: a path towards an "alternative" development?', paper presented at the Local Politics and Development Workshop, Centre for Development Studies, University of Oslo

Gregory, C. A. (1982) *Gifts and Commodities*, London and New York: Academic Press

Hacking, I. (1990) *The Taming of Chance*, Cambridge: Cambridge University Press

Harris, J. and P. de Renzio (1997) 'Policy arena: missing link or analytically missing? The concept of social capital', *Journal of International Development*, 9(7): 919–37

Hyatt, S. B. (1997) 'Poverty in a "post-welfare" landscape: tenant management policies, self-governance and the democratization of knowledge in Great Britain', in C. Shore and S. Wright (eds), *The Anthropology of Policy*, London: Routledge

James, W. (1999) 'Empowering ambiguities', in A. Cheater (ed.), *The Anthropology of Power*, ASA Monographs 26, London: Routledge

Korovkin, T. (1998) 'Commodity production and ethnic culture: Otavalo, northern Ecuador', *Economic Development and Cultural Change*, 47(1): 125–54

Martínez, J. A. (1996) 'Municipios y participación popular en América Latina: un modelo de desarrollo', La Paz: IAF/SEMILLA/CEBIAE

Mohan, G. and K. Stokke (2000) 'Participatory development and empowerment: the dangers of localism', *Third World Quarterly*, 21(2) April

Nelson, N. and S. Wright (1995) *Power and Participatory Development: Theory and Practice*, London: Intermediate Technology Publications

Polanyi, K. (1944) *The Great Transformation: The Political and Economic Origins of Our Time*, Boston, MA: Beacon Press

Posey, D. A. (1987) 'Alternatives to destruction: science of the Mebêngôkre', in A. Museau Goeldi (ed.), *Ciência de Mebengokre, alternativas contra a destruição*, Belem: Museau Goeldi, pp. 12–34

— (2000) 'Expolitation of bio-diversity and indigenous knowledge in Latin America: challenges to sovereignty and the old order', in C. Cavalcanti (ed.), *The Environment, Sustainable Development and Public Policies, Building Sustainability in Brazil*, Cheltenham: Edward Elgar, pp. 186–209

Rose, N. (1999) *Powers of Freedom: Reframing Political Thought*, Cambridge: Cambridge University Press

Rubin, J. W. (1997) *Decentering the Regime: Ethnicity, Radicalism and Democracy in Juchitan, Mexico*, Durham, NC and London: Duke University Press

Scott, J. (1998) *Seeing Like a State: How Certain Schemes to Improve the Human Condition Have Failed*, New Haven, CT: Yale University Press

Shore, C. and S. Wright (1997) *Anthropology of Policy: Critical Perspectives on Governance and Power*, London and New York: Routledge

Smith, C. (1984) 'Does a commodity economy enrich the few while ruining the masses? Differentiation among petty commodity producers in Guatemala', *Journal of Peasant Studies*, 11(3): 60–95

Stiefel, M. and M. Wolfe (1998) 'A voice for the excluded: popular participation in development: utopia or necessity?', Geneva: UNRISD

Tendler, J. (1997) *Good Government in the Tropics*, Baltimore, MD: Johns Hopkins University Press

Tonkinson, R. (1991 [1978]) *The Mardu Aborgines: Living the Dream in Australia's Desert,* Forth Worth, IL: Holt, Reinhart and Winston

Webster, N. and L. Engberg-Pedersen (2002) *In the Name of the Poor: Contesting Political Space for Poverty Reduction*, London and New York: Zed Books

13 | Ecological wealth versus social poverty: contradictions of and perspectives on indigenous development in Central America and Mexico

PABLO ALARCÓN-CHÁIRES

One of the characteristics of the current state of human civilization is significant scientific and technological progress. This progress has permitted humanity great conquests in the pursuit of dominance and supremacy over itself, nature, time and space. Biotechnology, deep knowledge of the cosmos, sophisticated communication systems, significant progress in medicine, etc., are examples of such development.

The basic problems of over 50 per cent of human beings are still to be solved, however. Consisting of what economists call extreme poverty, the ills affecting the planet, such as hunger, lack of basic healthcare and sanitary services, lack of educational opportunities, etc., are frequently found among the populations of the so-called 'developing' countries. Social strata in these countries are increasingly divided, with the worst positions being occupied by the rural population and, within this, the indigenous population. In spite of having in most cases a vast and rich natural environment, these populations have little or no economic wealth.

This chapter includes an overall assessment of environmental conditions in Mexico and Central America, in order to highlight the marked contradiction between the ecological and biological wealth in the region and the serious process of impoverishment of its population. It examines the contributions made by indigenous cultures to ecological management and conservation, as well as some proposals for alternative development based on these contributions. Finally, the chapter presents overall guidelines for development projects involving indigenous peoples and territories.

Social deterioration in the region

Ranked as the poorest region in the continent, Central America is currently facing a new challenge. The consolidation of recently inaugurated democratic regimes promises an improvement in the quality of life for its inhabitants. It is therefore a contradiction that, in spite of increased political and democratic stability in Central America since the 1970s and 1980s, the social indicators in the region continue to deteriorate. Poverty in Central America is so serious that over half the population is estimated to be living in poverty, and approximately a third in conditions of extreme poverty. In the case of Mexico, the situation is very similar: 60 per cent of Mexican people are poor and 44.7 per cent of this group are living in extreme poverty. In the case of Honduras, 70 per cent of the population is living below the poverty line (CEPAL 1997).

Land tenure is greatly unequal, even where the indigenous model of land tenure is still in force. For example, in Guatemala in 1989, 66 per cent of the land was held by 3 per cent of estate holders (Ascher and Hubbard 1989). In this context, there is a regional tendency towards the import of food, implying the abandonment of traditional primary activities and tending towards a process of agricultural industrialization (with marked use of pesticides and fertilizers) and cattle production.

The human development indices for the region show that there are significant differences between the countries in the region.[1] The degree of social precariousness also varies within each country. In Mexico, the illiteracy rate in the south-east region – where there are more indigenous inhabitants and greater indigenous cultural diversity – is higher by ten percentage points than the national average. This is a result of the great dispersion of population, school leaving due to family-related economic needs, and infant malnutrition. The lack of healthcare services and access to local sanitary facilities is also reflected in the following rates: only 29 per cent of households have piped water, 49 per cent have drainage services, 30 per cent have earth floors, 44 per cent use wood as the principal household energy source, and 18 per cent live in a single room. Seventy-four per cent of the Mexican indigenous population are living in this region, representing 16 per cent of the total population.

In short, the Mesoamerican region has a chronically disadvantaged population, including 15 million people who do not eat as they should, two-thirds of whom are located in the countryside. According to the United Nations' Food and Agriculture Organization (FAO), a fifth of Mesoamerican people suffer from malnutrition, a rate almost double the percentage for the whole of Latin America and which is more serious given that, while the rate decreased in the subcontinent by two points over the past decade, it increased by two percentage points in the isthmus countries.

In general, a large part of the active population is unemployed, or is on its way to unemployment. Access to healthcare services and education has diminished, basic human rights are violated, and children, women and indigenous peoples are the groups that are mostly affected by this social deterioration. In addition, Central America frequently confronts natural disasters such as hurricanes and earthquakes, which significantly affect the process of regional impoverishment.

Environmental deterioration

In 1995, Central America had a forest area comprising 522,443 square kilometres (km^2). According to some estimates, 18 per cent of those forests were conifers and the remainder was comprised of broadleaf forests. The conservation status of the Central American eco-regions revealed that 33 per cent were in a critical status; 33 per cent were in danger; 15 per cent were vulnerable; 15 per cent were stable; and 3 per cent were relatively undamaged (Dinerstein et al. 1995).

Mexico, for its part, has a forestry area of 141,745,169 hectares, with 21 per cent composed of forests, 19 per cent rainforests, 41 per cent desert areas vegetation, 3 per cent hydrophilic and halophitic vegetation, and 16 per cent disturbed areas (Secretaría de Agricultura y Recursos Hidráulicos 1994). At present, fewer than 15 per cent of rainforests and 50 per cent of forests have been conserved in Mexico. The status of its eco-regions is as follows: 12.5 per cent in critical condition; 16.6 per cent in danger; 16.6 per cent in vulnerable condition; 16.6 per cent stable; 12.5 per cent are relatively undamaged; and 25 per cent unclassified (Dinerstein et al. 1995).

There are indications of a tendency towards a lower quality and quantity of tree-bearing mass with consequent ecological implications. In Central America, the decreasing forest frontier, resulting from the pursuit of agrarian solutions, clearing for cropping and war-related activities, has entailed high environmental costs. In Nicaragua, for example, the colonization process and the changes in land use have meant that between 100,000 and 150,000 hectares have been deforested per year.

In general, the regional deforestation rate is estimated at 4,603 km^2 per year. In Mexico, climatic events and cutting result in a yearly loss of approximately 500,000 hectares of forests. This deforestation is also connected to a series of other environmental changes such as erosion (between 5 and 35 tons per hectare). If we consider that 70 per cent of this territory is made up of sloping hills (Girot 1997), the environmental and social cascading effect is obvious.

On the other hand, with nearly 7 per cent of the world's biodiversity, Central America is a pillar of the planet's biological wealth, not only in terms of the quantity of species it has overall, but also on account of the high number of endemic species that are found there. Costa Rica, Panama and Guatemala have over a thousand endemic species each. The biological specificity of the Central American eco-regions (based on the richness and complexity of the species, the endemic species, and the type of ecological functional processes) enables it to be ranked in the region as Outstanding in terms of its Bio-Regional Level, that is to say that the eco-regions included in it are closely dependent on each other (see Dinerstein et al. 1995). Mexico, for its part, has 212,900 distinct species, and these represent over 10 per cent of the planet's biodiversity. This situation, together with the sensitive attitude of Central American national governments, has facilitated the definition of legal regulations enabling the existence of protected areas all over the region.

Cultural diversity and diversity of species

According to estimates, there are currently 6,500 cultures worldwide within the total population of nearly 6 billion. What is important from the ecological point of view is that there is an overlap between the presence of indigenous populations and little-disturbed ecosystems. As Kuna Geodisio Castillo from Panama has put it, ' ... where there are forests, there are indigenous people, and where there are indigenous people there are forests' (see Figure 13.1). An indigenous population of approximately 19 million people distributed in something over a hundred groups is estimated to be living in Mexico and Central America (Table 13.1).

Conservation of nature and indigenous peoples

Various international organizations, researchers and scholars agree that indigenous groups are the naturally allied groups for conservation and good management of ecosystems. This occurs because, as Clad (1982) has pointed out, the lifestyles of indigenous cultures are based on the sustainable management of their local ecosystems.

Reichel-Dolmatoff (1976) argues that indigenous groups have a set of ecological principles combined with a social system and economic rules, contributing to a feasible equilibrium between nature and social requirements. According to Berkes et al. (1993), indigenous peoples' conservationist approach to the management of ecosystems is based on the protection of some biological communities, habitats and species, and the protection of some species development, as well as organized use of resources under the supervision of a local expert.

There are more deeply embedded reasons that highlight the role of indigenous peoples in the conservation of natural environments. To Toledo (1992a), the interaction between indigenous peoples and nature goes beyond physical observation and is closely linked to the indigenous perception of the world. This view of the world includes the whole set of beliefs represented and expressed by means of myths and rituals that allow them to explain themselves and, most importantly, to establish a relationship with their sacred nature. The song sung by the Huichol's shaman to the deer, the Chaa chak rain invocation of the Maya, the ceremonies celebrated by the Pipil after a good harvest, etc., are examples of the indigenous vision

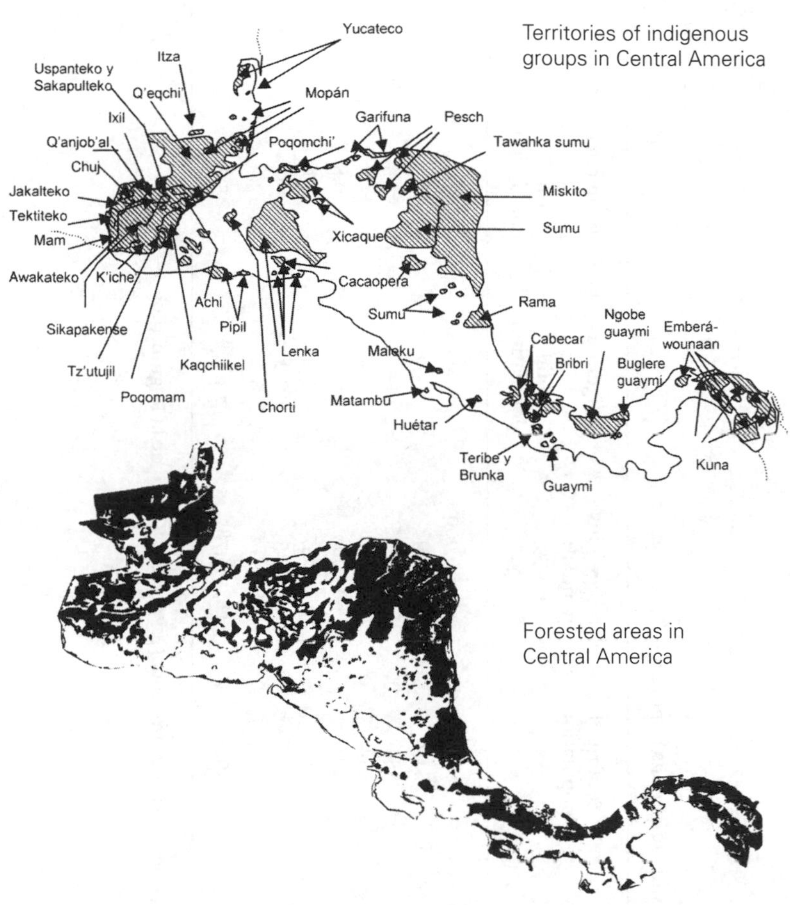

FIGURE 13.1 Indigenous presence in Central America

in pursuit of a reciprocal relationship with Mother Nature. The indigenous concept of nature implies a conceptualization of themselves, because they see themselves as part of nature – Mother Nature provides them with their food, their clothing, their housing, their own essential features.

Based on an ethical code, indigenous peoples use their natural resources with a view to the welfare of future generations. As an indigenous person told anthropologist Martin Von Hildebrand, '... the difference between you and us is that while you set aside a money inheritance for your children, we provide for an inheritance based on trees and animals'. And it is precisely this vision and attitude towards nature which have come to take second place in the dominant, 'civilized', 'modern' and 'progressive' society. Immersed in the 'individual self' and the 'here and now', the 'developed' world

TABLE 13.1 Mexico and Central America: total, rural and indigenous population

Country	Total population	Rural population	% of rural population	Indigenous population (1999)	% of indigenous population in relation to	
					total population	rural population
Mexico	100,294,036 [2]	24,540,000[1]	26.5[1]	12,000,000	12.00	50.5
Belize	233,000[4]	119,300[4]	51.2	30,000[1]	12.8	25.1
Guatemala	12,335,580[2]	6,584,300[4]	53.3	5,427,655[2]	44.0	82.4
Honduras	6,480,000[4]	3,564,000[1]	55.0	419,813[2]	6.4	11.7
El Salvador	6,031,000[4]	2,876,000[1]	47.6	600,000[3]	9.9	20.8
Nicaragua	4,807,000[4]	1,994,000[1]	41.4	235,857[2]	4.9	11.8
Costa Rica	3,840,000[4]	2,173,000[1]	56.5	36,745[2]	0.9	1.6
Panama	2,778,526[2]	1,209,000[1]	43.5	166,712[2]	6.0	13.7
TOTAL	136,799,142	41,850,600	30.6	18,916,782	13.82	45.2

Sources: 1 Toledo et al. 2001; 2 World Factbook 2000; 3 Rodríguez-Soriano 2000; 4 Proyecto Estado de la Región 1999

is increasingly losing itself in its pursuit of the fulfilment of pleasures, rather than the fulfilment of needs.

In addition to indigenous peoples' involvement in the management of protected natural areas, there is a silent ecological activism headed by indigenous groups in various locations in Mexico and Central America. In Honduras, for instance, the Misquito and Pesch indigenous groups, working together with the Garifuna and Ladinos,[2] have established the Comité de Vigilancia de Tierras (CVT). The CVT is a committee for the supervision of lands with the purpose of stopping the invasion of colonists, farmers and cattle raisers in the Plátano River Biosphere Reserve. The CVT also participates in marine turtle conservation programmes.

Protected natural areas and indigenous peoples

The International Union for the Conservation of Nature defines protected natural areas as land and/or sea regions specifically devoted to the protection and maintenance of biological diversity, and the associated natural and *cultural* resources managed by means of legal or other kind of procedures. According to IUCN/WCPA/WWF (2000), the advantage of using this term lies in the fact that it includes social, economic and cultural interests, as well as the values, rights and responsibilities of local communities living in or around protected natural areas (PNAs).

Indigenous populations live in 85 per cent of Latin American PNAs (Colchester 1994). PNAs in Mexico and Central America match the presence of several indigenous groups (Table 13.2). All indigenous groups in Belize, Nicaragua, Honduras and Costa Rica are to be found in a PNA, while half or more are living in a PNA in the other countries.

This indicates that indigenous peoples are among the major actors responsible for safeguarding the natural wealth of global and national societies. Some experiences in various worldwide locations where indigenous peoples participate in PNA conservation and management activities demonstrate that there is no conflict among indigenous groups, conservation and alternative development models. In general terms, the cases where the conservation of nature is a socialized act supported by participatory democracy, and where indigenous peoples play a significant role in conservation decision-making, can be considered successful – in spite of the small number of such cases. Moreover, progress in ecological research (evolutionary ecology) has shown that the interaction between the indigenous groups and nature is so close that, when indigenous management of nature ceases, the 'natural' system decays, requiring even greater time to attain stability.

Local indigenous groups' knowledge of PNA ecosystems provides opportunities for an improved quality of life. Such is the case with the Tawahka experience in the Tawahka Asagni Biosphere Reserve in Honduras (Benítez and Leyva 1998). And there are various other examples of indigenous peoples' management of natural areas; for instance, the Talamanca National Park and Indigenous Reserve in Costa Rica. There, the Bribri Territory Development Association, ADITIBRI, has designed a reserve management programme based on traditional systems which, at the same time, contributes to the conservation of national resources. Within this scheme there are conservation, agricultural, economic, cultural, communication and social activities in which indigenous peoples actively participate (García-Segura 1998).

Similarly, in the Kuna Yala region, Panama, the administrative, territorial and managerial control of natural resources is in the hands of indigenous peoples represented in the National Congress of the Kuna, a body governing all the activities in this territory (see Arias 1998). And in Nicaragua, some actions and zones of the Marine Biological Reserve of Cayos Miskitos and Franja Costera (regions of Mismakad, Karata and Laguna Woutha) are the responsibility of the Miskito, who, in addition to regulating access to natural resources, participate in the design of management programmes and explore economic alternatives for their communities (IUCN/WCPA/WWF 2000). Also in Nicaragua, the Mayagna Sumu have presented a proposal for the implementation of a management plan for the Bosawa Reserve,

TABLE 13.2 Presence/influence of indigenous populations in protected natural areas of Mexico and Central America

Country	Protected natural areas/presence of indigenous groups	Presence of indigenous groups in PNAs as per (total for the country)	PNAs with indigenous individuals, as per (total for the country)
Belize	9/3	3 (3)	9 (37)
Nicaragua	26/3	3 (3)	26 (75)
Panama	10/5	5 (8)	10 (37)
Honduras	17/6	6 (6)	17 (37)
Costa Rica	9/10	10 (10)	9 (123)
El Salvador	28/2	2 (3)	28 (94)
Guatemala	43/19	19 (22)	43 (104)
Mexico	33/31	31 (62)	33 (89)
TOTAL*		80	175

(* Neither ethnic groups nor repeated PNAs among countries are broken down in this total)

including historical and socio-economic research, mapping of the territory, passing of internal ecological regulations, and a conservation and sustainable development programme for shock-absorbing zones (Robins-Lino 2000).

In Belize, the Instituto de Manejo Indígena (Institute for Indigenous Management) of the Sarstoon-Temash National Park has greatly influenced the knowledge and traditional practices which, assessed on scientific criteria, have allowed for the inclusion of a wide range of the park's biodiversity in its management plan. The system of community co-management in Belize has facilitated the participation of the Q'eqchi in the Four Blues National Park and the Aguacaliente Sanctuary (Sánchez 2000). In Guatemala, the Itza have organized into cooperative groups in order to provide for the conservation and management of 80 per cent of their territory located within the Maya Biosphere Reserve. And in the Sierra de Las Minas Biosphere Reserve, external initiatives are promoting the integration of the Keckchi and Poqomchi indigenous groups and the conservation and management of the region's natural resources. These cases suggest a promising trend, and more research needs to be done to clarify the suggested linkage between indigenous peoples' management of natural areas and changes in the income/quality of life of these populations.

Conservation of nature and indigenous peoples: are they linked by a direct relationship?

The image of the 'noble savage' that has been usual in anthropological and ethnological research for many years is currently subject to debate. Various examples from all over the world indicate that the issues of conservation of nature and indigenous peoples are not always compatible. This situation should be analysed, however, in the light of the modern history of these peoples and the role of Western society in establishing new guidelines for behaviour.

In some cases, the abrupt incorporation of indigenous peoples into national and international dynamics through the tourist industry, or the demand for regional natural resources, has led to the acquisition of foreign values, contributing eventually to nature's exploitation. In other cases, the 'exclusion principle' typical of nature conservation activities in the region restrains access by local indigenous populations to the existing natural resources within the PNA, and disregards the fact that these peoples may have been living in the region for centuries. In the case of Honduras, the phenomenon of indigenous migration towards areas that differ from their own in ecological terms has turned some PNAs into open spaces and 'territories subject to predation', resulting in their progressive deterioration.

Thirty years ago, the International Union for the Conservation of Nature (IUCN) recognized the need to respect the right of indigenous peoples to their lands when establishing protected areas, recognizing the value of their lifestyles, and to design tools to turn their lands into conservation areas without the occupants giving up their rights or being displaced. Agreements resulting from the twenty-first Rio de Janeiro Summit agenda, particularly those related to the conservation of biodiversity, support this view on indigenous rights.

In spite of this, the vast majority of the protected areas established have violated these rights. According to scientific estimates, 1 million square kilometres of forests, savannahs, pasturelands and crop lands in Africa have been redefined as protected areas, but in most of them the indigenous rights to ownership, control and management of those areas have been denied. The number of people who have been displaced by these protected areas is unknown, and little has been done to reduce the resulting ills and poverty (Forest Peoples Programme 2003).

The region of Takarkunyala, located in the Darien National Park in Panama, is considered a sacred place by the Kuna because of a mountain bearing the same name. The ANAM (National Environment Authority) has forbidden the Kuna to use the territory in a traditional way. The park and the Humedal de Patiño PNA overlap the Emberá-Wounaan region, where the same restrictions apply. The traditional hunting and fishing activities carried out by the Maleku indigenous people from Costa Rica have been restricted by the establishment of the PNA and wildlife refuge of Caño Negro on indigenous lands.

In Mexico, the Cucapá, who have been living by the Colorado river located in the biosphere reserve of Alto Golfo and by the river's delta for thousands of years, are prevented from carrying out their main economic activity – fishing. This has led them to file a claim with the National Human Rights Commission over the pressure exerted on them by the environmental authorities.

The creation of new protected natural areas, where local authorities' involvement is relegated to second place, tends to 'encapsulate' these biologically wealthy zones for foreign interests. This occurs even when it implies the eviction and migration of local communities – more precisely indigenous communities – as with the Tzeltal, Tzotzil, Tojolabal, Chol and Lacandon communities in the Montes Azules Biosphere Reserve, Mexico. The vacation of the area by indigenous peoples is intended to further biological conservation. But if such plans are implemented, the displaced communities are likely to suffer from greater poverty and marginalization, as well as fewer development opportunities. In Cuetzalan, Mexico, an ecological reserve (an administrative structure with more concessions for the use and exploitation of nature) is being planned against the local community's will, and calls have already been made specifically targeting private initiatives for the creation of 'eco-tourism' projects in a region considered to be a priority for conservation by the CONABIO (National Commission for Biodiversity).

The Mesoamerican model for the management of natural resources

There are practical examples where the cosmology and knowledge of indigenous peoples are reflected in the management of ecosystems and natural resources. They generally differ from the modern model because they are based on rational thinking with different objectives. The economy of indigenous families is based on self-sufficiency in terms of basic consumer products and their production systems, implying space, time and biological diversification, so that different materials, energy and services are available from different sources throughout the year.

The creation of synergies contributes to an enhanced production system, in which the recycling of matter and energy generally results in a stable and independent system, meeting minimum food, housing and health needs. This model is not static, however. It is immersed in a continuous process of incorporation, removal, change and transformation of structure and operation. It is also influenced by the introduction of external agents and technological innovations.

Additionally, the incorporation of state-of-the-art technology (by means of geographical information systems, expanded digital services inside the community, ongoing update and training of indigenous staff, etc.) and the creation of internationally competitive indigenous community companies have in no way meant giving in to the current global development model. In contrast, they have implied the taming of the pervasive neo-liberal model by preserving features of the Mesoamerican model in which local institutions are in charge of decision-making and the production system is endogenous and self-supporting. There are many examples in Mexico of successful experiences of natural resource management and proposals for alternative development models designed by indigenous communities in what Toledo (2000) has called 'the other zapatism'.

Economic alternatives for indigenous peoples

Different classifications can be used to assign values to biodiversity, depending on the benefits provided to society. These values go beyond the economic sphere because they include aesthetic, cultural, spiritual, functional and ethical aspects, among the most important features (see de Alba and Reyes 1998). This section offers a 'utilitarian' translation of these values so that nature's value may be understood in the light of economic pragmatism. It is important to clarify that this utilitarian translation of the value of nature is intended merely to emphasize the economic opportunities of natural resource exploitation. It does not mean that it is the only value, or the most important one. The potential opportunities could include:

Sale of environmental services The policies implemented by most Latin American governments have undervalued the price and the actual importance of nature, particularly of the forest sector. Despite the insistent call for the need to incorporate nature-provided goods and services into national and international accounts, this rarely occurs. In an attempt to pay off the ecological debt that First World countries have with Southern countries, innovative government policies have been designed. For example, Costa Rica has sold carbon capture services totalling US$100 million per year, i.e. half the amount allocated to subsidies from the forest industry to other sectors in 1992. In Mexico, the value of the yearly capture of carbon per hectare is US$3,600 for forests and US$5,400 for rainforests (Muñoz 1994). In Costa Rica, the World Bank has estimated the yearly value of tropical forest at US$2,000 per hectare. The biodiversity preservation costs under sustainable conditions are estimated at US$77 per hectare per year (Aguirre-González 1997).

Among the environmental services provided by forest and rainforest conservation activities is the conservation of nutrients for the lands of small grain producers, which would save US$38.80 per hectare at national level. The reforestation of only half of the area sown with maize and beans entails a benefit for the natural capture of nutrients which would translate into thousands of dollars in savings (ibid.).

Bioprospecting studies The main arguments for bringing a halt to deforestation and the destruction of natural resources – particularly in developing countries (which paradoxically have great genetic wealth and little technological capacity) – are focused on the loss of opportunities for obtaining therapeutic drugs for various diseases. The World Health Organization estimates that 80 per cent of the population in developing countries (4 billion people) use traditional medicine for primary sicknesses. According to Morán (1999), the pharmaceutical industry pays between US$50 and 100 per sample for a potentially useful plant for the industry, although this sum may be doubled in the case of active ingredients.

Belize has allocated part of its territory to the establishment of the First World Ethnobotanical Reserve, which is intended to recognize and reinforce the relationship between the Maya peoples and nature. The Kuna from Panama regulate the research conducted on their territory by issuing permits and through a commitment to providing knowledge and technology transfer (Chapin 1991), in order to monitor authoring rights on the results of bioprospecting studies. It is estimated that the pharmaceutical value of forests in Mexico could be between US$26 million and 4.6 billion per year.

Agroforestry Some agroforestry production systems managed and designed by indigenous peoples have been more productive than modern systems. An example of sustainable resource management is provided by the Totonaco in Mexico. By means of their diversified management of the natural resources and the equitable distribution of land (smallholdings) they are able to obtain a US$8,000 annual return from agroforestry and cattle production. These kinds of practices combining maize crops, pasturelands, forests and *solares* (pieces of land for construction) contribute to the diversification of species – 355 in the case of El Totonacapa – which are efficiently used and managed (Toledo et al. 1994).

Something similar occurs with the production of coffee. Sixty-five per cent of organic coffee producers in Mexico are members of indigenous groups and their traditional production scheme (based on biodiversification, multiple use of the ecosystem, zero inputs, etc.) has caused the country to be ranked as the best producer of coffee at international level. This product generates nearly US$20 million per year given the added value of organic products in the international market (Moguel and Toledo 2000).

Conservation and management of protected natural areas The *Instituto de Manejo Indígena* (Indigenous Management Institute) from the Sarstoon-Temash National Park – with Q'eqchi and Garifuna members – was granted US$800,000 over three years by international organizations such as the World Bank and the Global Environment Facility for the development of a management programme, the elaboration of an inventory of resources, the elaboration of traditional ecological knowledge records, and the reinforcement of management ability (IUCN/WCPA/WWF 2000).

In the case of Mexico, there are studies indicating that individuals would be willing to pay US$10 per hectare in order to secure a natural legacy for generations to come, which in this country would translate into US$112 million (de Alba and Reyes 1998).

Foreign debt in exchange for nature One of the strategies sought by various international conservation agencies involves the purchase of the foreign debt of developing countries and its exchange for nature conservation. In 1991, Mexico and Costa Rica opted for this strategy through conservation organizations such as Conservation International, the World Wildlife Fund, the National Parks Foundation of Costa Rica, Nature Conservancy, the Rain Forest Alliance, the Monteverde Conservation League, as well as other Dutch and Swedish organizations. In Costa Rica, nearly US$12 million is spent every year to maintain national parks, but the exchange of foreign debt for nature generated US$330 million in 1991 (Phillips 1998), thus indicating that there is a positive economic balance to further conservation.

The conservation of nature under a traditional low-impact management scheme implies great savings in national accounts. According to estimates by Pimentel et al. (1995), the cost of (eolian and hydric) soil erosion and its environmental, sanitary and productive impact in the United States (no information is available for other countries) was US$44 billion per year, while prevention practices accounted for US$8.4 billion; that is, they were five times less expensive. In Mexico, it is estimated that the services provided by forests and rainforests as a result of water treatment would amount to US$160 per hectare, while the yearly cost of avoiding salinization caused by deforestation would be US$50 per hectare (UAES 1997).

Tourism Tourism is considered to be the second-most profitable industry after drug dealing, generating 10.9 per cent of the worldwide gross domestic product. This has been analysed by various indigenous organizations which are currently developing eco-tourism projects aimed at foreigners interested in nature. Some successful examples of this alternative type of tourism in Mexico are the Calakmul Biosphere Reserve (Maya), the Indigenous Community of Nuevo San Juan Parangaricutiro (Purepecha group), the Cancun–Tulum tourist corridor (Maya), Sierra de Juarez (Zapotec and Chinantec groups) and the Gulf of California (Seris).

Wild animals The economic value of many species that are illegally hunted in the tropical region is dramatically reduced. For instance, jaguars are often found to cause damage in rural areas, thus resulting in their illegal hunting. Under these circumstances, jaguar pelts can fetch as much as US$150. If hunting practices and the sale of fur had been carried out by sustainable means, the income from fur would have been US$20,000; while the sale price of 4,300 kilograms of meat of nine wild species obtained through traditional hunting practices would be nearly US$12,900. Controlled hunting of wild turkeys in communities from Quintana Roo, Mexico, generates between US$850 and 1,600 per hunting trip (Quinto-Adrián 2000). Based on the appropriate impact studies, the fauna may also be exploited by means of the sale of insects, ornate birds, marine shells, etc., for educational and academic purposes and for worldwide private collectors.

Some experiences from the Amazon region have demonstrated the feasibility of zoo breeding facilities for the production of meat for human consumption and fur for the international market. An example is the breeding of crocodiles, which may generate over US$14,500 per hectare per year (Nations and Coello-Hinojosa 1989).

Diversified use of ecosystems This includes the use of forests and rainforests to produce food, medicines, timber, tools, domestic power, forage, fibres, resins, drugs, colorants, rubber, flavouring and sweetener. Under this regime, the net value per hectare of rainforest was estimated at US$9,000 for 1992, comparatively higher than the US$3,184 income from plantations and the US$2,960 from cattle-raising activities in the same region (Toledo 1992b). In Mexico, the timber and non-timber use of its temperate forests may generate US$528 million in income, while income from its rainforests may amount to US$729 million per year (Gobierno de México 1996). Eco-tourism activities may generate approximately US$34 million per year (CSERGE 1993).

Development versus indigenous expectations?

Promoted by international funding agencies such as the Inter-American Development Bank and the World Bank, several production projects, including mining, hydraulic and energy engineering works, forest extraction and mass tourism, are under way in indigenous territories without the indigenous communities' consent.

The situation in Panama illustrates to a great extent what is happening in the region. The Ngöbe have been fighting the Cerro Colorado mining project developed for decades by PANACOBRE S.A., a Canadian company. The Ngöbe-Bugle indigenous community has also filed suit with the Supreme Court of Justice of Panama and has won protection rights against the implementation of the Tabasará hydroelectric project. This community has also been affected by the construction of the Chiriquí-Provincia Boca del Toro highway, and no compensation has been granted until now for the resulting environmental impact. The Kuna and Emberá-Wounnan have sued the government for breaching the compensation agreements and for the environmental damage caused by the construction of the Bayano hydroelectric dam. In spite of the recommendations by the World Commission on Dams and the public's opposition, Presidents Alfonso Portillo from Guatemala and Vicente Fox from Mexico announced the construction of a hydropower dam in the Altos del Usumacinta, including five small dams from El Petén, Guatemala, through Marques de Comillas, Chiapas, to Tabasco, Mexico. It is estimated that this will flood an area covering 10,000–12,000 square kilometres, including 800 archaeological sites (Yaxchilán, Piedras Negras and Altar de Sacrificios, etc.) and cooperative settlements of over 50,000 people, and will result in the loss of millions of precious trees and wildlife.

Another case is the construction of the 'El Cajón' dam currently under way in the western region of Mexico (Nayarit), which threatens not only to increase population density, but also to 'erase from the map' a great part of the sacred geography of the Huichol, Cora, Tepehuano and Mexicanero indigenous groups. Furthermore, electrification works in the region have been carried out against the will of these indigenous peoples and a struggle to stop such government actions aimed at indigenous 'development' has set in. Local peoples are aware that where such projects have been implemented there have been negative changes, from shifts in eating habits as a result of the increase in availability of low-nutrition products such as bottled soft drinks to the decline in ancient indigenous customs among young members of the population as result of the introduction of slot machines and television. To oppose this the Huichol in the indigenous community of Santa Catarina have presented a proposal for electrification to be carried out by means of solar panels. Such a system is more viable given the topographic conditions of the area. It is also less expensive and is able to limit the electrification of items that are causing problems in communities and threatening to change the environment, the internal social relationships and community institutions.

In this context, communities such as the independent municipalities of the state of Chiapas and Oaxaca are fighting to strengthen indigenous institutions. In the case of the Nahua indigenous community of El Coire on the Michoacan coast of Mexico, the processes imposed by the national government are markedly diminishing. Disregarding regulations that require the creation of party lists and membership, this community has recovered its traditions and customs through the spontaneous, open and free election of community representatives. Although it may seem simple, such action is a significant act of rebellion against government policies that have favoured disintegration in the surrounding communities.

Conclusion

There is an urgent need to pursue development alternatives based on the natural, knowledge-related and technological wealth of indigenous peoples. The approach may well be a hybrid one, incorporating viable modern options that offer improved standards of living. The challenge is to find a way in which the indigenous peoples may keep relevant cultural trappings while adapting to modern developments and change.

This does not mean reinterpreting 'sustainable development' per se. In fact, various experiences indicate that the indigenous populations were the ones that created and have been applying for hundreds of years what is now called sustainable development. This means that the task is to recover and reinforce indigenous peoples' culture of sustainability towards nature, and for knowledge of this to be disseminated.

The problems of indigenous peoples and poverty go beyond the socio-economic and political sphere and become an ethical issue. An initial step towards overcoming these problems may be to make worldwide public opinion aware of how important indigenous peoples are as owners of a great part of the planet's biological legacy, and how important their knowledge is as regards the sustainable management of ecosystems. Such recognition should include accepting that these peoples, in spite of their very different perspectives and ways of life, deserve respect.

Notes

1 The country rankings are as follows: Costa Rica, 34; Panama, 45; Mexico, 49; Belize, 63; Guatemala, 111; El Salvador, 114; Honduras, 119; and Nicaragua, 126.

2 People of mixed indigenous and Spanish ancestry.

References

Aguirre-González, J. A. (1997) 'Economic vs financial pricing of timber and its probable impact on national accounts: the Costa Rica case, 1980–92', in F. Smith (ed.), *Environmental Sustainability: Practical Global Implications*, Boca Raton, FL: St Lucie Press, pp. 87–106

Alarcón-Cháires, P. (2001) *Ecología y transformación campesina en la Meseta Purépecha*, Mexico: UMSNH

Altieri, M. (1995) *Agroecología: bases científicas para una agricultura sustentable*, Chile: CLADES

Arias, M. (1998) 'Panamá: the research project for the management of wilderness areas in Kuna Yala (PEMASKY)', in A. Gray, A. Parellada and H. Newing (eds), *From Principles to Practice, Indigenous Peoples and Biodiversity Conservation in Latin America*, Copenhagen: IWGIA Document 87, pp. 237–39

Ascher, W. and A. Hubbard (1989) 'Recuperación y desarrollo en centroamérica', *Ensayos del Grupo Especial de la Comisión Internacional para la Recuperación y el Desarrollo en Centroamérica*, San José, Costa Rica, pp. 111–20

Bartra, A. (2002) *Dos prioridades mesoamericanas: soberanía alimentaria y soberanía laboral*, América Latina en Movimiento, <http://alainet.org/active/show_text.php3?key=1607>

Benítez, E. and H. Leyva (1998) 'The Tawahka Asagni Biosphere Reserve in the context of ecological issues in Honduras', in A. Gray, A. Parellada and H. Newing (eds), *From Principles to Practice: Indigenous Peoples and Biodiversity Conservation in Latin America*, Copenhagen: IWGIA Document 87, pp. 215–27

Berkes, F., F. Folke and M. Gadgil (1993) 'Traditional ecological knowledge, biodiversity, resilience and sustainability', Beijer Discussion Paper Series no. 31, Sweden

Bodden, E. (1997) *Honduras: el beneficio de tener una finca de mariposas en la zona*, Primera Jornada Indígena Centroamericana sobre Tierra, Medio Ambiente y Cultura, Honduras, pp. 60–61

CEPAL (1997) *Género, pobreza y seguridad social en Centroamérica*, LC/Mex/L, p. 342

Chapin, M. (1991) 'How the Kuna keep scientists in line', *Cultural Survival Quaterly* (summer), pp. 15–17

— (1992) 'La Co-existencia de pueblos indígenas y el ambiente natural en Centroamérica', special map supplement to *Research & Exploration, a Scholarly Publication of the National Geographic Society*, Washington, DC: National Geographic Society

Clad, J. (1982) *Conservation and Indigenous Peoples: A Study of Convergent Interests*, World National Park Congress, Bali

Colchester, M. (1994) 'Salvaging nature: indigenous people, protected areas and biodiversity conservation', United Nations Research Institute for Social Development (UNRISD), Discussion Paper no. 55, Geneva

Comisión Centroamericana de Ambiente y Desarrollo (1997) *Estado del ambiente y los recursos naturales en Centroamérica*, CCAD/IUCN

Conklin, H. C. (1979) 'An ethnoecological approach to shifting agriculture', in A. P. Nayda (ed.), *Environmental and Cultural Behavior*, New York: Natural History Press

CSERGE (1993) 'Economic value of carbon sequestration. Watershed protection, value of pharmaceuticals from Mexico's forests, existence value', Draft Report to World Bank Latin America and the Caribbean-Country Department II, Centre for Social and Economic Research on the Global Environment, Annexes 3–6

De Alba, E. and M. E. Reyes (1998) 'La valoración económica de la diversidad biológica de México', in *La diversidad biológica de México: estudio de país*, Mexico: CONABIO, pp. 211–34

De Azueta, D. (1996) 'El conocimiento indígena', *Ecología Política*, Barcelona, 11: 103–10

Dillon, J. (2000) 'Deuda ecológica. El Sur dice al norte: <<es hora de pagar>>', *Ecología Política*, Barcelona, 20: 131–51

Dinerstein, E., D. M. Olson, D. J. Graham, A. L. Webster, S. A. Primm, M. P. Bookbinder and G. Ledec (1995) *Una evaluación del estado de conservación de las ecorregiones terrestres de América Latina y el Caribe*, Washington, DC: WWF/WB

Domínguez-Cervantes, E. (1999) 'El sistema nacional de Áreas Naturales Protegidas', *Biodiversitas* 27, México: CONABIO

Forest Peoples Programme (2003) 'Areas protegidas y pueblos indígenas', World Rainforest Movement, 73 <http://www.wrm.org.uy>

García-Segura, A. (1998) 'Costa Rica: the cases of Talamanca and Maleku', in A. Gray, A. Parellada and H. Newing (eds), *From Principles to Practice: Indigenous Peoples and Biodiversity Conservation in Latin America*, Copenhagen: IWGIA, Document 87, pp. 228–36

Girot, P. (1997) 'Uso del suelo en Centroamérica', in *CCAD. Estado del ambiente y los recursos naturales en Centroamérica, 1997*, mimeographed draft paper for review, CCAD/IUCN.

Gobierno de México (1996) *Programa forestal y de suelo: 1995–2000*, Mexico: SEMARNAP

Gobierno de México y Banco Mundial (1995) *Estudio del subsector forestal y de conservación de los recursos*, World Bank and Government of Mexico

Grimes, B. (ed.) (1992) *Ethnologue: Languages of the World*, 12th edn, Dallas: Summer Institute of Linguistics

Harmon, D. (1996) 'Losing species, losing languages: connections between biological and linguistic diversity', *Southwest J. Linguistics*, 15: 89–108

IUCN/WCPA/WWF (World Conservation Union/World Commission on Protected Areas/World Wildlife Fund for Nature) (2000) 'Indigenous and traditional peoples and protected areas: principles, guidelines and case studies', Best Protected Area Guidelines Series no. 4

Lázaro, H. (2000) 'Manejo de recursos naturals en áreas de amortiguamiento del Parque Internacional La Amistad', *Memoria de la Segunda Jornada Indígena Centroamericana sobre tierra, Medio Ambiente y Cultura*, conference proceedings, San José, pp. 405–7

Moguel, P. and V. M. Toledo (2000) 'Café, luchas indígenas y sostenibilidad; el caso de México', *Ecología Política*, Barcelona, 18: 23–36

Morán, K. (1999) 'Toward compensation: returning benefits from ethnobotanical drug discovery to native people', in V. D. Nazarea (ed.), *Ethnoecology. Situated Knowledge/Local Lives*, Tucson: University of Arizona Press, pp. 249–62

Muñoz, P. C. (1994) 'Manual de las cuentas satélites integradas económicas y ambientales', UN

Nations, J. D. and F. Coello-Hinojosa (1989) 'Cuyabeno Wildlife Production Reserve', in J. O. Browder (ed.), *Fragile Lands of Latin America*, Boulder, CO: Westview Press, pp. 139–49

Phillips, A. (1998) 'Economic values of protected areas: guidelines for protected areas managers', World Commission on Protected Areas, Best Practice Protected Area Guidelines Series no. 2

Pimentel, D., C. Harvey, P. Resosudarmo, K. Sinclair, D. Kurz, M. McNair, S. Crist, L. Shpritz, L. Fitton, R. Saffouri and R. Blair (1995) 'Environmental and economic costs of soil erosion and conservation benefits', *Science*, 267: 1,117–23

Prakash, A. and A. K. Gupta (1997) 'Ecologically sustainable institutions', in F. Smith (ed.), *Environmental Sustainability: Practical Global Implications*, Boca Raton, FL: St Lucie Press, pp. 47–65

Proyecto Estado de la Región (1999) *Estado de la región: resumen del primer informe*, San José

Quinto-Adrián, J. F. (2000) 'La fauna silvestre: una alternativa de desarrollo para las comunidades rurales en Quintana Roo, México', *Memoria de la Segunda Jornada Indígena Centroamericana sobre tierra, Medio Ambiente y Cultura*, conference proceedings, San José, Costa Rica, pp. 136–40

Reichel-Dolmatoff, G. (1976) 'Cosmology as ecological analysis: a view from the rain forest', *Man*, 2: 307–18

Robins-Lino, T. (2000) 'Los Mayangnas y la Reserva de la Biosfera de Bosawas', *Memoria de la Segunda Jornada Indígena Centroamericana sobre Tierra, Medio Ambiente y Cultura*, conference proceedings, San José, pp. 461–3

Rodríguez, N. (1980) *Imperialismo y descolonización*, vol. 2, Mexico: CIESAS/INI/SEP

Rodríguez-Soriano, R. (2000) 'El Salvador: solicitan ayuda internacional para el rescate de lenguas y culturas de comunidades indígenas en peligro de extinción', *El Diario*, Miami, 27 November

Sánchez, R. (2000) 'Manejo de áreas protegidas en Belice: el movimiento hacia el co-manejo comunal', *Memoria de la Segunda Jornada Indígena Centroamericana sobre Tierra, Medio Ambiente y Cultura*, conference proceedings, San José, pp. 464–7

Secretaria de Agricultura y Recursos Hidráulicos (1994) *Inventario Forestal Nacional Periódico, 1992–1994*, Mexico: Subsecretaría Forestal y Fauna Silvestre

Thompson, H. (2000) 'Pueblos indígenas y bosques de Nicaragua', <http//:www.puebloindio.org>

Toledo, V. M. (1992a) 'What is ethnoecology?: origins, scope and implications of a rising discipline', *Etnoecológica*, 1(1): 5–22

— (1992b) 'Bio-economics costs', in T. E. Downing, S. Hecht, H. A. Pearson, and C. García-Downing (eds), *Development or Destruction*, Boulder, CO: Westview Press, pp. 67–93

— (2000) *La Paz en Chiapas: ecología, luchas indígenas y modernidad alternativa*, Mexico: Editorial Quinto Sol

— (2001) 'Indigenous peoples, biodiversity and encyclopedia of biodiversity', vol. 3, San Diego, CA: Academic Press, pp. 451–63

Toledo, V. M., P. Alarcón-Cháires, P. Moguel, M. Olivo, E. Leyequien, A. Rodríguez and A. Cabrera (2001) 'El atlas etnoecológico de México y Centroamérica: fundamentos, métodos y resultados', *Etnoecológica*, 8/9: 7–41

Toledo, V. M., B. Ortiz and S. Medellín (1994) 'Biodiversity island in a sea of pastureland: indigenous resource management in the humid tropics of Mexico', *Etnoecológica*, 2(3): 37–49

UAES (1997) 'Valuación económica de la diversidad biológica', paper drawn up by the SEMARNAP Economic and Social Analysis Unit for CONABIO, Mexico

World Factbook (2000) Washington, DC: Central Intelligence Agency, <http://education.yahoo.com/reference/factbook/>

14 | Indigenous anti-poverty strategies in an Australian town

ROBYN EVERSOLE, LEON RIDGEWAY AND DAVID MERCER

Indigenous poverty and grass-roots strategies

Around the world, people who identify themselves as indigenous are consistently found to be among the most disadvantaged. Culturally distinct, often historically dispossessed and living within the influence of a dominant culture whose rules and values differ significantly from their own, indigenous peoples face a range of obstacles. Depending on their particular circumstances, they may lack access to appropriate services, suffer poor living conditions, and find that they have little say as individuals or groups in the decisions that affect them. Given the conditions of poverty of many indigenous peoples, the question becomes: how to overcome these obstacles and reverse situations of disadvantage.

Outsiders who want to assist with problems such as poverty generally recognize that solutions cannot be imposed, but must rather reflect indigenous peoples' own priorities and ways of doing things. Those people who know their communities' situation from the inside are often in the best position to identify what the important issues are, and what strategies are most likely to work to address these issues. This is even more clearly the case for indigenous peoples, who define themselves as culturally distinct from other populations, and whose values and ways of doing things may therefore be quite different from those of outsiders who come to them wanting to help (see, e.g., Simonelli and Earle 2003; Wilson 2003; Healy 2001).

An entire literature around 'grass-roots' and 'community' development recognizes the wisdom of supporting local solutions to local problems and valuing the insider knowledge of communities (e.g. Ife 2002; Healy 2001; Blunt and Warren 1996; Chambers 1994; Hirschman 1984). At the same time, there is also a growing recognition that, while 'bottom up' may be preferable to 'top down' social change, locals do not have access to all the resources they need to solve problems such as poverty (see, e.g., Keare 2001; Mohan and Stokke 2000). Partnerships and collaboration with outsiders, as well as the ability to influence the policy environment through self-advocacy and democratic processes, are thus necessary. For indigenous peoples, working with non-indigenous individuals and organizations can provide valuable resources and support – so long as they retain control of the processes that affect them.

What kinds of anti-poverty strategies do indigenous peoples themselves choose to pursue? Given the emphasis on the importance of indigenous peoples driving their own anti-poverty agendas, the dearth of practical studies on this topic is surprising. There is some work in the area of indigenous political movements and self-advocacy (e.g. Burgete Cal y Mayor 2000; Ramos 1998; Smith 1983) as well as a handful of studies dealing specifically with indigenous economic development (McBride 2001; Anderson 1997; Cornell and Kalt 1992), and several related explorations of the concept of 'ethno-development' in Latin America (Healy 2001; Partridge and Uquillas 1996; Plant 1998; van Nieuwkoop and Uquillas 2000; Radcliffe 2003). There is also a strong tradition of work in anthropology, and particularly economic anthropology, explicating the functioning and logic of non-Western social and economic systems. Some good research has been done on the changing economic strategies of indigenous peoples within their larger social and economic contexts (e.g. Korovkin 1998; Goldin 1996; Smith 1984). Yet much of this work has not addressed the preoccupations of those interested in the practical business of fighting poverty. International development professionals and governments, for their part, have tended to focus their analysis on anti-poverty programmes initiated, or at least funded, by outsiders, while indigenous peoples' own initiatives and strategies have remained largely invisible.

This chapter offers a closer look at 'insider' or community-driven anti-poverty strategies in one indigenous Australian community over a two-year study period (from April 2001 to April 2003). The context is urban, characterized by close daily contact with mainstream Australian culture. Thus, the context differs significantly from that of isolated/remote Australian indigenous communities. This is also a very diverse community, including people from the local country and linguistic group as well as indigenous Australians from other areas. There are also divisions among family groups, and a history of inter-family conflict. Thus, this is not the cohesive social unit that the label 'indigenous community' might suggest. Nevertheless, indigenous residents of the area do share a common indigenous identity (comprising only about 3 per cent of the town's population of about 30,000, with a total of about 2,800 people in the larger region). As a result, they often speak of the local indigenous people or indigenous community as a clearly defined – though clearly diverse – interest group.

This chapter details a range of initiatives that have been created by and for members of this indigenous community in order to address particular manifestations of poverty. The goal here is not to evaluate the effectiveness of each initiative – that would take many more pages than are available here, and also enter into eminently more political terrain. Rather, the aim is to provide a broad overview of what was done and what was proposed by indigenous people and organizations during the two-year study period. Such an overview allows us to highlight how members of indigenous groups in one local area define poverty and the kinds of actions and strategies they use to address it. It also provides an opportunity to explore the way in which relationships between the indigenous community and outsiders are often central to the process of social change.

Solving poverty from the inside? Indigenous initiatives in one town

Indigenous people comprise approximately 2 per cent of the total Australian population. Of this total, 30 per cent is registered as living in major cities, 26 per cent in remote or very remote areas, and the remainder in non-metropolitan regional centres such as the town that was the site of this study. Findings of a recently released Australian Commonwealth government report, *Overcoming Indigenous Disadvantage: Key Indicators 2003* (SCRGSP 2003), reflect the consistent conclusion that indigenous Australians are by far the poorest and most marginalized sector of the Australian population when judged by mainstream economic, housing, employment and related standards.[1] The average median family income for indigenous Australians is currently 68 per cent that of non-indigenous Australians, and an estimated 30 per cent of all indigenous households are income-poor. In addition, the indigenous unemployment rate is four times higher, the imprisonment rate is sixteen times higher, and life expectancy at birth is 25 per cent lower (Altman 2001; Yencken and Porter 2001) – about twenty years less than that of non-indigenous Australians.

Poverty among Australia's indigenous population is directly linked to processes of forced dispossession, and many have argued that the dramatic decline into poverty can be dated precisely to what Johnson (2000: 8) has called that 'single catastrophic event – the English colonisation of this country'. Prior to 1788 – and using such indicators as health and fitness, spiritual well-being, diet and available leisure time – historians such as Geoffrey Blainey (1985: 11) have mounted a strong argument that '... the standard of living in a normal year was high; higher than that of at least 70 per cent of the population of Europe in 1788'. Since 1976, when the Aboriginal Land Rights Act (NT) was enacted, both parliament and the courts have started to recognize native title rights, albeit tentatively. Following the High Court's landmark ruling in *Mabo*, in June 1992, the Native Title Act 1993 was enacted by the federal parliament. This was, however, significantly weakened by the Native Title Amendment Act in 1998. The recent experience in Australia has been that small advances have often been undermined following a change of government.

The following overview of indigenous-led anti-poverty initiatives in one Australian town over a two-year period reveals great diversity and creativity in addressing the poverty issues highlighted above. A review of these initiatives allows us to explore how indigenous people in this town define and talk about poverty, and the kinds of actions they themselves take to address poverty issues. Finally, these initiatives reveal the close interplay between indigenous initiatives and non-indigenous organizations, pointing to the pivotal role of such relationships.

The focus here is on specific, easily observable projects and activities. Some are formal projects and programmes; others are less formal activities. Over the course of the study, the importance of informal anti-poverty initiatives became clear: from an indigenous leader who took young people camping in his spare time, to a professional who extended her job description to include advocacy work. Informal anti-poverty actions – such as the strong mentoring and family leadership undertaken by older women known as 'aunties', or informal networking between indigenous and non-indigenous people – are clearly important, but they can be overlooked when the focus is on more formal and easily identifiable projects and programmes.

The research methods employed here were ethnographic observation and action research in the study town, carried out by two of the co-authors (one indigenous and one non-indigenous) during the period April 2001 to April 2003. The researchers were involved in a few of these projects and activities: planning, implementing or participating (and documenting them via action research). In many of the other initiatives, the researchers were not involved; these initiatives were documented via observations in the local community (ethnographic research). The small size of the study town and its indigenous population, and the extensive local networks of the researchers, made it possible to assemble a well-rounded picture of the kinds of initiatives that were taking place over this two-year period, and to take into account the diversity of interests and approaches within the local community itself.

Various indigenous community members and groups undertook anti-poverty initiatives during the study period. These initiatives were not centrally coordinated within the community, nor was there consensus about these initiatives and their benefits. As noted above, this community had many internal divisions. It was not at all unusual for local indigenous individuals and groups to criticize – often sharply – the projects and activities of other indigenous individuals and groups. Verbal conflicts often arose over the legitimacy of projects (did the proposed project or activity really involve the indigenous community?; was it appropriate to an indigenous way of doing things?; was it well and honestly managed?). The motivations of those who started or ran initiatives were also questioned (was the project or activity designed to benefit themselves or their family members, rather than the whole community?; had they shown favouritism in the allocation of rewards and benefits?). Criticism from some quarter was generally inevitable, and there was a frequent lack of coordination and support among different groups doing different things. Nevertheless, all were addressing the same basic issues.

Issues

Many meetings and informal discussions highlighted the 'issues' that were facing the local indigenous community locally over the two-year study period. *Poverty*, as a concept, was almost never mentioned. Local indigenous people talked about *issues* such as reliance on government-funded welfare-work projects (Community Development Employment Projects, known as CDEP) rather than mainstream employment, cyclical incarceration, family violence (particularly against women), health issues, housing issues, youth issues, cultural retention issues, access to financial capital, and so forth. The indigenous community members did not refer to these as discussions about 'poverty'. Yet these discussions nevertheless indicated a range of social and economic issues that fit clearly into both international poverty discourse and national discussions about indigenous poverty indicators.[2]

In their conversations, indigenous people clearly located these issues within a wider social and political context. Not surprisingly, there was often reference to historic conditions of marginalization and oppression, highlighted particularly with reference to the Stolen Generation, in which indigenous children of mixed descent were removed from their families and institutionalized or adopted by non-indigenous families.[3] The historical context was also reflected in discussions about the contemporary dependence of indigenous people on government programmes. Local indigenous people often expressed frustration with government support, perceived as bureaucratic, top-down, and with funding allocations going disproportionately to remote peoples. At the same time, there was also dispute over local indigenous organizations' ability to manage their own funding and programmes effectively. Finally, there were frequent statements about the limited recognition given to living indigenous culture, heritage and history in the local region.

Projects and actions

Over the two-year study period, indigenous Australians in the local area undertook a range of initiatives to address social and economic issues of importance to their local indigenous community. Some of these initiatives were new, some were ongoing, and some were only in the planning stages. Most were the result of efforts by local indigenous professionals or community leaders, who were often more adept than others in their community at moving between cultures. A local indigenous inter-agency network, Gnarlung Moort (Our People/Family), worked to ensure that efforts were not duplicated and that people were informed about the projects and activities that were taking place. In doing so, Gnarlung Moort played an important role in starting to address the lack of coordination among different groups doing different things.

An overview of projects and activities undertaken by local indigenous community members indicates that they were intended to address the kinds of 'issues' highlighted above. These initiatives also acknowledged – and sometimes attempted to change – the wider social context in which these issues were located. The strategies used to address both the issues themselves and their wider contexts can be divided roughly into the following four categories: Providing Social Support, Creating Economic Opportunities, Strengthening Cultural Visibility, and Exercising Leadership and Participation in the Wider Community.

Providing social support A range of projects and activities over the study period were geared to specifically address issues concerning people's health and well-being: particularly for young people, women and families as a whole. These were neither medicalized models of health promotion nor mainstream government-funded social services, but rather specific strategies of support (mentoring, counselling, visiting, providing practical/logistical assistance) and learning (via workshops, training) that were firmly based in the local indigenous community.

Such programmes were generally referred to as 'social' to distinguish them from projects with a more 'economic' or 'cultural' focus. Nevertheless, the distinction here is more one of strategy than of intent. Both 'economic' and 'cultural' projects and activities were also generally understood as strategies for addressing social issues. Economic strategies could provide employment and funds for social programmes. Cultural strategies could provide employment opportunities, support for youth and families, and increased recognition/decreased marginalization in the wider culture – which in turn could positively impact on social issues. Thus, social support strategies were only one approach to tackling social issues in the local indigenous community, and there was frequent overlap, particularly between social support and more overtly 'cultural' strategies. For instance, youth social programmes often had a strong cultural component, such as bush tucker walks, or the passing on of other kinds of traditional knowledge.

The indigenous-initiated and/or indigenous-run social-support projects and activities actually in progress during the two-year study period covered a wide range of topics: from crime and justice, to women's health, to recreation. These projects and activities included: a drug action team with outreach workers and various educational activities; an emergency cash fund; a prison visitors' programme; youth mentoring programmes; a fashion-modelling programme for children and youths; various school-holiday programmes, youth outings and camping trips; a family violence workshop; at least one local women's group; a women's camp; legal advocacy (via the Aboriginal Justice Programme); various kinds of advocacy with social-service providers (via the local staff of the Department of Indigenous Affairs); sports activities, visiting sporting personalities, a football carnival, and indigenous sports awards; other awards as part of NAIDOC (National Aboriginal and Islander Day Observance Committee) celebrations; various educational and social activities undertaken by the local Aboriginal school; and student support offered by indigenous centres at a local high school, the technical college and the local university.

In addition, during the study period a range of other projects and activities were proposed by indigenous community members. These included: a mentoring/training/ support programme for cyclical offenders (men who have been imprisoned multiple times) and their families; an indigenous night patrol and sobering-up shelter; and a drop-in centre to help with access to jobs and accommodation.

Creating economic opportunities In addition to those projects and activities that focused on providing social supports, another common strategy employed by indigenous community members was to focus on the creation of economic opportunities. Such projects focused on businesses that would generate employment from within the indigenous community itself. These businesses were variously conceived of as: the self-employment of individuals (such as Aboriginal artists), businesses run by individuals, businesses run by family groups, and businesses owned by the community as a whole (and which would provide funding for social programmes and spin-off businesses). There was also a focus on training and equipping people to take up economic opportunities, whether as business owners or employees. Finally, there was a close relationship between such economic strategies and the cultural strategies discussed below, as local indigenous people articulated a perceived competitive advantage in the art and tourism sectors owing to their cultural distinctiveness.

The indigenous-run economic initiatives observed during the study period included: an indigenous business magazine; a tour-guide training programme and a new indigenous tour-guiding business (run from the local technical college); projects to provide training to indigenous artists; projects to exhibit, promote and sell local indigenous artwork; an indigenous art-and-craft shop run through the CDEP programme and attempting to become independent; and a range of subsidized CDEP businesses providing training opportunities and opportunities for initial business development. These indigenous-run initiatives operated in addition to government programmes facilitating study, training and apprenticeships for indigenous people, as well as the courses on offer at the local technical college and university, which also had significant indigenous input and direction.

Other economic projects were also proposed during the study period. These included an indigenous business support group with paid facilitators; the purchase of property by local groups as an investment strategy generating rental returns; a community development foundation; a major indigenous tourism attraction (a cultural centre) with associated training and business opportunities; as well as various individual and small-group business proposals, ranging from furniture design to wine production.

Strengthening cultural visibility In addition to those anti-poverty strategies that took primarily a social-service or economic-opportunities focus, another group of projects and activities focused primarily on strategies of cultural affirmation, cultural education and strengthening the visibility of the local indigenous culture though emphasis on indigenous arts, language and traditional knowledge. As noted above, the links between cultural strategies and other strategies were very close, and many projects employed multiple strategies.

Indigenous-run cultural-visibility initiatives were diverse and varied. They included an annual festival of indigenous culture; a local indigenous dance group; indigenous language classes; school visits and presentations by indigenous people; and cultural sensitivity training programmes for agencies and employees. Some of the economic strategies detailed above, such as exhibitions of work by indigenous artists and the local tour-guide training programme, were also cultural-visibility strategies. The proposal to establish a major community-run cultural centre as a tourist attraction was conceived of both as a source of economic opportunities for indigenous people and as a way to make local indigenous culture more visible. Similarly, a local Careers and Culture Expo was a good example of how indigenous-run projects frequently addressed cultural, social and economic issues at the same time.

Leadership and participation in the wider community A final key anti-poverty strategy initiated by indigenous people in the study area involved bridge-building with the wider, non-indigenous local community. Such bridge-building was both formal and informal. The focus was on exercising leadership, participating in the wider community, supporting other indigenous people, and developing strong networks among non-indigenous people. Networks were particularly important here: both making them, and maintaining them for future benefit.

Formal leadership and participation activities during the study period included indigenous people taking on leadership roles within non-indigenous organizations and projects (particularly non-profit organizations) such as the local arts management board, the local university's advisory group, and an inter-agency youth project. Formal activities also included an indigenous woman running for local government.

Informal leadership and participation activities included active involvement at local events such as art exhibition openings, speaking at a major local conference, and participating in informal social occasions – for instance, Friday-afternoon drinks at the local hotel. Such networking activities helped establish relationships with non-indigenous people, including politicians, journalists, union representatives, government officials at all levels, and other key people. Informal networking also provided the opportunity to carry out cultural awareness training in enjoyable environments: providing information to non-indigenous people and creating positive experiences to combat the negative images reported in the press.

Conclusion: insider initiative and the complex terrain of social change

This chapter has provided an overview of anti-poverty initiatives by and for indigenous people in one diverse Australian town over a two-year study period. Both actual and proposed projects and activities have been included. The initiatives listed were those implemented independently by indigenous organizations, groups and/or individuals, as well as those implemented in collaboration with non-indigenous organizations. The latter organizations included the local art gallery, the local technical college, the education department, the local university, the local community house, state government departments, local government, and others.

A consideration of the kinds of indigenous-run anti-poverty initiatives observed in the study town is instructive. A review of these initiatives demonstrates that:

1. Although 'poverty' is not discussed per se, local indigenous people nevertheless identify the issues of importance to them and strategize ways to address them. Even in this incredibly diverse and often conflictive community, the issues identified were generally the same, and can be connected with elements in more general conceptualizations of poverty. These included reliance on government-funded welfare-work projects, cyclical incarceration, family violence, health issues, housing issues, concerns about the future of youth, loss of cultural resources, and lack of financial resources. There was also general agreement about the contextual factors that influenced these issues: including a history of disenfranchisement, the perceived ineffectiveness of both local indigenous and bureaucratic non-indigenous organizations, and a lack of recognition of local indigenous people and their history.
2. A range of strategies can be used to address poverty. In this case, various projects and activities could be classified as taking on a primarily social-support, economic-opportunity, cultural-visibility or wider-community-network approach to the issues at hand. It is also clear, however, that there was a considerable overlap among these different approaches. Many projects and activities, for instance, included at least some 'cultural' components. And most projects were intended, directly or indirectly, to address social issues. Meanwhile, people working on 'social' projects recognized that 'economic' issues were important – and vice versa. Sometimes, multiple approaches were integrated within a single project or activity: for example, in the successful annual Careers and Cultural Expo held in this town, which addressed social, cultural and economic issues using a range of strategies (for instance: providing cultural activities, exposing youth to economic, education and training opportunities, and cultivating links with non-indigenous organizations). Overall, a holistic approach to change was evident in the range of local indigenous anti-poverty strategies.
3. Informal activities were at least as important as formal projects. Nor should recreational and entertainment activities be overlooked when searching for indigenous anti-poverty initiatives. Many excursions and sports activities for children had a serious purpose: for instance, strengthening cultural identity and providing indigenous role models

for young people. Fun activities for adults, such as Friday-night drinks at the hotel, were also opportunities for networking and cross-cultural education.

4. Collaboration with non-indigenous individuals and organizations was often an important element of projects. In many of the indigenous initiatives mentioned here, non-indigenous organizations provided key infrastructure, staff time (of both indigenous and non-indigenous employees), and/or other kinds of logistical and funding support to indigenous initiatives. Thus, part of the success of indigenous initiatives hinges on establishing constructive relationships along these lines – while at the same time overcoming bureaucratic processes that can stifle dialogue. Informal social networks among indigenous and non-indigenous people are particularly useful in facilitating these sorts of constructive relationships.

To conclude, an in-depth look at indigenous anti-poverty strategies in one Australian town demonstrates the diverse and holistic ways in which local indigenous people addressed negative conditions and issues, while also grappling with the challenges of these issues' larger context. We see how a diverse range of factions and interest groups in the study town used both formal and informal strategies, working not only within their own indigenous community, but with non-indigenous organizations as well. Strategies to bridge indigenous and non-indigenous spheres of activity often played a key role: whether this was educating the non-indigenous locals about 40,000 years of indigenous history, sitting on the board of a predominantly non-indigenous community organization, or ensuring that indigenous youth could access mainstream employment. Given the importance of these cross-overs, there is clearly a role for non-indigenous people in supporting indigenous anti-poverty initiatives. For those who would do so, a good starting point is to understand the issues, to be aware of indigenous people's own strategies to address them – and then to be a part of the relationships that facilitate change.

Notes

1 Findings specifically on life expectancy, educational attainment, labour force participation and unemployment, household and individual income, home ownership, suicide, criminal victimization, and imprisonment rates.

2 See, for instance, Aboriginal and Torres Strait Islander Commission (2003) on 'headline' indicators of indigenous disadvantage. Three categories of poverty are defined: *subsistence*, *participation* and *absolute* poverty, with key indicators for each, giving a sense of the multi-dimensional nature of indigenous poverty.

3 Removal of Aboriginal children from their families was authorized in Western Australia up until as recently as 1972 (see HREOC 1997; Hall 1995: 11).

References

Aboriginal and Torres Strait Island Commission (2003) 'Submission to inquiry into poverty and financial hardship in Australia', Canberra: Senate Community Affairs Reference Committee

Altman, J. (2001) 'Overcoming indigenous poverty', *CEDA Bulletin*, March, pp. 56–60

Anderson, R. B. (1997) 'Corporate/indigenous partnerships in economic development: the First Nations in Canada', *World Development*, 25(9): 1,483ff

Blainey, G. (1985) 'Australia: a bird's eye view', in S. R. Graubard (ed.), *Australia: The Daedalus Symposium*, North Ryde: Angus and Robertson, pp. 1–27

Blunt, P. and D. M. Warren (eds) (1996) *Indigenous Organizations and Development*, London: Intermediate Technology Publications

Burgete Cal y Mayor, A. (2000) *Indigenous Autonomy in Mexico*, Copenhagen: International Work Group for Indigenous Affairs

Chambers, R. (1994) 'The origins and practice of participatory rural appraisal', *World Development*, 22(7): 953–69

Cornell, S. and J. P. Kalt (eds) (1992) *What Can Tribes Do? Strategies and Institutions in American Indian Economic Development*, Los Angeles, CA: American Indian Studies Center, UCLA

Goldin, L. R. (1996) 'Economic mobility strategies among Guatemalan peasants: prospects and limits of nontraditional vegetable cash crops', *Human Organization*, 55(1): 99–100

Government of Queensland (2002) 'Historic reparation offer to Indigenous Queenslanders to proceed', ministerial media statement, The Hon. Peter Beattie, Premier

Hall, S. (1995) 'No better than anyone else', discussion paper on the role of the churches and related organizations, religious orders and missionary societies in Aboriginal child removal and institutionalization, Social Responsibilities Commission of the Anglican Church in the Province of Western Australia

Healy, K. (2001) *Llamas, Weavings, and Organic Chocolate: Multicultural Grassroots Development in the Andes and Amazon of Bolivia*, Notre Dame, IN: University of Notre Dame Press

Hirschman, A. O. (1984) *Getting Ahead Collectively: Grassroots Experiences in Latin America*, Elmsford, NY: Pergamon Press

HREOC (1997) 'Bringing them home', report of the National Inquiry into the Separation of Aboriginal and Torres Strait Islander Children from Their Families, Sydney: Human Rights and Equal Opportunity Commission

Ife, J. (2002) *Community Development: Community-based Alternatives in an Age of Globalisation* (2nd edn), Frenchs Forest, NSW: Pearson Education Australia

Johnson, J. (2000) 'Sugar, tea-leaf, flour and meat', *Comment* (Brotherhood of St Laurence), pp. 8–9

Keare, D. H. (2001) 'Learning to clap: reflections on top-down versus bottom-up development', *Human Organization*, 60(2): 159–65

Korovkin, T. (1998) 'Commodity production and ethnic culture: Otavalo, Northern Ecuador', *Economic Development and Cultural Change*, 47(1): 125–54

McBride, J. (ed.) (2001) 'Our own vision – our own plan, what six First Nations organisations have accomplished with their own Economic Development Plans', Burnaby, British Colombia: Community Economic Development Centre, Simon Fraser University, <http: //www.sfu.ca/cedc/abced/Our_Own_Vision8.pdf>

Mohan, G. and K. Stokke (2000) 'Participatory development and empowerment: the dangers of localism', *Third World Quarterly*, 21(2): 247–68

Partridge, W. L., J. E. Uquillas and K. Johns (1996) 'Including the excluded: ethnodevelopment in Latin America', paper presented at the Annual World Bank Conference on Development in Latin America and the Caribbean, Bogotá

Plant, R. (1998) 'Issues in indigenous poverty and development', Technical Study no. IND-105, Indigenous Peoples and Community Development Unit, Sustainable Development Department, Washington, DC: Inter-American Development Bank

Radcliffe, S. (2003) 'Ethno-development in the Andes and the construction of culture in development', paper presented at the Association of American Geographers Annual Meeting, New Orleans

Ramos, A. R. (1998) *Indigenism: Ethnic Politics in Brazil*, Madison: University of Wisconsin Press

SCRGSP (Steering Committee for the Review of Government Service Provision) (2003) *Overcoming Indigenous Disadvantage: Key Indicators 2003*, Productivity Commission, Canberra

Sheldon, W. (2003) 'Indigenous situational disadvantage and sustainable development in Australia', Canberra: Capacity Building & Integrated Development Section, Aboriginal and Torres Strait Islander Services (ATSIS)

Simonelli, J. and D. Earle (2003) 'Disencumbering development: alleviating poverty through autonomy in Chiapas', in R. Eversole (ed.), *Here to Help, NGOs Combating Poverty in Latin America*, Armonk, NY: M. E. Sharpe

Smith, C. (1984) 'Does a commodity economy enrich the few while ruining the masses? Differentiation among petty commodity producers in Guatemala', *Journal of Peasant Studies*, 11(3): 60–95

Smith, R. C. (1983) 'A search for unity within diversity: peasant unions, ethnic federations, and Indianist movements in the Andean republics', in T. Macdonald Jr (ed.), *Native Peoples and Economic Development: Six Case Studies from Latin America*, Massachusetts: Cultural Survival Occasional Paper no. 16

Van Nieuwkoop, M. and J. E. Uquillas (2000) 'Defining ethno-development in operational terms: lessons from the Ecuador Indigenous and Afro-

Ecuadoran Peoples Development Project', Working Paper no. 6, Washington, DC: Latin American and Caribbean Regional Office, World Bank

Wilson, P. (2003) 'Market articulation and poverty eradication? Critical reflection on tourist-oriented craft production in Amazonian Ecuador', in R. Eversole (ed.), *Here to Help, NGOs Combating Poverty in Latin America*, Armonk, NY: M. E. Sharpe

Yencken, D. and L. Porter (2001) *A Just and Sustainable Australia*, Redfern: Australian Council of Social Service

15 | Sami responses to poverty in the Nordic countries

CHRISTIAN JAKOB BURMEISTER HICKS
AND ÁNDE SOMBY

The Sami are the indigenous people of Fenno-Scandinavia (Norway, Sweden and Finland) and the Kola Peninsula (north-western Russia). This chapter deals exclusively with the Sami of Fenno-Scandinavia owing to the contrasting economic conditions of the Fenno-Scandinavian Sami and those of the Kola Peninsula. The Fenno-Scandinavian or 'Nordic' Sami live in highly developed social welfare systems with governments that allow for greater autonomy than the Russian government. The Kola Sami do not share the same benefits as other Sami, owing to the limited political and economic control they have in Russia. The control that the Russian central government and the global markets hold over the Kola Sami makes it difficult for significant economic improvement even today.

There are also differences in the political and social situations of the Finnish, Swedish and Norwegian Sami. For instance, although the Finnish Sami do not have nearly such expansive rights as the Norwegian Sami, they did establish the first Sami parliament ten years before the Norwegian Sami and twenty before the Swedish Sami. The Finnish Sami also receive many of the same political privileges as the Norwegian Sami. Yet in Finland the Sami argue that there are no Sami-specific laws to secure them additional rights through their indigenous status.[1] In Norway, there are language laws that do allow the Sami greater latitude to teach their own language. In Sweden, on the other hand, Sami are far more disadvantaged legally than either of their eastern or western neighbours. Countless court rulings have gone against the Sami, despite the fact that prior to the nineteenth century Swedish Sami received the same rights as other citizens.[2]

This chapter will first trace the history of the Nordic Sami within the context of their current political/economic situation. It will then discuss their mechanisms and strategies for poverty alleviation within Finland, Norway and Sweden. The Nordic Sami have been extremely successful in their use of two distinctly different but co-dependent strategies. The first strategy has been to create a common Sami identity and culture during the last half-century and utilize the Nordic sense of morality and human rights to attract support for the Sami as a people. In this way, the Sami have effectively increased their ability to combat the social and economic ills that have plagued them for centuries. This strategy includes the use of public and governmental ethical principles to create pressure for increased rights and funding for the Sami, in order to correct and protect against poverty in northern Scandinavia. As an approach to combating poverty, this first strategy involves a range of activities that can together be termed 'cultural strengthening'. The second strategy is the Sami's effective use of the collective financial resources available from different sources, including ministries of the national government, municipal governments and Sami organizations.

Cultural strengthening

Arguably, in the early twenty-first century the political and societal standing of the Sami people is at its highest ever. There are vital Sami schools, social organizations, businesses and political parties. Poverty is at an all-time low in the northern parts of Scandinavia. In Norway and Finland, the Sami language is on track to be recognized as an official language in all government documents and in departments that pertain to Sami issues. The standard of living for the Sami is now nearly equal to that of other northern Scandinavian citizens.

The primary and most interesting reason for this transformation is the cultural creation of archetypal Sami traits, or 'Saminess', by the Sami elite from the 1950s to the early 1980s. The aim was to provide a stable basis for the development of a healthy indigenous community in northern Fenno-Scandinavia. In the late twentieth century, the Sami in Norway, and throughout Fenno-Scandinavia, have articulated a vision of pan-Sami identity based on ethnicity, culture, tradition and heritage, making putative ties to the past in an attempt to establish historical legitimacy. But although all such categories share in their normalized links with an imaginary past, in the ethno-political context they are invoked and reproduced tactically, and are 'created in the present, thus reflecting the contestation of interests more than the cultural essence of a purportedly homogeneous and bounded "traditional" group' (Conrad 1999: 1). This is not to say that there was no such thing as a standard Sami type, or even Sami cultural and ethnic traits, prior to the 1950s.

On the contrary, Sami culture was and has remained a distinct culture from the surrounding Nordic culture. The Sami are continually in conflict among themselves, however, owing to the fact that they see themselves as Norwegian or Swedish or Finnish first, and Sami second. The main reason for this dual identity is their assimilation into the dominant culture. It is also based on the fact that the Sami enjoy many of the benefits of being

Scandinavian and readily identify with the Nordic culture owing to these cultures' co-existence with each other over centuries. Nor has there been one common identifying basis for Sami culture. The coastal Sami of Norway differ in culture from the mountain Sami of Norway and Sweden, who differ from the Kola Sami of Russia. To make things more difficult, Sami cultural lines do not follow but rather transcend national boundaries. Sami in northern Norway have more in common with Finnish Sami than they do with southern Norwegian Sami. Through the building of Sami-ness, the elites made their cultures more uniform and less confusing for the outside cultures to understand. The Sami leaders wanted to be able to protect their people through the use of common cultural symbols that were common to most of the different Sami groups.

The movement towards a common Sami culture began in the 1950s and continued to be modified through the 1970s because the Sami elite found the need to promote and protect their communities in order to diminish discrimination and other hardships, including economic deprivation. Prior to the end of the Second World War many Sami hid their Sami identity in order to save themselves and their families from persecution. After the Second World War and the atrocities surrounding the Holocaust, however, world powers were concerned with human rights and colonial issues, allowing the Sami to benefit from a change in political sentiment.

> ... (A) culturally and politically fragmented Sami population characterized by the 'tutelage' of the majority population and by a lack of a collective 'ethnic spirit', under the leadership of a small cultural-political elite, beg [*sic*] building an organized and nationally unifying ethno-political movement which has been called 'The Sami Movement'. (Eidheim 1969: 3)

Their cultural strengthening involved promoting the Sami culture as a relatively cohesive culture which has particular cultural traits that set it apart from mainstream society. Indigenous identity is vital to cultural strengthening because it is particularly useful in showing the authenticity and legitimacy of the Sami as original inhabitants of Scandinavia and therefore entitled to special rights. 'In linking the present to the past, the "ethnogenetic function" gives the group the "terms to understand the present and *make claims on it*", and has, since the 1960s, been an effectively employed and well-recognized strategy of indigenous groups in the political disputes with "dominant powers" over land, resources, and self-determination' (Conrad 1999: 1).

In the Nordic countries, where equality and homogeneity were promoted over and above individuality, indigenous identity was both particularly difficult and important. The sameness of Nordic culture conflicts with and impedes differentness and made the Sami elite's task more difficult than might have been the case in countries with a more heterogeneous population.

> This publicly articulated, politically motivated, and ethnically determined Sami identity co-exists and, at times, conflicts, with other intersecting terms of identification: ones perhaps more individualized, or whose lines of identification are drawn more from social experiences than from an *a priori* ethnicity. Nonetheless, what can be seen as an ethnic identity consciously constructed by the Sami elite for ethno-political purposes cannot be dismissed on the basis of this same 'construction'. The terms of Saminess have sedimented deeply into popular enactment and individual conceptions of Sami identity, with the official terms of 'Saminess' tending to take on a 'powerful salience in the experience of those who bear them, often to the extent of appearing to be natural, essential, primordial'. (ibid.: 3)

Owing to the political climate in the 1960s and 1970s, however, this was less complicated and better received than previously.

By having a coherent and consistent Sami culture, the Sami asserted their difference from the Nordic majority culture and therefore demanded special rights and support. This meant that additional protections from racist policies could be formulated by the government and the public. The protection was also an attempt to reduce the poverty level for the Sami. It included resource ownership, or at least stewardship of fish, game and land rights (threatened by mining and logging interests from outside of Sapmi (the Sami name for their region) and even by the public's request for national parks in the north of Fenno-Scandinavia), as well as access to financial resources. The increased resource rights allowed the Sami to maintain a subsistence lifestyle and increased their legitimacy as an indigenous people. Most importantly, the grazing rights for reindeer on public lands meant that the Sami would not lose a major icon of their culture and significant amounts of income. The land rights issue became extremely contentious, based on the Sami's needs for pastoral land.

The most familiar form of Sami cultural representation is as reindeer herders. Today, reindeer herding is so closely tied to the Sami cultural identity that many traditionally non-herding Sami, such as the coastal Sami, identify with this pastoral lifestyle. This is due in part to the efforts of three different groups within the Sami people: the Sami artists, the political leaders and the reindeer herding organizations. Though many coastal and other traditionally non-herding Sami identify with reindeer herding, reindeer herding as a symbol of Saminess is not without its problems. Not all Sami identify with the reindeer lifestyle. Many of these groups resent the position that the reindeer-herding Sami have gained in politics. They feel that reindeer Sami have 'sold out' to mainstream society, and that other Sami have not been allowed a strong enough voice. This animosity among the Sami can be said to apply to southern Sami versus northern Sami and the linguistically different Sami groups.

At the beginning of the last century, there were many trade and social organizations representing the Sami, including reindeer herders' cooperatives. In 1947 the oldest and strongest reindeer-herding organization, the Sami Reindeer Herders' Association, was founded in Norway. This association has been a significant lobby group and trade organization for reindeer herders in dealings with the local and national governments. The Sami Reindeer Herders' Association helped bring reindeer herding to the forefront of agricultural politics in the highly agricultural country of Norway. The resurgence of such organizations in the post-Second World War period marked a renewed interest in reindeer herding for Sami and even other Scandinavians. The rise in membership of reindeer herders' organizations allowed for greater solidarity and visibility for what had always been a significant industry in the north. Currently, about 40 per cent of Norway's land is used for reindeer grazing (Brenna 1997).

The Sami political leadership also played a key role in bringing reindeer herding into the public's consciousness. The Sami leadership argued that reindeer herding should be the exclusive right of the Sami. Thus, the Sami could gain a monopoly on reindeer herding and thereby protect Sami agriculture. Reindeer would also provide a recognizable and distinct icon for the public to associate with Sami and Sami culture.

> During the 1960s, the commission in charge of revising the herding law (1964 års rennäringssakkunniga) [with some Sami impact] retained the emphasis on exclusivity to reduce the number of herders, distribute the work more equally, and allow each herder to achieve a higher standard of living. The commission reasoned that the problems of poverty and small-scale, labour-intensive family operations could be solved by rationalization in the manner of agricultural reforms taken during the 1950s ... Hence, the commission focused on reorganizing the Sami village into a producer association, proposed other structural measures to improve the efficiency of reindeer herding ... (Korsmo 1993: 34).

Reindeer herding eventually became an exclusively Sami endeavour by law and the Nordic governments provided at least some protection of public lands for grazing.[3]

Parallel to these changes there was a blossoming of artistic pursuits within Sami culture. The improved political voice of Sami allowed for greater expression among the Sami artistic community. Artists, poets and authors from within the Sami culture all presented the Sami as ecologically aware, peaceful and vibrant people. Even the dark and brooding portrayals of life and legends in such movies as *Pathfinder* showed the Sami as a positive culture, distinct from those that surrounded it.

People around the world associate reindeer with Santa or St Nicholas. The Finns contend that Santa lives in Finland near Rovaneimi. Here the elves are portrayed as having a distinctly Sami appearance, in their physical characteristics, clothing and other aspects of material culture. Many of the employees of Santa's Village are real Sami. By encouraging their image as the stewards of such lovable animals as reindeer, the Sami, and especially the artists, poets and writers, have engendered positive sentiments in the public psyche.

The Sami's success in providing cultural legitimacy and standardization through the symbolism of reindeer herding is even shown in the Norwegian government's documents and websites. On the official Norwegian government's website, there is a section on Sami reindeer herding which states, 'This objective involves making the business ecologically, economically and culturally sustainable – in other words, a business that can continue to provide a living for families connected with reindeer herding without undermining the distinctive character of the Sami' (Brenna 1997).

As the Sami cultural movement has gained momentum, additional symbols from material culture have been introduced.

> In the process of establishing a Sami identity that could encompass the various economic, linguistic, regional, ecological, cultural, subsistence, religious and political differences, a set of symbols was developed that was at once generalized and essentialized enough to appeal to the broad spectrum ... In terms of the present study, the symbols were emphatically non-Norwegian ... (Conrad 1999: 9)

A people's clothing helps define a people as having a common heritage. Universal Sami clothing was worn on different national holidays to display one's Saminess. In the past overt displays of individuality and indigenousness would have been frowned upon. In 1977, a Sami flag was created using the most common colours in Sami clothing (Bjørklund 2000: 27). Such a strong statement as a national flag created controversy in Scandinavia. Some people believed this was the start of a Sami movement to split from Scandinavia and create their own country. This was, however, not the real intention of the creation of the flag. In 1979 the Norwegian Sami Union, one of the two largest political Sami organizations in Norway, wrote in its manifesto: 'The Norwegian Sami Union should work on the basis of the principles of the Norwegian Constitution, showing respect for the King and his Government, the Storting [Norwegian Parliament], and other state authorities in a democratic manner' (ibid.: 27). Others viewed the flag as a sign of solidarity among Sami. After all the controversy, the Sami flag helped the Sami identity and spirit to coalesce.

The most important symbol of Sami religion is the 'magic drum'. This drum was traditionally used by Sami shamans in ceremonies and to relate the Sami history. This symbol had been outlawed in the nineteenth and twentieth centuries. Finally, in the 1950s, this was revoked and in the 1970s the symbol quickly became another accepted cultural indicator.

The Sami *joik* or music was often used in conjunction with the magic drum to tell stories and histories or to render other messages. With the social and political actions of the 1970s, including the Alta protests (see below), the *joik* became a widespread political as well as cultural symbol. Secret messages were transmitted through *joik*s. Often these messages had very controversial meanings, and the *joik*s were a good way to confuse the authorities. Although *joik*s are not usually sung in certain areas, such as pubs and restaurants, they are used proudly elsewhere to declare an identification with Sami culture, such as at the international music festival held in Finnmark, Norway, Riddu Riððu.

The educational systems in Fenno-Scandinavia have been a source of both oppression and freedom to the Sami. On the one hand, they have outlawed Sami language, clothing and music. On the other hand, many Sami activists were able to pursue higher education in the 1970s solely to advance the Sami movement. They understood the advantages of understanding the Nordic political system and specifically the need for greater understanding of Scandinavian law. When this generation graduated, they became a powerful force in Scandinavian politics and law. Not only were they well educated, but they were also young, energetic and inspired by the civil rights movements of previous years. The increased standard of living, including better educational systems in the Sami areas, allowed for increased cultural and political development, and the increased cultural and political development allowed for increased standards of living.

In Norway there are now Sami schools up to university level where Sami culture, art and language are taught. In Finland and Norway the Sami have the right to use their language in nearly all government business that pertains to their rights. Moves are being made to have the Sami language accepted and taught to all emergency personnel in Sami-inhabited areas.[4]

> Although issues of ethnicity, heritage, culture and tradition are essential to the ethno-political debate in northern Norway, it is arguable that these

are not, in the final analysis, what are being fought *about*, but what are being fought *with*. Ethnicity, tradition, and culture, are thus not what are primarily at stake, but what serve as a 'justification or a code for authentic and alternative groupness' and are the 'basis of entitlement of the group to certain other stakes and rights, which will be specific to each instance'. (Conrad 1999: 2)

Sami political organizations were perhaps the best advocates and creators of a homogenous Sami culture. The first major Sami political organization to be started was called the Nordic Sami Council (NSC).[5] This organization was a pan-Nordic Sami organization, started in 1957, with the purpose of furthering the interests of the Sami people in politics. It was to represent the Sami people at national and international levels. At these levels the representatives of the Sami organizations presented Sami culture as a unified culture. The NSC was successful in many of its objectives throughout the next forty-seven years, including sending delegations to the United Nations and representing the Sami people at the Arctic Council, and it was the political arm of the Sami until the introduction of the different Sami parliaments.

The Finnish Sami Parliament was the first national Sami parliament, started in 1973. Parliaments in Norway and Sweden followed later in 1989 and 1993 respectively. Though these parliaments did not have any legislative powers, they were advisory bodies for the national government. They provided input and expert advice for the issues that pertained to the Sami people. As representatives from the different Sami parliaments came together they also presented the Sami culture in a cohesive way to the Fenno-Scandinavian public. These parliaments have focused particularly on economic or land and resource issues throughout northern Scandinavia. In some rare cases national governments have disregarded the Sami parliaments completely, but most of the time changes have been made to national legislation in response to the recommendations of the Sami parliaments. As consultative organs of the national governments, they have proved to be effective tools for protecting Sami interests nationally and locally. In addition, the Sami parliaments continue to send delegations to international organizations such as the United Nations, the European Union and the Barents Council to represent Sami welfare.

In the late 1970s a new and significant event propelled the Sami cause to the forefront of Nordic politics and created a groundswell of international opinion in favour of the Sami situation. The Norwegian governments planned to dam the Alta-Kautokeino river in order to provide badly needed hydroelectric energy for the industrialized south of Norway. The Norwegian

Sami argued that the environmental and economic implications of this project would devastate the Sami communities of the northernmost part of Norway, Finnmark. Today the Sami protest and opposition to the Alta-Kautokeino Dam can be seen as the single most important catalyst for the Sami movement. They came at a time when national and international interest in indigenous and environmental rights was competing with energy issues in many countries around the globe. 'The Sami Movement's ethno-political participation in the Alta affair was founded upon the premise that tampering with the natural environment in Sapmi would entail the infringement of an old Sami enterprise and industry and would, therefore, constitute a violation of Sami culture' (Eidheim 1997: 48).

During the planning stages of the Alta-Kautokeino hydroelectric project in the early 1970s, southern energy needs were placed far above Sami territory needs.[6] Though the Sami brought their concerns to the rest of Norway, there was little or no dialogue with them regarding the issue. In the end, seven young Sami intellectuals brought the conflict to the heart of the Norwegian government. They became engaged in a prolonged hunger-strike on the steps of the Storting (Norwegian parliament). They used Sami cultural images to garner support, including sleeping in the traditional shelter, the *Lavuu*, a tent made of reindeer hides. Eventually public outcry at this hunger strike was so great that the Norwegian government agreed to discuss Sami demands. Among those demands were the incorporation of Sami rights into the Norwegian constitution, the creation of a representative political body for the Sami, more public attention to Sami issues, and the ending of the dam's construction.

As a direct result of the Alta movement and Scandinavia's overall re-evaluation of their indigenous policies, in 1980 the SRC (Sami Rights Committee) was established in Norway. This committee was to write a report evaluating the effects of Norwegian policies on the Sami. The SRC focused particular attention on whether Norwegian legislation was in line with current international indigenous policies.

> It was in Norway that the most politically intense confrontations took place over the Alta demonstrations which were to have far-reaching political consequences. Many Norwegian politicians and opinion-makes [*sic*] saw the Alta confrontation as some kin [*sic*] of a crisis of legitimacy for the Norwegian political system. Alta has served as a catalyst for the work of the royal commission [SRC] that was created in 1980 and for the reforms that followed the recommendations contained in its 1984 report. (Sillanpää 1994: 221)

Although not all of its recommendations were heeded, this report, entitled *Om Samenes Rettsstilling* (On the Sami Condition) (Norske Offentlige Utregninger 1984), has served as the benchmark for all Norwegian Sami laws since 1984.

Among the recommendations set out in this report was the creation of a Norwegian Sami Parliament. Though the Norwegian Sami Parliament was not able to revise or veto parliamentary legislation, it was able to allocate part of its budget and resources towards international activity. Norwegian Sami eventually attended many conferences and meetings on the environment, culture and other indigenous issues through the financial support of the Sami parliament, including the World Council of Indigenous Peoples, the Arctic Council and the Conference on Environment and Development in Rio de Janeiro.

For the Swedish Sami, the 'Taxed Mountain' case in northern Sweden mirrored the Norwegian Alta-Kautokeino Dam project. Sami from throughout Sweden rallied around those demonstrating in the Taxed Mountain case. This court case had similar consequences for the Swedish Sami. The case, which was decided by the Swedish Supreme Court in 1981, concerned land ownership and land-use rights in Sweden. The Sami contested the Swedish Crown's ownership of land in northern Sweden. The Sami asserted their reindeer grazing rights in the Jämtland area of northern Sweden and tried to stop land encroachment. Although, after nearly fifteen years of litigation, the Sami eventually lost their case for ownership rights (Kvist 1994: 213), the court acknowledged the Sami's usufruct (traditional usage). This acknowledgement created greater awareness within Sweden of Sami issues. Despite the outcome of the case, the Swedish courts, in making this ruling, had shown unprecedented respect for the Sami.[7]

The events surrounding the Alta-Kautokeino Hydroelectric Project, in particular, displayed to the Norwegian and foreign public what the Sami could do locally, regionally and, with time, internationally. The Sami discovered the importance of international media attention for their struggle for self-determination. Although the 1980s were not as volatile as the 1970s had been, the Sami made headway towards gaining additional rights. During this period the Alta case quickly motivated Sami activists to move into the international arena. With the help of well-educated young professionals, such as Leif Dunfjeld and Ragnhild Nystad, the Sami movement made its presence known at international level as never before.

Sami leaders have gained influence within the UN in an impressive way. They have utilized the features and mechanisms of the UN to augment their national activism to create a unified and potent force to change policy. The changes at international level have also brought about change at national level. Norway, Sweden and Finland all feel compelled to institute policies based on UN mandates. The Sami have long recognized this and have influenced the UN's indigenous proceedings in the General Assembly and the Economic and Social Council. Their changes have improved land, language, educational and cultural rights in the Nordic countries. With Sami political leaders holding the highest offices ever held by indigenous individuals, the Sami will certainly continue to have influence on indigenous politics at international level for years to come. Reflecting this influence, it is also likely that the national politics of Norway, Sweden and Finland will continue to strengthen Sami economic rights.

When Sweden and Finland were considering entry into the European Union (EU), Sami leaders raised opposition. They recognized that the agricultural laws governing the European Union would not protect the Sami's smaller-scale agricultural economies. Despite the fact that Sweden and Finland did eventually enter the EU, the Sami leadership was able to lobby effectively to include a special clause in the pastoral law of the EU. The reindeer economy of the Sami would be protected from other European interests. The courts in Brussels were sympathetic to the Sami conditions owing to the fact that the Sami are the only recognized indigenous group in the EU.

Fenno-Scandinavian human rights concerns have also contributed to Sami economic support for poverty alleviation. Finland, Norway and Sweden have founded an impressive number of human rights, development and poverty-relief non-governmental organizations (NGOs). Many of these organizations have had strong ties to African human rights and indigenous programmes over the last decade (Trollvik 1992: 4). The Norwegian Ministry of Foreign Affairs has also declared that 'Human rights will continue to be an integral part of Norway's [and Nordic] domestic, as well as our foreign policy' (Jaglund 2000: 1).

This statement is augmented and supported by the fact that Nordic representatives and delegates to the UN have been elected as chairpersons and rapporteurs for the Commission on Human Rights, the Permanent Forum on Indigenous Issues (PFII) and other human rights organizations. For instance, at the August 1983 meeting of the Working Group on Indigenous Populations (WGIP), Asbjørn Eide, a Norwegian attorney and currently a fellow at the Norwegian Institute of Human Rights, was elected as chairperson/rapporteur (United Nations Economic and Social Council 1983: 1). This choice was not made simply to placate indigenous peoples; Mr Eide was an indigenous expert and had a long history of minority rights promotion.

Despite their international human rights records, the Nordic states have been criticized for their indigenous policies. A Norwegian Sami scholar has observed that 'Internationally Norway was actively engaged in the human rights debate. Some people were made aware that Norway had supported principles concerning the protection of minorities which were not followed within the borders of the country' (Minde 1980: 2). Another author has recently made a similar observation: 'Norway is among the most committed champions of such international [indigenous] principles, and is therefore prone to be embarrassed when the discrepancy between its internationally propagated principles of aboriginal policies and its domestic fulfilment of these principles is exposed' (Thuen 2002: 293). In the 1960s Norway and Finland (and later Sweden), began examining the effects of their indigenous policies (Minde 1999: 72). The Sami political elite has been quite effective at bending the government's ear and gaining sympathy for their plight both politically and economically.

Financial resources

Though Finland, Norway and Sweden are not among the great political powers, they are wealthy social democracies. Owing to plentiful natural resources, successful tourism industries and booming high-tech markets, many of which are state owned, these three countries have significant funds available for government allocation. The citizens of these countries enjoy the highest standards of living on earth. For instance, the average per capita income in Norway is $30,800. In the United States, the average per capita income is $36,300. Norwegians enjoy many state-provided benefits, however, such as healthcare, social security and free post-secondary education. The Sami share these economic advantages, owing in part to the Nordic sense of equity. This economic equity has increased in recent years thanks to the Sami's successful indigenous rights campaign.

Indigenous peoples tend to be more economically disadvantaged than dominant cultures. For example, the UN reported that in 1997, of the indigenous populations in Bolivia, 64.3 per cent were below the poverty line compared to 48.1 per cent for the non-indigenous populations. Of the indigenous populations in Mexico, 80.6 per cent were below the poverty line, as opposed to only 17.9 per cent of the non-indigenous populations (United Nations 1998: 2; Central Intelligence Agency 2003). In the United States, 31.2 per cent of the indigenous population were below the poverty line, as opposed to 13 per cent of the non-indigenous population (United States Bureau of the Census 1990). It should be noted that the poverty levels for the non-indigenous populations in these countries were far worse than those in Western countries.

The Sami, on the other hand, have the advantage of living in prosperous nations and have enjoyed a far higher standard of living than most other indigenous groups. In general, the Sami have average per capita incomes similar to those of other Nordic citizens. Their situation is not perfect when compared with southern Nordic populations. Their relative wealth provides Sami organizations with larger budgets, however, allowing them to continue their work through the income gained both from individual and governmental coffers. The increased Sami self-determination has led to an increased input of financial capital from national and municipal governments into Sami communities in order to help offset their disadvantaged economic and social situation.

> The Norwegian State and the Sami Movement thus both ironically continue as partners in the homogenization of the Sami in their mutual expectation and perception of cultural difference, and in their respective funding and participation in such institutions as the Nordic Sami Institute and the Sami Education Council which are both based on, reinforce and recapitulate notions of a distinct Sami culture. (Conrad 1999: 3)

Owing to the Scandinavian ideals of altruism and charity and human rights/development schemes, the Sami are able to convince the Nordic majority to provide aid to the Sami communities through central and local government. As is often the case, local governments tend to be less sympathetic to increased Sami rights. This is due in part to the difficult economic situation that many northern municipalities face, making the doling out of additional economic benefits to a small minority more difficult for them than for the central governments. This resistance aside, the municipal and national governments have been increasingly forthcoming with their financial support for Sami communities.

Conclusion

Throughout the Sami's history, there has been a constant internal and external duality between being 'Sami' and being 'Nordic'. Nevertheless, many Sami and non-Sami alike argue that one cannot be Sami and Nordic, leading to ideological and social struggles between groups. Without distinct and shared cultural traits, the Sami would not be as socially and economically advantaged as they are now. This struggle to maintain Sami cultural distinction is not a new struggle, but a product of the last fifty years' advances in codifying cultural differences by the Sami leadership and others, in order to protect the Sami people. Owing to the current climate of acceptance of ethnic or at least cultural variation in the Nordic countries, Sami people are in a better situation than any other minority group in Scandinavia. This translates into direct economic advantage as well as cultural acceptance. Many Sami leaders are satisfied with the gains they have made for Sami rights.[8] They have managed to protect and promote their rights to education, language and self-determination. In turn, they have protected their communities through careful and effective strategies to combat poverty.

Despite the optimism on the part of many Sami leaders, however, and the significant achievement made by Sami in protecting their language, culture, livelihood and political rights, some in the Sami leadership feel that essential rights go unacknowledged. As late as April 2000, Sami leaders were still using the UN platform to call for recognition of their rights. Lars Anders Baer declared before the Working Group on Indigenous Populations (WGIP): 'The Norwegian authorities, by failing to recognise and protect our fundamental rights on our traditional territory, have violated Articles 1 and 27 of the Covenant [International Covenant on Civil and Political Rights]' (Baer 2000: 2). Given the atrocities and conditions Sami and other indigenous people have had to bear in modern states, the sentiments portrayed by Mr Baer are understandable. Even in the states of Norway, Sweden and Finland, where human rights have become precious ideals, racism and discrimination persist.

But what does all this mean for the Sami and more broadly for indigenous peoples' ability to combat poverty in their own communities? Perhaps the most universal and salient lesson that can be learned from the Nordic Sami experience is that through identifying themselves as a distinct but non-threatening community within the national cultural identity, the Nordic Sami have been able to secure a viable economic future for themselves. The Sami of Norway, Sweden and Finland have taught their respective countries the significance of not only recognizing but embracing and protecting cultural differences. This lesson is just now extending beyond the issue of indigenous people within Scandinavia, to issues involving new immigrants and linguistic minorities as well. In nations where homogeneity is promoted and preserved with such vehemence, difference is now also seen as a source of national pride. Certainly a lesson can be learned from the Scandinavian experience.

An extension of the Sami's success in promoting their cultural difference is the Nordic Sami organization's procurement of financial resources. These resources have been for their own benefit, as well as that of future generations of Sami and indigenous peoples at large. In the Nordic experience, at least, difference is an effective mechanism for poverty mitigation.

Notes

1 The one exception in any of these three countries would be reindeer herding laws which are granted only to traditionally pastoral Sami.

2 The most notable court case was the Taxed Mountain case, which will be talked about in greater depth later in this chapter.

3 As will be noted later, Norwegian and Finnish Sami were more successful at this than were their counterparts in Sweden.

4 Excluding Swedish Sami, whose situation is discussed in greater detail in Lewis (1998).

5 In 1994, reflecting the inclusion of Russian Sami, the Nordic Sami Council became the Sami Council.

6 The Alta-Kautokeino Dam affair refers to the damming of the Alta-Kautokeino river in northern Norway in the early 1980s. For a more thorough account of the Alta affair, see Paine (1982).

7 Prior to the nineteenth century, Swedish courts accepted Sami ownership just as they did non-Sami ownership. They actually ruled against non-Sami in favour of Sami agricultural and livestock land-use rights. This is a reference to the 'Lapp Codicil' of 1751, acknowledging certain Sami ownership rights under the Crown which were not seen again until the 1980s.

8 John Bernard Henriksen, Adviser, Norwegian Ministry of Foreign Affairs, Human Rights Division, e-mail communication to Christian Hicks (22 January 2003).

References

Baer, L. A. (1994) 'The Saami of Scandinavia and Russia: great strides towards self-determination since World War II', *Cultural Survival Quarterly*, spring

— (2000) 'Statement to the United Nations, Economic and Social Council, Sub-commission on the Prevention of Discrimination and Protection of Minorities, Working Group on Indigenous Population on behalf of the Saami Council', 11th Session, Review of Developments, Geneva: E/CN.4/Sub.2/2000/3

Bjørklund, I. (2000) *Sápmi: Becoming a Nation*, Torso: Tromsø University Museum

Brenna, W. (1997) *The Sami of Norway*, Norwegian Ministry of Local Government, <http://odin.dep.no/odin/engelsk/norway/history/032005–990463/index-dok000–b-n-a.html>

Central Intelligence Agency (2003) *Worldbook 2003*, <http://www.cia.gov/cia/publications/factbook/geos/us.html#econ>

Conrad, J. A. (1999) *Contested Terrain: Land, Language, and Lore in Contemporary Sami Politics*, Ann Arbor, MI: UMI

Eide, A. (2001) 'Legal and normative bases for Saami claims to land in the Nordic', in F. Andreas (guest ed.), *International Journal on Minority and Group Rights: Special Issue on Sami Rights in Finland, Norway, Russia and Sweden*, Dordrecht: Kluwer Law International, pp. 2–3

Eidheim, H. (1969) 'Stages in the development of Sami selfhood', Working Paper no. 7, in F. Barth (ed.), *Ethnic Groups and Boundaries*, Oslo: Universitetsforlaget

— (1997) 'Ethno-political development among the Sami after World War II:

the invention of selfhood', in G. Harald (ed.), *Sami Culture in a New Era: The Norwegian Sami Experience*, Karasjok: Davvi Girji OS

Jagland, T. (2000) 'Statement to the United Nations' Economic and Social Council's Commission on Human Rights on behalf of the Norwegian Ministry of Foreign Affairs', Agenda Item 5: Review of Recent Developments Pertaining to the Promotion and Protection of Human Rights and Fundamental Freedoms of Indigenous Peoples, Geneva, E/CN.4/Sub.2/2000/SR.35

Korsmo, F. (1993) 'Swedish policy and Saami rights', *Northern Review*, 11: 32–55

Kvist, R. (1994) 'The racist legacy in modern Swedish Saami policy', in *Canadian Journal of Native Studies*, 14: 2

Lewis, D. (1998) *Indigenous Rights Claims in Welfare Capitalist Society: Recognition and Implementation: The Case of the Sami People in Norway, Sweden, and Finland*, Rovaniemi: Arctic Centre, University of Lapland

Minde, H. (1980) 'The Saami movement, the Norwegian Labour Party and Saami rights', in T. Thuen (ed.), *Samene: Urbefolkning og Minorities*, Tromsø: Tromsø University Press

— (1999) 'Mot Rasediskriminering, for Urfolksretter – To Sider av Samme Sak?: Et Historisk Perspektiv på Samiske Rettsspørsmål', in H. Eidheim (ed.), *Samer og Nordmenn: Temaer i Jus, Historie, og Sosialantropologi*, Oslo: Cappelen Akademisk Forlag, p. 72

Norske Offentlige Utregninger (Norwegian Official Commission) (1984) *Om Samenes Rettsstilling* (On the Sami Condition), Oslo: Universitetsforslaget

Paine, R. (1982) *Dam a River, Damn a People? Saami (Lapp) Livelihood and the Alta/ Kautokeino Hydro-Electric Project and the Norwegian Parliament*, Copenhagen: International Work Group for Indigenous Affairs

Sillanpää, L. (1994) 'Political and administrative responses to Sami self-determination: a comparative study of public administrations in Fenno-Scandia on the issue of Sami land title as an aboriginal right', Helsinki: Finnish Society of Science & Letters

Thuen, T. (2002) 'In search of space: challenges in Saami ethnopolitics in Norway 1979–2000', in K. Karppi and J. Eriksson (eds), *Conflict and Co-operation in the North*, Umeå: University of Umeå

Trollvik, M. M. (former vice-president of Norwegian Saami Parliament) (1992) Statement on behalf of the Nordic countries to the United Nations General Assembly, New York, A/53/310, 10 December

United Nations (1998) *Indigenous People: Challenges Facing the International Community*, New York: Department of Public Information

United Nations Economic and Social Council (Commission on Human Rights, Sub-commission on the Protection of Minorities and Promotion of Human Rights) (1983) *36th Session, Agenda Item 11: Study of the Problem of Discrimination against Indigenous Populations, Report of the Working Group on Indigenous Populations on its 2nd Session*, Geneva, E/CN.4/Sub.2/1983/22, 23 August

United States Bureau of the Census (1990) *1990 Census of Population: 'Characteristics of American Indians by Tribe and Language'*, CP-3-7

16 | Conclusions: poverty, peoples and the meaning of change

JOHN-ANDREW MCNEISH AND ROBYN EVERSOLE

There is a growing international consensus that 'development' means doing something about poverty, and that *doing something about poverty* does not happen in a vacuum; rather, it requires the active participation of people who are poor. For diverse indigenous peoples around the world, these ideas are opening a significant policy space where their often long-standing quests for resources and recognition can be heard. In the rhetoric of participatory development, it is now possible to speak of indigenous peoples' own definitions of poverty (which may differ quite dramatically from the dollar-a-day or quantitative health indicators of non-indigenous policy-makers), and to consider indigenous peoples' own solutions to poverty.

Despite these apparently greater prospects for participation in development, there remain, however, serious impasses in the way in which indigenous peoples and development policy-makers express and understand their goals and aspirations. For indigenous peoples, terms such as 'economic development', 'capacity building' and 'social inclusion' often give way to political and legal concepts such as 'self-determination', 'autonomy' and 'rights'. This is not the language that development policy-makers expect. Consequently, it is not uncommon for indigenous peoples' own definitions and solutions – the conceptual bases of participatory development – to remain largely invisible to policy-makers, who are trained to think of poverty only as an economic or social development issue, rather than a legal or political issue. The coming of a more praxis-oriented rights-based language such as 'cultural liberties' (UNDP 2004), 'capabilities' (Sen 1999) and 'capacities' (Rao and Walton 2004) may help to address this limitation. For now, however, it is important to recognize that for indigenous peoples poverty is often all of the above.

This book has offered an exploration and analysis of how poverty currently affects indigenous peoples, and indigenous peoples' own responses and strategies. It has also contributed to a broader understanding of the causes and cures of poverty. As regards indigenous poverty specifically, the authors have shown how indigenous groups' demands for self-determination and land rights are central to the indigenous poverty issue, and need to be considered in the light of current anti-poverty and participatory development policies. Meanwhile, the book's in-depth exploration of poverty and indigenous peoples sheds light more generally on the dynamics of how poverty affects different population groups around the world. Ultimately, this permits us to suggest policy directions that may effectively reduce poverty.

In Part One, we discussed indigenous poverty as a process seated in social relationships. We saw that 'poverty' can be defined by quantitative indicators (for example, health and life expectancy, as per the chapters by Damman and Sánchez-Pérez et al.), as well as by qualitative experiences (for example, loss of rights and political powerlessness, as per Simon's contribution from Taiwan). Indigenous poverty, as with all poverty, is multi-dimensional; indigenous poverty specifically is related to the cultural differences between dominant and non-dominant groups, as well as to racism. Indigenous poverty is also exacerbated by a process of social and political marginalization in which indigenous peoples have little leverage to defend their rights and interests. These processes of discrimination are further worsened by governmental and international policies that fail to take into account or understand the importance of cultural difference to indigenous peoples' survival, or to deal effectively with indigenous peoples' marginalization.

In Part Two we reflected on some positive changes in international laws and policies towards indigenous peoples, and discussed the relationship between indigenous peoples and nation-states. For indigenous peoples, globalization has meant increased economic and social pressures due to the incursion of interest groups and practices from elsewhere. It has, however, also meant the opportunity to create pan-indigenist movements, and to use international forums to influence the actions of states and affect states' willingness to consider issues of indigenous rights. We can see that there has clearly been positive progress internationally in the recognition of indigenous rights. The UN draft declaration on indigenous rights is clearly an unfinished process, however, and we have seen that the current way in which indigenous rights are defined and enforced has its limitations. It may be possible to circumvent these limitations and reach a final agreement on the declaration, by considering both how the liberal foundations of rights-based discourses might be redefined, and how governance can become more truly participatory and inclusive. There are certainly now a range of proposals and ideas available that could help: for instance, Kymlicka's (1995) ideas on multicultural liberalism, Fung and Wright (2003) on participatory governance, and Pogge (2002) on rights-based approaches to development.

The relationship between indigenous peoples and nation-states is complex, yet there is clearly potential for indigenous peoples to achieve their oft-stated goal of self-determination within the borders of the modern nation-state. What is needed, however, is for states to critically consider their central assumptions about the citizen–state relationship. Must states continue to always view citizens as individuals in direct relationship with the state? Alternatively, what can be the role of collectivities – communities or peoples who wish to have a relationship with the state while maintaining a degree of self-governance and self-determination?

Ultimately, self-determination means the ability to determine one's own future without interference. Part Three discussed indigenous peoples' perspectives on development – which can be defined as the process of constructing desired futures. Clearly, indigenous peoples' *participation* in development does not mean that they simply join in to help realize other people's plans for them. Rather, self-determining participation means the opportunity to define both the goals of development and the processes required to get there. As the chapters in Part Three indicated, indigenous peoples have a variety of development goals – from preserving their language to ensuring jobs for their youth – and a variety of strategies for achieving these, from local networks to national parliaments. Specific development challenges clearly vary from place to place in different national and regional contexts; this book has only touched upon this diversity. Yet clearly, understanding indigenous peoples' own strategies in each context, and how these interact with non-indigenous spheres, is key. With this understanding, non-indigenous peoples, governments and international policy-makers can support indigenous peoples in achieving their development and poverty reduction goals.

Exploring the international pattern linking indigenous peoples and poverty also allows us to draw some conclusions about poverty more generally. While poverty may be described by economic measures or health indicators, it is ultimately seated in social relationships. The relationships that generate poverty play out at different levels:

- in political, economic, legal and other formal social institutions;
- in informal social institutions (such as attitudes, assumptions and everyday practices);
- at all spatial levels, from the international to the local and interpersonal.

The process of social change – in this case, fighting poverty – can be understood as a process of realigning relationships at these various levels. Where indigenous peoples are concerned, this may involve such actions as passing legislation preventing outside development on indigenous land. It may involve rewriting educational materials to include indigenous viewpoints, or restructuring government health and social services to place them under greater indigenous community control. At the international level, it may involve multilateral agreements that further insist upon and regulate respect for indigenous rights and multiculturalism. At the interpersonal level, it may mean a critical rethink of racist attitudes and assumptions among neighbours. And within indigenous communities themselves, it can involve resolving issues such as the most appropriate political or governance institutions and how they will represent the community in dialogue with those outside.

It is important to understand that change does not happen only within the formal institutional structures of a society. Informal institutions also matter. Culturally internalized attitudes and assumptions about gender and race need to be openly discussed, studied and debated. Categories of identity, and culturally accepted practices of inclusiveness and exclusiveness, often go unquestioned, even when they perpetuate discrimination and disadvantage – both within indigenous communities and in the larger society. Informal institutions exert a powerful influence, and formal changes in development practice, policies and laws targeting indigenous peoples will continue to have a limited effect so long as there is no further foundation for accepting difference in the societies where these peoples live. From a governance perspective, the development of a more inclusive 'politics of difference' will require resolving the disjuncture between indigenous peoples' aspirations for cultural autonomy, and the persisting assumption that the citizens of a nation-state must be loyal, uniform and modernized.

In sum, this book offers a multi-disciplinary review of indigenous poverty, drawn from many different contexts around the world. It focuses on the specificity of indigenous poverty, but also demonstrates the close relationship this has with the poverty of other marginalized and minority groups. As such, this book makes it clear that the future reduction of indigenous poverty depends on the formation and continuance of cooperation and alliances between such groups. It provides yet another indication of the vital importance of marginalized and minority groups and their perspectives to any serious pursuit of social equity. The book also offers a useful resource that indigenous peoples, indigenous rights organizations, policy-makers and academics can draw upon as they grapple with the issue of indigenous poverty. It is hoped that this book will assist them to critically analyse poverty-creating processes, redefine challenges, and ultimately help create conditions in which indigenous peoples can achieve their own visions of prosperity.

References

Fung, A. and E. Olin Wright (eds) (2003) *Deepening Democracy: Institutional Innovations in Empowered Participatory Governance*, London: Verso

Kymlicka, W. (1995) *Multi-cultural Citizenship: A Liberal Theory of Minority Rights*, Oxford: Clarendon Press

Pogge, T. (2002) *World Poverty and Human Rights: Cosmopolitan Responsibilities and Reforms*, Cambridge: Polity Press

Rao, V. and M. Walton (2004) *Culture and Public Action*, Palo Alto, CA: Stanford University Press

UNDP (2004) *Human Development Report 2004, Cultural Liberty in Today's Diverse World*, New York: United Nations Development Programme

About the contributors

Pablo Alarcón-Cháires is a biologist who holds a Master of Science degree from the Universidad Michoacana de San Nicolás de Hidalgo. He has conducted research projects on the conservation of species, rural production, indigenous groups and environmental issues in association with university institutions and national and international organizations. He is currently working at the Ethnoecology Lab of the Centro de Investigaciones en Ecosistemas/UNAM (Centre for Ecosystems Research, UNAM). He was acknowledged by the World Wildlife Service-US in 1993 for his marine turtle research and conservation work, and was awarded the second 1997 National Prize to the Best Research Work on Mexican Farms, and in association with other researchers the second 1998 National Prize for Agrarian Studies.

A. Carolina Borda Niño is a political scientist from the Universidad Nacional de Colombia. She has five years of academic experience in the field of cultural minorities and their relations with the state. Her papers include analyses of the political development of indigenous communities in Colombia from the perspective of power theories; studies related to government transfers to indigenous reservations and their effects on the concept and practices of autonomy of Colombian indigenous communities since 1994; studies related to ethno-education as a public policy in Colombia; analysis of the Emberá-Katío problem, Alto Sinú, in connection with the firm Multipropósito URRA; and a comparative analysis of the Zapatist armed indigenous movement in Mexico and the U'wa indigenous movement in Colombia, among others. She is a member of the research group Relaciones interétnicas y minorías culturales (Interethnic Relations and Cultural Minorities), School of Law, Political and Social Sciences, Universidad Nacional de Colombia.

Alberto D. Cimadamore has a PhD in International Relations from the University of Southern California, Los Angeles, and a Masters in International Relations from the Latin American School of Social Sciences, Argentina. He is currently Professor and Acting Director of the Masters Programme in Regional Integration Processes, MERCOSUR, Centre for Advanced Studies, University of Buenos Aires, Argentina; Professor of Theories of International Relations, Political Science Department, School of Social

Sciences, University of Buenos Aires; Researcher of the National Council of Scientific and Technological Research of Argentina; and Institutional Adviser of the Latin American Council of Social Sciences (CLACSO). He has published on regional integration, international relations and poverty, among other topics.

Stephen Cornell is Professor of Sociology and of Public Administration and Policy and Director of the Udall Center for Studies in Public Policy at the University of Arizona, where he also is a Faculty Associate of the university's Native Nations Institute for Leadership, Management, and Policy. He co-founded and today co-directs the Harvard Project on American Indian Economic Development. His PhD is from the University of Chicago. He taught at Harvard University and the University of California, San Diego, before joining the Arizona faculty in 1998.

Siri Damman is a doctoral student preparing her thesis on indigenous peoples and their right to food, based on field work in Argentina and Canada. Damman is a nutritionist with additional training in social anthropology. After her masters degree, for which she looked into elements of food security and coping strategies in a community of traditional fishermen in Mali, West Africa, she was a research assistant at the Department of Nutrition (Nutrition Institute), University of Oslo. For the last two years she has been part of an interdisciplinary team called the International Project on the Right to Food in Development, which is a collaborative undertaking between the Department of Nutrition and the Norwegian Centre for Human Rights, Faculty of Law, University of Oslo, and the Akershus University College, Kjeller, Norway.

Robyn Eversole is Research Fellow at RMIT University's Centre for Regional and Rural Development in Hamilton, Victoria, Australia. Originally from West Virginia, USA, she holds a PhD in anthropology from McGill University, Canada, and has conducted research on economic and social development issues in South America, Western Australia, and currently in south-western Victoria. Her publications include the book *Here to Help, NGOs Combating Poverty in Latin America*, a range of articles in international scholarly and practitioner journals, and five books for children.

Christian Jacob Burmeister Hicks is a Master of Arts candidate at the University of Alaska, Fairbanks. He has a Bachelor of Arts in History and a Bachelor of Arts in Anthropology from Hamline University in Saint Paul, Minnesota. His masters thesis is about the impacts of Nordic Sami on international institutions.

Louise Humpage is formerly from New Zealand and a post-doctoral research fellow at RMIT University, Melbourne, Australia. Her research interests include ethnic relations, social policy and citizenship, which were reflected in her doctoral research, entitled 'Closing the Gaps? The Politics of Māori Affairs Policy'. She is currently working on several projects relating to refugees, indigenous affairs policy and Third Way politics.

Josep María Jansá holds a degree in medicine and surgery and a doctorate in medicine from the University of Barcelona. He specializes in preventive medicine and public health. He is currently head of the Community Health Service at the Barcelona Public Health Agency. His work focuses on epidemiological surveillance and epidemiology in infectious diseases, particularly tuberculosis, AIDS and legionellosis. He is also an expert in international health, health in war conflicts and health and immigration. He has been involved in and acted as project leader in several projects in Latin America, Africa, eastern Europe and Latin America.

Don McCaskill has taught for many years in the Native Studies Department of Trent University in Canada. He has published a number of books on topics pertaining to native people in Canada and indigenous people in South-East Asia, including *Development or Domestication? Indigenous People of Southeast Asia* (with Ken Kampe). He has been involved with research and development in Thailand for more than fifteen years and is currently a researcher at the Social Research Institute at Chiang Mai University, where he is involved in a comparative study of the impact of globalization on indigenous people in Thailand, Lao PDR, Vietnam and China. He is also the director of the Native Studies Thailand Year Abroad Programme.

John-Andrew McNeish is a post-doctoral researcher at the Institute of Anthropology, University of Bergen. He is currently working on the Norwegian Research Council funded project: 'Poverty politics: current approaches to its production and reduction'. Before joining the Institute he was a Researcher at the Comparative Research Programme of Poverty (CROP), responsible for the coordination and development of CROPs research in Latin America and the Caribbean. John has lived in Norway for five years and has worked as a Guest Researcher at the Institute of Social Anthropology, University of Oslo and as Researcher on Regional Development, Business and Innovation at the Norwegian Work Research Institute (AFI) in Oslo before moving to Bergen. He holds a PhD in Social Anthropology from Goldsmiths College, University of London and has published a number of papers looking at the impact of political reform, political crisis and globalisation in Bolivia.

Dario J. Mejía Montalvo is a political scientist from the Universidad Nacional de Colombia. He is a member of the Zenú ethnic group. He has three years of experience working with indigenous organizations, and five years of academic experience in the field of political and cultural analysis associated with the relations between the state and ethnic groups in Colombia, including analysis of the impact of government transfers on the exercise of autonomy of Colombian indigenous communities since 1994; the implications of homogenization of speech on human rights in Colombian indigenous communities in their legal and self-determination practices; interpretation of the Emberá-Katío problem, Alto Sinú; analysis of the indigenous upheaval in Ecuador in January 2000; and following up the representative position of indigenous people in light of the peace talk process in Colombia, among other issues. He is a member of the research group Relaciones interétnicas y minorías culturales (Interethnic Relations and Cultural Minorities), School of Law, Political and Social Sciences, Universidad Nacional de Colombia.

David Mercer has degrees from Cambridge and Monash universities. He is currently Associate Professor in the School of Social Science and Planning, RMIT University, Melbourne, Australia. He is Co-ordinator of the Master of Social Science (International Urban and Environmental Management) Programme. Prior to moving to RMIT University in 2002 he was Associate Professor in the School of Geography and Environmental Science at Monash University, Melbourne. Dr Mercer is an elected fellow of the Environment Institute of Australia and New Zealand and is the author of over 130 publications on many topics in the general area of social science and natural resource management, mainly with a focus on Australia. His most recent book (2000) is *'A Question of Balance': Natural Resource Conflict Issues in Australia* (Federation Press, Sydney).

Indra Overland is Senior Research Fellow at the Norwegian Institute of International Affairs. He wrote his D.Phil. thesis at the University of Cambridge. The thesis was on the Russian Saami, an indigenous people in north-western Russia. He has previously worked as Higher Executive Officer for the Saami, Minority and Aliens Department of Norway's Ministry of Local government and Regional Development. He has published extensively on indigenous peoples in Russia.

Leon Ridgeway is a Miaangle man from New South Wales and holds a Bachelor of Arts in Aboriginal and Intercultural Studies from Edith Cowan University, Perth, Western Australia. He works in the areas of indigenous education and community development, where his interests lie in indigenous economic development, history and youth issues. He is currently Programme Coordinator for Kurongkurl Katitjin Nyungar Student Centre in the Faculty of Regional Professional Studies at Edith Cowan University.

Jeff Rutherford is a researcher with the Social Research Institute and a lecturer with the International Sustainable Development Studies Institute, both of Chiang Mai University in northern Thailand. He has lived, worked and studied in South-East Asia for more than ten years, with an interest in indigenous people and the environment, especially in the theoretical and practical intersection between rights, security and ethics. E-mail: <tjeffrutherford@hotmail.com>

Héctor Javier Sánchez-Pérez is Researcher and Full Professor of Population and the Health Sector at the Colegio de la Frontera Sur, San Cristóbal de Las Casas, Chiapas, Mexico. He graduated as a doctor (MD) from the Universidad Autónoma de Barcelona (UAB), and has an MS in Public Health (UAB) and an MS in Public Health Research (Universidad Nacional Autónoma de México). He conducts research projects on poverty and health, tuberculosis in areas of high socio-economic marginalization, and human rights and health. He is a member of the National Association of Researchers of Mexico.

Scott Simon received his PhD in Anthropology from McGill University, Montreal, in 1998. He is currently Assistant Professor of Sociology at the University of Ottawa, Canada, where he specializes in development and globalization. He has lived for more than five years in Taiwan, and has been affiliated with both the Institute of Sociology and the Institute of Ethnology at Academia Sinica. Most recently, he is author of *Sweet and Sour: Life Worlds of Taipei Women Entrepreneurs* (Lanham, MD: Rowman & Littlefield, 2003) and francophone editor of the *Canadian Journal of Development Studies*. He is currently doing research on ethnic relations and economic development in Taiwan.

Ánde Somby is a Norwegian Sami from Finnmark, Norway. He comes from a reindeer-herding heritage and has family members who are famous authors, artists, thespians and political activists. Dr Somby has been active in the Sami rights movement since the 1970s. He was involved in the Alta-Kautokeino protest and internationally in indigenous work within the United Nations. Ánde Somby has a law degree from Oslo University. He is currently a Professor of Law and Indigenous Studies. He has taught at Oslo University, the University of Tromsø, Norway, the University of Alaska, Fairbanks, and the University of Arizona.

Guadalupe Vargas Morales graduated as a pharmacological biochemist from the Universidad Autónoma de Chiapas. She is a professor at middle-level and high-level educational institutions in Chiapas. She conducts research on the bacteriological quality of water for human consumption and intestinal parasitosis in children living in very poor rural areas.

Index